DRESS UP KIT

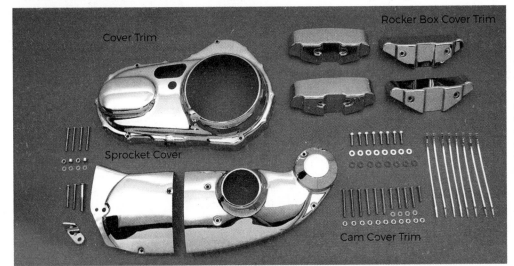

42-0947

2004-Up

V-Twin Chrome Dress Up Kits include chrome primary cover trim, cam cover trim, rocker box cover trim, master cylinder cover and chrome sprocket cover. Also included is chrome brake pedal and chrome shift lever to add a finished touch. Note: 2004-up models require purchase of primary derby cover available separately.

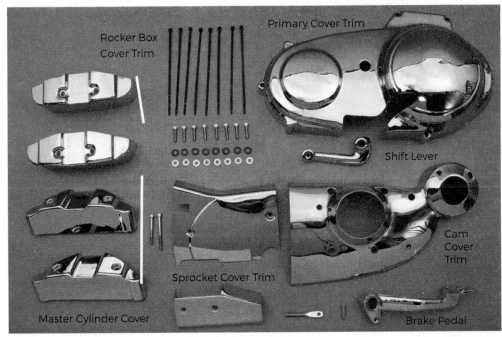

42-0799

1991-2003

VT No.	Item	Year
42-0799	with Brake/ Shift Pedal	1991-03
42-0846	w/o Brake/ Shift Pedal	1991-03
42-0947	w/o Brake/ Shift Pedal	2004-up

XLCH Motor Plaque features 1971 style Ironhead Sportster.

VT No. 48-0372

1991-2003 Right Side

Left Side

1

1991-2003 PRIMARY COVER

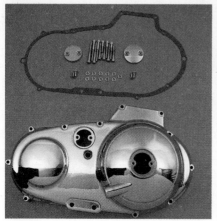

43-0234

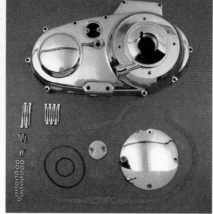

43-0235

Outer Primary Covers

Available as cover only or kit which includes cover, allen screw set, inspection covers and gasket.

Form Fitting Chrome Steel Covers fit over stock primary covers to mirror the contour for a skin tight fit. Covers are held in place by existing hardware. Installation takes less than 10 minutes.

Chrome	Black	Kit	OEM	Year
43-0221		43-0234	25430-89	1991-1993
43-0220	43-0375	43-0235	25460-94	1994-2003

Primary Cover Trim

Fully covers the existing aluminum primary and is secured in place by the 5 of the existing screws. 1994-2003 type available as cover with choice of derby as listed on this page. 42-0996 requires the re-installation of clutch cable for installation and purchase of derby.

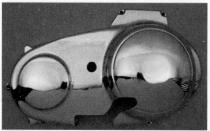

42-0750

42-0750 Installed

42-0996

VT No.	Year	Type
42-0750	1991-2003	Full
42-0996	1994-2003	Open Derby

Clutch Inspection Covers

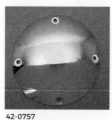

42-0757

42-0951

42-0952

42-1031

42-0678

42-1018

42-1019

42-0142

VT No.	Finish/Style	Year
42-0757	Chrome, Smooth	1994-2003
42-0951	Chrome Eagle Spirit	1994-2003
42-0952	Gold Eagle Spirit	1994-2003
42-0678	Chrome, Raised Chrome Skull	1994-2003
42-1018	Chrome Skull	1994-2003
42-1019	Chrome Flame	1994-2003
42-1031	Chrome USA Flag	1994-2003
42-0142	Black, Raised Chrome Skull	1993-2003
14-0570	O-Ring for 42-1031	25463-94

Inspection Cover Set

Chrome set for 1991-93 models.

37-8992

VT No.	Item
37-8992	Cover Set
42-0868	Cap, each
42-0047	Cap, each
14-0917	O-Ring for Cover
37-8701	Screws, chrome
14-0547	O-Ring for Screws

Chrome Chain Inspection Cover fits 1994-2003 models.

42-0756

VT No.	OEM	Item
42-0756	34761-94	Chain Cover Inspection
14-0917	11188	O-Rings for above
37-8701	41171-74	Screws for above

Black Primary Covers

43-0372

43-0375

Outer Primary Cover for XL. Order hardware, derby cover and gaskets separately.

Chrome	Black	Fits
43-0220	43-0375	1994-2003
43-0287		2004-2006
43-0285	43-0372	2007-Up
42-0996	42-0360	Primary Cover Trim 1994-2003
42-0939	42-0359	Primary Cover Trim 2004- Up

42-0789

Rocker Box Top Cover

Includes 4-piece D-ring kit..

Chrome	Black	Fits
42-0789	42-0362	1986-1990
42-0946	42-0393	1986-2003
42-1063	42-0352	2004-2006
42-0364	42-0353	2007-2012

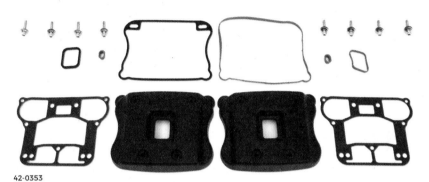

42-0353

Black Wrinkle Finish Primary Covers

VT No.	OEM	Fits
43-0463		2004-2005
43-0464	25307-06	2006-Up

43-0464

Engine Dress Kit

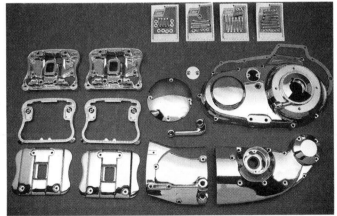

42-0690

Dress Kits for XL's include all die cast replacement parts as pictured.

VT No.	Year
42-0690	1994-2003
42-1055	1991-1993

42-0933

42-0996

42-0845

42-9975

43-0185

42-0930

42-0939

43-0149

42-0359

Chrome	Black	Item	Chrome	Black	Item
42-0933	42-0357	Cam Cover Trim	43-0185	43-0329	Sprocket Cover
42-9975	42-0358	Cam Cover Trim	43-0149	43-0330	Sprocket Cover
42-0939	42-0359	Primary Cover Trim	42-0845	42-0383	Trans. Sprocket Cover Trim
42-0996	42-0360	Primary Cover Trim	42-0930	42-0384	Trans. Sprocket Cover

2004-UP PRIMARY COVER

Outer Primary Cover

43-0275

Available as chrome cover only or kit which includes chrome cover, chrome allen screw set, inspection covers and gasket. **Note: Black Wrinkle Finish.

Chrome	Black	Kit	OEM	Year
43-0263		43-0275	25460-04	2004-2005
43-0287*	43-0376		25460-04	2004-2005
43-0462	43-0464**		25460-06	2006- Up
43-0285*		43-0284	25539-06	2006-Up
	43-0372			2007-Up

*Note: Perma Chrome Brand

** Black Wrinkle Finish

Form Fitting Chrome Steel Covers fit over stock primary covers to mirror the contour for a skin tight fit. Covers are held in place by existing hardware. Installation takes less than 10 minutes.

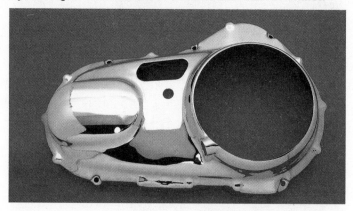

2004-up XL Trim bolts over existing stock primary cover. Order inspection and derby cover separately. Clutch cable must be removed and reinstalled for installation.

Chrome	Black	Item
42-0939	42-0359	Cover
37-1201		Screw Set

2004-Up Derby Covers, Chrome

42-0713   42-0728   42-0967   42-1017

42-1045   42-0141   42-0192   42-1266

42-0468   42-0469   42-0968

42-1251   42-1255   42-1256   42-0193

VT No.	Style	VT No.	Style
42-0713	Eagle Spirit, Gold inlay	42-0468	Chrome with chrome flame
42-0728	Eagle Spirit, Chrome	42-0469	Black with chrome flame
42-0967	Smooth	42-1251	Black with chrome skull
42-1017	Flame	42-1255	Chrome with skull
42-1045	USA	42-1256	Chrome with black skull
42-0141	Skull	42-0968	Inspection Cover
42-1266	Chrome skull	42-1374	Chrome Air Flow
42-0192	Chrome, smooth	42-1378	Black Air Flow
42-0193	Black, smooth	42-1278	Black/Chrome Skull
42-1033	Maltese		

SNAP CAP™ Easy to Install!

Chrome Bolt Cap Cover Kit

37-9532

VT No.	Model	Kit Qty
37-9532	2004-Up	77
37-9534	2004-Up Engine	63
37-9533	1984-2003	74

For Sportster.

These bolt cover kits will make any bike look great and are also for custom builders use. Easy to install these new kits have beautifully designed pieces to cover the raw OE bolt heads on engine, transmission, primary and more, each kit includes detailed instruction for installation on each model as listed, all covers in each kit are individually packed and numbers for identification. Installation has never been easier.

Chrome Caps

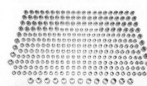

300 Piece Assortment!
37-1505

  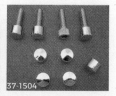

37-1502   37-1503   37-1504

- Snap On
- Tight Fit
- Easy Installation
- Universal Use

VT No.	Fits
37-1502	1/4"
37-1503	5/16"
37-1504	3/8"
37-1505	Assortment

Chrome Caps snap on knurled allen screws for ease of installation. Packs of 100.

1986-90 DRESS UP KIT

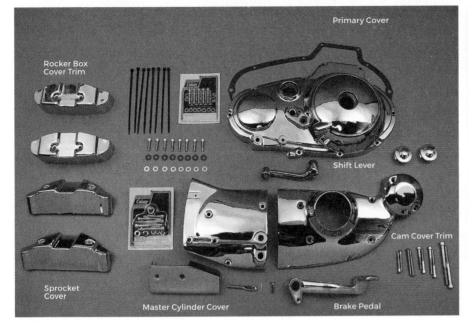

Primary Cover

Rocker Box Cover Trim

Shift Lever

Cam Cover Trim

Sprocket Cover

Master Cylinder Cover

Brake Pedal

43-0316

Left Side

Right Side

VT No.	Type
43-0316	With brake/shifter pedal
42-0847	Without brake/shifter pedal
42-8690	With brake/shifter

V-Twin Chrome Dress Kits for 1986-90 XL models includes chrome primary cover with inspection covers, cam, rocker box, master cylinder and sprocket covers. Also included is chrome brake pedal and chrome shift lever to add a finished touch. Hardware for installation included.

1986-90 Gold Show Kit

includes all acorn nuts for engine.
VT No. 7919-G

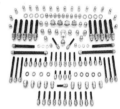

TAPPET BASE COVER

Chrome Cylinder Base Cover

42-1171

42-1171 Installed

Fits the area cylinder base on left side of engine. Fits 2004-up.
VT No. 42-1171

42-0447 Installed

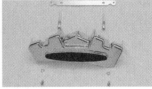

42-0447

Chrome Tappet Base Cover is die cast one piece covering the area from the pushrod tube base to the cam cover. Fits 1991-2003.
VT No. 42-0447

Chrome Tappet Bar Base Cover fits 2004-up XL.

VT No.	Item
10-0565	Base Set
2224-8	Screw Set
37-1504	Gasket and Pushrod Tube O-Ring Kit

Chrome Tappet Covers fit 1986-90, four piece. Presses onto tappet block.
VT No. 42-0113

Chrome Tappet Block Cover Set

Features contour for perfect fit over existing stock style lifter blocks, securely held in place by 4 chrome allen screws supplied. Pushrods must be removed for installation. Original design by Motoy-Cycle™ Accessories. 1957-85 XLH-XLCH.
VT No. 42-0115

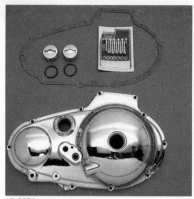

43-0236

Chrome Outer Primary Covers

Available as chrome cover only or kit which includes chrome cover, chrome allen screw set, inspection covers and gasket. Replaces 25430-86.

VT No.	Item
43-0128	Chrome
43-0371	Black
43-0236	Chrome Kit

37-8991

37-8690

Chrome Inspection Cover Set for clutch and chain on primary cover for 1986-90.

VT No.	Colony	U/M	Style
37-8690		Pair	Stock
37-8991		Pair	Hex
8776-2T	8776-2	Each	Hex
	2558-1	Each	Allen

PRIMARY HARDWARE

Screw Sets for Sportsters

Stock Screw

Acorn Screw

Allen Screw

Chrome	Cadmium	Type	Years	Model
9852-5	9853-5	Stock	1952-56	K
–	9851-5	Stock	1957-66	XL-XLH
8890-20	8891-20	Stock	1964-69	XLCH
8892-12	8893-12	Stock	1967-70	XLH
9753-9		Allen	1957-69	XLCH
8785-12		Allen	1971-76	XLCH-XLH
8785-12T		Allen	1971-76	XLCH-XLH
8788-11		Allen	1977-85	XLCH-XLH
8788-11T		Allen	1977-85	XLCH-XLH
9749-11		Allen	1986-90	XL
9749-11T		Allen	1986-90	XL
9767-15		Allen	1991-93	XL
9767-15T		Allen	1991-93	XL
9769-17		Allen	1994-2003	XL
9769-17T		Allen	1994-2003	XL
2220-24		Allen	2004-up	XL
7149-11		Acorn	1971-76	XLH, XLCH
9768-15		Acorn	1991-93	Evolution XL
8869-13		Acorn	1986-90	Evolution XL
9770-17		Acorn	1994-2003	Evolution XL

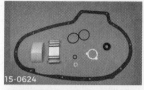
15-0624

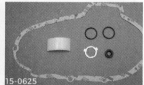
15-0625

15-0627

15-0674

15-0698

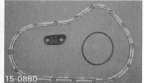
15-0880

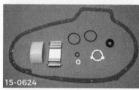
15-0624

Primary Cover Gasket Kits

Include gaskets and small parts for left side repairs. Available with paper or aluminum with rubber coating.

Rubber Coated	Paper	Fits
15-1639	15-0624	1967-76 XL, 1971-76 XLCH
15-1640	15-0625	1977-79 All
15-1641	15-0627	1980-89 All
	15-0674	1990
15-1643	15-0698	1991-2003 All
15-1644	15-0880*	2004-up

*Note: Paper with silicone beaded primary cover gasket.

Primary Cover Gaskets

GB No.	James	OEM	Fits
15-0388	15-1398	34955-04	2004-up Primary Cover
15-0056	15-1399	As Above	Metal with foam rubber coating
15-0307	15-0913	34955-89A	1991-2003 XL Primary Cover
15-0143		Pair	1991-2003 XL Primary Cover
15-0647	15-1154	34955-89X	1991-2003 XL Primary Cover with Bead (.030")
15-0057		As Above	Metal with foam rubber coating
	15-1423	As Above	Foamet® with Bead
15-0646	15-1153	34955-75X	1977-90 XL/XR 1000 Primary Cover with Bead (.030")
15-0170	15-0912	34955-75	1977-90 Primary Cover
15-0058		As Above	Metal with foam rubber coating
	15-1425	As Above	Foamet® with Silicone Bead
15-0211		34624-77	1977-90 Footpeg Stud
15-0169	15-0911	34955-67A	1967-76 XL Primary Cover
15-0406		As Above	With Silicone Bead
	15-1424	As Above	Foamet® with Silicone Bead
15-0168	15-1042	34952-52A	1952-69 XL Primary Cover
15-1215			52-69 XL Primary Cover Thick
15-1540		34986-04	2004-Up Inspection Cover
15-0190	15-1046	35169-52	1952-84 Mainshaft Plate
15-0212	15-1053	37762-52	1954-70 Clutch Cover
15-0178	15-0920	60567-36	1958-69 Inspection Cover
15-0663		63858-49	1984-98 Evo Rocker Cover Bolt Washer

1971-85 DRESS UP KIT

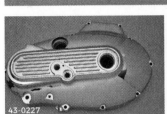

V-Twin ™ Engine Dress Up Kit for XL

1971-83 type kits include primary cover with plugs, sprocket/ kicker cover and cam cover trim. Chrome hardware is included to facilitate assembly. Rocker boxes are not included.

VT No.	Years	Model	Starter
43-0310	1971-76	XLCH	Kick
43-0311	1971-76	XLH	Kick and Electric
43-0312	1977-78	XLCH	Kick
43-0313	1977-78	XLH	Kick and Electric
43-0317	1979	XLH	Kick and Electric
43-0314	1980	XLH	Electric
43-0315	1981-82	XLH	Electric
43-0318	1984-85	XLH	Electric with Alternator

43-0227 43-0226

XLH-XLCH Outer Primary Covers available as cover only. VT No. 43-0328 fits Iron Head models with alternator in clutch drum.

43-0225

VT No.	OEM	Finish	Fits
43-0227	34949-75A	Chrome	1977-83
43-0105	34949-75A	Polish	1977-83
43-0328	25430-84	Chrome	1984-85
42-0225	34949-71	Polish	1971-76
43-0226	34949-71	Chrome	1971-76

Inspection Plugs

Primary Cover Chrome Caps for 1971-84. Available as sets or each, in stock, slotted or hex design.

Hex Type   Stock Type

Hex Type

Set	Each	Year	Fits
37-8999		1971-76	Filler Cap and Clutch Adjuster
	7600-4	1971-76	Filler Cap
	7600-4T	1971-76	Filler Cap
	2559-1	1971-76	Filler
	7601-2	1971-76	Clutch Adjuster
	7601-2T	1971-76	Clutch Adjuster
37-8989		1977-84	Filler Cap and Clutch Adjuster
	2557-1	1971-76	Clutch Adjuster
	7809-2	1977-84	Filler Cap and Clutch Adjuster
	7809-2T	1977-84	Filler Cap and Clutch Adjuster
	2879-1	1971-76	Filler Cap

Stock Type

Set	Each	Year	Fits
37-0050		1971-76	Filler Cap and Clutch Adjuster
37-7176		1971-76	Set
37-7784		1977-84	Filler and Clutch Adjuster
	37-0451	1952-70	Filler, Alloy
	37-0452	1952-70	Filler, Chrome

1971-85 Primary Cover Kit

43-0238   43-0237

Chrome Primary Cover Kits for 1971-83 XLH-XLCH models. Kits include chrome die cast outer primary cover with bearing installed, inspection cover, clutch adjuster cover, gasket and chrome allen screw set.

VT No.	Years	Fits
43-0237	1971-76	Generator
42-0238	1977-83	Generator
43-0254	1984-85	Alternator

XLCH

Primary Cover Inserts feature adhesive back. Fits 1971-76.
VT No. 48-1985

Inserts for 1971-76 Primary are chrome steel with double-stick adhesive strip to fit in recess in aluminum primary cover, sold each.
VT No. 42-0609

Primary Cover is constructed of stamped steel. Inspection cover included. Replaces 34949-64. Fits 1958-69 XLCH.
VT No. 42-0700

DRESS UP KIT

V-Twin™ Dress Up Kit fits right side on XL models. 1983-03 kits include chrome steel cam cover trim, chrome die cast sprocket cover, chrome master cylinder cover and hardware. 1980-82 kits include chrome sprocket cover, chrome master cylinder and cam cover trim with hardware. 1971-78 kits include chrome sprocket cover and cam cover trim with hardware. 2004-up kit includes chrome dress trim to fit over sprocket and cam cover.

42-0894

42-0932 Installed

42-0896

42-0932

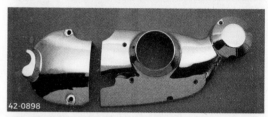
42-0898

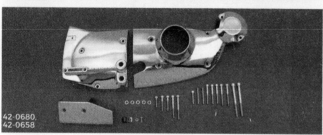
42-0680,
42-0658

42-0895

42-0899

VT No.	Year	Model	Type
42-0894	1971-76	Chain	Kick
42-0898	1971-76	Chain	Electric
42-0895	1971-76	Chain	Kick and Electric
42-0896	1977-78	Chain	Kick
42-0899	1977-78	Chain	Electric
42-0897	1977-78	Chain	Kick and Electric
42-0914	1979	Chain	Kick and Electric
42-0680	1980	Chain	Electric
42-0658	1981-82	Chain	Electric
42-0650	1983-90	Chain	Electric
42-0651	1991-2003	Belt and Chain	Electric
42-0932	2004-up	Belt	Electric

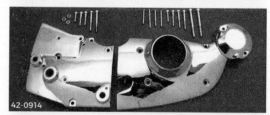
42-0914

Tool Kits for XL

VT No.	Fitment
16-0849	1957-70
16-0846	1977-84
16-0746	1986- Up

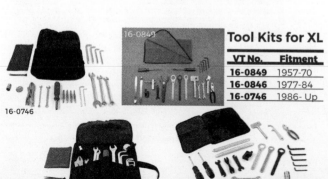
16-0746
16-0846

42-0650

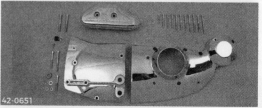
42-0651

CAM COVER TRIM

Dress Up Set

42-1052   42-1050   42-1051

Features brilliant chrome covers to fit over original aluminum covers. Formed to mirror the contour for a skin-tight fit. Order derby and points cover separately for 42-1052 and 42-1051.

VT No.	Years
42-1050	1991-2003
42-1052*	1991-2003
42-1051	2004-Up

*Note: Open Derby Access

Cam Cover Trim

42-0138

42-0138 Installed

42-0137

42-0137 Installed

Cam Cover Trim installs over original cover for 2004-up XL

VT No.	Finish	VT No.	Finish
42-0138	Alloy	42-0137	Black

Chrome Right Side Cam Cover / Sprocket Cover

43-0450

43-0457

Chrome Right Side Cam Cover/Sprocket Cover Set for XL's includes both pieces with gasket and chrome allen screws for assembly.

VT No.	Year	VT No.	Year
43-0449	1986-1990	43-0450	1991-2003
43-0457	2004-Up		

Form Fitting Chrome Steel Covers

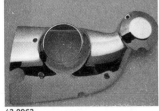

42-9962

42-9963

42-0110

42-9968

42-0933

42-9975

Installed on 1998 XLH

Form Fitting Chrome Steel Covers fit over stock cam cases on XL models. No need to remove cam case or disturb cams or gears. Covers held in place by existing screws and related hardware as supplied. Note: 42-9962 is kickstart only. All other numbers are for electric start.

VT No.	Fits	VT No.	Fits
42-9961	1971-1978	42-9962	1971-1978
42-9968	1979-1980	42-9963	1981-1982
42-0110	1983-1990	42-9975	1991-2003
42-0933	2004-Up		

1986-UP ROCKER COVERS

Rocker Box Top Cover includes D-ring four piece kit.

42-0789

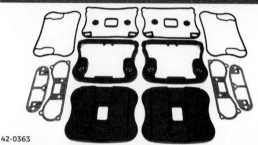

42-0363

Chrome	Black	Fits
42-0789	42-0362	1986-1990
42-0946	42-0363	1991-2003
42-1063	42-0352	2004-2006
42-0364	42-0353	2007-up

2004-up Top Rocker Cover Set.

VT No. 10-0566

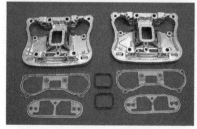

Lower Rocker Box Set

Chrome Lower Rocker Box and Gasket Set fits 1991-03 models.
VT No. 42-0220

Gloss Black Rocker Box Lower Sprocket Housing

Fits 2004-up XL.
VT No. 43-0387

Rocker Cover Screw Kits

Acorn or allen type for 1986-up.

VT No.	Item
8868-16	Acorn
8931-16	Allen
9788-24	Button Head Allen

Sifton Evolution Rocker Box Breather Upgrade Kit includes tap, drill bit, breather tubes and instructions. Fits 1992-03.
VT No. 16-0916

Chrome Rocker Box Dress Cover Sets fits over rocker box assembly without disassembly of engine. Chrome allen screws included. Fits 1986-up.

42-0796

VT No. 42-0796

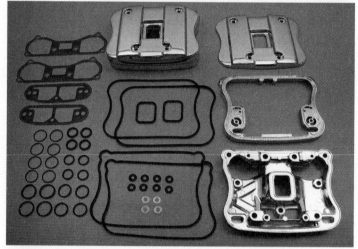

Rocker Cover Sets. Kits include gaskets for both heads.

Chrome	Black	Fits	Pc.
42-0788		1986-1991	6
42-0792	42-0368	1991-2003	6
42-5520	42-0352	1986-2006	4
42-5524	42-0353	2007-Up	4

Chrome Rocker Box Covers for 1986-up models.

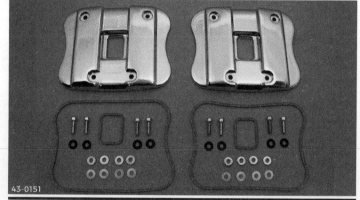

43-0151

VT No.	OEM	Item	Finish	Fits
43-0151	17501-86	Top Cover	Smooth	1986-2003
10-0566	17551-04	Top Cover	Finned	2004-Up
10-0579		Top Cover	Smooth	2004-Up
11-0585	17533-90	D-Ring		1991-2003
43-9130	17533-86	D-Ring		1986-90

Stock Style Hardware Kit contains all the stock engine nuts, bolts, washers and studs for the engine in choice of chrome or cadmium plating. Kit includes primary cover screws, lifter base screws, timing plug, cam cover screws, cylinder base nuts and washers, generator screws, head bolts and washers as required for each application.

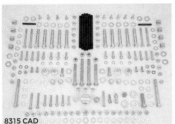

8315 CAD

Chrome	Cadmium	Fits
8315 CHR	8315 CAD	1957-66 XLH
8316 CHR	8316 CAD	1657-69 XLCH
8317 CHR	8317 CAD	1967-70 XLH, 1970 XLCH
8319 CHR	8319 CAD	1971-73 XLH - XLCH
8320 CHR	8320 CAD	1974-76 XLH - XLCH
8321 CHR	8321 CAD	1977-80 XLH - XLCH
8322 CHR		1981-86 XLH

HARDWARE KIT

37-9533

37-9532

- SNAP ON!
- TIGHT FIT!
- EASY INSTALL!

Chrome Bolt Cap Cover Kit for Sportster

VT No.	Model	Kit Qty
37-9532	2004- Up	77
37-9534	2004-Up Engine	63
37-9545	2004- Up	109
37-9533	1984-2003	74

These new bolt cover kits will make any bike look great and are also for custom builders use. Easy to install these new kits have beautifully designed pieces to cover the raw OE bolt heads on engine, transmission, primary and more, each kit includes detailed instruction for installation on each model as listed, all covers in each kit are individually packed and numbers for identification. Installation has never been easier.

Gardner & Wescott Allen Sets

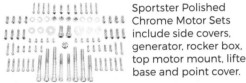

Sportster Polished Chrome Motor Sets include side covers, generator, rocker box, top motor mount, lifter base and point cover.

VT No.	Fits
37-9082	1991- Up Evolution XL
37-2087	1986-Up Evolution XL
37-2088	1984 1/2 -1985 Iron Head Alternator
37-2089	1977-1984 1/2 Sportsters
37-2090	1971-76 Sportsters
37-2091	1957-69 XLCH
37-2092	1967-70 XLH and 1970 XLCH

37-1201

37-1205

VT No.	Fits
37-1201	Primary-Derby
37-1202	Timing Cover
2226-4	Sprocket Cover
37-1204	Tappet
37-1205	Rocker Box

Chrome Allen Screw Sets fit 2004-up XL's.

Factory Type Studs for Stock Applications

12-2117

Show Kits

COLONY

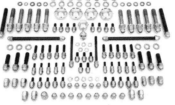

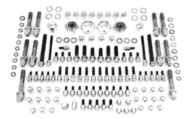

Cam and Primary Chrome Screw Sets include inspection and sprocket screws. By Gardner Wescott.

VT No.	Year
37-8508	1991-Up
37-8509	1986-1990
37-8510	1977-1985
37-8511	1971-1976

Allen	Gold	Year
	7900-G	1957-64
	7901-G	1965-70
1017-P		1971-73
1017-P	7903-G	1974-76
1016-P		1977-84
1015-P	7919-G	1986-90
1014-P		1991-93
1013-P		1994-2003

Caps Show Bike Kits in chrome finish.

VT No.	Fits
8517	1984-1986 Evolution 4 Speed
8518	1985-1986 Evolution 5 Speed

37-8505

VT No.	OEM	Fits
12-2117	24751-75	1975-up XL Right Front Peg
12-0552	24752-75	1975-85 XL Left Front Foot Peg
12-2111	24811-59A	1965-72 Starter
12-1151	24817-52	1952-81 XL Right Case
8814-15	24819-52	1954-76 XL Oil Pump Set
12-1150	24825-82	1982-up XL Right Case
18-3123	37584-67	1952-70 XL Clutch Hub
12-1186	40018-77	1977-up XL Adjuster Shoe, each
8813-4	45840-48	1949-76 Glide Leg, pair
8826-6	45998-73	1977 up Glide Leg, pair
	72341-48	1973-up FX Leg Stud, pair

FLYWHEELS

Complete Flywheel Assembly is shipped complete, assembled and trued with shafts.

VT No.	OEM	Fits	Type
10-1130	23900-57A	1957-76 XL	Motor Shop
10-1010	23900-75	1977-80 XL	S&S
10-1131	As Above		Motor Shop Ready
10-1132	23900-75B	1981-85 XL	Motor Shop Ready

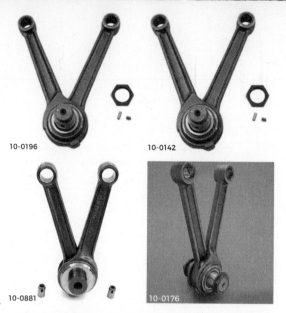

10-0196   10-0142

10-0881   10-0176

10-0179

S&S Rods are heavy duty replacement rod sets included wrist pin bushings, rod races, matched rods, pins, rollers-cages, and nuts, for stock or stroker use. Use "Heavy Duty" or "Supreme" which is recommended for drag strip applications.

Heavy Duty	Supreme	Fits
10-0179	10-0191	1957-81 XL
10-0180	10-0194	1981-85 XL
10-0187		1986-99 XL-Evolution 883-1200

V-Twin™ Stock Replacement Rods

V-Twin™ Replica Stock Replacement Rod Sets include new rods, crank pin, nuts, cages and standard rollers which are fitted and assembled. Piston pin bushings are installed and honed for stock wrist pin.

VT No.	OEM	Fits
10-0176	24275-57	1957-80
10-0196	24275-80	1981-85
10-0142	24275-86A	1986-99
10-0881		2000-Up

9878-13

Engine Case Bolt Kit includes the necessary hardware to bolt together the motor cases of the years listed in cad plated finish.

VT No.	Fits
9878-13	1657-76
9879-31	1977-90

CASE BOLTS

Chrome Engine Case Allen Bolt Kit fasten engine case halves. Fit 2004-up.

VT No. 2217-8

TRUETT & OSBORN

Truett & Osborn flywheel sets feature original weight for both right and left sides.

VT No.	Fits
10-1012	1957-80
10-1030	1981-85

Rear Engine Case Studs. Set of 3.

VT No.	OEM	Years
12-1151	24817-52	1952-81
12-1150	24825-82	1982-90

8610-1

9402-1

A. Timing Plug

Fits all Sportster timing plug holes and oil tanks.

B. Allen Style Plug use on all 1970-up replaces 720.

A. Timing Plug	
VT No.	Finish
8610-1	Chrome
8611-1	Cadmium

B. Allen Style Plug	
VT No.	Finish
94021	Chrome
9403-1	Cadmium
37-9206	Chrome by Garner Westcott
9960-1	Chrome (Oversize)

10-0550　　10-1210

Crank Pins are made of 8620 steel with .062 heat treated penetration. *Note: One Hole.

Years	OEM	Jims 3 Hole	Eastern 3 Hole	V-Twin 2 Hole	V-Twin 3 Hole
1954-81	23960-54	10-8359	10-0550		10-0552
L1981-99	23960-80A	10-8361	10-0192	10-1210	

Rod Bearing Sets With Set of 3 Cages fitted with standard size Torrington rollers for connecting rods. The cage material is noted.

VT No.	OEM	Cage	Years
10-0140	24370-52B	Alloy	1952-86
10-2567	Cage Set	Alloy	1952-86
10-2557	24354-87A	Steel	1987-99

Crank Pin Lock Kits

Include 2 nuts, 2 locks and mount screws. Nuts and locks are also available separately. Fits 1954-81.
VT No. 10-0183

Alloy Cage Connecting Rod Roller Sets for 1957-99 XL.

Size	1957-Early 86
STD	10-0160
.0002 Oversize	10-0161
.0004 Oversize	10-0162
.0006 Oversize	10-0163
.0008 Oversize	10-0164

Connecting Rod Race Sets made from 52100 steel and hardened. Fits 1957-85.

VT No.	Size
10-0137	STD
10-0827	.010 Oversize

Crank Pin Nut Lock Plate. Fits 1957-81.
VT No. 17-0914

CRANK PIN

Sifton Crank Pin Kit includes crank pin, rod races, standard rod rollers, and retainers.

VT No.	Years
10-2572	1954- Early 1981
10-2573	Late 1981-1986

Wrist Pin Bushings are available in bronze replica type or Sifton Ampco 45 for all XL. Replica type sold in pairs. Sifton type sold each.

Size	VT No.	Type
STD	10-0760	Replica
STD	10-0766	Sifton
.005	10-0762	Replica
.010	10-0763	Replica

CRANK PIN FLYWHEEL WASHER

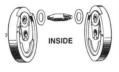

INSIDE

10-1150

Crank Pin Flywheel Washers sold in pairs.

Inside	OEM	Type	Fits	Size
10-1150	6506	Bronze	L 1979-86	STD
10-1149	6506B	Bronze	L 1979-86	.005 OS
10-1167	6508	Bronze	1987-99	STD
10-1151	23972-57	Steel	1957-71	.072
10-1273	23972-72	Bronze	1657-72	.073 w/ fly cut
10-1164	23972-72	Bronze	1972- E 79	.062
10-1168	23972-72	Bronze	1972- E 79	.005 OS
10-1285	23972-72A	Bronze	1972- E 79	.060 w/ fly cut

Crank Pin Nut Sets.

Eastern	Jims	OEM	Fits
12-0522	12-0604	23967-54A	1954- E 81
12-0565	12-0600	23901-81	L 1981-1999

100 Quantity Pack Roller Bearings

Size	Long	OEM	Short	OEM
STD	12-4561	9150A		9441A
.0002	124562	9152A	12-4554	9442A
.0004		9154A	12-4555	9443A
.0006	12-4564	9156A		9444A
.0008	12-4565	9158A		9445A
.001	12-4566	9160A	12-4558	9446A

PINION AND SHAFT HARDWARE

Sprocket & Pinion Shaft Key

Sold in 10 pack. Replaces 23985-12. Fits 1954-81.

VT No. 12-0200

Cam Thrust Washers

For 1958-up.
VT No. 17-0921

1987-up Pinion Bearings

10-1281

Case Race

Machined and ground to factory specifications.

Pinion Shaft Gears. White is largest, green is the smallest.

12-1394

*Note: Motor Shop Brand.

	1952-76	1991-99
Color	24011-37	
STD	12-1394*	
STD	12-1473	
White		12-1469
Red		12-1468
Blue		12-1467
Green		12-1470

Pinion Bearing Sets

VT No.	Item
10-2536	Kit
12-0403	Cage
Bearing Only	
12-0321	1977-86
10-2531	1977-84 Race for above

For 1954-76 XL right side includes rollers and cages. Washers and snap rings included when required.

VT No.	OEM	Item
10-8530	8881	Outer Race
12-0946	11177	Retaining Ring
10-1279	24647-87	Blue Bearing Assy
10-1280	24650-87	Red Bearing Assy
10-1283	24658-87	Inner Ring
10-1281	24659-87	White/Grey Bearing Assy
10-1282	24660-87	Green Bearing Assy

Jims	Eastern	Size	Year
10-0252	10-0200	Standard	1954-76
	10-0201	.002	1954-76
10-0253	10-0202	.005	1954-76
10-0254	10-0203	.010	.010 1954-76
	12-0250	10 pack	1954-76 Set Screw
	10-0755	Standard	1986
	10-8530	Standard	1987-up
	10-8531	.002	1987-up
	10-8534	.005	1987-up

Nut Sprocket & Pinion Shaft Taper End. Sold 5pk.

VT No.	OEM	Fits
12-0531	8011	1954-80
12-0516	23902-81	1981-85

Nut, Pinion Shaft Gear End

Eastern	OEM	Fits
12-0536	7913	1977-90
12-0577	7916A	1991-up

10-0404

Pinion Shafts are precision ground for fit.

Jims	Eastern	VT No.	Item	Year	OEM
10-8330	10-0404		Pinion Shaft	1957-76	24005-57
	10-0405		With Race	1977-E81	24008-75A
10-8354	10-0399		With Race	L1981-85	24005-80
	10-2531		Race Only	1977-86	24009-77
		12-0321	Bearing Only	1977-86	24648-77

XL Cam Gear Bushing Kits

Include bushings for #1, 2, 3 and 4. Cams. Standard size. Fits 1957-90.

VT No. 10-0711

Cam Bushing Kit

10-8265 10-8266
10-8267 10-8273

VT No.	Fits
10-8265	1986-90
10-8266	1977-85
10-8267	1957-77
10-8273	1991-96

Genuine Torrington Bearing Set

VT No.	Brand	U/M
10-8285	V-Twin	4
10-8283	Torrington	4
12-0425	V-Twin	Ea

4 piece set for XLS 1957-85.

Lock Plate, Sprocket and Pinion Shaft

VT No.	OEM	Fits
17-0913	24016-36A	1957-80 XL
17-0917	24018-72	1972-81 Big Twin

Sold in 10 pack.

Quick Change Cam Gear Gasket and Seal Kit

Fits XL and Evolution motors, includes both cork and quad seals for pushrods to fit all year range.

GB No.	Fits	GB No.	Fits
15-0752	1957-81	15-0755	1991-99
15-0753	1982-85	15-1265	2000-03
15-0754	1986-90	15-1266	2004-up

PINION PARTS

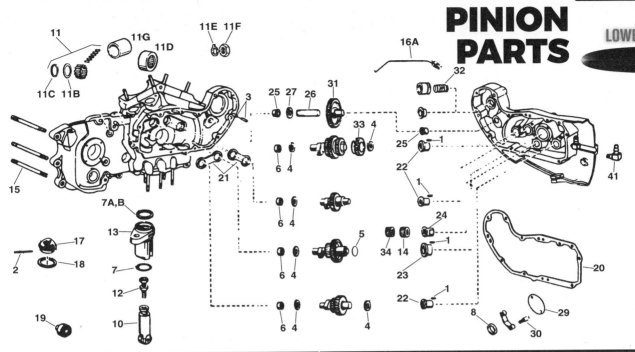

VT No.	#	OEM	Item	Year
12-1184	1	275	Pin, Bushing	1954-90
12-1173	2	333	Pin, Strainer	1952-76
12-1172	3	375	Pin, Casing	1957-76
12-0705	4	6769	Shims Cams .007	1952-85
12-0706		6770	As Above .005	1952-85
12-0716		6771	As Above .015	1952-85
12-0717	5	6773	Shim #2 Cam .005	1952-85
12-0718		6775	As Above .010	1952-85
12-1258		6778	As Above .015	1952-85
12-0315	6	9057	Bearing cam	1952-90
10-2552	6	25598-91	Bushing Cam	1991-Up
14-0500	7	11100	O-Ring Block	1952-85
15-0501	7A	11101	O-Ring Pushrod	1979-85
15-0116	7B	17955-36	Cork, Pushrod (12)	1952- E 79
14-0100	8	11124	Seal, Cam Cover	1957- Up
10-0502	10	18508-52B	Cam Follower Standard	1957-86
10-0503			Cam Follower .005 OS	1957-86
10-2536	11		Pinion Bearing Kit	1954-76
10-1154	11B	24692-54	Washer	1954-76
12-0913	11C	24701-54	Retaining Ring	1954-76
12-0321	11D	24648-77	Bearing	1977-84
10-2531	11G	24009-77	Race	1977-84
17-0918	11E	7044A	Lock	1979- Up
12-0536	11F	7913	Nut	1977-90
12-0577	11F	7916A	Nut	1991- Up
10-0517	12	18554-57	Tappet Adjusters	1957-85
10-0522	13	18607-57A	Tappet Block (Jims)	1957-85
10-0182	13	18607-57A	Tappet Block Set	1957-85
12-1394	14	24011-37	Pinion Gear	1957-76
12-1473	14	24011-37	Pinion Gear	1957-76
Note:	14	24059-74	Pinion Gear	1977- Up
12-1151	15	24817-52	Stud (3) Casing	1954-81
12-1150	15	24825-82	Stud (3) Casing	1982- Up

VT No.	#	OEM	Item	Year
40-0121	16A	24912-52A	Breather Pipe, Chrome	1954-82
12-1512	17	24975-37	Oil Strainer	1954-72
12-1511	19	25075-55	Breather Valve	1952-76
15-0121	20	25224-52	Gasket, Cam Cover	1952-81
15-0124		25263-81	Gasket, Cam Cover	1981-85
15-0245		25263-86	Gasket, Cam Cover	1986-90
17-0921	21	25551-58	Cam Thrust Plate	1958-90
10-0709	22	25586-37	Bushing Cam	1952- Up
10-2540	22	As Above	.005 Oversize	1952- Up
10-0710	23	25588-57	Bushing #2 Cam	1952-90
10-2541	23	As Above	.005 Oversize	1952-90
10-8538	23	25588-91	Bushing #2 Cam	1991- Up
10-0712	24	25593-57	Bushing Pinion	1957-76
10-2544		As Above	.005 Oversize	1957-76
10-0713	24	25593-74	Bushing Pinion	1977- Up
10-0715	25	25597-57	Bushing Idler	1952-85
10-2546	25	As Above	.005 Oversize	1952-85
10-2499	26	25787-57	Stud, Idler Gear	1957-85
15-0217	27	25811-11	Washer, Idler Gear	1957-85
10-0197	26/27		Idler Stud Kit	1957-85
	29	32591-70	Gasket, 2-Hole	1970-79
15-0156		32591-80	Gasket, 4-Hole	1980-95
32-0051	30	32601-78	Stud, Ignition	1972-79
12-1451	31	25776-57	Idler gear	1957-84
13-0106	32	25287-37	Breather Spring	1957-62
12-1400	33	25517-71	Tach Drive Gear	1971-80
12-1290	32A	25265-63	Breather Deflector	1963-78
12-0421	34	25618-37	Oil Pump Drive Gear	1957-76
12-1380	34	26318-75	Oil Pump Drive Gear	1977-87
12-1377	34	26318-88A	Oil Pump Drive Gear	1988- Up
17-0519	41	62375-57	Vent hose Fitting	1970- Up
12-0215	42	11219	Oil Pump Drive Key	1988-89
12-0213	43	11204	Rear Intake Key	1980-85

Cam Cover Screws for Sportster

Chrome Acorn	Chrome Allen	Cadmium Stock	Chrome Stock	Year
		8895-9	8894-9	1954-70
	8783-8	2062-8	2061-8	1971-84
8865-11	9751-11			1986-2003
	9751-11T			1986-2003
	37-1202			2004-up
	2222-11			2004-up

Cam Cover Gaskets (#20)

GB No.	James	OEM	Fits
	15-0214	24978-57	1957-81 Oil Strainer
15-0564	–	Pair	1954-Early 81 Cam Cover
15-0121	15-1078	25224-52A	1954-Early 81 Cam Cover
15-0124	15-0931	25263-81	1982-85 Cam Cover
15-0245	15-0932	25263-86	1986-90 Cam Cover
	15-1255	As Above	With Silicone Bead
15-0308	15-1256	As Above	1991-99 Cam Cover
			With Silicone Bead
–	15-0933	25263-90A	2000-up Cam Cover
15-0385	15-1223	25263-00	2000-up Cam Cover w/Bead

SPROCKET SHAFT

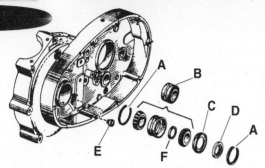

12-0322

12-0323

Jims	Eastern	Years	OEM
10-8319	10-0420	1957-76	24000-57
10-8320	10-0421	1977-E 81	24000-75
10-8321	10-0434	L 1981-85	24000-80

Sprocket Shafts fit as listed. Machined and hardened to factory specifications.

Left Crankcase Bearing by Timken.
Factory assembled with correct spacer for proper end play.

12-0322

Left Crankcase Bearing and Race Only.
Two Required. Order snap ring and the correct spacer separately. Replaces 48302-85. Fits 1991-96.

VT No.	#	OEM	Year	Item
12-0912	A	24701-52	1952-76	Ret Ring
12-0322	B	24729-52	1952-76	Timken Bearing
12-0323	B	24729-74	1977-03	Timken Bearing
12-0422	B	48302-85	1985-03	Cup and Cone
12-0989	ACD	Kit	1952-76	Spacer Kit
12-0990	ACD	Kit	1977-90	Spacer Kit
10-0470	C	24781-54	1954-76	Spacer, each
10-0460	C	40240-89	1991-01	Spacer
14-0118	D	35151-52A	1954-E76	Seal, 5 pack
14-0119	D	35151-74	1977-up	Seal, 5 pack
12-1511	E	25075-55	1957-76	Oil Transfer Valve
12-0713	F		1952-76	Shim .003
12-0714	F		1977-up	Shim .003

12-0989

12-0990

VT No.	OEM	Years
12-0322	24729-52	1954-76
12-0323	24729-74	1977-2003
12-0768	24605-07	2004-Up

VT No.	Timken	Years
12-0430	12-0322	1954-76
12-0431	12-0323	1977-2003
12-0768		2004-Up

10-0470

Motor Sprocket Nuts

VT No.	OEM	Year	Item
12-0502	8025	1957-69	Nut
12-0505	40387-70	1970-88	Nut
12-0149	7652	1989-up	Nut
10-0460	40240-89	1989-up	Spacer

12-0505

12-0912   12-0714   12-1511   14-0119

SIFTON CAMS FOR XLH-XLCH

Timken Bearing Spacer Shims

Available in 5 packs.1977-up Sportster.

VT No.	OEM	Size	VT No.	OEM	Size
10-1260	9142	.100	10-1265	9147	.110
10-1261	9143	.102	10-1266	9148	.112
10-1262	9144	.104	10-1267	9149	.114
10-1263	9145	.106	10-1268	9155	.098
10-1264	9146	.108	12-0983	9119A	Retaining Ring, 10 pk

Sifton Cam Set features PB & configuration, 4pc.

VT No.	Years	Timing	Duration @.053	Duration @.020	Max Lift	TDC	Fits
10-0662	1971-80	43/31	254	298	.410	.208	Bolt in Street Cam for more Power
10-0661	1981-84						No Head Work Required and can be used with stock springs

Sifton 205 Minus Titan Cam Set will produce excellent results in well aspirated or very large motors. Timing is taken at .053 of lift off the low spot on the heel of the cam @ tappets. Tappet clearance : zero to .002.

VT No.	Years	Titan Cam	Degrees @.053		Valve Lift Total	Spring Info		Free Travel
			Opens	Closes		TDC	Travel To Coil Bind	
10-0628	1971-80	Inlet	33°	55°	.436	.220	.475	.500
10-0666	1984-84	Exhaust	52°	25°	.436	.194	.475	.500

10-4014

XLH-XLCH CAM

VT No.	Years	Grind	Timing	Duration @.053	Duration @.020	Max Lift	TDC	Fits
10-4010	1957-70	PB+4/1	34/40	257	298	.410	.200	4/1 Kit consists of exhaust cams only for use with stock P intakes. Bolt-in power for Sportsters with no head work, 2pc set.
10-4014	1971-80	PB+4/1	43/31	254	298	.410	.192	
10-4020*	1981-84	PB+4/1						
10-4025	1984-85	w/ alternator						
10-4040	1957-70	PB+	34/40	254	298	.410	.208	Sportsters w/ P or Q cams, bolt-in more power with great street grind. No head work needed. More power through RPM range w/ stock springs. To 7000 RPM.
10-4045	1971-80		43/31	254	298	.410	.208	
10-4050*	1981-84							
10-4055	1984-85	w/ alternator						
10-4075	1957-70	Y	35/47	262	310	.425	.206	Street 900/1000 biggest cam available for no head work installation. Some 1982 engines may require spring spacing. Stock springs are OK. Great mid and upper end power.
10-4080	1971-80		53/29	262	310	.425	.182	
10-4085*	1981-84							
10-4090	1984-85	w/ alternator						
10-4105	1957-70	R5	33/41	254	306	.445	.209	Street Drags modified 900/1000 motors and small strokers. Big boost in torque over stock cams (2000/7500 RPM). Stock springs are OK, but head set up required.
10-4110	1971-80		43/31	254	306	.445	.200	
10-4115*	1981-84							
10-4120	1984-85	w/ alternator						
10-4135	1957-70	X	35/55	270	314	.450	.210	Street Drags for stroker motors to 76". More mid range and upper end power. Lowe lift results in easier installation in 1977 and later engines w/ extended pinion bearing housing. Stock springs recommended.
10-4140	1971-80		57/33	270	314	.450	.206	
10-4145*	1981-84							
10-4150	1984-85	w/ alternator						

*Note: 1981-84 Cam gear Kit differs from 1971-80 only on the #4 cam which does not have a tachometer drive gear. Tachometer Gear 25517-71 is available separately as VT No. 12-1400.

1986 - Up 883 1100 1200 XL Engine Cams

		Stock	02/41	223	270	.458	.094	Listed for comparison. Note: 1985-87 Exhaust cam lift is .414
			41/02	223	270	.458	.094	
10-8120	1986-90	V2	16/44	240	290	.465	.180	Bolt-in cams for stock 883, 1100, 1200. More duration and lift means extra power through RPM range. Stock springs and hydraulic lifters recommended. 2000-6000 RPM.
10-8125	1991-99	N2	46/18	244	290	.440	.155	
10-8122	2000-Up							
10-8140	1986-90	V4	30/46	256	296	.490	.216	Street Drags stock or modified 883, 1100, 1200. Slightly higher idle speed but stock springs and hydraulic lifters recommended. 2500-6000 RPM.
10-8145	1991-99	N4	52/24	256	296	.490	.189	
10-8123	2000-Up							
10-8180	1986-90	V8	32/44	256	296	.490	.226	Modified 1100-1200, stroked 883 with stock springs and hydraulic lifters. Great mid-range power. 2000-6000 RPM.
10-8185	1991-99	N8	56/28	264	302	.500	.212	
10-8124	2000-Up							
10-8160	1986-90	V6	34/50	264	302	.500	.241	Modified 1200 to 80" and/or high comp pistons. Same intake as N8 but more exhaust duration. Stock springs and hydraulic lifters recommended. 2500-6500 RPM.
10-8165	1991-99	N6	56/28	264	302	.500	.212	
10-8128	2000-Up							

XL 1971-Up Cam Covers

10-0554

10-0558

10-0559

10-0560

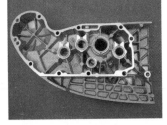

Year	Chrome			Polished			Screw Sets
	Kick Start & Electric	Kick Start Only	Electric Only	Kick Start & Electric	Kick Start Only	Electric Only	Cam & Primary
1971-76	10-0377	10-0572		10-0559	10-0591		37-8511
1977-80	10-0378	10-0573		10-0558	10-0592		37-8510
1981-85		10-0379		10-0560			37-8510
1986-90			10-0791	10-0857		10-0857	37-8509
1991-2003		10-0554				10-0555	37-8508
2004- Up		10-0563					37-1202

Motor Shop Cam Cover Bushing Service will install new bushings in right side case and cam cover for 1957-up XL models.
VT No. 60-0131

Cam/ Sprocket Cover Sets, 2004- Up XL

10-1431

Set	Finish	Cover Only
10-0348	Black	10-1431
10-0489	Chrome	10-1432

TAPPET KITS AND PUSHROD SET

Stock Solid Alloy Tappet Kit includes tappets with adjuster screws, pushrods and tappet blocks. Fits 1957-84.

VT No. 11-0588

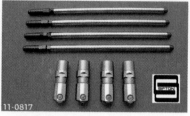

VT No.	Year	Type
10-0821	1957-85	Solid
10-0823	1986-90	Solid
10-0822	1986-90	Hydraulic
10-0817	1991-99	Hydraulic
10-0818	2000-03	Hydraulic

Sifton Tappet Kits include roller tappets and are fully adjustable, pushrod set included with hydraulic or solid type tappets.

Tapered Adjustable Pushrods

VT No.	Year
11-9703	1984-90
11-0574*	1991-03

Tapered Adjustable Pushrods are manufactured from 4130 steel with hardened adjusters and ball ends. Designed to be installed without removing gas tank or camshaft cover. Set of four for solid or hydraulic tappets. **Note:** Requires the use of VT No. 11-0935 pushrod covers.

Sifton Quick Install

Pushrod Sets are designed to be installed without removal of rocker boxes or cylinder heads. Precision made from 4130 chromoly tubing. Fit 1991-03.

VT No. 11-9544

Sifton Taper Pushrod Set

Constructed of chromoly extruded tapered tubing for 1991-up XL. Order Andrews Cam Set separately. **Note:** Modified 1200 to 80" and/or high compression pistons. Stock springs and hydraulic tappets recommended. RPM : 2500-6500.

Sifton Pushrod Sets are constructed of aluminum alloy with heat treated steel ends. Fits 1957-85.

VT No.	Item	Year
11-9544	Pushrod Set	1991-03
10-8160*	Cam Set	1986-90
10-8165*	Cam Set	1991-99
10-8128*	Cam Set	2000-up

Sifton	Colony
11-9529	7123-4

Solid Pushrod Kits include four alloy pushrods and adapters to convert stock hydraulic tappets to solid. Fits 1986-up 883-1200 Sportster.

VT No.	Year
11-9547	1986-90
11-9538	1991-03
11-1964	2004- Up

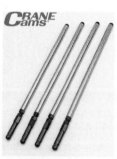

Crane Adjustable Pushrods made from 3/8" aircraft grade seamless 4130 chromoly steel tubing and heat treated to 128,000 psi tensile strength for a stronger and lighter than stock pushrod. Style adjuster helps minimize the effects of poor pushrod geometry found in stock pushrods, 3/8" diameter eliminates pushrod "rub" completely. Set contains 2 intake and exhaust pushrods. These are not time saver type. 1991-03.

VT No. 7132-65

Andrews Pushrods available in chromoly steel or aluminum, adjustable of fixed type as noted. All are stock diameter, so there is no cover interference.

VT No.	Fits	Style
11-9867	1986-90	Adjustable Aluminum
11-9868	1986-90	Adjustable Chromoly
11-9869	1991-03	Fixed Aluminum
11-9870	1991-03	Fixed Chromoly
11-9952	1991-03	Adjustable Aluminum
11-9953	1991-03	Adjustable Chromoly
11-9874	1957-85	Fixed Chromoly
11-9876	1957-85	Fixed Aluminum

S&S Hydraulic .612 Tappet Limited Travel Kit. Designed to maximize the efficiency of the stock hydraulic tappets. Kit consists of 4 machined heat treated and ground spacers when installed in the tappets reduce the travel of the hydraulic unit in high rpm situations thereby eliminating potential damage to the engine due to high RPM valve float.

Fits 2003-up.

VT No. 10-8532

PUSHROD COVER SET

Chrome Pushrod Cover Kits include all pieces and seals.

11-0905

11-0941

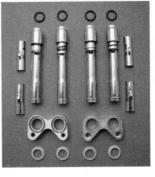

Billet Pushrod Cover and Mount Base Set allows adjustable covers to be used on 1991-2003.

VT No.	Item
11-0944	Complete Kit
14-4171	Lifter Base Seal Kit

11-0935

11-0933

Pushrod Cover Components fit 1957-85.

VT No.	Years
11-0905	1957-Early79
11-0937	Late1979-85
11-0933	1985-89
11-0935	1990-2003
11-1205	2004-up
11-0930	Adapts 11-0933 to 1990-up
11-0941	1990-2003 one piece design
11-1965	2004-up one piece design

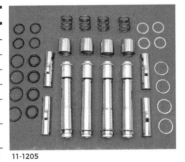

11-1205

Colony	V-Twin	Item	Fits
7507-20	11-0929	Upper Kit	1957-85
9887-20	–	Upper Kit	1986-90
–	11-0916	Clip Only (4 piece)	1957-85
–	11-0932	Clip Only (4 piece)	1986-89
7808-4	–	Inner Tube	1957-78
–	11-0908	Inner Tube	1979-85
7822-12	11-0923	Lower	1957-78
–	11-0936	Lower	1979-85

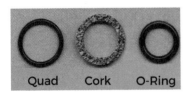

Quad   Cork   O-Ring

Pushrod Cork-Seal Kit

Include enough pieces to seal 4 complete pushrod covers on years listed. Available in cork, OEM-type Quad, or Buna-N machined rubber seals.

James	GB No.	Type	Fits
14-0668	15-0626	Cork	1957-79
14-0670	14-0953	Quad	1979-84
	14-0971	Rubber	1957-79, Blue Silicone
14-0671	14-0951	Rubber	1986-89
14-0672	14-0952	Rubber	1991-up XL 883 1200 Evo
	8729-12	Rubber	1957-79 (Colony)

14-0971   14-0951   14-0671

Pushrod Tube Seals

VT No.	OEM	Type	Years
14-0501	11101	Lower	1979-85
14-0512	11132	Middle	1979-90
14-0550	11145	Lower	1986-90
14-0532	11157	Upper	1984-90
14-0912	11190	Upper	1991-up
14-0935	17944-89	Lower	1991-03

37-9078 Installed

Pushrod Cover Cups

Die-cast construction in chrome or gold, set of four.

37-9078

37-9079

VT No.	Item
11-1073	Brass Hex
11-0024	Chrome Skull
37-9078	Chrome Skull
37-9079	Gold Skull

11-1073

ROCKER ARM

Include bushings installed.

11-9511

11-9512

VT No.	OEM	Type	Brand
1986- Up Evolution			
11-9511	17360-83	As Above.	Sifton
11-9512	17375-83	As Above.	Sifton
1957-85			
11-0522	17394-57A	F. Ex	VTwin
11-0523	17395-57A	R. Ex	VTwin
11-0524	17396-57A	F. In	VTwin
11-0525	17397-57A	R. In	VTwin
11-1066	Set w/shafts		VTwin

Rocker Arm Shaft

VT No.	OEM	U/M	Brand
1957-85			
11-0518	17435-57A	Each	Sifton
11-1068	17435-57A	Set 4	Sifton
11-0541	As Above	Each	Jims
1986- Up Evolution			
11-0571	17611-83	Set of 4	Sifton
11-0576	17611-83	Set of 4	Jims
11-0814	17611-83	Each	.005 OS Sifton

Rocker Arm and Shaft Kit by Sifton

Fits 1986-up models. Includes (2) 17375-83 rocker arm, (2) 17360-83 rocker arm and (4) 17611-83 shafts.

VT No. 11-0572

11-0855

Rocker Box available with polished finish for Iron Head Sportster. Fits 1957-85 XL.

VT No.	Finish	Note
11-0855	Polish Set	Bare
11-0867	Polished Set	Assembled

Sifton Rocker Arm Seals are machined of nylon to replace rubber O-rings on 1957-85 models.

VT No. 14-0148

Spacers and Shims

14-0501

VT No.	OEM	Item	Fit
12-2116	17451-57	Spacer	10pk
13-0100	17483-57	Springs	10pk
14-0501	11101	O-Ring	10pk
12-0704	.005	Shim	1957-85
12-0710	.007	Shim	1957-85
12-0715	.015	Shim	1957-85

Rocker Arm Bushings

Replace 17428-57. Use on 1957-up models. 8 pc.

VT No.	Item
10-0700	Stock Split Type
10-2106	As Above, Sifton

Sifton Rocker Arm and Shaft Kit fits 1957-84 XL Iron Head models and includes four rocker arms with bushings installed, four shafts, shims, spacers, chrome replica end caps and nuts.

VT No. 11-0820

Rocker Shaft End Plugs

VT No.	Fits
7142-4	1971-84
7143-4	1957-70

Installation or removal is much easier than original slotted part. Packaged four per set.

8224-8

Rocker Shaft End Caps

Rocker Shaft End Cap Kit for Sportster as replica type with hex caps for left side. *Note: Feature 1/2 x 20 thread to be used on later type rocker shafts.

VT No.	Year	Finish	Nut Type
2019-8*	1957-84	Chrome	Slot
2020-8*	1957-84	Cadmium	Slot
8222-8	1957-70	Chrome	Slot
8223-8	1957-70	Cadmium	Slot
8224-8	1971-84	Chrome	Allen
8225-8	1971-84	Cadmium	Allen

Chrome Allen Rocker Shaft Plugs. Set of 4. Fit 1971-84 XL models. Includes sockets and cups.

VT No. 37-0025

Rocker Box Bolts for both heads, includes washers. Available in stock hex type, acorn or allen.

Colony	VT No.	Year	Finish	Type
9829-28		1957-76	Chrome	Hex
9830-28		1957-76	Cad	Hex
7136-14		1957-76	Chrome	Acorn
8789-28		1957-76	Chrome	Allen
9831-28	37-9395	1977-85	Chrome	Hex
	9831-28T	1977-85	Chrome	Hex
9832-28		1977-85	Cad	Hex
8790-28		1977-85	Chrome	Allen

8400-8

8730-8

Rocker Shaft End Nut Kit includes four acorn or cap style nuts and washers for replacing.

VT No.	Type	Finish
8400-8	Cap	Chrome
8401-8	Cap	Cadmium
8730-8	Acorn	Chrome
12-1193	Washers	Zinc

8614-4

Chrome Rocker Shaft End Caps provide ease of installation with ample clearance between gas tank.

VT No. 8614-4

VT No.	Size
10-0514	STD
10-0515	.005
10-0527	.010

Lightning Tappet

Lightning Tappet Assemblies. Complete units precision machined and drilled for early motors. Holes allow better lubrication in valve train. Screws included. Fits 1957-85.

10-0542   37-8866

Tappet Adjusting Screws

VT No.	QTY	Year	Item
10-0542		1957-85	Kit
10-0517	4 pk	1957-85	Screw
10-0523	10 pk	1936-52	Split Nuts
8780-4	4 pk	1936-52	Split Nuts

Replacement Nuts

Fit each brand of pushrods or tappets.

VT No.	Type	U/M
8780-4	Colony 5/16-24	4 pk
37-8866	V-Twin 6/16-32	4 pk
12-0524	Eastern 9/32-32	10 pk

Jims Big Axle

Jims Big Axle Tappet Assemblies include roller assembly installed. Jims does not include adjuster screws or nuts where necessary. Jims available with Big Axle Roller Assy. Sold each.

10-1806

VT. No	Size	Year	Fits/Type
10-0657	STD	1986-90	Hydro Solid
10-0658	.002	1986-90	Hydro Solid
10-0659	.005	1986-90	Hydro Solid
10-8276	STD	1991-99	Power Glide
10-1803	STD	1991-99	Hydro Solid
10-8282	.005	1991-99	Power Glide
10-1806	STD	2000- Up	Power Glide
10-0568	STD	2000- Up	Power Glide
10-0571	.005	2000- Up	Power Glide
10-1811	.010	2000- Up	Power Glide
10-0569	STD	2000- Up	Hydro Glide

V-Twin Replacement Tappets

VT. No	Size	Year	U/M
10-8277	STD	1991-99	Each
10-0820	STD	2000- Up	Each
10-0824	STD	2000- Up	4 pk

TAPPET ASSEMBLY

Solid Tappet

Big Axle

Solid Tappet Assemblies

Include roller assembly installed. Jims does not include adjuster screws or nuts where necessary.

Jims are available with Big Axle Roller Assembly. Fit 1957-85.

Jims	Eastern	Size
10-0632	10-0502	STD
10-0633	10-0503	.005
	10-0524	.010
	10-0451	.015
	10-0452	.020

10-0520   10-0934   10-0934

Tappet Roller Repair Kit includes 4 pins and 4 roller assemblies for 1957-85 XL.

VT No.	Item
10-0520	V-Twin Brand
12-1179	Pins Only, 10 pk
10-0934	Big Axle

10-8526   11-9544

Evolution Solid Tappets can only be used with adjustable pushrods. Jims brand sold each. Sifton™ sold in set of 4.

Jims	Sifton™	Size	Fits
10-0636	10-8256	STD	1986-90
10-0637	10-8257	.005	As Above
	10-8258	.010	As Above
10-8370	10-8376	STD	1991- Up
11-9544		Pushrods	1991-03

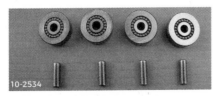

10-2534

Tappet Roller Repair Kit includes 4 pins and 4 roller assemblies.

VT No	Year/Model	Brand
10-2534	1986-99 Evo XL	V-Twin
10-0529	1986-99 Evo XL	Crane

10-0852

Sifton Solid Tappet Assembly Sets of 4, feature centrifugal surface fine grinding and max-axle precision fit rollers and pins. Solid units include adjuster screws & lock nuts. Fit 1957-85.

VT No.	Size
14-0784	Standard - Adjuster screw & nuts not included
10-0852	Standard
10-0774	.005
10-0775	.010

Solid Lifter Kit includes four standard tappets with adjusters and four lifter blocks.
VT No. 10-0474

Evolution Hy-Rev™ Hydraulic

V-Thunder tappet features a unique anti-pump up race retainer, designed to replace the normal clip so as to precisely limit travel of the plunger during operation, this allows the valve train to perform more like a mechanical stern allowing higher RPM operation with quiet and precision of hydraulics. Fits 1991-99. Standard size.

VT No.	U/M
10-8280	Ea
10-8281	4

V-Thunder Tappet Set of 4.
VT No. 10-7391

Crane Hydraulic Roller Tappet provides improved RPM capability, superior reliability and quieter operation. Features use of a precision, hardened ball-type valve to provide superior sealing and lash control. Rotating check ball prevents localized wear and pitting. Fits 1999-up. VT No. 10-2200

REPLICA VALVE

11-0609   11-0617   11-1111

Model and Year	Type	OEM	Sifton™ Nitrate Steel	Sifton™ Steel	Sifton™ Nitrate Steel	V-Twin™ Chrome Steel	V-Twin™ Stainless Steel Nitrate
Ironhead Sportster 1958-69	Intake	18070-58					
	Exhaust	1808-58A	11-1107		11-0617	11-0631	
Ironhead Sportster 1970-85	Intake	18070-70	11-1106		11-0609	11-0628	
	Exhaust	18080-58A	11-1107		11-0617	11-0631	
	Exhaust	1/8" OS			11-9646		
Ironhead "R" 1970-85	Intake 1 15/16	18070-70R		11-0665			
	Exhaust 1 3/4	18080-70R		11-0676	11-0618		11-0623
Evolution 883cc 1986-2003	Intake	18031-86	11-1109		11-0671		
	Exhaust	18030-86					
Evolution 1100-1200 1987-2003	Intake	18023-87	11-1111		11-0667		
	Exhaust	18024-87					

*Note: All XL valves with an "R" after OEM part number denote racing stem lengths. They are .080 longer than the stock valves, and have tulip shape head for maximum flow. Valve face diameters are larger which require a larger seat ground in the head.

TAPPET   BASE

10-0540

VT No.	OEM	Brand
10-0522	18607-57	Jims, ea.
10-0182	18607-57	V-Twin, 4pc
10-0540	18607-57	Sifton Set
8782-4	Screws	Chrome set, Allen
9846-4	Screws	Cadmium Bolt Set, Hex

Tappet Block for 1957-84 in polished finish.

Tappet Base Screws

	1957-85	1986-90	1991-94	1995-03
Acorn		8867-4	9765-4	9766-4
Allen	8782-4	8782-4	9759-4	9760-4
Hex	9846-4	(cadmium)		

Tappet Block Set fits 1986-90 XL models. Set of 4.
VT No. 10-0593

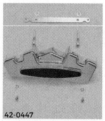

Chrome Tappet Base Cover is die cast one piece covering the area from the pushrod tube base to the cam cover. Fits 1991-2003.
VT No. 42-0447

42-0447

Chrome Tappet Cover fit XL models, 2004-up.

VT No.	Item
10-0565	Cover
15-0544	Gaskets

Chrome Tappet Covers fit 1986-90 XL, 4 piece 42-0113 style presses onto tappet block.

VT No. 42-0113

Chrome Tappet Block Cover Set features contour for perfect fit over existing stock style tappet blocks, securely held in place by four chrome allen screws which are supplied. Pushrods must be removed for installation. Original design by Motoy-Cycle™ Accessories. Fits 1957-85 XLH-XLCH.
VT No. 42-0115

VALVE BY ROWE & KIBBLEWHITE

Rowe or Precision Machining (Kibblewhite). Intake valves are made of 8645 heat treated valve steel and the exhaust valves are made of 21-2N heat treated non-magnetic stainless steel. These valves are available with the following stems and heads:

1. **Roller Burnished Stem:** Roller burnishing smooths the finest grind finish (16 micro-inch) to a 4 micro-inch.
2. **Melonite, Special Black Stem:** This is a heat treating process developed and patented in Germany. Gives the valve a Black Smokey look. Very hard and slippery. Currently being used on O.E.M. valves available in Rowe or Black Diamond brands.
3. **Titanium Nitride Gold Coated Stem:** Absolutely top of the line. Extremely hard and slippery. Gold in color, known by the scientific abbreviation TiN, this is the same coating used on Carbide cutters for high heat applications
4. **Razor Back by Kibblewhite** are one piece forged Evolution-8 stainless steel, fully CNC machined with hard chrome stems.
5. **Rowe Pro:** Forged one piece stainless steel valve precision CNC machined. Features special black melonite finish, swirl polished tulip area and heat treated water tip.

| Model / Year | Application | ROWE VALVES | | | | | KIBBLEWHITE | |
| | | Forged & Shot Peened Head | Fully Machined Head | | | | Stainless | |
		1. Roller Burnish	2. Melonite Special Black	2. Melonite Special Black	3. TiN Gold Coat	4. Rowe Pro	Black Diamond™	5. Razor Back
Ironhead Sportster 1958-69	Intake 18070-58						11-6003	11-6079
	Exhaust 1808-58A	11-6033					11-6010	11-6080
Ironhead Sportster 1970-84	Intake 18027-80	11-6034	11-6041				11-6004	11-6081
	1/16" OS						11-6107	
	Exhaust 18033-80	11-6033					11-6010	11-6080
	1/16" OS						11-6108	
Ironhead Sportster XLR 1970-85	Intake						11-6006	11-6082
	Exhaust						11-6013	
Evolution 883cc 1986-2003	Intake 18031-86					11-6109	11-6091	
	Exhaust 18030-86						11-6092	
Evolution 1100-1200 1986 Only	Intake 18023-86						11-6005	
	Exhaust 18024-86						11-6012	
Evolution 1100-1200 1987-2003	Intake 18023-87			11-6065			11-6093	
	Exhaust 18024-87				11-6071		11-6094	
Evolution 833 2004- Up	Intake 18053-84							
	Exhaust 18059-04			11-6116				
Evolution 1200 2004- Up	Intake 18690-02			11-6117				
	Exhaust 18691-02							
Conversion 883 to 1200 Evolution	Intake						11-6072	
	Exhaust						11-6073	

Oversize Valve Seats

Oversize Valve Seats can be used with unleaded gas. Replacement size is actual size of seat supplied by V-Twin Number. Stock size is noted as reference only.

VT No.	Item	
Intake		
11-0642	1957-69	1.690 Port Size
	Replacement size 2 x 1.687 x 9/32"	
11-0643	1970-85	1.650 Port Size
	Replacement size 2 1/16 x 1.687 x 9/32"	
11-0787	1986- Up	1.815 x 1.398 x .384
	Replacement size 36.5mm x 47mm x 10mm	
Exhaust		
11-0659	1957-85	1.405 Port Size
11-0789	1986- Up	1.579 x 1.107 x .340
	Replacement size 1 3/16 x 1 5/8 x 3/8"	

ONE PIECE VALVE

Manley Stainless Valves are machined from one piece forging with a swirl polished finish and chrome plated stem. Sold pair.

VT No.	Years	Type	Head Diameter	Stem Diameter	OEM
11-9000	1970-85	Exhaust	1 9/16" stock	.3385 stock	18080-58A
11-9032	1970-85	Stock length from factory			
11-9032	1970-85	Intake	1 15/16" stock	.309 stock	18080-70
11-9000	1958-69	Exhaust	1 9/16" stock	.3385 stock	18080-58A
11-9034	1958-69	Intake	1 13/16" stock	.309 stock	18070-58
11-9083	1986-03 883	Exhaust	1.345 stock	.3095 stock	18030-86
11-9080	1986-03 883cc	Intake	1.585 stock	.3105 stock	18031-86
11-6093	1988-03 1200cc	Intake	1.715 stock	.3105 stock	18023-87

 # VALVE GUIDE

For Evo Sportster

1986-Up.

Size	ROWE Ampco 45 Intake/Exhaust	Precision Machine Ampco 45 Intake/Exhaust	Precision Machine Cast Iron Intake/Exhaust
STD		11-1019	11-1014
+.001		11-1020	11-1015
+.002			11-1016
+.003		11-1022	11-1017
+.004	11-1898	11-1023	11-1018
+.006	11-1899		

Rowe Unhoned Cast Iron

Intake and exhaust is same unless noted.

Size	1983-Up Intake	1983-Up Exhaust	1957-82 Intake	1957-82 Exhaust
STD	11-2144		11-2154	11-2155
+.001	11-2146		11-2156	11-2157
+.002	11-2148		11-2158	11-2159
+.003	11-2150	11-2151	11-2160	
+.004	11-2152			
Top Dia.	.531	.531	.531	.531
Seal #	14-0143	14-0144	14-0143	14-0144
Overall Lgth	1.73	1.86	1.73	1.86

11-2158   11-2157   14-0143

Embroidered patch can be sewn or ironed on.
VT No. 48-1523

For Evo Sportster

Size	V-Twin™ Cast Iron Intake	V-Twin™ Cast Iron Exhaust	Rowe Cast Iron Intake	Rowe Cast Iron Exhaust	Rowe Ampco 45 Intake	Rowe Ampco 45 Exhaust
1957-82						
STD	11-0718	11-0722				
+.001	11-0719	11-0723				
+.002	11-0720	11-0724			11-1907	
+.003	11-0721	11-0725		11-9828		
+.004	11-1898	11-1023	11-1018			
+.006	11-0687					
1983-85						
STD			11-1913			
+.001						
+.002					11-1915	11-1918
+.003						11-1925

For 1957-82

Size	Precision Bronzonium Intake	Precision Bronzonium Exhaust	Precision Ampco 45 Intake	Precision Ampco 45 Exhaust	Precision Cast Iron Intake	Precision Cast Iron Exhaust
STD			11-1024	11-1029	11-1034	11-1039
+.001			11-1025	11-1030	11-1035	11-1040
+.002			11-1026	11-1031	11-1036	11-1041
+.003	11-0767	11-0771	11-1027	11-1032		
+.004	11-0685	11-0684		11-1033		

VALVE SEAL

14-0143   14-0143

Valve Stem Seals in 10pks for years listed. Installation tools and plastic 10pk sleeves available separately.

VT No.	Fits	Mfg. No.	Size
14-0143	Intake XL 1957-85	1404	5/16"
14-0144	Exhaust XL 1957-85	1405	11/32"
14-0164	Evolution 883-1200	1400	5/16"
16-1751	Sleeve		5/16"
16-1752	Sleeve		11/32"
Installation Tools			
16-0134	1957-84 XL		Tool
16-1746	1984-Up XL		Tool Only

16-0134   16-1746

Valve Stem Oil Seal Kits include four pieces of proper guide seal and installation tool for XL. Tool sold separately.

VT No.	Fits
16-1745	1985-Up Kit
16-0405	1957-84 Kit
16-0134	1957-84 Tool, White
16-1746	1984-Up Tool, Red

SIFTON VALVE SPRING KITS

Sifton XL Lower Valve Collar and Seal Kit for all 1957-85 models. Kit includes four special lower collars machined to accept K-line style seals. Two intake seals and two exhaust seals. Top of guide must still be machined to accept seals. Seal installation tool included.

VT No. 11-0821

Sifton Lightweight Valve Spring Kits include springs, keepers, retainer, and lower collars unless noted. Fits 1970-84 XL for 160 lb seat pressure, up to .460" valve travel. Hard-anodized aluminum retainers. May require "R" model valve to achieve installed height.

VT No. 13-2210

Sifton™ Lightweight Valve Spring Kits include springs, keepers, retainer, and lower collars unless noted.

VT No.	Type
13-2080	170-180 lb seat pressure up to .600" valve travel. Titanium retainers.
13-2085	170-180 lb seat pressure up to .600" valve travel. Heat treated steel retainers.
13-2093	170-180 lb seat pressure up to .600" valve travel. Hard anodized aluminum retainers
13-2140	170-210 lb seat pressure up to .800" valve travel. Titanium retainers.
13-2142	170-210 lb seat pressure up to .800" valve travel. Heat treated steel retainers.

Sportster .490" Lift Kit (not Evolution)

The .490 lift kit features stock OD springs, interference fit to reduce harmonics and control spring surge. No machining required for installation. Springs have 20% more pressure than stock. Use with stock lift cams to .490. Supplied with steel top collars. Uses stock lower collars.

VT No.	Combined Loads	Coil Bind	Recommended Cam Lift
11-9609	85 @ 1.310 .500 @ .820	.790	Stock -.490

Sifton™ Valve Spring Set

For High Lift Cams can be used with stock retainers and lower collars.

VT No.	Fits
13-2090	1985-90 up to .600" valve lift
13-2215	1970-84 Stock replacement

Sifton™ Valve Spring Keeper

Keepers are CNC machined and then heat treated.

VT No.	Fits
11-2096	1986- Up
11-4276	1957-84 includes retainer

Valve Spring Kits

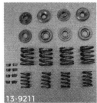

Includes all springs, collars and keepers necessary for each application.

VT No.	Year	Spring Only
13-9211	1957-81	13-0102
13-9199	1981-83	13-0102
13-9207	1983-85	13-9175
13-9196	1986-01	

Valve Keeper Keys

Split type Packaged and sold in four pairs per package enough for one engine.

VT No.	Mfg.	Year
11-0514	V-Twin	1957-85
11-9614	Manley	1957-85
11-9610	Manley	1986-2001
11-0805	V-Twin	1986-2001

Steel Valve Collars. Precision Machined and heat treated. Black oxide finish.

VT No.	OEM	Use	Year	Model
11-0806	18220-57	Lower	1957- E 81	900, 1000
11-0807	18220-81	Lower	1981 - E 83	900, 1000
11-0808	18220-83	Lower	L 83 - 1985	900, 1000
11-0809	18221-57B	Upper	1957-84	900, 1000
11-0810	18222-83	Lower	1986-01	883, 1100, 1200
18-0811	18219-83	Upper	1986-01	883, 1100, 1200

Andrews Valve Gear

VT No.	Item	Fits
11-9881	Low profile - .060" more spring travel. 4 pc set	1957-85
13-9251	Hi-Lift Springs .550+ No machining required	1986-2001 XL Evo

HEADS AND HARDWARE

UPPER ENGINE

3

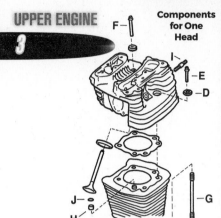

Components for One Head

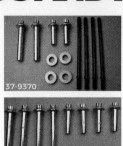
37-9370

37-8141

37-9265

Head Bolts and Hardware Kits

1986-up XL Models for one head.

VT No.	#	OEM	Item
37-9370			Hardware Kit (D,E,G)
2011-8	E	16478-85A	Head Bolt Chrome, 8 pk
	F	16480-85A	Screw Set, L 1985-91 Big Twin
2012-8	E	16478-85A	Head Bolt Chrome, 8 pack
	F	16480-92	Screw Set 1993-up XL
9507-8	G	16832-86A	Colony Stud Evolution, 1986-up XL
37-9260	G	As Above	Sifton
37-8935	H	16573-83	Insert, 8 pack
12-1187	I	16715-83	Exhaust Stud, 5 pack
14-0516	J	26432-76	O Ring, 10 pack
37-9075	D	16482-85	Washer Late1985-92, Zinc, 4 pack
37-9265	D	As Above	Chrome, 8 pieces
2017-8	D	As Above	Chrome, 8 pieces

Chrome 12 Point Head Bolt Set includes 8 washers and 8 head bolts for 1986-92 XL.

VT No. 37-9019

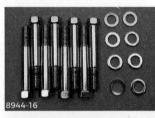
8944-16

COLONY

Head Bolt, Nut & Washers

Cad	Chrome	Fits	Type
8945-16	8944-16	1957-72	Hex
	9747-16	1957-72	Allen
8212-16	9211-16	1973-85	12 point
	9748-16	1973-85	Allen

Highest quality available. Machined from high strength steel and hardened to original factory specifications to prevent stretching. All bolts feature rolled threads for superior strength and fit.

Head Bolt Washer Kit
Fits 1957-85 Sportster models.

8170-10   8488-10

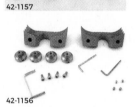

42-1158

42-1157

42-1156

Finned Head Bolt Bridge

Bolts on! 2004- Up XL.

VT No.	Finish
42-1158	Chrome
42-1157	Black
42-1156	Silver

37-9131 Installed

37-9131

37-8799

Chrome Head Bolt Covers fit 1986-2003 XL.

VT No.	Type
37-9131	Grooved
37-8799	Smooth

Headbolt Covers

9000-4

9110-9 Installed

9001-4 installed

Fit over 12 point headbolts on 1973-85 XL Sportster, 1986-up Evolution 883-1100-1200 Sportster. Evolution styles include four pieces for left side only 1973-85 Sportster kits include eight covers. Styles include hex acorn or cap with a gold or chrome plated finish. Allen wrench included.

Chrome	Gold	Model	Type
9000-4		1986-99 Evo	Acorn
9002-4		1986-99 Evo	Cap
9110-9	9111-9	1973-85 XLH	Acorn
9112-9		1973-85 XLH	Cap

1986-03 Head Bolt & Spark Plug Covers

Die cast and chrome plated to cover entire head bolt area and spark plug base. Held in place by rubber boots on spark plug wires. Fits 883-1200 XL models.

VT No. 42-0741

BIG BORE CYLINDER KIT

Big Bore kits on this Page Do Not Require Any Machining!

No Head Work Necessary

11-0473

Each kit includes
- 2 Pre-Fit Cylinders with pistons and matching Hastings Piston Rings
- 9.5:1 Compression

1200cc XL Conversion Cylinder and Piston Set includes 2 silver finished cylinders or black wrinkle with milled edge fin cylinders with fitted Wiseco or Sifton moly 9.5:1 reverse dome piston and ring set. Order Rocker box gasket set separately.

9.5:1 883-1200

VT No.	Item	Type	Finish	Years
11-0473	Cylinder/Piston Kit	Wiseco	Silver	1986-03
11-0355	Cylinder Piston Kit	Wiseco	Black	1986-03
11-0595	Cylinder/Piston Kit	Sifton Moly	Black	1986-03
11-1115	Cylinder/Piston Kit	Sifton Moly	Silver	1986-03
11-1118	Cylinder/Piston Kit	Sifton	Black	1986-03
11-1104	Cylinder/Piston Kit	Sifton	Silver	1986-03
11-1105	Cylinder/Piston Kit	Sifton	Black	1986-03
11-0346	Cylinder/Piston Kit	Wiseco	Silver	2004-up
11-0347	Cylinder/Piston Kit	Wiseco	Black	2004-up
11-0377	Cylinder/Piston Kit	Sifton Moly	Silver	2004-up
11-0378	Cylinder/Piston Kit	Sifton Moly	Black	2004-up

We recommend use of adjustable pushrods with installation of Big Bore Kits

11-0595

Each kit includes
- 2 Pre-Fit Cylinders with pistons and matching Hastings Piston Rings
- 10:1 Compression

The Sifton cylinders have a very thick, large O.D., "cast in" liner which has been proven to be an important factor to maintain thermal stability which is the ability to retain the important cylinder bore dimension through repeated heat cycles.

1200cc XL Conversion Cylinder and Piston Set includes 2 silver finished cylinders or black wrinkle with milled edge fin cylinders with fitted Wiseco 10:1 piston and ring set.

VT No.	Finish	Fits
11-0565	Silver	1986-2003
11-0589	Black	1986-2003
11-0336	Silver	2004- Up
11-0337	Black	2004- Up

10:1 883-1200 Big Bore Conversion Cylinder Kit

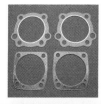

Cylinder Base/Head Gasket Set.

VT No.	Fits
15-0389	1986-2003 XL
15-0394	2004- Up XL

Power Stroke Hone Precision Fit! & **Kwik-way Boring Bar**

IRONHEAD CYLINDER KITS

1957-85 Cast Iron Cylinder & Piston Kit

11-2607

9:1	10:1 Wiseco	Year	CC
11-2605		1957-71	900
11-2606		1972- E 73	1000
11-2607	11-2617	L 1973-85	1000

VT No.	OEM	Year
8858-8	16830-72	1972-85
12-2102	16830-54	1954-71
12-2103	16830-72	1972-85

Cylinder Base Studs feature heat treating and interference thread at cylinder base. Sets of eight.

Cylinders are for stock bore, stock stroke and compression. Must be honed to standard size for proper fit.

Front	Rear	OEM	Year	CC
11-0482	11-0492	16464-58	1957-70	900
11-0488	11-0489	16464-72	1972 E 1973	1000
11-0504	11-0505	16464-73A	L 1973 - 85	1000

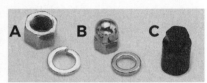

Base Nut Wrench

For 1957-85.

VT No. 16-0108

Cylinder Base Nuts for 1957-84.

Chrome	Cad	Parker-ized	#	Type
7018-16			B	Acorn
7623-8			C	XLR
		7624-8	C	XLR/Black Oxide
8106-16	8107-16	9624-16	A	Stock Hex

Rocker Cover Gasket Kits for Evolution

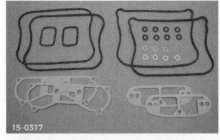

15-0317

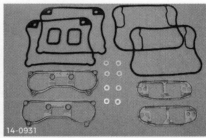

14-0931

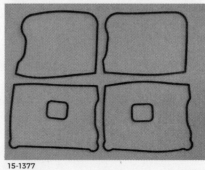

15-1377

Include upper and lower gaskets in cork or molded O-ring type with bolt seals and washers for both heads.

VT No.	GB	OEM	Type	Fits
15-0862	15-1377	17030-89	O-Ring	1986-90 883-1100-1200
	15-0317	17030-86R	Cork	1986-90 883-1100-1200
15-0863	14-0931	17030-91	O-Ring	1991-03 883-1200

Collapsible Pushrod Cover

11-0944

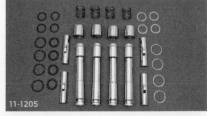

11-1205

Allow for ease of pushrod change or adjustment.

VT No.	Year
11-0944	1991-2003
11-1205	2004- Up

REPLICA CYLINDER - 1986-UP XL

11-0344 11-0343 11-0342

Cylinders for Evolution XL Models

Cylinders sold without pistons and are not honed for final fit. Sold each.

VT No.	OEM	Model	Finish	Years
11-0341	16446-86A	883	Silver	1986-03
11-0343	16447-88	1200	Black Wrinkle	1988-03
11-0344	16447-88	1200	Silver	1988-03
11-0342	16447-88	1200	Silver	1988-03
11-0334	16463-04	1200	Silver	2004-Up
11-0335	16463-04	1200	Black Wrinkle	2004-Up

CYLINDER KIT

11-2609

Replica Evolution XL Cylinder & Piston Set

Pre-fitted with cast pistons and Hastings Rings.

VT No.	Model	Finish	Years
11-2608	883	Silver	1986-03
11-2609	1200	Silver	1988-03
11-2626	1200	Black	1988-03

Each kit includes two pre-fitted cylinders with pistons and matching Hastings piston rings, two head gaskets, two base gaskets and wrist pins.

Motor Shop 1200cc Cylinder

11-1203

VT No.	Finish	Ratio
11-1200	Black	9:1
11-1204	Silver	9:1
11-1202	Black	10.5:1
11-1203	Silver	10.5:1

Sets include Wiseco fitted piston and ring sets to be used with 1200cc heads only. Fits 1988-03 1200cc as stock replacement on 1200cc only. Can not be used as Big Bore Kit for 883 models.

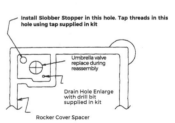

Sifton™ Evolution Rocker Box Breather Upgrade

Kit includes tap, drill bit, breather tubes and instructions. Fits 1992-up.

VT No. 16-0916

Install Slobber Stopper in this hole. Tap threads in this hole using tap supplied in kit

Umbrella valve replace during reassembly

Drain Hole Enlarge with drill bit supplied in kit

Rocker Cover Spacer

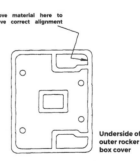

Remove material here to achieve correct alignment

Underside of outer rocker box cover

11-1682 11-1684 11-1685

OE Breather Valves

Front	Rear	Year
11-1682		2004-07
11-1684	11-1685	2007- U[
14-0955		Valve Flap

WISECO FORGED PISTON KITS

11-9885

Note: For our Product Descriptions "XL" denotes for Sportster models (including XLH, XLCH, XLS).

Wiseco High Performance Forged Piston Sets include 2 pistons that are forged from a high Silicone alloy, 2 ring sets (either Wiseco XC or Hastings X style), 2 wrist pins and 4 circlips. Wiseco rings sold per piston.

Notes:
1. Piston Kits Include Hastings X-Ring.

2. 2009- Up cylinders cannot be over-bored. Requires the purchase of 1200cc cylinder to be used with piston kit.

3. Piston Kits include Wiseco XC Ring.

	Note	Item	STD	.010	.020	.030	.040
1972-85 1000 Sportster 10:1 Compression 3 3/16" Bore	1	Piston Kit	11-9720	11-9721	11-9722	11-9723	11-9724
		Rings	11-9748	11-9749	11-9750	11-9751	11-9752
1986- Up 883 XL Evolution Overbore to 1200cc Rev Dome 8.5:1 Compression 3 1/2" Bore	1,2	Piston Kit	11-9945				
		Rings	11-9759	11-9762	11-9760		
1986- Up Piston Kits 883 XL Overbore to 1200cc 9.5:1 Rev Dome Compression 3 1/2" Bore	1,	Piston Kit	11-9885	11-9886	11-9887	11-9888	11-9889
		Rings	11-9759	11-9762	11-9760	11-9764	11-9765
1986- Up 883 XL Overbore to 1200cc Rev dome 10:1 Compression 3 1/2" Bore	1	Piston Kit	11-9846	11-9847	11-9848		
		Rings	11-9759	11-9762	11-9760		
1988-2003 1200 XL, 1986-87 1100 XL Piston Kit 1200cc XL Evo 9:1 Compression w/ flat top piston	1	Piston Kit	11-9890	11-9891	11-9892	11-9893	
		Rings	11-9759	11-9762	11-9760	11-9764	11-9765
1988-2003 1200 XL, 1986-87 11XL Evo 10.5:1 Compression	1	Piston Kit	11-9913	11-9914	11-9915	11-9916	11-9917
		Rings	11-9759	11-9762	11-9760	11-9764	11-9765
2004- Up 1200 XL Evolution 10.5:1 Compression	1	Piston Kit	11-9954	11-9955	11-9956		
		Rings	11-9759	11-9762	11-9760		
			.07	.017	.027	.037	.047
1986- Up 883 XL Evo Overbore to 1200cc Rev Dome 9.5:1 Compression 3 1/2" Bore	3	Piston Kit					11-9719
		Rings				11-9863	11-9775
1988-2003 1200 XL, 1986-87 1100 XL Evo Flat Top 9:1 Compression	3	Piston Kit					11-9861
		Rings				11-9863	

Wiseco Replacement Parts

Circlips fit all 3 1/2" bored pistons, sold pair.
VT No. 11-9779

Wrist Pins are sold each.

VT No.	Year
11-9776	3 3/16" and 3 7/8"
11-9852	3 1/2" 883 Evolution

S&S Button Style Keepers

Control wrist pin end play which varies with bore size. Button style keepers must be fully supported by wrist pin hole. Sold in pairs. 3 3/16" bore, standard to +.070, Aluminum.

VT No. 11-2170

11-2240

KB
PERFORMANCE
PISTONS

*Note: 2009-up cylinders cannot be over-bored. Requires the purchase of 1200cc cylinder to be used with piston kit.

The Keith Black 390 Hypereutectic alloy is cast in a permanent steel mold which makes it possible to build a light weight piston that makes more power, runs quietly, uses less fuel and lasts longer than any other type of piston being made today. We can now forget about running loose, noisy, oil-burning pistons. The low heat transfer of the alloy keeps the skirts cool so piston expansion is minimal. The KB piston will make maximum power at 2 to 4 degrees less total timing than conventional pistons. All KB pistons sets are supplied with Hastings Moly Ring sets.

Application	Ring End Gap Factor	Piston To Wall Clearance
Street Normally Aspirated	.0065"	.00075"-.0015"
Street Nitrous or Supercharged	.0080"	.0015"-.0025"
Flat Track Gasoline	.0080"	.0010"-.0030"
Flat Track Alcohol	.0060"	.0010"-.0030"
Drag Gasoline	.0075"	.0010"-.0030"
Drag Alcohol	.0065"	.0010"-.0030"
Drag Supercharged or Nitrous Gas	.0095"	.0015"-.0030"
Drag Supercharged Alcohol	.0085"	.0010"-.0030"
Drag Supercharged Fuel	.0115"	.0020"-.0040"

Note: It is important to use our ring end gap instructions to avoid ring butting.
Safe top ring end gaps can be found by multiplying the bore diameter by the appropriate ring gap factor from the adjoining chart.
Example: 3.5" bore "Street Normally Aspirated" = 3.5" bore x .0065" = .023" top ring end gap.
Note: Second ring end gaps do not need extra clearance.

	1000cc Sportster	1200cc Evo	1200cc Evo	883-1200cc Conversion
	XLH/XLCH	XL	XL 1988- Up	XL
Years	1972-85	1988 -Up	w/ High Cams	1986- Up
C.I.D	61"	74"	74"	74"
Bore	3.188"	3.498"	3.498"	3.498"
Stroke	3.812"	3.812"	3.812"	3.812"
Head Type	Dome	Flat Top	Flat Top	Dish
Cyl. Hght.	5.330"	4.650"	4.650"	4.650"
Comp. Ratio	8.2	9.0:1	8.9:1	10:1
STD	11-2240	11-2210	11-2245	11-2228
.005		11-2211	11-2246	11-2229
.010	11-2241	11-2212	11-2247	11-2230
.020	11-2242	11-2213	11-2248	11-2231
.030	11-2243	11-2214	11-2249	11-2232
.040	11-2244	11-2215	11-2250	11-2233

V-TWIN PISTON KIT

Over 100,000 Kits Sold Since 1978!

V-Twin Piston Kits include two cast alloy pistons, genuine Hastings three piece ring set, two wrist pins and four circlips.

UPPER ENGINE 3

Replica type piston sets use 22588-78 Pin Lock, VT No. 12-0929.

Dia.	STD 9:1 900cc XL 3" Bore	STD 9:1 1000cc XL 3 3/6" Bore	LC 8.4:1 1000cc XL 3 3/6" Bore	STD 883cu V2 Evolution	STD 1100cc V2 Evolution	STD 86-03 1200cc V2 Evolution
STD	11-0200	110208	11-0300	11-0241	11-0246	11-9761
.005				11-0242	11-0247	11-9849
.010	11-0201	11-0209	11-0301	11-0243	11-0248	11-9767
.020	11-0202	11-0210	11-0302	11-0244	11-0249	11-9768
.030	11-0203	11-0211	11-0303	11-0245	11-0250	11-9768
.040	11-0204	11-0212	11-0304	11-0440	11-0441	11-9712
.050	11-0205	11-0213	11-0305			
.060	11-0206	11-0214	11-0306			
.070	11-0207	11-0215	11-0430			

Wrist Pin & Locks

VT No.	Year/Model
11-0869	1957-85 XL
11-0872	1986-03 1100-883 XL
11-0873	1988-03 1200 XL

Wrist Pin Locks

VT No.	Year	U/M
12-0929	1978-85	10 pk
12-0949	1986- Up	10 pk

12-0929

12-0949

BIG BORE PISTON KITS

Cylinder & Piston Conversion Kit

Fits 1986-2003 1200cc XL.
VT No. 11-1118

See Tool section for more about our Motor Shop Services!

Piston Sets

11-9885

11-1680

11-1700

Include rings, wrist pins, and circlips for 1986- Up. Note: 2009-Up cylinders cannot be over-bored. Requires the purchase of 1200cc cylinder to be used with piston kits.

VT No.	Item	Brand
11-9885	Piston Kit	Wiseco
11-1680	Piston Kit, STD	Sifton
11-1700	Piston Kit, .005 OS	Sifton Moly
11-0852	Piston Kit, STD	Sifton Moly

Top End Gasket Set for Big Bore Kits

Head base gasket set with .040 gasket, beaded, blue Teflon with 4 O-Rings. Fits 1986-2003.
VT No. 15-0393

HASTINGS® RING SETS

HASTINGS H Piston Rings

Hastings Piston Rings

Replacements for OEM ring sets and will also fit our cast pistons. Available in standard or oversize versions with either a cast or moly compression ring and 3-piece oil ring in cast or moly construction. Sold in sets for two pistons.

XL/ XLCH

1000cc XLH/XLCH

3 3/16" Bore
Comp Ring 1/16"
Oil Ring 3/16"

	Cast	Moly
Mfg. #	7003	2M7003
STD	11-0109	11-1377
.010	11-0110	11-1378
.020	11-0111	11-1379
.030	11-0112	11-1380
.040	11-0113	11-1381
.050	11-0114	11-1382
.060	11-0115	11-1383
.070	11-0116	11-1384

900cc XLH/XLCH

3" Bore
Comp Ring 1/16"
Oil Ring 3/16"

	Cast	Moly
Mfg. #	6457	
STD	11-0100	
.010	11-0101	
.020	11-0102	
.030	11-0103	
.040	11-0104	
.050	11-0105	
.060	11-0106	
.070	11-0107	

One Piece Cast Iron Ring Sets

For 2 Pistons w/ 1pc oil ring		
Dia.	1000cc XL 3 3/16"	
Bore	61"	
STD		
.010	11-0161	
.020	11-2515	
.030	11-2516	
.040	11-2517	
.050	11-2518	
.060	11-2519	
.070	11-2520	

883cc XL Evolution

Bore	3"
Comp Ring	1.5mm
Oil Ring	2.8mm
	Moly
Mfg. #	2M6198
STD	11-0160
.005	11-0161
.010	11-0162
.020	11-0163
.030	11-0164
.040	11-0174

EVOLUTION

1200cc XL Evolution 1988-03

3 1/2" Bore
Comp Ring 1/2"
Oil Ring 5/36"

	Cast	Moly
Mfg. #	6164	2M6164
STD	11-0190	11-1357
.005	11-0191	11-1358
.010	11-0192	11-1359
.020	11-0193	11-1360
.030	11-0194	11-1361
.040	11-0195	11-1362

1200cc XL Evolution 2004- Up

Bore 88.85mm (3.498)
Comp Ring 1.2mm (top) 1.5mm (2nd)
Oil Ring 2.5mm

	Cast	Moly
Mfg. #		
STD		11-1394
.005		11-1395
.010		11-1395

1100cc XL Evolution

Bore 3.350mm
Comp Ring 1.5mm
Oil Ring 2.8mm

	Cast	Moly
Mfg. #		2M6199
STD		11-0165
.005		11-0166
.010		11-0167
.020		11-0168
.030		11-0169
.040		11-0175

Total Seal Ring Sets

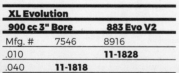

Include rings for 2 pistons with a top ring of ductile cast iron, the gapless middle ring and Gold Poser 3-pc design oil rings.

XL Evolution		
900 cc 3" Bore		883 Evo V2
Mfg. #	7546	8916
.010		11-1828
.040	11-1818	

GASKET

Evo Rocker Cover Gasket Kits

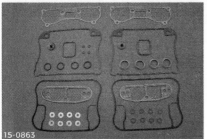

15-0863

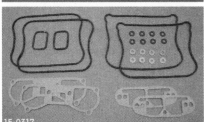

15-0317

Both upper and lower gaskets in cork or molded O-Ring type with bolt seals and washers for both heads.

James	GB	Type/Fits
15-0862		O-Ring 1986-90 883-1100-1200
15-1363		As Above, Includes metal Rocker Base Gaskets
	15-0317	Cork 1986-90 883-1100-1200
15-0863	14-0931	O-Ring 91-03 883-1200
	15-1621	As Above w/ 1pc Est Lower Rocker Gaskets
15-1454		2004-06 883-1200
15-1455	15-0786	2007- Up
	15-1622	As Above w/ 1pc Est Lower Rocker Gaskets

GB Top End Gaskets for Sportster models.

15-1612

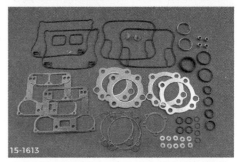

15-1613

GB Head/Base Gasket Sets

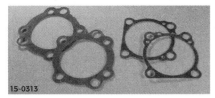

15-0313

.040 special copper head gaskets and .007" thick aluminum base gaskets, will not compress or torque. Kits include two head and two base gaskets.

VT No.	Year	Model
15-0313	1986- Up	1200
15-0675	1989- Up	883

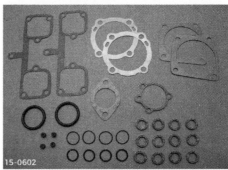

15-0602

GB No.	James	OEM	Fits
15-0257			86-2000 883 Fire Ring
	15-0970	16665-86	1986-87 1100 Blue Teflon *Fire Ring
15-0258*			
15-0366	15-1082	16773-86B	1988-00 1200 Fire Ring
15-0380	15-1083		Above, .045"
	15-1132		Above, .030"
15-0643			Graphite .030"
	15-1012	16769-57	1957-71 Teflon
15-0101	15-0973	16769-72A	1972 E73 Copper
	15-1130	16769-73T	1973-85 Copper
15-0102	15-0974	16769-82	1973-85 1100 Copper .045"
14-0516		26432-76A	1986-00 Stud O-Ring

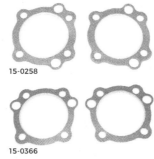

15-0258

15-0366

Cylinder Head Gaskets

V-Twin Cylinder Head Gaskets Copper. **VT No. 15-0102**

VT No.	OEM	Years	Fits
15-0600	17030-57	1957-71	900cc
15-0601	17030-72	1972-E73	1000cc
15-0602	17030-73	1973-76	1000cc
15-0603	17032-79	1977-81	1000cc
15-0618	17032-82	1982-90 1983	1000cc XR-1000
15-0635	17030-86	1985-90	883 Evolution
15-0636	17030-86A	1986-89	1100 Evolution
15-0639		1988-90	1200 Evolution
15-0053	17032-86B	1991-03	883 Evolution
15-0662	17032-91	1991-03	1200 Evolution
15-0054	17027-04	2004-up	883
15-0055	17049-04	2004-up	1200 Evolution

GB No.	James	OEM	Fits
15-0105	15-0982	16774-57	1957-71 Front and Rear, 900cc
15-0106	15-0983	16774-72	1972-85 Front and Rear, 1000cc
15-1126			Above, Metal w/ seal Coating and Bead
	15-1121	16774-86AC	1986-2003 w/ seal coating
	15-1373		As Above, .016" thick
	15-1374		As Above, .010" thick
15-0235	15-0984	16774-86D	1986-2003 Black
15-1534		16789-04	2004-up Black
15-1287		16774-86D	1986-03 Beaded

Cylinder Base Gaskets.

15-0235

15-0105

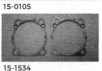

15-1534

15-0106

15-1287

15-1126

Top End Kits XL Models. Fits 2004-up. Replaces 17049-04. **VT No. 15-1616**

GASKET KITS FOR XL *Genuine*

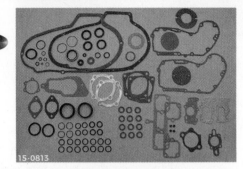

15-0813

Sportster Complete Gasket by James

VT No.	OEM	Years	Fits	Includes
15-0809	17026-71	1957-71	XLH, XLCH	Teflon Head Gasket
18-0813	17026-73	1972-85	XLH, XLCH	.032 Copper Head Gasket
15-1178	17026-86	1986-90	883-1200 XL	Teflon Head gaskets/ Rubber Rocker Gaskets
15-1366*	17026-86	1986-90	1200XL	MLS Head Gaskets
15-0818	17026-91A	1991-03	883-1200 XL	Graphite Head gaskets/ Rubber Rocker Gaskets
15-1367*	17026-91A	1991-03	1200 XL	MLS Head Gaskets
15-1450	17047-04	2004-06	883-1200 XL	
15-1451	17047-07	2007- Up	883-1200 XL	

*Note: for 883 applications, order head gaskets separately.

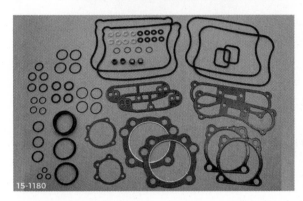

15-1180

Top End Sets by James

VT No.	OEM	Years	Fits	Includes
15-0827	17030-57	1957-71	XL	Teflon Head Gasket
15-0828	17030-72	1972-85	XL	Copper Head Gasket
15-1180*	1703086B	1986-90	1200 XL	Teflon Head Gaskets/ Rubber Rocker Gaskets
15-1365*	17032-86	1986-90	1200 XL	MSL Head Gaskets
15-0835*	17032-91	1991-03	1200 XL	Graphite Head gaskets/ Rubber Rocker Gaskets
15-1368*	17032-91	1991-03	1200 XL	MLS Head Gaskets
15-1452*	17049-04	2004-06	1200 XL	
15-1453*	17049-07	2007- Up	1200 XL	

*Note: 883 applications order head gaskets separately.

GB Evolution Sportster 3pc Rubber Coated Gaskets

15-0475

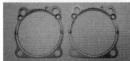

15-0487

Features a stainless center sandwiched between two rubber coated stainless spring steel outer layers. The outer layers are embossed at the oil drain hole and cylinder bore area that provides a correct seal. Sold in pairs.

Size	3 1/2" Bore	3 5/8" Bore	3 13/16" Bore	3 3/4" Bore
Cylinder Base Gaskets 1986-99 XL, 883-1200				
.010	15-0487	15-0489		
.020	15-0488	15-0490		
Head Gaskets 1986-99 XL				
.030	15-0475	15-0477	15-0479	15-0481
.040	15-0476	15-0478	15-0480	15-0482

VT No.	James	OEM	Year
15-0112	15-1003	17536-70	1957-84
15-0640		Beaded	1957-84
	15-1270	Metal w/bead	1957-84
15-0366	15-1134	17353-86	1986-up
15-0260	15-0991	17353-86	1986-up Lower (Cork)
	15-0993	17354-86A	1986 Upper
15-0386	15-1135	17354-86A	1986-90 Upper
14-0933	15-0992	17353-89	1989-up Lower
	15-0994	17354-89	1991-up Upper

Engine Gasket for Sportster by GB

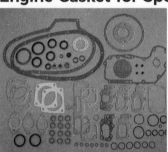

15-0501

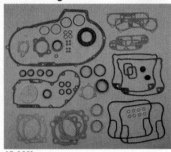

15-0661

VT No.	OEM	Years	Models
15-0500	17026-70	1957-71	900cc
15-0501	17026-71	1972-E73	1000cc
15-0502	17026-73	1973-76	1000cc
15-0503	17026-79	1977-78	1000cc
15-0634*	17026-82	1982-85	1000cc
15-0523	17026-83	1983	XR-1000
15-0633	17026-86	1985-89	883 Evolution
15-0632	17026-86A	1986-89	1100 Evolution
15-0691	17026-88	1988-90	1200 Evolution
15-0661	17026-91A	1991-03	1200 Evolution

*Note: Contains the thick low compression type head gasket. VT No. 15-0603 or 15-0504 can also be used for this application if a higher compression ratio is desired.

Rocker Box Gaskets

Metal Cylinder Base Gasket has a steel base metal which has been coated on both sides with a specially formulated high temperature oil resistant rubber compound. Silicone beading around the inner and outer perimeter forms a seal on both sides of gasket, pairs. Available from James. 1986-Up XL Evolution.

VT No. 15-1121

Motor Shop Services Sportster 4-Speed Mainshaft Gear Cluster Assemblies

17-1252

Each shaft is assembled with correct thickness thrust washers and snap ring for proper gear clearance. Also included is shaft end play washer assortment for proper end play shimming during installation.

VT No.	Year
17-1250	1956-69 XLCH
17-1251	1967-70 XLH Only
17-1252	1971-E84
17-1253	Late1984-86
17-1254	1987-90

TRANSMISSION 4

4-SPEED TRANSMISSION INSTALLATION TIPS

VT No. 17-0028, 17-0027, 17-0032, 17-0030, 17-0033, 17-0034, 17-0031, 17-0029

All XL Transmission assemblies are bench tested for positive gear engagement and disengagement but it is always best for a final check after unpacking transmission before being installed.

All V-Twin Transmissions are assembled with late style shifter cam plate that uses welded in pin for neutral switch indicator. On some early(Pre 1974) case this pin may have to be shortened or removed to allow cam plate to move freely. Failure to check this will cause transmission to not completely shift through all gears. This should be checked first prior to assembly.

Gear Engagement Check

Rotate pawl carrier (EE) until pawl carrier contacts lifter arm (Y+X). Hold the shifter cam (D) with opposite hand to prevent cam follower (I) from completing gearshifts. If hand pressure is released from shifter cam the gears will be drawn into complete engagement and all inspection procedures will be performed incorrectly.

Shift transmission into first gear then check gear to dog Pocket Engagement. Correct engagement should be 25%.

Shift transmission into all other gears checking Pocket Engagement, which must be at least 50%.

Filing of lifter arms (Y+X) will produce changes in Pocket Engagement.

Establishing Mainshaft and Countershaft Endplay

Use the thinnest low gear washer and mainshaft washer. On 1954-early 84 models the mainshaft thrust washer must be installed with Tang Down. For 1954-early 1984 models the mainshaft needle bearing will have to be installed. Temporarily install access cover to crankcase with all transmission parts. Carefully align Cover Dowel Pins and with a rawhide mallet tap into position and install four cap screws.

When installing transmission into case check shift fork shaft for correct alignment to case. Do not force transmission into case if shift fork shaft will not go in to case. If shift fork shaft is forced into case damage or bending to shaft will happen causing shifter roller finger to bind against shifter cam plate or shifter fork binging on shaft or with pawl carrier assembly.

On 1954-E84 Models Inspect case race and rollers, if badly pitted scored or worn they should be replaced. Correct fit of main bearing is .0006in-.0014in. If clearance is beyond specified limit a new race and bearings must be installed, and line lapped for proper fit. Note: Fitment of door to case may sometimes requires reaming of holes in access door or removal of alignment pins from case. If removal of dowel pins is necessary tapping dowel pin holes and use of additional bolts is suggested.

Note also that even during factory assembly process several access doors were tried before final assembly.

Using a Dial Indicator measure mainshaft endplay from sprocket side of shaft, press against clutch gear so that bearing seats against lock ring in access cover. Move shaft back and forth and measure endplay while holding clutch gear in. If endplay is not with specification (see chart) install thrust washer of suitable size.

With access cover still in place bend a discarded spoke or other suitable wire and wedge into hole on end of countershaft. Push and pull countershaft and measure endplay with dial indicator. If endplay is not within specification (see chart) install countershaft washer of suitable size.

After countershaft endplay has been established install oiler plug in access cover with oil hole up.

Note: On 1959-early 84 models the clutch must be temporarily installed and the 1984-85 models the Stator spacing ring and the Stator must be installed on access door before above Endplay clearances can be established.

When Mainshaft and Countershaft end play established install new shifter shaft into the crankcase so that the shifter lever arm is centered. Using a grease pencil mark the shaft at the 12 o'clock position by marking the shaft you can tell if the shifter lever arm position changes when installing the transmission. Correct shaft to shifter pawl yoke engagement is important for proper gear shifting. Install transmission and rotate countershaft slowly to check that the gear shift arm is engaged with shifter pawl. To do so rotate shift lever, a noticeable resistance to movement indicates proper engagement.

4-SPEED TRANSMISSION

TRANSMISSION

4

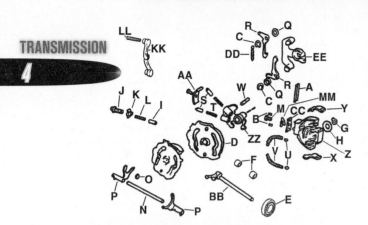

Transmission End Play Specifications

	1956-78	1979-Early84	Late1984-85
Countershaft	0.004-0.009	0.007-0.015	0.004-0.015
Mainshaft	0.003-0.009	0.003	0.003

1984-90 Sifton Units with Billet Door

17-0039   17-0029

17-0031

17-0028

17-0030

17-0027

17-0033

17-0034

17-0032

Complete XLH-XLCH 4 Speed Transmission Gear Assembly Unit includes gears, mainshaft, countershaft, shift forks and shafts assembled to trap door. Order right side case races, rollers, shims and bearings separately. Shift selector shaft included.

Note: Main and countershaft end play and trap door alignment with case must be established and adjusted prior to final assembly.

VT No.	Years	VT No.	Years
17-0028	1956-66 XLH, XLCH 1967-69 XLCH	**17-0027**	1967-70 XLH, 1970 XLCH
17-0032	1971-72 XLH, XLCH	**17-0030**	1973-74
17-0033	1975-76	**17-0034**	1977-84
17-0031	L 1984-85	**17-0039**	1986
17-0029	1987-90		

BATCH OF ASSEMBLED TRANSMISSIONS

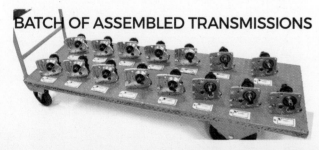

5-SPEED TRANSMISSION GEAR

17-9110

17-9101

17-9103

17-9104

17-9144

17-9105

17-9180

17-9170

17-9153

5-Speed Parts for 1991-2003 by Andrews

VT No.	OEM	Item	Fits	Brand
17-9110	2 pc Set	2.61 close ratio 1st gear set	1991-03	Andrews
17-9101	35771-89	2nd main/ 3rd counter	1991-03	Andrews
17-9103	35772-89	3rd main/ 2nd counter	1991-03	Andrews
17-9104	35773-89	4th gear/ Main	1991-03	Andrews
17-9144	35775-89	4th gear/ Counter	1991-03	Andrews
17-9105	35034-89	Main drive gear (1989-03)	1989-03	Andrews
17-9153	35633-89	Counter drive gear, (1989-03)	1989-03	Andrews
17-9180	35640-89	Mainshaft, (1989-03)	1989-03	Andrews
17-9183	35640-89	Mainshaft, (1989-03)	1989-03	V-Twin
17-9182	35641-89	Countershaft, (1989-03)	1989-03	V-Twin
17-9170	35641-89	Countershaft, (1989-03)	1989-03	Andrews
17-0723	35163-06	Mainshaft (2006- Up)	2006-up	V-Twin

Drain Plug

COLONY

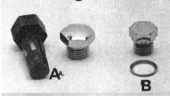
A

B

A. Chrome Dome head plug with an oversize thread and one tap for rethreading the stripped out drain hole. Fits 1965-up O.H.V. Big Twin and 1967-up 4-speed Sportster.

B. Stock Style of drain plug and brass gasket used on Sportster transmission and motor case also oil tank with 1/2"-13 thread.

VT No.	Type	Letter
7502-2	Plug and Tap	A
7503-1	Plug Only	A
8494-1	Chrome	B
8495-1	Cadmium	B
8495-1T	Cadmium	B
15-0194	Gasket, Brass	B
15-1158	Gasket, Brass (James)	B

Medium Close Ratio

1st and 2nd for 1991-2003 drags and modified street bikes needing closer ratio shifts through 1st and 2nd gear, ratio "S" gear sets will be a distinct advantage. Set of 2 gears.

VT No.	Ratio/Fits
17-9816	2.368 1st gear set
17-9724	1.876 2nd gear set

5 Speed			
Main Drive	Drive	Seal	Spacer
17-9105	Belt	14-0962	17-0560
17-9105	Chain	14-0616	17-9851

Super Close Ratio 1st, 2nd, 3rd, 4th "Y" gear sets will put more usable torque where it belongs-at high RPMs. 2 gears per set. Fits 1991-03.

17-9717

VT No.	Ratio	Gear
17-9717	2.026	1st
17-9727	1.670	2nd
17-9737	1.364	3rd

1991-03 5-Speed Gear Sets

Available as kits which include: 1st gears, 2.68, counter and main, 2 pieces; 2nd gears, counter and main, 2 pieces; 3rd gears, counter and main, 2 pieces; 4th gears, counter and main, 2 pieces; 5th gears, counter and main, 2 pieces, countershaft,1 piece; and mainshaft, 1 piece.

VT No. 17-6015

17-0956

1994-2003 5-Speed Trans Doors Stock.			
VT No.	OEM	Item	Type
17-0956	25238-94	Door	Stock
37-8935	16573-83	Insert	Stock

1991-up 5-Speed Transmission Hardware.			
VT No.	OEM	Item	Years
12-1159	11019	Retaining Ring	1991-03
12-0905	11031	Retaining Ring	1991-03
12-0968	33653-90	Retaining Ring	1991-03
13-9225	34481-91A	Spring	1991-03
13-9232	34491-91	Spring	1991-03
17-9853	6003	Thrust washer	1991-Up
12-0366	8876A	Bearing, 4 pc	1991-Up
12-0339	8977	Bearing, closed end	1991-Up
12-0361	8996A	Ball Bearing	1991-Up
12-0928	11067	Retaining Ring	1991-Up
12-0952	11161	Retaining Ring	1991-Up
14-0534	11165	Quad Seal	1991-Up
14-0918	12030	Oil Seal	1991-Up
14-0962*	12067B	Oil Seal	1991-Up
17-0560*	33344-94	Spacer, Belt	1994-Up
17-0586	35020-89	Retainer, Countershaft	1991-Up
12-9997	35051-89	Needle Bearing	1991-Up
17-0588	35063-89	Spacer	1991- Up
17-9851**	33334-85	Spacer	1985-1993

*Note: Use on 1991-up with rear belt.
**Note: Use on 1991-up with rear chain. Requires 14-0616 seal.

4-SPEED XLH-XLCH GEARS

17 Tooth Clutch Gears for Sportsters

Includes bushing and Torrington needle bearing.

Andrews	VT No.	#	OEM	Fits
	17-1140	A	37449-56	1956-66 XLH-XLCH
				1967-69 XLCH
	17-1141	B	37448-67	1967-70 XLH, 1970 XLCH
17-8710	17-1142	C	37448-71	1971-E79 XL
17-8711	17-9760	D	37448-79	L1979-E84 XL
	17-9826	E	37448-84A	L1984-86
17-4850	17-9146	F	37448-87	1987-90, 18T

4-Speed Gear Sets for Sportster

Available as kits which include: 1st gears, counter and main, 2 pieces; 2nd gears, counter and main, 2 pieces; 3rd gears, counter and main, 2 pieces; 4th gears, counter and main, 2 pieces; the countershaft, and mainshaft, must be ordered separately.

1973-78	1979-84	Evolution, 4-Speed	Brand	
17-6011	17-7654		Andrews	"W" 1st. Stock 4th
17-6012	17-7655	17-7656	Andrews	"W" 1st, "C" 4th
17-6013	17-7657		Andrews	Stock 1st, Stock 4th
	17-0761		V-Twin	
17-6014	17-7658	17-7659*	Andrews	Stock 1st, "C" 4th

*Note: Requires use of early countershaft 35613-58, **VT No. 17-0328, 17-1151 or 17-8248**

Needle Bearings

Feature full compliment roller design.

VT No.	Torrington	OEM	Type/Use
12-0461	12-0326	35690-54	Closed Transmission
12-0396	12-0327	35961-52	Open, Transmission

1st and Countershaft Drive Gear

VT No.	Andrews	#	OEM	Teeth	Shaft	Fits
17-1122		A	15277-52A	27	Main	1954-90
17-1053			Sifton	27	Main	1954-90
17-0168*		B	25760-54	17	Counter	1954-72
17-1119	17-1060	C	35760-73	17	Counter	1973-83
17-9825		D	35760-84A	17	Counter	1984-90
	17-8580	E	35695-58	27	Counter	1958-86
17-5621	17-5620	F	35695-87	26	Counter	1987-90
17-1143		E	Sifton	27	Counter	1958-86

*Note: Includes speedometer drive gear

2nd Gears

VT No.	Andrews	#	OEM	Teeth	Shaft	Fits
17-1126	17-8241	C	35750-58A	20	Counter	1958-90
	17-8242	B	35296-56A	23	Main	1956-90
17-1123	Sifton		35296-56A,	23	Main	1956-90

3rd Gears

VT No.	Andrews	#	OEM	Teeth	Shaft	Fits
	17-8243	D	35709-54B	23	Counter	1954-90
17-1124	Sifton	D	35709-54B	23	Counter	1954-90
17-1120	17-8244	A	35305-56A	20	Main	1956-90

Andrews "C" Ratio Gear Sets

Provide true close ratio shifting for XL gear boxes.

*Note: From 1987-90 all XL models have "C" Ratio Main Drive Gears as stock parts. Also fits late 1984 alternator 1000cc models.

VT No.	Fits	Gear	Stock Ratio	"C" Ratio
17-8721	1979- E 84 XL	1st	2.52	2.29
17-4850*	L 1984-90 XL	2nd	1.83	1.66
17-5622*	L 1984-90 XL	3rd	1.38	1.26
		4th	1.00	1.00

Andrews Wide Ratio 1st Gear Sets changes 1st from 2.52 ratio to 2.68 for more low end torque with 21T or 22T trans sprocket. Fits 1973-85. Can also be used on 1986-90 models if early type countershaft is used.

VT No. 17-9856

4-SPEED MAIN SHAFT HARDWARE

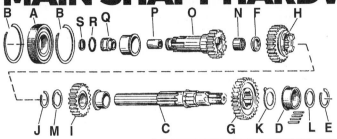

Main Shaft Hardware

VT No.	OEM	#	Years	Item
12-0308	9025A	A		Ball Bearing, each
12-9936	9025A	A		As Above, Torrington
12-0378	35030-89	A	1989-up 5-Speed	Ball Bearing
12-0958	11006	B	1986-up	Retaining Ring Inner,
12-0965	11180	B	1984-90	Retaining Ring Outer
12-0930	35112-52	B	1954-E 84	Retaining Ring,
12-0966	35112-84	B	L 1984-85	Retaining Ring Inner
17-1165	35044-56	C	1956-69 XLCH-XLH 1967-69 XLCH	Mainshaft
17-8080	As above	C		Andrews
17-1166	35046-67	C	1967-70 XLH	Mainshaft
17-1167	35046-71A	C	1971-E84, XL	Mainshaft
17-8120	As above	C		Andrews
17-9982	35036-84A	C	1984-90 XL	Mainshaft

Main Shaft Oil Seals

17-1160			1952-E1984	
14-0150			L 1984-1990	

XL Trans Main Bearing Race

VT No.	OEM	#	Years	Size
17-1136	35105-52	D	1954-83	Standard
17-1178	As Above	D	Jims	Standard
17-1137		D	1954-83	.002
17-1138		D	1954-83	.005
17-1180	As Above	D	Jims	.005
17-1139		D	1954-83	.010
17-9912		D	1954-83	.020
17-9924	35105-83	D	E 1984 only	Standard
17-9925		D	E 1984 only	.005
17-9927		D	E 1984 only	.002
12-0359	9118	DD	1984-90	Bearing
12-0361	8996	DD	1991-2005	Bearing
17-1182	35041-84	D	L 1984-90	Standard
17-1183		D	L 1984-90	.002
17-1184		D	L 1984-90	.005
12-0931	35113-52	E	1954 E84	Retaining Ring
17-9913	35216-79	F	Thrust Washer	.212
17-1125	35361-56	F	Thrust Washer	

Main Shaft Hardware

VT No.	OEM	#	Years	Item
17-1122	35277-52A	G	1954-86	M.S. First Gear, 27 T
17-1050	As Above	G		Andrews
17-8242	35296-56A	H	1956-90,	Andrews M.S. Second gear, 23 T
17-1120	35305-56A	I	1956-90	M.S. Third Gear, 20 T
17-8244	As above	I		Andrews
12-0932	35337-56	J	1956-up	Snap Ring
17-1128	35326-73	K	1954-78	Thrust washers .080, 5pk
17-9752	35326-Set	K	1954-78 Right	.030-.125 -15 pc
17-9236	35385-84	K	1984-90	.067 Right Side, 5 pk
17-9237	35384-84	K	.072 As above	
17-9238	35383-84	K	.079 As above	
17-9239	35382-84	K	.084 As above	
17-9240	35381-84	K	.090 As above	
17-9241	35380-84	K	.096 As above	
17-9247	35385-Set	K	1984-90,	.067-.096, 6 pc
17-9930	35360-Set	K	1979-83,	.098-1.25, 4 pc
17-1129	35363-52	L	Thrust washer	
17-1127	35364-56	M	Thrust washer	
17-0089	35356-86	M	Thrust washer	
12-0327	35961-52	N	Needle Bearing	
17-1140	37449-56	O	1956-66 XLH-XLCH, 1967-69 XLCH	Clutch gear
17-1141	37448-67	O	1967-70 XLH, 70 XLCH	Clutch gear
17-1142	37448-71	O	1971-E79 XL	Clutch gear
17-8710	As above	O		Andrews
17-9760	37448-79	O	L 1979-E 84 XL	Clutch gear includes P, N, F installed
17-8711	As Above	O		Andrews
17-9826	37448-84A	O	L 1984-86, All	Clutch Gear
17-9146	37448-87	O	1987-90	Clutch Gear
17-4850	As Above	O		Andrews Set 2 pc
10-0751	37458-52	P		Bushing, Clutch Gear
10-0764	37538-56	Q		End Bushing Clutch Gear
14-0502	11103	R		O-Ring
14-0127	37531-56B	S		Seal

XL Transmission Rollers

23 Pack	100 Pack	OEM	Size
17-1147		9095	STD
17-1148	12-4588	9096	.0004
17-1149	124589	9097	.0008

Oil Seal and Retainer Kit

Metal retainer with seal. Replaces 35150-52, includes gasket and screws. Fits all 1952-Early 1984.

VT No. 17-1160

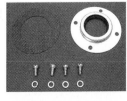

17-1167

17-1166

XL Mainshaft

Andrews	VT No.	OEM	Fits
17-8080	17-1165	35044-56	1956-66 KH-XL-XLH-XLCH 1967-69 XLCH
	17-1166	35046-67	1967-70 XLH, 1970 XLCH
17-8120	17-1167	35046-71A	1971-E84 XLH-XLCH
	17-0143	35046-71A	As Above, Sifton
17-8121	17-9982	35036-84A	1984-90 XLH
17-9180	17-9183	35640-89	1991-05 XLH
	17-0723		2006-up XL

4-SPEED XL COUNTERSHAFT

17-1261

Countershaft Assemblies

VT No.	Year
17-1260	1954-72
17-1261	1973-E 84
17-1262	L 1984-86
17-1263	1987-90

1954- E 84 Sportster Countershaft Hardware

Washers sold in 5pks unless noted.

VT No.	OEM	#	Item	VT No.	OEM	#	Item
17-9200	35818-72	A	.020	17-9231	35821-52	A	.055
17-9228	32327-73	A	.025	17-9232	35824-52	A	.060
17-9201	35818-72	A	.030	17-9233	35825-72	A	.065
17-9229	35328-73	A	.035	17-9203	35828-72	A	.070
17-9202	35821-72	A	.040	17-9234	35829-52	A	.075
17-9227	35329-73	A	.045	17-9204	35830-72	A	.080
17-9230	35820-52	A	.050	17-9205	35326-86	A	.085

VT No.	OEM	#	Item
17-1132	Set of 12	A	.020, .025, .030,.035, .040, .045, .050, .055,.060, .065, .070, .075
12-0326	35960-54	B	Countershaft Bearing
17-9253	35836-55	C	.075 Washer
17-9254	35838-55	C	.085 Washer
17-9206	35839-55	C	.100 Washer
17-9235	35840-52	C	.065 Washer
17-1133	Set of 4	C	.065, .075, .085, .100 Washer
17-1151	35613-58	D	Countershaft
17-8248	As above	D	Andrews
17-0328	As above	D	Sifton
17-8580	35695-58	E	Countershaft Drive, 27T Andrews
17-8243	35709-54B	F	Countershaft Third, 23T, Andrews
17-1126	35750-58	G	Countershaft Second
17-8241	As above	G	Andrews
17-0168	35760-54	H	Countershaft Low 1958-72 with Speedometer Gear 17T
17-1119	35760-73	H	Countershaft Low Gear, 17T 1973-Early84
17-1060	As above	H	Andrews
10-2516	35787-52	I	1st Gear Bushing, 1954-Early72
10-0752	35787-72	I	1st Gear Bushing, Late1972-Early84
17-9771	35631-54	J	Oiler Plug 1954-72
17-9871	35631-73	J	Oiler Plug 1973-86
17-1135	35809-58	K	Thrust washer
17-1134	35841-58	L	Thrust washer
12-0327	35961-52	M	Countershaft Bearing, Open

L 1984-85 Sportster Countershaft Hardware

VT No.	OEM	#	Item
17-9200	35818-72	A	.020 Washer
17-9228	35327-73	A	.025 Washer
17-9201	35819-72	A	.030 Washer
17-9229	35328-73	A	.035 Washer
17-9202	35821-72	A	.040 Washer
17-9227	35329-73	A	.045 Washer
17-9230	35820-52	A	.050 Washer
17-9231	35821-52	A	.055 Washer
17-9232	35824-52	A	.060 Washer
17-9233	35825-72	A	.065 Washer
17-9203	35828-72	A	.070 Washer
17-9234	35829-52	A	.075 Washer
17-9204	35830-72	A	.080 Washer
17-9205	35818-72	A	.085 Washer
17-1132	Set of 12	A	.020, .025, .030,.035, .040, .045, .050, .055,.060, .065, .070, .075
12-0326	35960-54	B	Countershaft Bearing
17-9929	Set of 4	C	.047, .056, .066, .080
17-9831	35613-84	D	Countershaft
17-8580	35695-58	E	Countershaft Drive, 27T, Andrews
17-8243	35709-54B	F	Countershaft Third, 23T, Andrews
17-1126	35750-58	G	Countershaft Second
17-8241	As above	G	Andrews
17-9825	35760-84A	H	Countershaft Low, 17T
12-0368	8888	I	Low Gear Bearing
17-9871	35631-73	J	Oiler Plug
17-1135	35809-58	K	Thrust washer
17-1134	35841-58	L	Thrust washer
12-0327	35961-52	M	Countershaft Bearing, Open

1986-90 Sportster Countershaft Hardware

VT No.	OEM	#	Item
17-9221	35865-86	A&C	Thrust washer .030,
17-9223	35864-86	A&C	.035 As Above
17-9224	35863-86	A&C	.040 As Above
17-9225	35862-86	A&C	.045 As Above
17-9226	35861-86	A&C	.050 As Above
17-9251	35860-86	A&C	.055 As Above
17-9928	Set of 6	A&C	.030, .035, .040, .045, .050, .055
12-0326	35960-54	B	Bearing
17-9831	35613-84	D	Countershaft, Sifton
17-5621	35695-87E	E	Countershaft Drive 26T
17-5620	As Above	E	Andrews
17-8243	35709-54B	F	Third Gear, 23T, Andrews
17-1126	35750-56	G	Second Gear
17-8241	As above	G	Andrews
17-9825	35760-84A	H	Low Gear, 17T
12-0368	8888	I	Low Gear Bearing Countershaft
17-1135	35809-58	K	Thrust washer
17-1134	35841-58	L	Thrust washer
12-0327	35961-52	M	Bearing, Open

Sifton ™ Countershafts

17-0328

VT No.	OEM	Year
17-0328	35613-58	1954- E 84
17-9831	35613-84	1984-90
17-9182	35641-89	1991- Up, 5 Speed

4-SPEED XLH-XLCH TRANSMISSION

17-1172

17-1164

17-1189

17-1162

17-1171

Gear Selector Shaft

1954- Up Sportster models. *All are splined on shift lever end.

VT No.	OEM	Year
17-1164*	34628-54A	1954-74
17-1186	34628-54	1954-74
17-1162*	34627-75	1975-76
17-1189*	34628-75	1977-85
17-1171*	34628-86	1986-90
17-1172*	34015-91	1991-2003
17-0987	34014-06	2006-up
10-1259	35404-74	1977-up, Thrust washer
14-0102	12010	1986-up Oil Seal
10-0733	40520-63	1979-up Bushing
10-0724	34037-52	1954-74 Bushing
14-0160	37101-84	1984-up Oil Seal
12-1292	16825-48	1954-74 End Plug

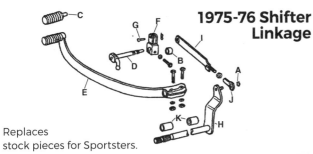

1975-76 Shifter Linkage

Replaces stock pieces for Sportsters.

VT No.	#	OEM	Item
12-0938	A	11016	Retainer
10-2483	B	34037-75	Bushing
21-0901	C	34611-65	Rubber
17-1162	D	34627-75	Shaft, Shifter
21-2034	E	34666-75	Lever, Chrome
17-0065	F	34670-75	Inner Lever
23-0421	G	42269-30	Clevis Pin washer and Cotter Pins
17-9758	H	42548-75	Cross Shaft
17-9780	I	42583-75	Shift Link
17-9781	J	42585-75	Pivot End, 5/16"x24
10-2505	K	47757-52	Bushings, 2pk

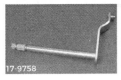

17-9758

17-9781

17-0065

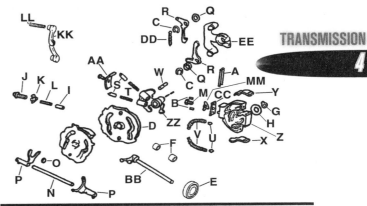

VT No.	OEM	#	Item
12-0974	638	B	Pin Arm Support
12-0939	11036	C	Retaining Ring
17-0061	34012-52C	D	Cam Plate 1952-76
17-0502	34012-75B	D	Cam Plate 1977-90
14-0116	34035-52	E	Oil Seal, 5 pack
10-0724	34037-52	F	Shifter Shaft Brush, pair
12-0917	34040-52	G	Cam Retainer Ring
17-0086	34060-52	H	Thrust Washer 1954-76, each
17-9911	35336-74	H	Thrust Washer 1977-90, each
17-0076	34062-52	I	Shifter Cam Follower
17-0067	34065-52	J	Cam Follower Bolt, each
17-0923	34067-52	K	Cam Bolt Lock Tab
17-0751	Kit	I,J,K	Cam Follower Kit
17-9845	34063-84	KK	Shifter Cam Follower
13-0130	34068-52	L	Cam Follow Spring
13-9161	29980-84A	LL	As Above 1984-up
17-0227	4621	M	Shifter Cam Bolt 1954-Early 84
17-0231	3854	M	Shifter Cam Bolt Late 1984-90
17-0919	34069-71	MM	Bolt Lock, Shift Cam
17-1159	34141-52A	N	Fork Shaft
17-0118	34168-52	O	Roller, Shift Fork, pair
17-1152	34291-52B	P	STD Steel Shift Fork
17-9793			+.005 Steel Fork
17-9792			-.005 Steel Fork
17-1153			+.010 Steel Fork
17-1154			-.010 Steel Fork
17-1155	34292-72		+.020 Steel Fork
17-1156	34293-72		-.020 Steel Fork
17-9790			+.030 Steel Fork
17-9791			-.030 Steel Fork
17-1175			Standard Forged Brass Shift Fork
17-1173			+.010 Forged Brass Fork
17-1174			-.010 Forged Brass Fork
17-1176			+.020 Forged Brass Fork
17-1177			-.020 Forged Brass Fork
17-0058	34461-72	Q	Shift Pawl Spacer
17-0953	34476-72	R	Shift Pawl (2), Sifton
17-0073	34477-53	S	Shift Pawl Left, each
	34478-53	S	Shift Pawl Right, each
13-0133	34482-53	T	Shift Pawl Spring
17-0056	34485-52	U	Plug Retainer
13-0134	34500-52A	V	Pawl Carrier Spring
17-0055	34503-52	W	Pawl Carrier Pin
17-0054	34506-52A	X	Pawl Lifter Arm, Low
17-0053	34507-52A	Y	Pawl Lifter Arm, High
17-0233	Set	XY	Pawl Lifter Arm Set
	34514-75A	Z	Pawl Support, 1977-90
17-9847	34514-75A	Z	Pawl Support, 1977-90
	34489-52A	ZZ	Pawl Carrier 1954-71
17-9949	34494-74C	EE	Pawl Carrier 1972-90
17-0052	34525-70	AA	Pawl Retainer
17-1164	34628-54A	BB	Shift Shaft 1954-74
17-1162	34627-75	BB	Shaft 1975-76
17-0051	35891-66	CC	Shim, Pawl Support
13-0137	37222-52	DD	Shift Pawl Spring, 1972-90
13-9232	34491-91	DD	Shift Pawl Spring, 1991-up

TRANSMISSION COMPONENTS

TRANSMISSION 4

17-1175

17-1152

Shifter Forks

Shifter Forks are steel type or brass forks available in standard or offset dimension. Both are one piece forged, heat treated and machined to stock specification.

Use on all 4 Speed 1952-90. Sold each.

Brass	Steel	Size
17-1175	17-1152	Standard
	17-9793	+.005
	17-9792	-.005
17-1173	17-1153	+.010
17-1174	17-1154	-.010
17-1176	17-1155	+.020
17-1177	17-1156	-.020
17-9794	17-9790	+.030
17-9795	17-9791	-.030

17-9847

17-0087

Pawl Carrier

Pawl Carrier Support only. Fits 1977-90, Replaces 34514-75A.

VT No. 17-9847

Pawl Carrier Assembly is an exact replica of forged aluminum as original and includes all internal parts assembled for XL 1952-90 4-Speed models. Replaces 34016-77. Order bolt separately.

VT No.	Item
17-0087	Assembly
17-9949	Pawl Carrier
17-0227	Bolt 1954- E 84
17-0231	Bolt for L 1984-90

Shifter Pawl Assembly

Includes shifter pawl carrier, Shifter pawls, pawl springs, pawl spacer and retaining rings. Fits 1972-90 all XL models.

VT No. 17-9801

Crank Case Vent Fitting

Replaces 34744-77. Fits 1977-80.
VT No. 40-0513

17-1187

17-9919

17-0956

XLH-XLCH Transmission Products

Guaranteed for quality and fit.

VT No.	Years	Item	Type
17-1161	1957-83	Door	Replica
17-1187		Door w/Bearing	Replica
17-9148	1984-90	Door w/Alternator	Sifton
17-0956	1994- Up	Door	Stock
37-8935	1991- Up	Insert	Stock
12-1154	1957-90	Dowel	Pin, Standard
12-1155	1957-90	Dowel	.010 Oversize

37-8935

Shifter Cam Follower

Replaces 34063-84 on 1985-90, made of durable steel.

VT No.	Item
17-9845	Shifter Cam Follower
13-9161	Spring

Cam Follower Kit includes steel follower and two springs Fits 1985-90.
VT No. 17-0850

Shifter Finger Roller

Replaces 34168-52. Fits 1954-90, sold in pairs.
VT No. 17-0118

Shifter Fork Shaft

VT No.	OEM	Years
17-1159	34141-52A	1952-84
17-1170	34141-84A	1985-Up

Case Repair

Weld In Case Repair Section fits 1957-83 cases.
VT No. 43-0116

VT No.	OEM	Size	Use
37-0096	707	1/2- 13	XL Transmission
37-0098	720, 706A	5/8 - 18	Oil Tank and Time Hole
37-8961	718	1/4 - 18	NPT Chain Cover

Drain Plugs

Magnetic drain plugs prevent metal particles from circulating through engine and transmission cases, oil tank, etc.

Front

Back

17-9148

Is 7775-T6 aluminum and tempered 83, 000lb tensile strength

ACCESS DOORS

17-9148 Door Production

COVER 1971-76

43-0109 43-0173 43-0125

Sprocket cover features starter motor cut out, fits 1971-76 XLCH-XLH kick and electric start or electric start only models. Stock replacement type, not reinforced.

Polish	Chrome	Type
43-0108	43-0109	Kick / Electric
	43-0173	Electric Only
	43-0125	Electric Only

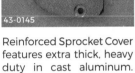

43-0145 43-0180

Reinforced Sprocket Cover features extra thick, heavy duty in cast aluminum. Fits 1971-76 XLH-XLCH.

Polish	Chrome	Type
43-0117	43-0145	Kick Only
43-0118	43-0180	Kick/ Electric

1971-78 Kick Starter Return Spring Stud

VT No.	Finish
17-0156	Chrome
9900-1	Chrome
9901-1	Cadmium

COVER 1986-UP

43-0185 43-0186 43-0150

TRANSMISSION 4

43-0129 43-0130 43-0130 Installed

43-0080 43-0149 43-0166 43-0167

Sprocket Covers

Covers are die-cast as original. Order hardware separately. Fits XLS-XLH.

Polished	Chrome	Black	OEM	Year
43-0166	43-0167		34911-81B	1986-90
43-0129	43-0130		34911-81A	1981-85
	43-0080		Belt	1986-90
43-0149	43-0150	43-0330	34911-91	1991-03
43-0185	43-0186	43-0329	34932-04	2004-up

SPROCKET COVER 1977-80

43-0111, 43-0138   43-0112, 43-0144   43-0172   43-0177   43-0119, 43-0178   43-0120, 43-0152

1977-78 Sprocket Covers for XLCH kick only, and XLH kick and electric. Has foot peg stud hole. Replaces OEM 34850-77 kick, 34870-75A kick and electric.

Polish	Chrome	Type
43-0111	43-0138	Kick
43-0112	43-0144	Kick/Electric
	43-0172	Electric Only

1979-80	Polish	Chrome	OEM	Year	Type
	43-1195	43-0177	34870-79	1979	Electric
		43-0178	34872-79	1979	Kick/Electric
	43-0119		34888-79	1979	Kick/Electric
	43-0120	43-0152	34911-80A	1980	Electric

Mount Kits

ALLEN STYLE   ACORN   STOCK

Chrome	Chrome	Cadmium	Years	Type
8888-2		8889-2	1971-76	Stock
7155-4			1971-76	Acorn
8784-7	8784-4T		1971-76	Allen
8786-5	8786-5T		1977-80	Allen

1979 Kick Starter Return Chrome Spring Stud

9902-1

1981-UP SPROCKET COVER

Cam/Sprocket Cover Sets, 2004-Up XL

10-1431

Set	Finish	Cover Only
10-0348	Black	10-1431
10-0489	Chrome	10-1432

27-0832 Installed

Outlaw Sprocket Cover Kit and Belt Guard

27-0833

For 2004-Up XL. Replaces stock pulley cover, fills in the center of pulley for clean, detailed, high-performance look.

43-0388   43-0389

Chrome	Black	Item
43-0388	43-0389	Pulley Cover Kit
27-0832	27-0833	Pulley Cover Guard

Chrome Sprocket Cover Trim fits over existing cover for XL as noted. Includes hardware.

VT No.	Years	VT No.	Years
42-0840	1986-90	42-0845	1991-03
42-0843	1981-85	42-0930	2004 Up

42-0840

42-0843

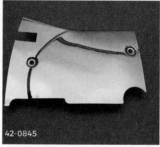

42-0845

42-0930

Sprocket Cover Screws

ALLEN STYLE

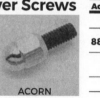

ACORN

Acorn	Allen	Years
	8786-5	1981-85
8866-8	9750-6	1986-2003
	9750-6T	1986-2003
	2226-4	2004 Up

Sprocket Cover Hardware for XLS, XLH

23-1728

23-3080

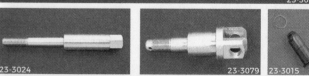

23-3024   23-3079   23-3015

VT No.	OEM	Years	Item
23-3024	24866-86A	1986-90	Mount Stud
23-3015	42441-80	1980-90	Pivot Stud
23-3079	42441-90	1991-2003	Pivot Shaft
23-1728	34909-83	1983-90	Master Cylinder Support Bracket
23-3080	34933-96	1991-2003	Master Cylinder Support Bracket

*Note: Fits belt and chain drive.

KICK STARTER GEAR KIT

XLCH Internal Kick Starter Gear Kit

17-1146

Includes parts pictured, matched ratchet gear set with sleeve, crank gear, spring, rivets, locks, shaft and the hard to find hardware for XLCH repair or XLH conversion. Only needed parts are a cover, kick starter spring and arm assembly. 1980-up Sportsters are not drilled to accept a kicker shaft.*Note: Must be used with early style one piece kicker arm (VT No. 17-0308).

VT No.	Years	VT No.	Years
17-1144	1954-70	17-1145	1971-72
		17-1146*	1973-79

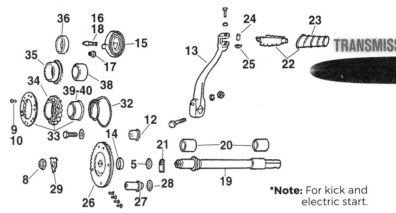

TRANSMISSION

4

*Note: For kick and electric start.

Kick Starter Hardware for 1954-79 Sportsters

VT No.	#	OEM	Years	Item
12-0709	5	6802	All	.007 Shim
12-0528	8	7926	All	Shaft Nut
17-1111	9	8215	1957-70	Rivet, 25 pack
17-1112	10	8216	1971-up	Rivet, 25 pack
17-9844	12	24577-68	1968-up	Hole Plug
17-0018	13	33052-71	All	Kick Arm
14-0115	14	33076-37	All	Oil Seal
13-0122	15	33084-41	All	Chrome Spring
17-0155	16	33088-52	1952-70	Spring Stud Zinc
17-0156	18	33088-71	1971-79	Spring Stud Chrome
17-1114	19	33094-57	1957-76	Kicker Shaft
17-1115		33094-77A	1977-79	Kicker Shaft
10-0718	20	33099-52A	All	Bushing Shaft
10-0719	20	As Above with seal		
17-1113	21	33110-54	All	Thrust Plate
17-0301	22	33175-16B	All	Kick Pedal
28-0213	23	33182-63A	All	Black Rubber
10-2494	24	33213-31	All	Pedal Bushing
13-9184	25	33215-30	All	Spring Washer
17-1106	26	33348-57	1957-77	Large Kick Gear
17-1107		33348-77	1978-79	Large Kick Gear
17-9833	27	33356-52	All	Gear Stop
37-9239	28	6469	All	Washer for Above
17-0911	29	33362-52	All	Lock Tab
17-1116	30	33379-57	1957-70	Ratchet Plate 9T
17-1109	31	33379-71A	1971-79	Ratchet Plate 9T
13-0127	32	33390-52	All	Ratchet Spring
17-1103	33	Cpt. Kit	1954-70	Ratchet Gear Kit
17-1104	33	Cpt. Kit	1971-72	Ratchet Gear Kit
17-1105	33	Cpt. Kit	1973-79	Ratchet Gear Kit
17-0998	34	33432-73	1973-79	Ratchet Gear 9T
10-0722	35	33442-57	57-E73	Bushing
10-0723	36	33442-73	L73-79	Bushing
17-1101	38	37753-76	1957-70	Spacer XLH, electric start only
17-1100*	39	37754-74	1957-72	Spacer 1.047 long
17-1102*	40	37755-73	1971-79	Spacer 1.153
16-0466			1980-85	Kick Starter Drill Fixture Tool

17-1105

XLCH Ratchet Gear Kit

Includes gear, plate, rivets, machined spacer and spring for appropriate year. Spacer supplied as noted.

VT No.	Years	Spacer
17-1103	1954-70	17-1100
17-1104	1971-72	17-1100
17-1105	1973-79	17-1102

17-1116

17-1109

17-1108

9T Starter Ratchet Plates

Mesh with stock gear. *Note: Machined type.

VT No.	OEM	Year
17-1116*	33379-57	1957-70
17-1109	33379-71A	1971-79
17-1108*	33379-71A	1971-79

Ratchet Plate Rivets

Two lengths 5/32 x 13/16 x 9/32 dia (8215) use on 1957-70 XLCH and 5/32 x 7/16 x 9/32 dia (8216) use on 1971-79 XLCH. 25 pk.

VT No.	OEM	Type
17-1111	8215	Early
17-1112	8216	Late

Ratchet Plate Riveting Fixture and Alignment Tool clamps plate to drum while setting rivets on 1971-79 XL clutch drum.
VT No 16-0165

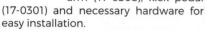
KICK PEDAL AND ARM

Stainless Steel Arm Kit

17-0982

ARMS & SHAFTS

Kick Starter Arms

Constructed of forged steel for durability for 1954-84 FX-FL.Kit Includes heavy forged offset kick arm (17-0308), kick pedal (17-0301) and necessary hardware for easy installation.

17-0308

17-0309

VT No.	OEM	Finish	Type
17-0309	Kit	Complete	
17-0308	33052-71	Chrome	Heavy
17-0310	As above	Stainless	Heavy
17-0018	As Above	Chrome	Standard
17-0322	33052-71	Black	Polished
17-0344	Natural	Replica	Black
17-0601	Bolts	Chrome	Kit
17-0602	Bolts	Chrome	Kit

17-9921

Stroker Kick Starter Arm Kit includes I Beam, 1" longer chrome kicker arm with chrome rail type buffalo kick pedal and hardware.

VT No.	Item
17-9921	Complete Kit
17-0160	Arm Only
17-9150	Pedal Only

Stock

17-0307

Flat

17-9934

Chrome Fold-Out Kick Starter Arms for 1977-79. 17--0307 is stock,17-9934 features flat kicker pedal that spins.

Kick Start Spring Studs

A   B

Zinc	Chrome	Cad	#	OEM	Year
17-0155	9898-1		A	33088-52	1952-70
	17-0156			33088-71	1971-78
	9900-1	9901-1		33088-71	1971-78
	9902-1		B	33098-79	1979

Spool Kick Start Pedal

17-0046

17-0459

17-0461

Order bolt kit separately, except where noted.

Chrome	Black	Brass	Style
17-2124	17-0046		Smooth
	17-0979		Spool w/ Bolt Kit
17-0461	17-0459	12-0747	Holes
	17-0957		Hex
		17-0343	Holes
		17-0837	Ventilated w/ Bolt Kit

PEDALS

Alloy Billet Kick Starter Pedals

17-0765

17-0355

17-0386

17-0651

17-0359

VT No.	Style
17-0386	Knuckle
17-0765	Maltese, Natural
17-0651	Red Baron with Chrome Axle Shaft
17-1491	Knuckle Only Alloy
17-0359	Polished Alloy Assembly
17-0355	Bronze Assembly

28-0213

28-0214

Rubber Kick Pedal

H-D Logo Kick Starter Pedal
VT No. 17-0315

A stock replacement of rubber, for old style Popsicle kick starter pedal in either white (28-0214) or black (28-0213).

Pedal Assembly for 1936-76

17-0301

17-0311

17-2123

17-0302

17-0329

17-0303

17-0306

VT No.	FITS
17-0301	Flat Rubber Complete
17-0311	Flat Rubber White
17-2123	Shaft Only
17-0302	Chrome Skeleton (USA)
17-0306	Bolt Kit
37-0992	Chrome Bolt (5 pack)
17-0771	Bolt, Each
37-0964	Bolt, Each, Chrome

Kick Start Return Spring 1954-1979

13-0122

13-9248

VT No.	OEM	Finish
13-0122	33084-41	Chrome
13-9248	33084-41	Black

Flat Kick Start Pedals

17-0299

17-9150

Available in O-Ring or Rail design.

VT No	Type
17-0299	O-Ring
17-9150	Rail

1952-84
XLH
KICK
STARTER
CONVERSION

XLH Complete Kick Starter Kits. All parts included as illustrated. Check ratchet gear spacing before assembly. Available in kick only sprocket cover or kick and electric sprocket cover with cut away for starter motor. Available with chrome or polished sprocket cover.

V-Twin Original Since 1980!

VT No.	Years	Type	Finish	VT No.	Years	Type	Finish
22-1050	1952-70	Kick only	Polish	22-0204	1973-76	Kick only	Polish
22-0200	1967-70	Kick and Electric	Polish	22-0211	1973-76	Kick only	Chrome
22-0201	1971-72	Kick and Electric	Polish	22-0205	1977-78	Kick and Electric	Polish
22-0202	1971-72	Kick only	Polish	22-0210	1977-78	As Above with Cover	Chrome
22-0203	1973-76	Kick and Electric	Polish	22-0206	1977-78	Kick only	Polish
22-0209	1973-76	As Above with Cover	Chrome	22-0207	1979-only	Kick and Electric	Polish
				22-0783*	1980-84	Kick Only	Polish

Note: 1980-up Cases are not machined from factory to accept kick starter components and can not be fitted with a kick starter. *We offer a drill fixture for 22-0783.

22-0458

Components for 1991- Up Kicker Kits

22-0459

17-0723

22-0459 Installed

VT No.	Years	Item
17-0466	1991-06	Mainshaft
17-0723	2006-Up	Mainshaft w/ Gears
17-0467	2004- Up	Cover
17-0468	2006- Up	Bracket
22-0215	1986-1990	Kickstart Conversion Kit

TRANSMISSION 4

1991-UP KICKER KIT

Kicker Kits fit 1991-Up XL 5 Speed models. Sprocket cover features logo.

22-0213

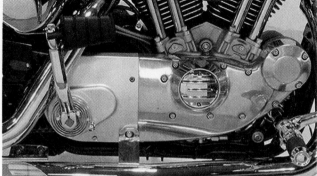

22-0213 Installed

22-0218

22-0218 Installed

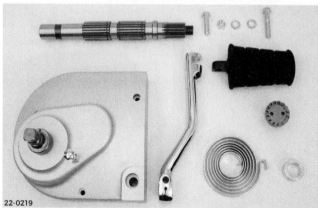

22-0219

22-0219

22-0458

Alloy	Chrome	Black	Years
22-0213	22-0218	22-0655	1991-2003
22-0562	22-0563	22-0591	2004-2006
22-0458	22-0459	22-0589	2007-Up

1991-UP CLUTCH COMPONENT

Complete Clutch Pack includes all parts shown except clutch ramp.

For Sportster

VT No.	Year
18-0177	1991-93
18-0178	1994-03

TRANSMISSION 4

VT No.	OEM	#	Item	VT No.	OEM	#	Item
37-9161	3583	A	Bolt	18-8327	36785-91	M	Clutch Hub, replica
12-0158	8873	B	Ball; 25 pack	18-8326	36790-91	N	Clutch Shell with P & V, 1991-03
12-0353	8885	C	Bearing	18-0792	36790-04	N	Clutch Shell with P & V, 2004-up
12-0961	11046	D	Adj. Screw Ret. Ring	18-8296	36792-91	O	Diaphragm Spring
12-0567	11730A	E	Nut Adj. Screw	18-5052	37924-04A	O	2004-up Diaphragm Spring
12-0986	11250	EE	Ret. Ring, 1994-up	12-9998	36799-91	P	Ball Bearing
18-3206	11735B	F	Adjust Screw, 1991-93	17-0932	36802-84B	Q	Filler Plug Lock Plate
18-3242	11752	F	Adjust Screw, 1994-03	12-9915	37495-91	R	Main Shaft Nut
18-3210	25453-87A	G	Ramp, Inner 1994-up	18-8298	37870-91	S	Spring Washer
18-0351	Kit		Ramp Assembly 1991-93	18-8256	37872-90	T	Inner Spring Seat
18-0352	Kit		Ramp Assembly 1994-up	18-8258	37904-90	U	Retaining Ring
18-0834	Kit		1994- Up Tamer	18-8259	37905-90	V	Retaining Ring
18-1111	25409-86A	H	Outer Ramp, 1991-93	18-8260	37908-90	W	Retaining Ring
18-3243	25409-94B	H	Outer Ramp, 1994- Up	18-8261	37909-90	X	Retaining Ring
18-3211	34920-86	I	Cable Coupling	18-3230	37910-91	Y	Clutch Plates (8) Set
17-0931	25448-84	J	Lock Tab 1991-93	18-8255	37912-91	Z	Pressure Plate
18-3647	—	K	Ring Gear	18-3231	37913-90	AA	Steel Plate (6)
13-9158	36715-84	L	Clutch Adjuster Spring, 1991-93	18-8297	37918-91	BB	Release Plate
13-9257	36715-94	L	Clutch Adjuster Spring, 1994-up	18-8313	37977-90	CC	Spring Plate
				18-0834	Kit		Tamer, 1994- Up

1985-90 CLUTCH HARDWARE For Sportster

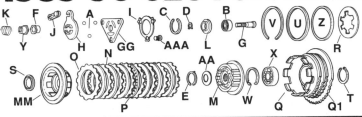

VT No.	OEM	#	Item	VT No.	OEM	#	Item
37-9161	3583	AAA	Bolt	18-1146	36787-84	N	Steel Drive Plate, 5 Piece Set
18-8269	5707	AA	Spacer	18-3665	36788-84	O	Friction Plate, 7 Piece Set
12-0158	8873	A	Ball, 50 pack	18-3216	36789-84	P	Spring Plate, Center
12-0353	8885	B	Bearing	18-8324	36791-84	Q	As Above V-Twin Brand
12-0960	11045	C	Retaining Ring, Guide	18-3646		Q-1	Ring Gear Only
12-0961	11046	D	Adjusting Screw Retaining Ring	18-3233	36792-84	R	Spring Pressure Plate
12-0962	11164	E	Clutch Hub Retaining, 10 pack	18-8227		R	As Above, Barnett
12-0567	11730A	F	Nut, Adjuster Screw	18-8219	36794-84		Clutch Internal Spring Seat Kit
18-3206	11735B	G	Adjust Screw	12-0964	36795-84	T	Ret. Ring, Clutch Hub
18-0351	25408-84	GG	Ramp Kit	18-3660	36797-84	V	Retaining Ring Press. Plate, 10
17-0931	25448-84	I	Lock Plate, Ramp	12-0963	36798-84	W	Retaining Ring Clutch Hub
18-3211	34920-86	J	Cable Coupling	12-0352	36799-84	X	Bearing, Clutch
13-9158	36715-84	K	Clutch Adjuster Spring	17-0932	36802-84B	Y	Filler Plug Lock Plate
18-3659	36730-84	L	Bearing Guide	18-8266	36793-84	Z	Spring Seat Center
18-8244	36785-84	M	Clutch Hub	18-0179		A-Z	Complete Kit
18-8268	36786-84	MM	Pressure Plate				

18-1211

18-3619

18-0352

18-0351

Clutch Ramp Assemblies

Full Kits include all necessary hardware for installation.

VT No.	Year
18-0352	1994-Up
18-0351	1986-93
18-3619	1971-84
18-1211	1954-70

1970 & EARLIER XL CLUTCH

18-3157   18-3161   18-3640

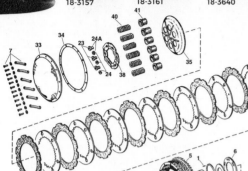

VT No.	#	OEM	Item
17-1111	4	8215	5/32 x 13/16 / 9/32 Rivet
18-3640	5	33162-67	Starter Ring Gear
17-1116	6	33379-57	Starter Ratchet 9T
18-2331	7	34897-53	Screw Retainer
18-1140	8	37201-54	Release Worm and Lever
18-1138	9	37210-47	Release Worm Cover
13-0137	10	37222-52	Worm Lever Spring
17-1158	12	37279-56	Release Rod Set 56-66 XL 1967-69 XLCH
17-1157	12	37280-67	Release Rod Set 1967-69 XLH, 1970 XLCH
14-0125	15	37339-53	Release Rod Oil Seal
N/A	16	37345-52	Release Rod Oil Seal Ret.
12-0539	17	37526-56A	Clutch Hub Nut
12-0540	18	37527-67A	Clutch Hub Nut
17-0912	19	37533-52A	Clutch Hub Lockwasher
17-0090	20	37535-52	Clutch Hub Spacer
18-3157	21	37556-57B	Hub Assembly, 1957-69 XLCH
18-3161	21	37557-67	Hub Assembly, 1967-70 XLH, 1970 XLCH
18-3164*			Nuts for Above *Note: Required
12-0372	22	37568-67	Clutch Hub Bearing Inner Race
12-0510	23	37581-52	Large Hub Stud Nut
12-0574	24	37582-52	Small Hub Stud Nut
12-0551	24A		Nut Set 3 each, #23 & #24
18-8232	25	37584-64	Clutch Hub Stud (6) 1964-66
18-3123	25	37584-67	Clutch Hub Stud (6) 1967-70
17-0091	28	37721-54	Sprocket Hub Washer
12-0328	29	37722-52	Clutch Sprocket Needle Bearing
17-0020	30	37731-52	Washer, Sprocket Bearing, 0.0955" thick
17-0021	30	37732-52	Washer, Sprocket Bearing, 0.0975" thick
17-0022	30	37733-52	Washer, Sprocket Bearing, 0.0980" thick
17-0024	30	37735-52	Washer, Sprocket Bearing, 0.0925" thick
17-0023	30		Washer Sprocket Bearing, 0.1010" thick
17-0092	30		As Above Assortment, 1 each of above
14-0128	31	37740-57	Clutch Hub Oil Seal, Kick Start
14-0129	32	37741-67	Clutch Hub Oil Seal, Electric Start
18-3637	33	37760-52	Clutch Cover
15-0212	34	37762-52	Clutch Cover Gasket
18-3635	35	37876-52	Releasing Disc
18-1113	36	37985-52A	Friction Plate Raybestos (7)
18-1115	37	37992-52	Drive Plate (7)
18-1141	38	38013-52	Pressure Plate
18-1116	39	38016-52	Backing Plate
13-0140	40	38076-52	Spring (6)
18-3642	41	38101-52	Backing Plate, Spring Cup (6)
18-1139	42	38130-54	Adjusting Screw
12-0519	43	38135-50	Adjusting Screw, Locknut

Replica Clutch Adjuster Sleeve. Fits 1954-71, 7/16" hole levers. Zinc plated.

VT No. 37-8460

Cadmium Clutch Adjuster Sleeve. Fits 19574-71

VT No. 2576-1

1952-70 Clutch Cable with adjuster.

VT No. 36-0406

Cable Oiler Boot

Rubber Cable Oiler Boot replaces 38690-55, for XL 1955-80. 5 pack.

VT No. 28-0401

Clutch Rod Installation

Assembly Order Illustration

17-1158   17-1157

For transmission mainshafts 17-1166, 17-1165.

VT No.	Years
17-1158	1956-66 XLH 1967-69 XLCH
17-1157	1967-69 XLH 1970 XLCH

Early XLH/XLCH Sprocket Cover

43-0114

Kick and electric with starter cut out. Replaces 34871-67B, kick only replaces 34782-57A on 1952-70 Sportsters. Complete cover assembly includes cover, release worm adjuster screw, nut, oil deflector, spring and kicker spring stud.

VT No.	Type
43-0114	Polished Kick & Electric Cover
43-0135	Polished Kick Cover Only
43-0136	Chrome Kick Cover Only
43-0115	Chrome Kick and Electric Cover
18-1211	Release Kit

Stock Sprocket Kick Start Cover Screws

VT No.	Years	Type
8884-2	1954-70	Chrome
8885-2	1954-70	Cadmium
8886-2	1952-70	Pipe Mount Stud
8887-2	1952-70	Above, Cadmium

43-0133

1952-67 XLCH Sprocket Cover

Cast Sprocket Cover features early Rib design, includes worm and hardware, replaces 34874-52A.

VT No. 43-0133

1954-70 Clutch Release Kits

18-1211

VT No.	OEM	Part
18-1211		Kit
18-1138	37210-47	Cover
18-1139	38130-54	Screw
12-0519	38135-50	Nut
18-1140	37201-54	Worm
13-0137	37222-52	Spring, 10pk

1971-84 CLUTCH HARDWARE

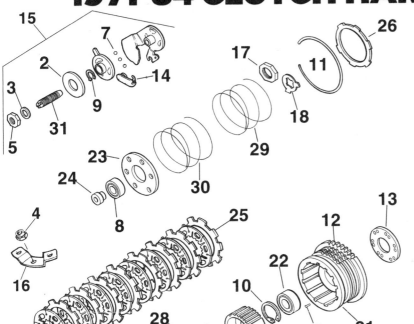

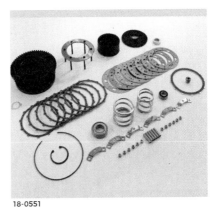

18-0551

Complete Clutch Pack

Includes all parts shown, except clutch release kit #15.

VT No.	Year / Type
18-0551	1971-80 Kick and Electric
18-0552	1971-80 Kick Only
18-0553	1981- E 84 Electric

VT No.	OEM	#	Item
18-1212	5995	1	Spacer Standard 1.525 (6)
18-1214	5996	1	-.040 (6) under
18-1215	5997	1	-.080 (6) under
18-3655	6860	2	Washer, each
37-0516	7130W	3	Lock Washer
12-0511	7686	4	Nylon Lock Nut, 10 pack
12-0513	7803	5	Adjuster Nut
17-1112	8216	6	Rivet, 25 pack
12-0157	8860	7	Balls
12-0341	9073	8	Bearing
12-0903	11005	9	Snap Ring, 10 pack
12-0909	11052	10	Snap Ring, 10 pack
18-3260	11053	11	Retainer, 10 pack
18-3640	33167-67	12	1967-80 Ring Gear
18-3645	—	12	1981-Early 84 Ring Gear
17-1109	33379-71A	13	Ratchet Plate
18-3650	34920-71	14	End Coupling
		15	Kit, assembly
12-0540	37527-67	17	Hub Nut, each
17-0912	37533-52A	18	Lockwasher, 10 pack
12-1967	Kit	17-18	Nut Kit
18-2321	37499-71	16	Retainer, Releasing Disc Nut-Set of 6 retainers with nuts
18-1142	37561-71	19	Clutch Hub
18-3162	37701-71A	21	As Above 71-80 Clutch Drum, Kick Only with Ratchet Plate
18-3163	37716-71A	21	71-80 Clutch Drum Kick and Electric with Ratchet Plate
18-1131	37716-81	21	Clutch Drum 1981-E84 with Ring Gear
18-0833			Ring Gear (Special)
18-1219		21	1981-E84 Kick and Electric
12-0329	33722-71	22	Bearing
18-3208	37878-74	23	Release Disc
18-2330	37879-71	24	Thrust Collar
18-3651	37985-71	25	Drive Plate, 8 pack
18-1119	37987-71	26	Outer Drive, each
18-1118	37992-71	27	Steel Drive, 8 pack
18-2322	38005-74	28	Stud Plate
13-0141	38079-72	29	Outer Spring
Set	38080-71	30	Inner Spring
18-3618	31830-71	31	Screw Kit (Includes 3 and 5)
18-1213	38130-71	31	Screw only

18-8155

18-3618

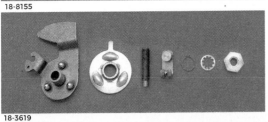
18-3619

18-3163

1971- Early 1984 XL Clutch Adjuster Parts Kit

VT No.	OEM	Item
18-8155	Kit	Complete Kit
18-3619	37203-71A	Ramp Kit
	37202-71A	34920-71
18-2332	37202-71A	Inner Ramp
18-3618	31130-71	Adjuster Screw Kit
18-3650	34920-71	End Coupling
12-0903	11005	Snap Ring, 10 pack
12-0157	8860	Balls, 50 pack

Includes parts illustrated. Other items available separately. Screw kit includes adjuster screw and nut only.

CLUTCH SET

Steel Sets

18-8284

VT No.	Year	QTY	VT No.	Year	QTY
18-8283	1957-70	7 pc	18-8285	1984-90	5 pc
18-8284	1971-83	8 pc	18-8286	1991- Up	6 pc

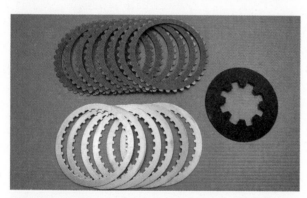

Heavy Duty Wet Type Clutch Kit for XL

VT No.	Year	Spring
18-1734	1984-90	Without
18-1735	1984-90	Without
18-3686	1991- Up	With

Heavy duty factory "wet" type complete kit includes our original bonded police clutch steel plates and spring plate. For XL models.

Clutch Spacer

Fits 1971-83. Set of 6 spacers to provide adjustment of pressure plate and adequate clearance on inside diameter of friction plates.

*Note: Use with Barnett Clutch Plates SK3K (VT No. 18-1117).

VT No.	Colony	Size	Type
18-1217*	1952-70	1.525"	Barnett
18-1212	2756-12	1.530"	Stock
18-1214	2765-12	.040"	Under
18-1215	2775-12	.080"	Under

Clutch Adjusting Screws (sold each)
VT No.	Year	Model
18-1139	1952-70	XL and K
18-1213	1971-84	XL
18-3206	1985-94	XL
18-3242	1995-03	XL
18-3262	2004-up	XL

Clutch Hub Nuts
VT No.	Fits	Item
12-0539	1956-69	Nut
2738-4	1956-69	Kit
12-0540	1967-84	Nut
12-1967	1967-84	Kit
12-9915	1991-up	Nut

Hub Nuts secure clutch hub to main shaft.

12-0539 12-0540 12-9915

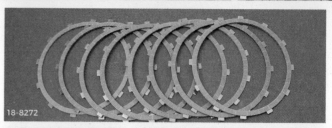
18-8272

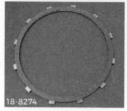
18-8274

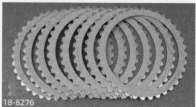
18-8276

Alto Clutch Sets

Kevlar or Red Eagle type. Both are bonded to steel.

VT No.	Year	Type
18-8271	1957-70	Red Eagle
18-8272	1971-83	Red Eagle
18-8273	1971-83	Kevlar
18-8274	1971-83	Red Eagle Outer Drive Plate, each
18-8275	1984-90	Red Eagle
18-8300	1984-90	Kevlar
18-8276	1991-up	Red Eagle
18-8299	1991-up	Kevlar

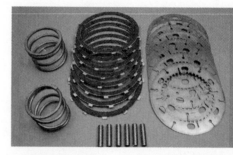

Clutch and Spring Kit

Kit includes 8 friction plates, 8 steel plates, spacer set and spring set. Fits 1971-E84.

VT No. 18-1150

18-1120

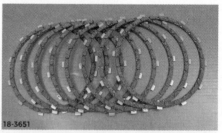
18-3651

Replica Clutch Set
VT No.	Year	Type	Set of
18-1113	1952-70	Raybestos Friction	7
18-0155	1971-84	Kevlar Friction	8
18-3651	1971-84	Steel Friction	8
18-1120	1971-84	Alloy Friction	8
18-3263	1991- Up	Steel Drive	6
18-0154	1991- Up	Kevlar Friction	8

Tamer Thrust Collar fits 1971-84. Eliminates jerking and lunging while in gear. Works on belt and chain drive, replaces bearing thrust collar.

VT No. 18-2323

BARNETT CLUTCH KIT *Barnett*

Carbon Fiber Clutch Sets

Barnett carbon fiber clutch sets for wet clutch feature excellent lubricity and very good energy absorption. Order steel plates separately.

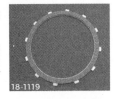
18-1119

Series K Kevlar & Steel Clutch Plates

Barnett Series K Kevlar Clutch Plates and Steel Plates for Sportster. The ultimate in durability, smoothness and strength. Steel backed plates give smooth precise launches and shifting even under extreme heat. 100% asbestos free. Barnett friction clutch sets and steel plates, sold in sets only.

TRANSMISSION

4

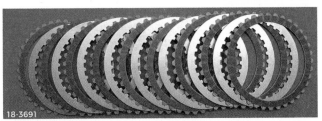
18-3691

VT No.	Year	VT No.	Year
18-3688	1971-84	18-3689	1984-90
18-3690	1991 Up	18-3691*	1991- Up

*Note: 9 Friction plates, 8 steel drive plates. Adds 12% more surface area. Double steel drive plate not used.

18-3230

VT No.	Year	Type	U/M
18-1115	1952-70	Steel, .047 thick with key hole slots	7
18-1116	1952-72	Steel Backing Plate	1
18-1117	1971-84	Friction Wet Only, supplied with spacers	8
18-1118	1971-84	Steel, Inner/Outer slots keep plate flat and true	8
18-1119	1971-84	Alloy, bonded one side outer drive plate	7
18-3665	1984-90	Friction Kevlar bonded	7
18-8248	1984-90	9 Friction, 8 Steel plates - adds 14% surface area	
18-1146	1984-90	Steel	5
18-3230	1991- Up	Friction, Kevlar bonded	8
18-3231	1991- Up	Steel, re-use stock double riveted drive plate	6
18-3233	1991- Up	Extra Plate, 9 Kevlar Friction, 8 Steel plates - adds 12% more surface area. Double riveted drive plate not used.	

Barnett Scorpion Clutch Kit

18-3742

VT No.	Years
18-3722	1971-83
18-3732	1984-90
18-3742	1991 Up

Features over twice as much friction surface area compared to stock clutch. Scorpion Clutches provide a positive engagement and release. The kit incorporates six heavy duty coil springs. In addition, an extra spring set with a different spring rate is included which allows the clutch to be tuned for street or race application depending on usage. Tunability is easy without removal of the primary cover. Barnett friction plates are compatible with any primary oil. Each kit is designed to be used with stock type clutch basket.

13-0141

13-9204

13-0140 / 13-9254

Stock Style Clutch Spring Sets

VT No.	Year	Brand	QTY	VT No.	Year	Brand	QTY
13-0141	1971-84	V-Twin Mfg	2	13-0140	1952-70	V-Twin	6
13-9204		Heavy Duty	1	13-9254		Barnett	6
13-2007		Sifton	1				

1971-84 Barnett Friction Plate Set

Original compound.

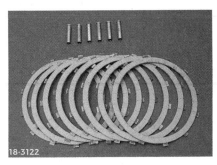
18-3122

20-0211

16-0310

Pro-Clutch

VT No.	Item
20-0211	1991- Up Chain
16-0310	Puller Tool

THROTTLE CABLE KIT

Throttle & Cable Kits include grips, throttle and idle. Barnett cable with ends attached for S&S 'E' & 'G' carburetors.

VT No.	Item
35-9246	38" Complete Kit
35-0212	Handle and Grips only

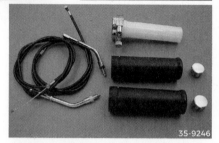

S&S Super 'E' & 'G' Cables for Dual Stock Type Throttle Handles

Stainless	Black	Len.	Type	Years
36-1504	36-2464	38"	Throttle	81-95
36-1506	36-2466	38"	Idle	81-95
36-1561	36-0744	38"	Throttle	96-up
36-1562	36-0746	38"	Idle	96-up
36-1563	36-2545	42"	Throttle	81-95
36-1564	36-2544	42"	Idle	81-95
36-1565	36-0732	42"	Throttle	96-up
36-1566	36-0734	42"	Idle	96-up

Chrome Throttle Clamps & Tube Set

Feature smooth design, upper and lower pieces with screws and nylon throttle tube, for single or dual cable applications.

VT No.	Item		VT No.	Item
35-0253	Single		35-0254	Dual

Chrome Hand Grip Hole Plugs

Replace 56238-62 on 1960-up, using stock grips, 10 pk.
VT No. 28-0618

Nylon Throttle Tubes

VT No.	Type	Year
35-9073	Single	1976-81
28-1981	Dual	1982-95
35-9870	Dual	1996-up

Throttle Kits

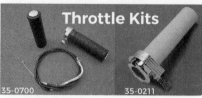

Available in single or dual units with or without grips and chrome end plugs. Single 1974-80.

VT No.	Item
35-0215**	Kit with 2 grips
35-0700	Cable Assembly Kit, Single
35-0211*	Throttle Only
35-9073	Nylon Tube Only
35-0210	Adjuster Only

*Note: Includes nylon tube with chrome clamps
**Note: Includes chrome end plug.

Bendix Carburetor Throttle

Kit includes single cable throttle assembly, cable with adjuster and chrome bracket.
VT No. 35-0070

Carburetor Cable Brackets

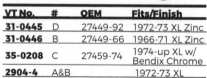

VT No.	#	OEM	Fits/Finish
31-0445	D	27449-92	1972-73 XL Zinc
31-0446	B	27449-66	1966-71 XL Zinc
35-0208	C	27459-74	1974-up XL w/ Bendix Chrome
2904-4	A&B		1972-73 XL

Universal Throttle Sets

Feature chrome housing w/ adjuster, metal twist tube. Use universal cable

VT No.	Item
35-0071	1" with Anderson Rubber Grips
35-0232	As Above without Grips
28-0116	Grips for Above
35-0213	1" with Plastic Grips and Cable
35-0214	7/8"with Plastic Grips and Cable
36-0104	Cable only, barrel end, 48"
36-0112	Cable only, barrel end, 60"
36-2538	Handle Ferule with nut

*Note: Does not include left side grip order 28-0215.

Dual 1981-Up (Push-Pull)

VT No.	Item
35-0237	Kit with grips
35-0212**	Kit with grips
35-9352**	Kit w/black cables, 1981-89
35-9350	Kit w/black cables
35-9351	1996-up Kit w/black cables
35-9149*	Throttle only
35-9218	All Friction Spring

*Note: Includes nylon tube with chrome clamps
**Note: Includes chrome end plug.

Chrome Throttle Cable Router

Directs cable on Tillotson carburetor.
VT No. 35-0500

Throttle Adjusting Kit

Includes chrome knob and spring. Fits 1974-up.

VT No.	Item
35-0210	Adjuster w/ Spring
13-9197	Spring
12-0980	Retaining Ring

Keihin Throttle Cable End

Brass cable fitting end. Replaces 56508-76, 10 pk.
VT No. 36-2480

Throttle Thumbwheel Screw

1" diameter for throttle return on 1974-up models. Spring included.
VT No. 35-0372

Chrome Throttle Cable Support Bracket

For all Twins with Bendix carburetor. Replaces 27459-74.
VT No. 35-0208

THROTTLE CABLE SET

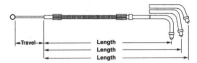

Cables are constructed with the Supra™ stainless steel braid which is tightly woven for a bright, quality consistent finish. The clear coat is UV resistant, heat bonded, non-yellowing grade for long service life. All applications include the correct fittings, adjuster and inner lengths for an exact installation and fit.

CABLES 5

36-0856

36-0857

Stainless Steel Braided Cable Set

36-0114

36-0102

VT No.	XL Year	Make	Length
36-0857	1996-98		Stock (35")
36-0856	1990-95		Stock (34")
36-0866	1990-96		+8" (42")
36-0855	1981-89		Stock (38")
36-0827	1999-up		Stock (33")
36-0114	1982-95	S&S	42"
36-0115	1982-95	S&S	54"
36-0857	1996-up	S&S	34.25"
36-0129	1996-up	S&S	38"
36-0128	1996-up	S&S	42.50"
36-0119	1996-up	S&S	47"
36-0131	1996-up	+12"	52"

Handlebar Cable and Brake line Kit

VT No.	Len.	XL Fit
36-1608	12"	2014-17
36-1609	14"	2014-17
36-1610	12"	2007-13
36-1611	14"	2007-13

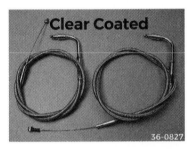

Clear Coated

36-0827

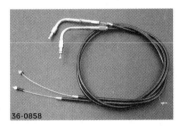

36-0858

Black Matched Stock and Idle Cable Sets

For Big Twins include correct throttle and idle cable assembly.

Stock	+8"	+12"	Years
36-0858	36-0861		1996- Up
36-0859	36-0862		1990-1995
36-0860	36-0863	36-2561	1981-89

Throttle/Idle Cables

Available in black vinyl or braided stainless covering with correct end fitting for each application, also available in over stock length. All are assemblies unless noted.

36-0101

V-Twin Stainless	V-Twin Black	Barnett Stainless	Barnett Clear Coat	Barnett Black	OEM	Length	Fitment
				36-2460	56389-74	Stock	1974-75
				36-0107		+6" Extension	1974-75
		36-1501		36-2461		+8" Extension	1974-75
36-0901	36-0102		36-1502	36-2462	56313-76	Stock	1976-80
	36-0103					+6" Extension	1976-80
	36-0357		36-1503	36-2463		+8" Extension	1976-80
				36-0948		+12" Extension	1976-80
36-0903	36-0101		36-1504	36-2464	56324-81	Stock	1981-85 Throttle Cable
	36-0357		36-1505	36-2465		+8" Extension	1981-85 Throttle Cable
	36-0356			36-2558		+12" Extension	1981-85 Throttle Cable
36-0902	36-0100		36-1506	36-2466	56323-81	Stock	1981-85 Idle Cable
			36-1507	36-2467		+8" Extension	1981-85 Idle Cable
	36-2557					+12" Extension	1981-85 Idle Cable
			36-1520		56308-86	Stock	1986-87 Throttle Cable
36-8022					56308-96	Stock	1996-03 Throttle Cable
			36-1521	36-2473	56309-86	Stock	1986-87 Idle Cable
			36-1522	36-2490	56308-88	Stock	1988-95 Throttle Cable
			36-1523	36-2491	56309-88	Stock	1988-95 Idle Cable
			36-1524	36-0703	56308-96	Stock	1996-01 Throttle Cable
			36-1525	36-0705	56309-96	Stock	1996-01 Idle Cable
			36-1568	36-0762	56400-96	Stock	2002-Up Throttle Cable
			36-1569	36-0763	56401-96	Stock	2002- Up Idle Cable

Barnett Clear Coat Braided Stainless Throttle Cable Sets

By Barnett. Sets include throttle & idle cable.

VT No.	Year	Model	Length
36-0832	1981-95	S&S Super E.G. Screamin' Eagle	40.125"
36-0829	1996- Up	S&S Super E.G. Screamin' Eagle	40.375"
36-0830	1981-95	S&S Super E.G. Screamin' Eagle	45.375"
36-0831	1996- Up	S&S Super E.G. Screamin' Eagle	41.5"
36-0832	1981-85	XL	Stock
36-0833	1981-85	XL	+8"
36-0851	1986-87	XL	Stock
36-0852	1988-95	XL	Stock
36-0853	1996-01	XL	Stock

Chrome Dual Throttle Cable Separator

Two piece design.
VT No. 31-9942

Spiral Chrome Throttle Cable

Stock length fits 1976-80 all throttle.
VT No. 36-0511

CLUTCH CABLE

Clutch Cable Assemblies feature heavy duty construction designed for reliability and longer service. By V-Twin or Barnett in black vinyl or braided stainless covering

36-0408

36-2353

36-8085

V-Twin		Barnett		OEM	Length	Fitment
Stainless	Black	Clear Coat	Black			
36-0504	36-0406	36-1534	36-2350	28619-57	Stock	1957-70 All XL
	36-0407				+4" Extension	1957-70 All XL
			36-2351		+8" Extension	1957-70 All XL
36-0506	36-0408	36-1536	36-2352	28619-71	Stock	1971-85 All XL
	36-0409				+4" Extension	1971-85 All XL
		36-1537	36-2353		+8" Extension	1971-85 All XL
			36-2495		-5" Under	1971-85 All XL
			36-2354		Stock	1971-85 All XL, Nylon Lined
	36-2425			28619-06	Stock	1986-90 XL 883
36-2513				28621-86	Stock	1986-90 XL 1100, 1200
		36-1538	36-2485*	28619-86A	Stock	1986-03 XL 883
		36-1539	36-2486*	38621-86A	Stock	1986-03 XL 1100, 1200
		36-1540	36-2487*		+6" Extension	1986- Up XL 1100, 1200
36-8061	36-2432	36-1541	36-0539	38620-96	Stock	1996-03 XLH 1200cc
	36-8089				-2" Under	1996-03 XLH 1200cc
36-8064	36-8085		36-8087	38699-04	Stock	2004- Up XL
36-8078	36-8086		36-8088		+4" Extension	2004- Up XL

*Note: Uses eyelet style end. Hand lever pin is supplied.

Stainless Steel Braided Clutch Cables

36-8052

VT No.	Casing Len.	Len.	OEM	Application
36-8050	52.75"	Stock	38619-86A 38663-00	1986-03 XLH 883 Std., 87-91 XLH 883 Deluxe, 00-03 XL 833C/1200CC, 2002-03 XL 883R, 1996-2003 XL 1200S
36-8052	61.25"	Stock	38621-86A	1986-87 XLH, 1992-95 XLH 833 Deluxe, 1987-95 XLH 883 Hugger, 1988-95 XLH 1200
36-8053	47-06"	Stock	38619-84	1970-85 XLH, 1981-85 XLS, 1970-79 XLCH
36-8061	57.25"	Stock	38662-00 38620-96	1996-03 XLH 883 Hugger, XLH 1200, 1999 XL 883Cc 1996-99 XL 1200CC
36-8064	54.75"	Stock	18699-04	2004- Up XL, 883C, 1200R
36-8078	59.25"	+4"		2004- Up XL, 883C, 1200R

Chrome Clutch Cable Adjuster Cover

Before

After

36-0578 · 36-0579

Fits 1987-up Big Twin and installs over adjuster at clutch adjustment cover. Locks in place with stainless set screw. Will retro fit Barnett or stock cables.

VT No.	Type	Style	VT No.	Type	Style
36-0578	1982-up	Upper	36-0579	1987-up	Lower

60" Chrome Cable Wrap

Classic 1950's style dresser trim item. Inner diameter size noted. Sold each.

36-0621

VT No.	Size	VT No.	Size
36-0520	5mm	36-0525	10-11mm
36-0521	6-7m		

ReplicaClutchAdjusterSleeve

Fits 1954-71.7/16" hole levers. Zinc plated.
VT No. 37-8460

26-2130 · 26-0505 · 26-2138

26-2132 · 36-2559

Lever Pins / Bushings

VT No.	OEM	Item	U/M
26-2130	45036-82	1982-87	10
26-0505	45036-68	1965-72 with Bushings	10
26-2138	45039-68	Nylon Bushing	25
26-2132*	45036-88	1988- Up with Bushings	Ea
36-2559	45423-92	Lever Bushings	10

*Note: Teflon pin fits 1988-up eyelet clutch cables.

Rubber Cable Oiler Boot

Replaces 38690-55, for XL 1955-80. 5 pack.
VT No. 28-0401

BRAKE CABLES

Brake Cable Clamp

Cinches cable to brake arm.
VT No. 26-0508

Cable Clamp

Fitted to hand lever for emergency or permanent use. Easy to install .460" diameter, pair.
VT No. 26-0509

Front Brake Cable

Replacement core and casing for 1949-71 FLH Glide 1952-72 Sportster models. Replaces 45073-51 60" long, must be cut to proper length.

36-2385

VT No.	Item	VT No.	Item
36-2385	Stock	36-0501	Stock Type, Barnett
36-2565	Stock		
36-0545	Replica 1949-52, 26"	36-0509	Replica
		36-2489	Braided Steel

SPEEDO CABLE & CLAMP

36-2531

36-0601

36-0603

36-0959

Front Wheel Drive Speedometer Cables

Choose by application or by length and top nut size.

1984-87 XLH, 1986-87 XLH 1100, 1984-85 XL 1983-85 XR

Black Vinyl	Stainless	OEM	Len.	Top Nut
36-0606	36-2528	67078-85A 67051-73 67052-78A	40"	16mm
36-0813		Barnett		
	36-0120	Coated		

1973 XL, 1988-94 XLH, 883 HUG-DLX and XLH 1200

Black Vinyl	Stainless	OEM	Len.	Top Nut
36-2414	36-2529	67048-83A	43"	16mm
	36-0121	Coated		
36-0815		Barnett	42"	
36-0608		67052-78B	49"	

1973 XL Only

Black Vinyl	Stainless	OEM	Len.	Top Nut
36-0604		67051-76	42.5"	16mm
36-0602		+4"	46.5"	

1983 XLS Only

Black Vinyl	Stainless	OEM	Len.	Top Nut
36-2410	36-2530	67054-83A	46.5"	16mm

1974-83 XL Models

Black Vinyl	Stainless	OEM	Len.	Top Nut
36-0603	36-0819	67051-74	39"	12mm
	36-0123	Coated		
36-0814		Barnett		
36-0959		With Elbow	41"	16mm
36-0604		+4"	43"	
36-0605	36-2534	+6"	44.5"	12mm
	36-0124	Coated		

1979-82 XLS Models

Black Vinyl	Stainless	OEM	Len.	Top Nut
36-2411	36-2533	67060-79A	38"	12mm

36-2570

Transmission Drive Speedometer Cables

Black Vinyl	Metal Zinc	OEM	Len.	Top Nut	Fits
36-2570	36-2577	67051-52A	46"	5/8"	1957-70 XL Trans Drive
36-0992		67051-70	46"	16mm	1970-72 XLH
36-0512		Custom	50	12mm	1952-70 XL, Mini Speedo Kit 39-0365/39-0314

Replacement Speedometer Cable Nuts

For front wheel drive cables and sold in 5pk.

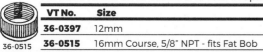
36-0397   36-0515

VT No.	Size
36-0397	12mm
36-0515	16mm Course, 5/8" NPT - fits Fat Bob

37-8911   37-9119

31-9943

37-9341   37-8912   37-8915

37-8914   37-8976   37-8913

31-1010   37-9396   37-9359

Chrome Cable Clamps

2-piece design for securing cables or wires to frame and forks. Sold each. As noted for cable type.

VT No.	Size	Holes	Type
37-8911	1"	1	Clutch
37-9119	1"	2	Throttle
31-9943	1"	Slot	Throttle (2)
37-8976	1-1/4"	Slot	Throttle (2)
37-9396	1-1/4"	2	Throttle (2)
37-8915	1-1/8"	1	Clutch
37-9359	1-1/4"	1	Clutch
37-8913	35mm (1-3/8")	1	Clutch
37-8914	39mm	1	Speedometer
37-9341	41mm	1	Speedometer
31-1010	49mm	1	Clutch

37-0883   37-0887

Chrome Billet Cable Clamps

Sold each.

VT No.	Size	Type
37-0833	1"	Throttle, Single
37-0887	41mm	Clutch
37-0897	39mm	Clutch

Kwik-Klip

Attaches brake line or speedo cable to fork leg.

VT No.	Inner Dia.
24-1023	39
24-1024	49
24-0497	41

31-0315   31-0316

41mm Push On Fork Tube Clamps

VT No.	Style
31-0315	Smooth
31-0316	Groove

Cable Adapter

Allows use of 5/8" cable on 12mm threaded speedometers.
VT No. 36-0507

CHOKE CABLE

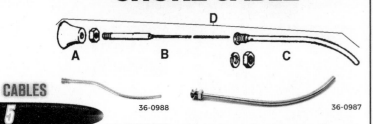

36-0988

36-0987

36-2391

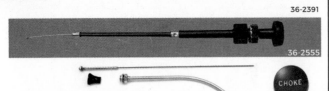

36-2555

36-0989   36-0994

Choke Cable Assemblies

VT No.	#	OEM	Fits
36-0989	D	Kit	1967-70 XL
36-0946	D	Kit	1972-79 XLH-XLCH
36-2555	D	29229-88D	1988-up XL
36-0987	C	29220-67	1967-70 XL
36-0988	C	29220-72 29219-78	1972-78 XL - 1979-E80
36-2391	B	29216-72	1972-78 XL
36-0994	A	29214-67	1971-84 XL Knob Black plastic

Chrome Choke Knob

Fits 1989-up CV model carburetors.
VT No. 36-0551

Choke Knob Insert

Polish stainless, pack of 5. Fits 1989-up.
VT No. 36-0555

Block Off Plug

Plug for speedometer drive hole plug fits 1952-72.
VT No. 2057-2

SPEEDOMETER DRIVE

Speedometer Drive Units

36-2526

Right

Spacer

Fit front wheel only, have .750 axle hole, for right and left side as noted, spacer length note. (A) Overall (B) Spacer length. 2.1 Ratio.

VT No.	OEM	Spacer	Length	Fits	Side
36-0800	67127-73	.268	.789	All 1973-83 XL-XLS-XLCH	Right
36-2526	Chrome	.268	.789	As Above	Right
36-0802	67127-84A	.361	.940	1984-94 XL	Left

Chrome Speedometer Drive Cover

Fits perfectly over the existing drive units. Fits 1987-95 with 39mm Forks.
VT No. 42-0434

Speedometer Drive Spacers

Replace drive units. Fits 1973-83 XL.
VT No. 44-0390

Speedometer Cable and Cable Mount

28-1998 Installed

31-0149

For front wheel drive models 1973-95. 5 packs.

VT No.	OEM	Item	VT No.	OEM	Item
31-0149	38623-68	Chrome Bracket	28-1998	66996-85	Cable Boot

Electronic Speedo Sending Unit

1995-up XL Electronic Speedometer Sending Unit replaces 74402-95B.
VT No. 17-0589

Speedometer Sending Unit Wrench

Features a shortened 3/16" ball end hex bit for removal or installation of hex screw used on all models equipped with electronic sending units.
VT No. 16-6738

Speedometer Calibrator

36-0250

36-0422

Programmable Transmission Speedometer Sensor

Fully adjustable sensor assembly for all 5 & 6 Speed transmissions with electronic drive speedometer. Allows fast and accurate adjustments for any tire size, pulley on gear ratio change.
VT No. 36-0150

Corrects readings of stock electronic speedometers when using oversized rear tires or when other drive train modifications have been done that effect final drive ratio. Use on all Big Twins.

VT No.	Brand	VT No.	Brand
36-0250	S&S	36-0422	VT

39-0435

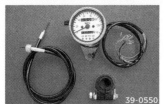
39-0550

39-0437

39-0556

39-0438

39-0576

39-0435, 39-0436, 39-0550 Turn Signal Light, Pre 90 models tap into orange wire exiting turn signal flasher. 1991-up models signal indicator light cannot be used.

39-0456

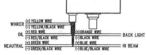

Mini Gauges includes cable and mount clamp and 4 LED indicators on 60mm types only. Note: 39-0556 & 39-0437 include left side speedometer drive.

- Blue-High Beam
- Green-Neutral
- Red-Oil
- Yellow-Turn Signals

*Note: Does not have LED indicators.
**Note: Does not have LED indicators and includes 2:1 ratio left side speedo drive unit.

White Face

48 mm	60 mm	Ratio	Item	Year
39-0435	39-0550	2:1	Speedometer	1973-94
39-0437**	39-0556**	2:1	Speedometer	Custom
39-0438*	39-0576*		Tachometer	Electric
39-0456	39-0456	Knob	Speedometer	

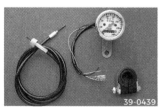
39-0439

39-0578

39-0441

39-0580

LED

48 mm White Face 3-LED	60 mm Black Face 4-LED	Ratio	Item	Year
39-0439	39-0578	2:1	Speedometer	1973-94
39-0441	39-0580	2:1	Speedometer	1995-99

MINI GAUGE

28-0325

31-9997

39-0858

39-0859

39-0593

39-0860

60mm Mini Electronic Speedometer and Tachometer

Speedometer features a 12 volt LED back-light and easy push button recalibration and re-settable trip meter. The 8000 RPM tachometer has LED lamp. All units have black face and include clamp.

VT No.	Ratio	Drive	Item
39-0858	2:1	Mechanical	Speedometer
39-0859	2240:60	Mechanical	Speedometer
39-0593*		Electronic	Speedometer
39-0860	0-8000 RPM		Tachometer
31-9997	Y		Bracket
28-0325			Clamp

*Note: For use with stock type electronic speed sensor.

39-0563

39-0789

80mm Electronic Gauge

Features stainless housing and Y bracket.

VT No.	Type		Year
39-0563	Tachometer	1978-up	Speedometer
39-0789	Speedometer	1995-up	Speedometer

Stock Replacement Speedometer and Tachometer Gauges for XL

VT No.	OEM	Fits	Item
39-0933	67037-85A	1985-90 1200	Speedometer
39-0937	67016-86A	1986-91 883	Speedometer
39-0936	67111-85	1985-94 All XL	Tachometer
39-0321		1965-73	Tachometer

CABLES 5

MINI GAUGE

Multi-Colored Mini Gauges

60 mm gauge features a 2.4" polished stainless body with a white face, total length of 2.7". Units include a chrome bezel with choice of red, orange, blue, yellow, white, green or purple by the push of a button. Works on 12 v systems. Tach adapter required for use with single fire ignition. Speedometer accepts 12 mm drive cable.

VT No.	Gauge	Ratio
39-0417	Speedometer	2:1
39-0433	Speedometer	2240:60
39-0434	Tachometer	Electric

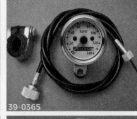

Chrome 60mm Tachometer Housing Kit

Includes bracket (to mount to XL 39mm 1988-up fork stem bolt) and 60 mm electric tachometer. Housing which is available separately may be fitted with any 60mm electric speedo or gauge.

VT No.	Item
39-0202	Tachometer Kit, (Includes housing & bracket)
39-0204	Speedometer Kit, (Includes housing & bracket)
39-0290	Magneto Tachometer Kit (Includes bracket)
39-0292	Tachometer Kit (Includes bracket)
39-0203	Housing Only
24-0367	Stem Bolt

48mm Deco or 60mm Mini Speedometer and Tachometer Kits

Kits include gauge, chrome bracket and rubber handlebar clamp and proper cable which can be installed without any adapters or modifications. 1995-99 kits for XL includes drive and cable.

Speedometer			
48mm Deco	60mm Mini	Ratio	Fitment
39-0365	39-0314	2:1	1952-72
39-0368	39-0315	2:1	1973-94
39-0554	39-0555	2:1	1995-99
	39-0575	Electric	1995-up (Not a Kit)
Tachometer			
39-0366	39-0317		1971-80
39-0367	39-0392*		Electric 3-wire type
31-9997		Fits All	Chrome Y mount
33-2008		Fits All	Light socket with bulb
33-2047		Fits All	12 Volt bulb, 10 pack

Note: For use on 1978-up models with coil triggered tach, Green Negative wire goes to negative side of coil. Red wire goes to ignition side of key switch. Tach head must be grounded by black wire.
Cable 36-0512 fits 39-0314 & 39-0316 kits.
Cable 36-0603 fits 39-0315 kits.

Digital Speedometer/Tachometer

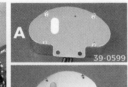

Front View of 39-0599 and 39-0685

Digital Speedo/Tachometer has the following functions:

· Bar Graph Tach
· High Beam
· Neutral
· Oil Pressure
· Turn Signals
· Digital Odometer
· Trip Meter

Measures: 110mm ((L)x57mm (H) x 38mm(W).

VT No.	Item
39-0599	Gauge (A) Requires an installation bracket
39-0685	Gauge (B) No bracket necessary for installation
31-0984	Bracket
31-2145	Bracket
31-1262	Bracket

Chrome Billet Housing

Accepts 48mm electronic tachometer or speedometer.
VT No. 39-0116

OE Mechanical Tach

0-8000 RPM.
Mounts in 3-1/4" dia. hole. Fits 1965-73 XL.

VT No. 39-0321

GAUGE MOUNT

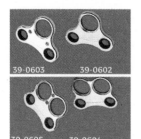

Chrome Billet Gauge Holder

Fits 48mm or 60mm gauges for T-type bars 1" or 1-1/4" with 3-1/2" center

48mm	60mm	Holes	Type
39-0602		0	Single
39-0603		2	Single
39-0604	39-0613	0	Dual
39-0605	39-0614	2	Dual

Chrome Speedometer & Tachometer Brackets for XL

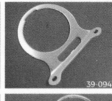

VT No.	OEM	Lite	Years	Type	VT No.	OEM	Lite	Years	Type
39-0142	67053-83	3	1983-91	Single	39-0141	67110-83	3	1983-91	Dual
39-0397	67053-86	4	1986-91	Single	39-0400	67036-86	4	1983-91	Dual
39-0941	67083-92	Slot	1992-94	Single	39-0942	67167-92	Slot	1992-94	Dual
39-0212	67293-95		1995-up	Single	39-0213	67294-95A		1995-up	Dual

Speedometer Visor

Fits 1995-up XL models.
VT No. 39-0223

Chrome Gauge Covers

Fit FXR models.

VT No.	OEM	Year	Type	Type
39-0162	Set	1984-90	Tach and Speedometer	Dual
39-0395	67092-85	1984-94	Tachometer	Dual
39-0394	67090-85	1984-90	Speedometer	Dual
39-0943	67091-91	1991-94	Speedometer	Dual
39-0955	92061-83	1983-up	Rubber Cushion	
39-0956	67104-83	1984-91	XL Rubber Cushion	

Chrome Billet Fork Tube Gauge Bracket

Permits quick and easy installation of mini 48 mm gauges to exposed fork tubes. Gauges are sold separately.

VT No.	Fork Size
31-0876	39mm
31-0877	41mm

3/8" Indicator Lamps

VT No.	OEM	Color	Type	Fits
33-2022	68489-86	Red	Oil Pressure	1986-up XL
33-2023	68574-86	Green	Neutral	1986-up XL
33-2024	68023-92	Blue	Hi Beam	1986-up XL
33-2025	68695-91	Green	Turn Signal	1991-up XL
33-2026	68002-92A	Red		1991-up XL
39-0956	67104-83		Rubber Cushion	1984-91 XL

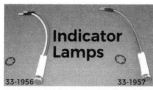

Indicator Lamps

VT No.	OEM	Color	Type
33-1956	67851-75	Green	Neutral
33-1957	68536-75	Red	Oil Pressure

Fit visors and dash for high beam, neutral and generator. Fitment for 1975-83 XL models.

Speedometer and Tachometer Brackets, 1973 Only

VT No.	OEM	Type
39-0143	67181-73	Single Gauge
39-0139	92074-73	Tachometer-Speedometer
39-0140	67180-73	Cup for Speedometer and Tachometer

REAR CHAIN

530 Diamond STD

The mainstay of motorcycle chains.

VT No.	Links	VT No.	Links
19-0320	100	19-0327	108
19-0321	102	19-0324	110
19-0322	104	19-0325	112
19-0323	106	19-0326	120

530 XDL Self Lube

Eliminates the possibility of hit-and-miss lubrication due to its constant and consistent lubrication in the pin bushing area.

VT No.	Links	VT No.	Links
19-0330	100	19-0334	108
19-0331	102	19-0335	110
19-0332	104	19-0336	112
19-0333	106	19-0337	120

530 XLO O-Ring Chain

Includes a .214 pin which has been produced using a special alloy steel and case hardened for optimum strength.

VT No.	Links	VT No.	Links
19-0354	102	19-0357	110
19-0355	104	19-0358	112
19-0348	106	19-0398	120
19-0349	108		

530 Nickel Plated Chain

Offers rust-proof protection in a bright finish. Each part of the nickel plated chain is individually plated before assembly. 50ENP.

VT No.	Links	VT No.	Links
19-0340	100	19-0344	108
19-0341	102	19-0345	110
19-0342	104	19-0346	112
19-0343	106	19-0347	120

V-Twin 120 by 530

VT No.	Finish	Type
19-0723	Nickel	Standard
19-0725	Nickel	Standard
19-0726	Parkerized	Standard
19-0457	Natural	Heavy Duty
19-0458	Natural	O-Ring
19-0823	Silver	O-Ring
19-0824	Nickel	O-Ring

Master Links

Replacement link for #50 530 chain. Note: sold in 10 packs unless noted otherwise.

VT No.	Fits Chain Type
19-0350	Standard
19-0351	Nickel
19-0375	XDL Self Lube
19-0353	XLO O-Ring, each
19-0376	N.O.S. Repair Link with 2 Master links OEM, 40052-15

Rear Chain Tensioner by LBV

Reduces chain vibration and frequency of adjustment by utilizing a durable urethane roller which revolves on sealed bearings mounted on chrome anchor plates.

VT No.	Year	Model
19-0432	1957- Up	XL, XLH
19-0436	Roller Only	

Rear Chain Adjuster Set

Heat treated and include nuts. 1952-78.

VT No.	Finish
7703-2	Chrome
9020-2	Cadmium

530 HQR Tsubaki Super

An ultra high-performance, solid roller chain with 10,500 lbs. average tensile strength.

HQR	Links	HQR	Links
19-0500	102	19-0505	112
		19-0552	130
		19-0553	150
19-0504	110	19-0507	Con. Link

530 QR Solid Roller Chain

An economical, high quality solid roller chain.

HQR	Links	HQR	Links
19-0510	104	19-0514	110
19-0512	108	19-0515	120
19-0513	110	19-0559	130

530 HSL

A virtually maintenance-free chain with heavy duty shot-peened side plates, sintered metal bushings, and quad staked riveting. Nickel-plated HSL/NP available in a gleaming rustless finish.

HSL	HSL/NP	Size
19-0524	19-0532	102
19-0526		106
19-0528	19-0536	110
19-0529	19-0537	112
19-0530	19-0538	120
19-0531	19-0539	Connecting Link

Sigma O-Ring Chain

10,600 lbs. tensile strength, features heavy-duty, wide-waist link plates for increased durability.

VT No.	Links	VT No.	Links
19-0540	102	19-0544	110
19-0541	104	19-0545	112
19-0542	106	19-0546	120
19-0543	108	19-0554	130
19-0547	Link	19-0555	150

Diamond Spare Parts Kit

Includes two master links, one link and one offset link for all 530 heavy-duty chain.
VT No. 19-0352

PRIMARY CHAIN

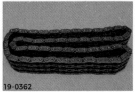

Diamond Endless Primary Chain

With oval side plates.

VT No.	Year	Sprocket	Link
19-0362	1957-2003	34	94
19-0369	2004 Up	38	96

Primary Chain features endless construction, oval shape side plates. Fits 1957-2003 XL (35 x 3 x 94) for 34T sprocket. Primary chain link measures 35" x 3" for XL primary chains.

Chain	Master Link
19-0932	19-0271

BELT & CHAIN

6

PRIMARY CHAIN ADJUSTER

Chain Tensioner

Includes pad, clip, and 39980-54 brace. Replaces 39975-54A on 1957-69 XLCH or 39975-54B on 1971-76 XLH-XLCH.

VT No.	OEM	Item
18-3155	39975-54A	A
18-3156	39975-54B	B,C (2pc)
18-3228	39980-54	C (Offset bracket)

VT No.	OEM	Model
28-0224*	Kit	1957-76 XLH-XLCH
28-0227	39978-58A	1957-76 XLH-XLCH
18-3643	39979-58	Retainer For Above

Primary Chain Nylon Adjuster Pads

Nylon Adjuster Pads for 1957-76.
*Note: Includes metal retainer 18-3643.

York Self-Adjusting Chain Tensioner

Fits 5 speed models with wet clutch. Replaces factory type detent adjuster shoe assembly. Tensioner kit includes all hardware and instructions for complete conversion. Fits 1991-up.

VT No. 18-3684

18-3684 Installed

XLCH Motor Sprocket

VT No.	OEM	Fits	Teeth
19-0009	Special	1957-76	23
19-0123	40288-58	1954-69	34
19-0067	40235-70A	1970-76, 76-78	34
19-0381	20435-74	1977-78, 79-90	34
32-0030*	32493-02A	2004- Up	34
19-0451	40241-02	2004- Up	34
Nuts			
12-0502	8025	1957-69	Nut
12-0503	40387-70	1970-88	Nut
12-0149	7652	1989- Up	Nut
10-0460	40240-89	1989- Up	Spacer

12-0502

19-0067

Note: 2004-up models requires purchase of sprocket/alternator rotor assembly
*Note: Rotor Assembly

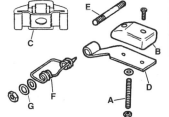
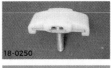

18-3220

18-0250

18-0119

Primary Adjuster Shoe Kit, 1977 -Up

VT No.	#	OEM	Year	Item
18-3220	Kit		1977-85	All Shown
18-3249	Kit		1986-90	As Above
18-3221	A	3250	1977-90	Adjuster
18-0250	C&A	39975-90A	1991-2001	Pad & Adjuster
18-0119	C&A	40039-02B	2002-up	Pad & Adjuster
28-0226	B	39966-80	1980-90	Pad
18-3222	D	39973-86	1977-90	Carrier
12-1186	E	40018-77	1977-85	Stud
12-2121	E	40018-86	1986-90	Stud
13-9163	F	40019-80A	1977-85	Spring
13-9164	F	40019-86A	1986-90	Spring
37-0588	G	6033	1977-85	Copper Washer

Motor Sprocket

Compensator Sprocket Components. 1957-76 XL.

VT No.	#	OEM	Item	Year
19-0437	A-F	—	Complete Kit	1967-74
19-0438	A	40273-67	34T Sprocket	1967-76
19-0439	B	40297-57	Cam Extension	1957-76
13-9238	C	40302-55A	Spring	1957-76
19-0440	D	40325-57	Sleeve	1957-76
19-0441	E	40376-57	Shaft Extension	L 1957-E 74
19-0443	E	40377-74	Shaft Extension	1974-76
19-0442	F	40386-57	Nut	1957-76

NOTE:
FOR DESCRIPTIVE PURPOSES XL= FOR SPORTSTER

REAR SPROCKET

19-0672 19-0673

1979-1981 Rear Sprockets

Zinc	Chrome	Teeth
	19-0047	43
	19-0049	44
	19-0032	45
19-0048	19-0033	46
	19-0035	47
	19-0037	48
	19-0039	49
19-0040	19-0041	51

Replaces 41470-73. Used on 1979-81 XL, XLCH & XLS, cast or wire wheel. Dish type sprocket with 9.8mm offset.

1982-92

VT No.	OEM	Teeth	Type
19-0042	41470-82	48	Offset
19-0043	41464-81	51	Offset
19-0120	41470-78	48	Flat
19-0124	—	49	Flat
19-0121	41464-86	51	Flat

1982-92. Chrome finish. Offset types have 6 mm offset. Note: VT No. 19-0120, 19-0124, 19-0121 are flat. 19-0042, 19-0043 have 6.0mm offset. 19-0032 through 19-0048 have 9.8mm offset.

5-Spoke Chrome Sprockets

Offset models have 9.8 mm offset. **Note:** Offset is measured from sprocket bolt mount surface to center line of teeth as shown

Offset	Flat	Teeth	Fits
19-0672	19-0674	48	1986-1999
19-0673	19-0675	51	1986-1999
19-0218	19-0251	48	2000- Up
19-0250	19-0221	51	2000- Up
Shim:	23-0320		1986-1999
Shim:	20-0346		2000- Up

Chrome Lazer Style Sprocket

Feature milled center design and 9.8 mm offset fit 1979-81. Flat fits 1986-up.

Offset	Flat	Teeth
19-0129	19-0047	48
19-0130	19-0049	49
19-0131	19-0032	51

Note: Sprocket offset measured from bolt mount surface to center of teeth.

Rear Sprocket Kit

For brake drums with rivet on sprockets. Includes rivets and dowels. Fits 1952-78. 51 tooth. Replaces 41470-70.

VT No.	Item	VT No.	Item
19-0011	Kit	19-0114	Rivets

TRANSMISSION DRIVE SPROCKET

A
19-0125

B
19-0064

C
19-0384

1952-1978 A	1979-1983 A	1984-1990 B	1991- Up C	# of Teeth
19-0125				18
19-0090			19-0446	19
19-0091		19-0072	19-0383	20
19-0092	19-0096	19-0063	19-0384	21
19-0093	19-0097	19-0064	19-0385	22
19-0589	19-0589			22
19-0094	19-0098	19-0073	19-0386	23
19-0095	19-0099			24

19-0589 has offset for 200 tire

Offset Sprockets

19-0422

19-0128

Fit models which allow use of a 150 series tire. Order rear sprocket spacer separately.

VT No.	Teeth	Speed	Year
19-0419	19	4	1984-90
19-0409	21	4	1984-90
19-0410	22	4	1984-90
19-0421	19	5	1991- Up
19-0422	20	5	1991- Up
19-0128	3/16"		Spacer

19-0211

19-0215

Offset transmission drive sprockets fit 1991-up XL with chain drive conversion. 500" Offset Counter Shaft Sprocket. Order flange nut separately.

VT No.	Teeth
19-0164	22
19-0402	23
19-0122	24

.810" Offset Countershaft Sprocket

19-0214	22
19-0215	23
19-0216	24
20-0324	Nut

Drive Sprocket Nut

VT No. 12-0529 includes seal in nut.

*Note: Does not include lock tab.

VT No.	OEM	Years
12-0529*	35047-53	E 1953-70
12-0530	35047-71A	1971-E84
12-0566*	7855W	1984-90
20-0308	35211-91	1991-Up
17-0910	Lock Tab	1952-E84

Oil Seal & Retainer Kit

Metal retainer with seal. Replaces 35150-52, includes gasket and screws. Fits all 1952-E84.

VT No.	OEM	Item
17-1160		Kit
15-0190	35169-52	Gasket
14-0118	35151-52	Seal

PULLEY

20-0376 20-0377 20-0378 20-0379

VT No.	Fits	Teeth	Finish
20-0376	1991-1999	61	Chrome
20-0377	2000-2003	61	Chrome
20-0765	2000-2003	61	Natural
20-0379	2004-2006	61, 18 spoke	Chrome
20-0767	2004-2006	61	Natural
20-0378	2007- Up	68 5-Spoke, 1"	Chrome
20-0766	2007- Up	68, 1"	Natural

Chrome Pulley/ Sprocket Bolt Kit

Year	Wheel Type		Drive Type		#	Style	Includes	
	Cast	Spoke	Belt	Chain			Nuts	Washers
1979-91	9857-10		◊	◊	A	Collar		
1979-91		9856-15		◊	A	Collar	◊	◊
1979-91		8836-10		◊	A	Acorn		
1979-91				◊	B	Cap	◊	
1979-91		8834-10		◊	C	Allen	◊	
1979-91		37-8131		◊	D	Hex	◊	
1979- Up			◊	◊	E	Acorn		◊
1979- Up			◊	◊	F	Cap		◊
1979- Up	8835-10		◊	◊	G	Allen		◊
1979- Up	9608-10	9609-15	◊	◊	H	Dome	◊	◊
2000- Up	2053-10	2053-10	◊		I	Hex		◊

Rear Drive Pulley

42-0670 42-0934 42-7512

42-1132

Rear Pulley Cover

VT No.	Year	Teeth	Finish
42-0670	1991-03	61	Chrome
42-0934	2004- Up	68	Chrome
42-7512	2004- Up	68	Chrome
42-1132	2004 - Up	68	Black

29T Front Drive Offset Pulley, 1991-2003

20-0512 20-0648

VT No.	Off-set
20-0512	.750"
20-0648	1"

Pulley Indexing Flange Nut

Allows drilling and tapping of additional set screw locations. Fits 1991-up XL.

VT No.	Type
20-0215	Belt
20-0324	Chain

Chrome Guard/Rear Pulley/Dress-up Kit

Includes belt guards, upper and lower, and rear pulley cover for 5-Speed belt drive models with hardware.

27-0619 27-0541

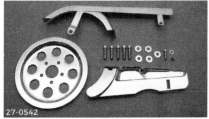

27-0542

VT No.	Year
27-1645	1991-2003
27-0788	2004-Up
20-0784	2004-Up

Final Drive Front Pulleys

20-0526

20-0341

1986-up 5 Speed models as supplied by V-Twin or BDL. All BDL pulleys are 1/3" lighter than stock and include spacer, seal, lock plate and screws. *Stock Size Pulley.

VT No.	BDL	Teeth	Finish
20-0328		27	1986-90
	20-0650	28	1991-03
20-0526*	20-0651*	29	1991-03
20-0341		30	2004- Up
	20-0652	30	1991-03

Pulley Lock Tool fits 1991-up XL.
VT No.
16-0588

BELT

Chrome Belt Guards

27-1667

1991-1999

27-0123

2000-2003

27-1745

2004- Up

27-0862

2004- Up

Chrome Lower Belt Guard

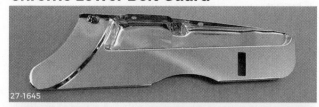

27-1645

27-0788

27-0788 Installed

Includes belt guards, upper and lower, and rear pulley cover for 5-Speed belt drive models with hardware.

VT No.	Year	Pulley
27-0541	1991-1999	61 Tooth
27-0542	2000-2003	61 Tooth
27-0619	2004- Up	68 Tooth

Final Drive Belt for XL

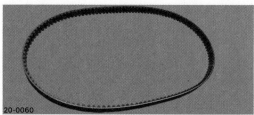

20-0060

Carlisle	Dayco	BDL	Width	Tooth	Tooth/Model
20-3999		20-0456	1.125"	125T	XL Ratio Change
20-4000		20-0060	1.125"	128T	1991-92 XL 883 Deluxe XL 1200, 1993-03 All XL and 1986-92 XL Rear Belt Conversion Kit
20-4001			1.125"	133T	1993-2003 XL Ratio Change
		20-4004	1.125"	136T	2004-06 883 XL
		20-0688	1.125"	137T	2004-06 1200 XL
		20-4005	1.000"	136T	2007-10 883 XL
20-4003	20-0788		1.000"	137T	2007-up 1200 XL 2011-up XL

Note: There is no warranty on belts sold as part of kit or individual replacements.

Rear Chain Conversion Sprocket

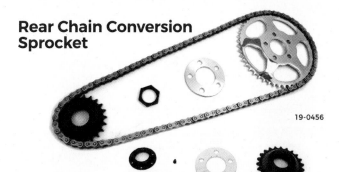

19-0456

19-0761

Sprocket Kit for converting 1991-up XLs to chain drive. Includes 120 link chain, front and rear sprockets.

VT No.	Front Tooth	Rear Tooth	Years
19-0456	22	48	1991-1999
19-0761	23	51	2000- Up
19-0763	24	48	2000- Up

Front Belt Lock Plate and Nut Kit

20-0308

VT No.	Item
20-0308	Kit
17-0934	Lock Only
12-0579	Nut Only
37-0429	Set Screw

Includes 2 allen screws, sprocket lock nut and lock plate. Fits 1991-up XL models.

SHIFTER LEVER & PEGS

Chrome Shifter Lever Assemblies

Include cats paw shifter peg. 21-0571 has smooth bore.

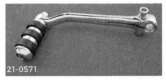

21-0571

21-0572

21-0573

21-0574

21-0579

21-0576

21-0575

21-0577

VT No.	Year	VT No.	Year	VT No.	Year
21-0571	1957-70	21-0574	1975-76	21-0577	1991-03
21-0572	1957-70	21-0575	1977-85	21-0579	2004-up
21-0573	1971-74	21-0576	1986-90		

21-0612 **1991-03**

21-0614 **2004- Up**

Chrome Billet Shifter Lever and Footpeg Kit includes arm and cats paw shifter footpeg.

Short Stud Shifter Pegs

21-0872

VT No.	#	Year	VT No.	#	Year
27-1633	A	Railer	21-0640	F	O-Ring (Rotates)
21-2025	B	Cats Paw	21-0402	F	O-Ring
21-1665	C	Cats Paw, extended	21-0872		Skull Shifter
21-0407	E	Chrome Cap			

Chrome Shifter Levers

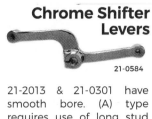

21-0584

VT No.	#	Year
21-2013	A	1952-70
21-0310	A	1952-70
21-0301	B	1971-74
21-0314	B	1971-74
21-2034	C	1975-76
21-0304	D	1977-85
21-2012	E	1986-90
21-0643	E	1986-90
21-2032	F	1991-03
21-0578	H	2004-Up
21-0584	Heel-Toe	2004-Up
21-0823	Heel-Toe	1991-03
21-0359	Zinc	1952-70

21-2013 & 21-0301 have smooth bore. (A) type requires use of long stud shifter footpeg as hole is not threaded.

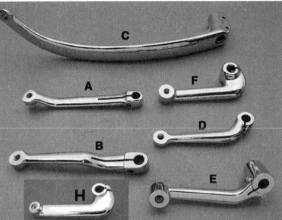

1991-Up 5 Speed Shift Lever

21-0387

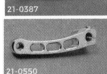

21-0550

VT No.	Year
21-0550	1991-2003
21-0387	2004 -Up
21-0590	1991-2003 Black with highlighted aluminum

Chrome Diamond Shape Shifter Peg includes diamond shape rubber insert and short stud (1/2").

VT No. 21-0260

Stock Rubber Shift Pegs

21-0901

21-0902

21-0903

21-0904

21-0908

7/8" long stud is used when the lever is unthreaded and stud accepts a nut. Short 5/8" thread screws into lever.

VT No.	Color	Type
21-0901	Black	Short, 1/2"
21-0902	White	Short, 5/8"
21-0903	Black	Long, 7/8"
21-0908	Black	Long, 7/8"
21-0904	White	Long, 7/8"

2004-UP FORWARD CONTROL

22-0731 Installed

22-0457 Installed

22-0731

22-0457

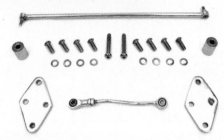

Reduced Reach Forward Control Adapter Kit

Fits 2004-13 XL. Brings forward controls closer to rider.

VT No. 27-1731

22-0721 Installed

2004-up forward control includes brake pedals and mount plates as shown. 22-0731 includes soft peg set.

22-0731

22-0721

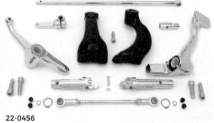

23-0777

22-0456

Extended Reach Forward Control Conversion

Conversion for 2004-13 XL forward controls, to move 6" forward.

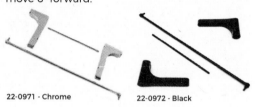

22-0971 - Chrome   22-0972 - Black

Shifter Linkage

For 2004-Up XLC with forward controls.

21-0452

21-0452 Installed

21-0453 Installed

VT No.	Type	Size	Year
22-0721	Without Footpegs	Stock	2004-05
22-0731	With Footpegs	Stock	2004-05
22-0900	Chrome w/Footpegs	Stock	2006-13
22-0799	Black w/Footpegs	+2"	2004-13
22-0456	Chrome w/o Footpegs	Stock	2014-up
22-0457	Black w/o Footpegs	Stock	2014-up

23-0856

Hardware	
21-0787	Shaft Arm
23-0856	Brake Rod

21-0452

21-2081

21-2087

Forward Control Footrest Support

Chrome support fits 2004 - up XLC models with forward controls.

VT No.	Item
27-0010	Support
21-0746	Footpeg Yoke

Forward Control Peg Adapters

Allow use of male pegs on OE style forward controls.

VT No.	Item
27-0974	Stock
27-0999	+2"

27-0974   27-0999

VT No.	Style	VT No.	Style
21-2081	Round SS	21-0452	Black Hole
21-2087	Maltese	21-0453	Black Talon

Note: For descriptive purposes XL= For Sportster

BILLET FORWARD CONTROL KIT

Chrome Billet Forward Control Kit   Master cylinder included. Order brake line and related parts separately.

22-0769 RIGHT

22-0769 Installed Right

22-0769 LEFT

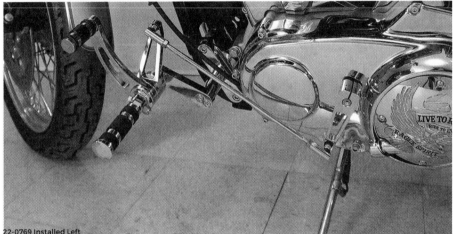

22-0769 Installed Left

VT No.	Item	Year
22-0769	Kit	1986-03
22-0828	Kit	2004-13
23-0688	Brake "T"	
23-8060	21" Line	
23-0612	10mm Bolt	
23-4047	Straight Banjo	
23-4051	90° Banjo	

22-0785

22-0797

Black	Polish	Fits	Black	Polish	Fits
22-0784	22-0785	883 1991-2003 XL	22-0796	22-0797	883 2004-2013 XL

Billet Forward Control Kit

1986-2003 FORWARD CONTROL KIT

22-0766 Left Side Shift

22-0766 Right Side Brake

22-0588
+2" EXTENDED

BRAKES 7

Chrome Forward Control Kit for XL models, featuring XLC styling. Kit includes Cats Paw™ Foot and Shifter Pegs. 22-0718 & 22-0588 order pegs separately

VT No.	Item	Years	Speed	VT No.	Item	Years	Speed
22-0766	Control Kit with pegs	1986-90	4	27-1582	Foot Peg Set	All 1991-03	
22-0719	Control Kit with pegs	1991-2003	5	21-2025	Shift Peg	All 1991-03	
22-0718	Control Kit without pegs	1991-2003	5	23-0465	Brake Pedal	All 1991-03	
22-0588	Control Kit +2" without pegs	1986-2003	4/5	21-0830	Shifter Arm		

1986-2003 Billet Forward Control Kit

Features Big Twin style controls. Order related brake parts separately. Will not work with stock exhaust.
VT No. 22-0790

Left

Right

Brake Related Parts for 22-0790

VT No.	Item
23-4279	90° Fitting
23-8342	36" Hose
23-0571	"T"
23-0426	Switch
23-8362	16" Hose
23-4050	Banjo
23-3005	Master Cylinder
23-0859	MC Rebuild
23-0773	Plunger

Rear Sprocket Rivet Tool

Will hold sprockets in place to install rivets by hammer or press. For 1957-78 XL.
VT No. 16-1267

Rear Sprocket Kits

For brake drums with rivet on sprockets. Includes rivets and dowels. Fits 1952-78. 51 tooth. Replaces 41470-70.

Kit	Rivets
19-0011	19-0114

VT No.	# Type	Finish
8811-16	Bolts	Chrome Set - 5pk
19-0011	Sprocket	51T Black with Rivets
19-0114	Rivets	Set
23-0817	Shoe Kit	1952-72
23-0818	Shoe Kit	1973-78

1957-2003 FORWARD CONTROL

22-0957

22-0958

Forward Mid-Control Kits

Positioned slightly forward than stock for comfort.

VT No.	Item
22-0460	1986-2003 Mid Forward Control, Chrome
22-0461	2004- Up Mid Forward Control, Chrome
22-0957	Forward Control Kit, Chrome
22-0958	Forward Control Kit, Black
22-0961	Forward Control Kit with footboards, Chrome
22-0962	Forward Control Kit with footboards, Black

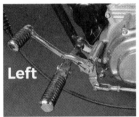

Left

Right

Left
22-0700

Right
22-0701

XLH-XLCH Forward Controls

Chrome plated and complete as pictured for right and left sides for 1957-78 models with mechanical brakes. Purchase longer motor mount bolts separately. Note: Front Pipe may have to be indented for clearance

VT No.	Fits	Brake	Shift
22-0700	1957-74	Left	Right
22-0701*	1977-78	Right	Left

*Replacement Part for 22-0701:

22-0375 Chrome Brake

883-1000-1100-1200 Forward Control

VT No.	Year	Speed
22-0395	1984-85 Only	4
22-1048	1986-90	4
22-0396	1991-2003	5
22-0383	1991-2003	5, w/o pegs

For Sportster models with alternator. Includes chrome brake and shifter assemblies, complete with all necessary brackets, pedals, linkage, O-Ring pegs and hardware for installation. Use existing master cylinder for assembly.

21-2014

21-2018

21-2052   22-1046

21-2058

Replacement Parts

VT No.	Item
23-9202	Brake Pedal only
22-1046	Bracket Only
21-2058	Shift Foot Lever only
21-2014	Shift Lever Arm, 5 Speed
21-2018	Inner Shift Lever, 5 Speed
21-2052	Two Piece Shift Arm, 4 Speed
21-0957	Shifter Arm Extension
21-0956	Shifter Pedal Mount
21-0402	Shifter Peg
27-1580	Footpegs

Daniel Boone Forward Controls

22-0391

Controls fit models as listed. 1977-78 models are cable operated and include cable. 22-0391 includes master cylinder and stainless brake line.

Brake Side

Shift Side

VT No.	Fits	Brake	Shift	Brake Type
22-0391	1979-83	Right	Left	Hydraulic
21-0923	1957-74			Lever

7408-10T

Front Motor Mount Bolt Kit

VT No.	Type	Style
7141-18	Stock	Acorn
37-9207	Stock (no Spacers)	Hex
9797-20	Stock	Allen
7408-10	X-Long	Acorn, 7.5"
7408-10T	X-Long	Acorn, 7.5"
37-9086	Chrome	Spacer Set
37-9158	Washers, 4pk	Locating

Stock length kits include chrome spacers and washer. Extra length kit are bolts only, excluding spacers. Use extra length kit for installing forward controls or hi-way bars. Fit 1957-84.

Brake Pedal

21-0671

27-1519

27-1520

Brake Pedal can be used as a replacement for Daniel Boone or Davey Crockett controls. The 3/8" - 16 threaded stud can also be used as rigid mount foot pegs.

VT No.	Item	U/M
27-1519	Rubber Covered	Set
27-1520	O-Ring	Set
21-0671	Cats Paw	Each

1980-UP REAR BRAKE PART

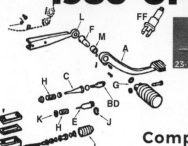

Chrome Brake Pedal

Includes bushings.

VT No.	Year
23-0401	1980-2003
23-0680	2004- Up

Rear Brake Pedal Components

For 1980-2003.

VT No.	#	OEM	Item
23-0401	A	42459-80B	1980-2003 Pedal
23-0405	A-1	542400-80	Pin for Pedal
23-1741	B	42445-80A	1980-2003 Rod End and
	C	42448-80	Plunger Assembly
23-1986	B&D		Rod End with Pin
23-3016	B	42445-80A	1980-E87 Rod End only
23-9173	B	42437-87	1987-up Plunger Rod End
23-3017	E	42448-E87	1982-E87 Plunger
23-3015	F	42441-80	1980-90 Pivot Shaft
23-3079	FF	42441-90A	1991-03 Pivot Shaft with Clevis
12-0972	G	11093	1980-89 Pivot Retainer
13-9165	H	40920-79	1980-84 Return Spring
13-9166	H	40920-82	1984-E87 Return Spring
28-0505	I	40922-79	1979 Pushrod Boot
12-0971	J	40918-82	1984-up Retaining Ring
23-1758	K	44126-82	1982-up Washer, Spring
23-1728	L	34909-83	1983-90 Bracket
23-3080	L	34933-96	1991-03 Bracket, Chrome
10-1256	M	42443-80	1980-up Bushing

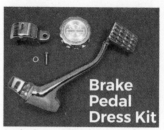

Brake Pedal Dress Kit

Includes pedal and reservoir cover. Fits 2004-07 XL.
VT No. 23-0962

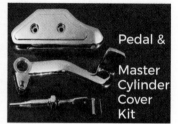

Pedal & Master Cylinder Cover Kit

Includes plunger and mount hardware. Fits 1982-2003.
VT No. 23-0672

Rear Brake Lines

Sportster master cylinder to TEE, rear hose is rubber with chrome STEEL end from TEE to rear caliper.

23-2310

VT No.	OEM	Years	Item
23-0696	44437-77	1979	Tube
23-0729	42484-81	1981-85	Tube
23-2310	44438-87B	1987-03	Hose
23-8076		1987-03	Stainless Braided Hose

23-8076

*Note: Single piece hoses, use this line only.

XLS-XLH Sprocket Cover Hardware

23-3079 23-3015 23-3024 23-1728 23-3080

VT No.	OEM	Years	Item
23-3024	34866-86A	1986-90	Mount Stud
23-3015	42441-80	1980-90	Pivot Stud
23-3079	42441-90	1991-up	Pivot Shaft
23-1728	34909-83	1983-90	M.C. Support Bracket
23-3080	34933-96	1991-2003	M.C. Support Bracket

Brake Caliper Inserts

37-8968

37-8969

37-8970

Chrome finish. Easily installed with double faced tape supplied. Sold each.

VT No.	Diameter	Fits	Type
37-8968	1.80"	1987-99	Hayes Rear
37-8969	1.47"	1984-99	Front
		1982- E 87	Girling Rear
37-8970	1.40"	1977-83	Dual Disc Front
		1972-84	Banana Rear
		1977-81	Rear

Rear Caliper Parts
1979-81

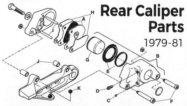  

23-9239 23-0140 23-0125

VT No.	#	OEM	Item
23-9239			Caliper Assembly, Chrome
23-1746	F	44175-77 44176-77	Screw Set
23-0414	I	44186-77	Caliper Pins, 10pk
23-9199	H	44182-77 44185-77	Plate, Inner Plate, Outer
23-2276	E	44152-77	Seal Kit
23-0510	A	43395-80	Pad Set
23-2280	G	44181-77A	Caliper Piston
23-1731	D	44146-77	Bleeder
23-9198	C	44141-77	Brake Hose Set
23-0135	J	45861-79 15862-79	Bushing, Set
28-0718	K	44199-79	Rubber Bumper

Bolt Set

Chrome	Black
37-0508 1982-E 87	
23-0140 L 1987-99	23-0125 L 1987-99
2081-3 2000-2007	

Rear Caliper Seal Kits

VT No.	Year
23-2276	1979-81
23-2277	1982-86
23-9022	1987-99
23-0533	2000-03
23-0276	2004-13
23-0293	2014- Up

*Includes seal kit.

Rear Caliper Pistons		Rear Caliper Pistons	
VT No.	Year	VT No.	Year
23-2280	1979-81	23-0532	2000-03
23-2281	1982-86	23-0275*	2004-13
23-1999*	1987-99	23-0290	2014- Up

MASTER CYLINDER

23-1717

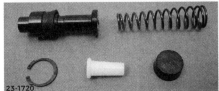
23-1720

23-0586

3-1828   23-9177   23-9201

42-9945 Installed

42-0890

42-9945

23-0757
23-0758

23-9262

BRAKES 7

Rear Master Cylinder Rebuild

VT No.	OEM	Fits
23-1717	42374-77B	1980-81
23-1720	42874-82A	1982-Early87
23-9177	42382-87A	Late 1987-2003
23-1211	42810-04	2004-07
23-1212	42810-07	2007-13
23-1828	41700097	2014-up
23-0586	42436-87 Pushrod	Late 1987-2003

Rear Master Cylinder Covers, Chrome Finish

VT No.	Year
42-9945	1980-2003
42-0890	1982-2003

Rear Master Cylinder Boots
Sold each.

VT No.	OEM	Fit
28-0503	41764-79	1979
28-0505	40922-79	1980-86
28-2005	40922-87	1987- Up

Rear Master Cylinder

VT No.	OEM	Finish	Fit
23-0757	42453-82B	Natural	1982-E 87
23-0758	42453-82B	Chrome	1982-E 87
23-9262	42456-87	Chrome	L 87-2003

Rear Master Cylinder Top Covers

Available as listed in Eagle Spirit chrome or gold inlay, finned, or smooth

23-9190

24-0632

24-0629

23-0617   24-0601

Smooth	Eagle Spirit Chrome	Eagle Spirit Gold	Finned	Years
23-9187	24-0629	24-0632		1987-96
23-9190				1982-87
23-0617			24-0601	1979-81

 15-0203   15-0188
 15-0242   15-0250

Big Twin Gaskets
Master cylinder and reservoir top gaskets

GB No.	OEM	Year	Type
15-0188	45012-72	1972-81	Master
15-0204	45012-82	1982-84	Master
15-0242	45005-85	1985-95	Master
15-0250	45005-96	1996-up	Master
Rear			
15-0202	41766-58	1958-78	Master
15-0203	42455-80	1979-81	Master
15-0248	42455-82	1982-E87	Reservoir
15-0540	42455-99	2000-up	Reservoir
15-0242	45005-85	1985-95	Master
15-1379	Gasket	2004-06	Master
15-1380	Gasket	2007-up	Master

Stainless Steel Master Cylinder Top Screws

25 pack.

VT No.	OEM	Years	Type
37-8947	2628	1972-81	Front Master - Top, Countersunk
37-8948	2579	1982- Up	Front Master - Top, Countersunk
37-9082	2622	1970-78	Points Cover
37-9083	2625	1979- Up	Points Cover
37-8821	42534-82	1982- Up	Reservoir Cover

Warranty All Brake/Calipers/Master Cylinders sold as individual pieces or in kits are covered under our warranty "Replacement Only" Provision. All item part numbers begin with a 23 prefix. No credit will be issued for these items as they are exchange only.

1952-78 BRAKE

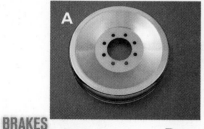

Brake Shoe Sets

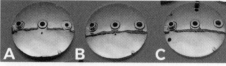

23-0450

1954-78 XL models. Include linings riveted on. Order spring set separately

VT No.	Item	Type
23-0505	Lining Set	Standard
23-0450	Lining Set	.025 Oversize
13-0146	Spring Set	—
23-0503	Shoe Set	Standard
23-0390	Shoe Set	.025 Oversize

Rear Brake Drum

Includes sprocket riveted on for use on 1955-78 XLH-XLCH Sportster models. Order mounting bolts separately.

VT No.	#	Type	Finish	VT No.	#	Type	Finish
45-0403	A	Cover	Chrome	8811-16		Bolts	Chrome Set
23-0437	B	Drum	Chrome	19-0011		Sprocket	51T Black w/ rivets
23-0438	B	Drum	Black	19-0114		Rivets	Set
8812-16		Bolts	Cadmium Set	23-0817		Shoe Kit	1952-72
				23-0818		Shoe Kit	1973-78

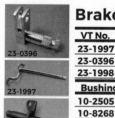

Available in chrome or polished finish. Order anchor bolt kit separately.

Rear Backing Plate

Polished	Chrome	#	Year	Type
	23-9013	A	1954-72	Rod
	23-9014	B	1973-74	Rod
23-2268	23-9015	C	1975-78	Cable

Rear Wheel/Brake Drum Assembly

Includes 16" all chrome wheel, brake drum, chrome backing plate assembly and chrome axle kit. Order chrome brake arm VT No. 23-0397.

VT No.	Year
52-1050	1954-72
52-1051	1973-74
52-1052	1975-78

Brake Operating Shafts

Splined to accept brake pedal.

23-0396

23-1997

23-1998

VT No.	OEM	Years
23-1997	42549-52	1952-74
23-0396	41620-75	1975-76
23-1998	42549-75	1977-79
Bushings	OEM	Years
10-2505	47757-52	1952-76
10-8268	25594-75	1977- E 81
10-0748	34898-79	1979 Pivot Shaft

Rear Backing Plate

22-0728

Chrome assembly includes chrome backing plate, shoes, springs, cam, pivot stud and related hardware.

Order rear arm separately.

VT No.	Year
22-0728	1954-72
22-0729	1973-74
22-0730	1975-78

Rear Brake Linkage

22-0812

Kit includes chrome rod with nut, chrome pedal, chrome rear arm, brake spring, cross shaft, clevis pin and hardware. Order rear arm separately.

VT No.	Year	VT No.	Year
22-0812	1952-66	22-0811	1967-74

Brake Pedals

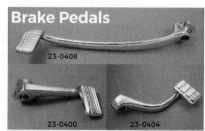

23-0408

23-0400

23-0404

VT No.	OEM	Years
23-0408	42410-52	1952-74
23-0931	42410-52	1952-75 Zinc
23-0400	42420-75	1975-76
23-0404	42410-75A	1977-79

1952-72 Drum Front Brake

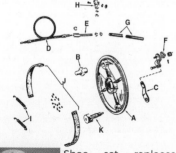

Shoe set replaces 41849-64 for 1964-72 models. VT No. 23-0525

VT No.	#	OEM	Item
	A	44148-64	Polished Backing Plate
24-0116	B	44156-64	Pivot Stud, 1964-72
24-0609	C	44307-52	Zinc Lever
36-2385	D	45060-54	Cable Assembly
36-2565	D		Cable Assembly
8818-3	E	45159-50	Adjuster, Zinc
9741-2	E		Adjuster, Chrome
37-8676	F	45174-64	Clevis, Zinc
24-0095	G	45203-52	Chrome Front Brake Tube
24-0646			As Above, Cadmium
2041-7	H	45218-53	Parkerized Throttle Cable Bracket
13-0146	I	41835-69	Spring Set
23-0505	J	44432-54	1952-63 Linings
23-0450	J	OS	1952-63 Linings
23-0506	J	41848-64	1964-72 Linings
23-0519	K	44264-64	Brake Cam, 1954-72

Clutch and Brake Lever Assemblies

Include cable pin. Available chrome or polished with 5/16" hole sizes for cable entry. VT No. 26-2167 and 26-2168 accept front brake switch.

Chrome	Polish	OEM	Years
26-0525	26-0526	45002-65	1952-68 Brake
26-2167	26-2168	45002-69	1969-72 Brake

1954-78 MECHANICAL BRAKE PART

23-0127

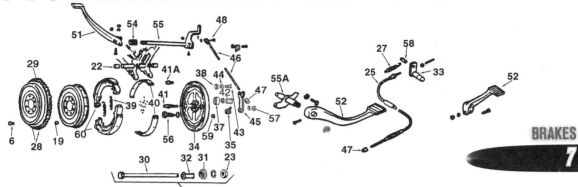

Chrome Rear Brake Arm replaces 41925-52. Fits 1952-78.

VT No. 23-0397

BRAKES

7

XL Rear Brake Components, Drum Type

VT No.	#	OEM	Item /Type	VT No.	#	OEM	Item /Type
10-2505	22	47757-52	Bushing, pair	23-0127	37-41-52		Pivot Stud Kit 3pc 1952-72
44-0326	23	7986	Axle Nut Kit, Chrome	23-0410	41A	41876-73	Pivot Stud 1973-78
36-1975	25	38634-75	Cable Assembly 1975-76	23-0412	42	41882-52	Stud Nut 1954-72
36-1977	25	38634-77	Cable Assembly 1977-78	9207-4	37-41-42		Pivot Stud Kit, Chrome
13-0205	27	40521-75	Spring, Stop Light & Switch	9208-4		As Above	Pivot Stud Kit, Cadmium
23-0438	28	41401-52	Drum and Sprocket, Black	23-0397	45	41925-52	Rear Lever Chrome
23-0437	28	Complete	As above, Chrome	23-0322			Rear lever Zinc
19-0011	29	41470-70	Sprocket only, Black with rivets	23-0399	46	42252-52	Brake Rod, 54-66 Short, Chrome.
8811-16	6-19	Chrome	Lug Bolt Set	23-0324		42252-52	As above, Cad w/nut
8812-16	6-19	Cadmium	3970B and 7725 Nut	23-0326		42252-52	As above, Parkerized
44-0217	30	41551-52	Rear Axle, Chrome	23-0398	46	42253-67	Brake Rod, Long 67-74, Chrome
44-0565	30A	—	Rear Axle Kit	23-0325		42253-67	As above, Cad w/nut
44-0317	31	41598-52	Collar, Zinc	37-8461	47	42264-52	Adjuster Nut 1952-78
44-0500	31	41598-52	Collar, Chrome	23-0421	48	42269-30	Clevis Pin 1954-74
44-0324	32	41600-55	Spacer, Chrome	23-0408	51	42410-52	Pedal, Chrome 1952-74
23-0396	33	41620-75	Splined Arm 1975-76	23-0400	52	42420-75	Pedal, Chrome 1975-76
23-2267	34	41662-54	Side Plate 1954-72	23-0404	52	42410-75A	Pedal, Chrome 1977-79
23-2268	34	41662-75	Side Plate 1975-78	13-0153	54	42427-52	Return Spring 1954-78
13-0144	35	41667-75	Spring, Lever, each	23-1997	55	42549-52	Cross Shaft 1954-74
13-0146	39	41835-69	Shoe Springs, pr	23-1998	55A	42549-75	Operating Shaft 1977-79
23-0411	37	41730-52	Locating Block, Zinc	23-3066	56	44264-54	Cam Brake 1954-78
8937-3	38	41730-73	Spacer Pivot Stud Kit	23-0505	40	44432-54	Lining and Rivet Set 1954-78
	43	41882-73	Bolt, 3 Piece	37-9172	58	45052-75	Cable pin
	44	41883-73	Washer, Cadmium	23-0503	60	44401-49B	Brake Shoe Set
8936-3			As Above, Chrome 3 Piece Kit				

32-7785   32-0547   32-0424

XLCH Switch Kit

1958-1969 XLCH switch kit replaces 72011-59 bracket, 5902 (2) spacer.

VT No. 32-9161

Rear Brake Cable Assembly

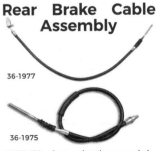

36-1977

36-1975

1975-78 drum brake models, 2 types.

VT No.	OEM	Years
36-1975	38634-75	1975-76
36-1977	38634-77	1977-78

Chrome Brake Light Switches

VT No.	#	OEM	Type	Fits
32-7785	A	72004-52	Push	1959-66
32-0547	B	72004-75	Pull	1975-76
32-0552	B	Black	Pull	As Above
32-0424	C	72004-70	Push	1967-74
32-0572	D	Kit	Pull	1975-76
32-0551	E	Kit	Push	1977-78
13-0218		Spring		1969

Brake Rod Adjuster Nut fits 1952-78.

VT No. 37-8461

Mechanical Brake Lamp Switch

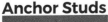

32-0421

32-1155

32-1156

Universal fit. Includes clamp and spring. Pull type, black. Pull is on.

VT No.	Type
32-0421	
32-1155	Oval
32-1156	Rectangle

Anchor Studs

9207-4/ 9208-4

23-0410

8936-3/ 8937-3

For backing plates in chrome or cadmium finish.

VT No.	Years	Finish
9207-4	1954-72	Chrome
9208-4	1954-72	Cadmium
8936-3	1973-78	Chrome
89.7-3	1973-78	Cadmium
23-0410	1973-78	Zinc

23-1150

23-1097

23-1092

23-0369

22-0366

Rear Caliper Kit

Chrome finish. Fits XL models and includes complete chrome replica 4-piston caliper assembly with pads and polished stainless steel drilled brake disc with chrome mount bolts.

VT No.	Year	2004- Up
23-1150	2005-up	
23-1097	2004	23-0680 Rear Pedal
23-1092	2000-2003	21-0578 Chrome Shifter Lever
22-0369	1987-1999	27-0817 Footpeg Support, Left
22-0366	1982-1986	23-0780 Footpeg Support, Right

22-0363

Rear Caliper Kit

22-0356

Includes GMA Caliper with bracket and either a polished or standard 11-1/2" stainless steel rotor with mount bolts. Use with 5/8" master cylinder.

VT No.	OEM	Year
22-0361	22-0354	1979-81
22-0362	22-0355	1982-E 87
22-0363	22-0356	L 1987- 99

11.5" Chrome Caliper Kit fits XL Rigid frames with 3/4" rear axle. Kit includes polished 11.5" disc, bolts, chrome 4-piston caliper complete with integral bracket and weld on frame tab for left side.

VT No. 22-0370

Vibration Shims for Rear Pads

23-9238

1982-86
OEM 41665-82

23-0137

1987-99
OEM 43959-86

23-0147

2000-03
OEM 44337-00

23-9268

2014-Up
OEM 42521-04

REAR CALIPER

Rear Caliper Set

Chrome replica style includes bracket and caliper with pads. Uses stock brake lines. Fits 1987-99 XL.

VT No. 22-0379

23-9221

23-0633

Chrome Caliper Assemblies

23-9052

VT No.	OEM	Year	VT No.	OEM	Year
23-0587	40925-00	2000-2003	23-9221	44198-87	L 1987-99
23-0633	40968-04	2004	23-9052	44052-82A	1982-E 87 Caliper, Complete
23-0236	40968-05	2005-07			
23-0855	40968-08	2008- 2010	37-0508	44201-82	Bolt Kit for Above
23-1316*	40968-11	2011-Up	*Note: Black		

GMA Rear Billet Aluminum Brake Calipers

23-4519

23-9209

23-9208

Machined from billet aluminum and clear anodized. Feature dual pistons which are internally connected, brake pads and brackets, when provided. Include spacers and hardware necessary for installation. Hoses and brake disc not included. Use 5/8" bore master cylinder.

23-9209 Caliper Installed

VT No.	GMA	Model
23-4519	203	1979-81 XL
23-9208	204	1982- E 1987 XL
23-9209	205	L 1987-99 XL w/ Banjo Bolts

GMA Components		
23-4520	PA2	GMA Caliper Piston, pair, fits 23-4519, 23-9208, 23-9209
23-4510	RB1	Caliper O-Ring Seal Kit fits ,23-4519, 23-9208, 23-9209
23-4514	B-Pad	SBS Brake Pad Set fits Calipers: 23-4519, 23-9208, 23-9209
23-9237	R879SPT	GMA Ductile Iron Brake Disc Rear
23-9936	R79FXL	GMA Floating Brake Disc1979-99 Rear

Chrome Bracket for Calipers

Sold separately. Replaces 40929-87. Fits L 1987-99.

VT No. 23-9047

FRONT CALIPER 1984-99

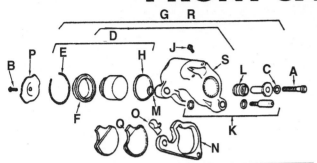

11-1/2" Chrome Left Side Front Caliper

Kit includes polished stainless steel Dura brake disc with bolts and chrome caliper half with brake pads and hardware. 39mm. Fits 1984-99.

VT No. 23-0563

Front Calipers and Components

VT No.	#	OEM	Item/Type
37-8822	A	855	Screw
	B	3517	Screw, Kit
	C	6019	Washer, 1983-92
37-0800		As Above	1993-99
23-2279	D	44020-83	Piston Rebuild Kit
12-0977	E	44021-83	Retainer
23-2275	F/H	44047-83	Dust Boot with Seal
23-3061	G	44046-84C	1984-99 All, Black
23-3082	G	As Above	Caliper Left, Chrome Complete
23-1731	J	44048-83	Bleeder
23-2274	K	44053-83	1984-92
23-9226	K	44053-92	Guide Pin Kit for 1993-99
28-2133	L	44054-83	Boot, each
14-0563	M	44059-83	O-Ring
23-2308	N	44072-92A	Bracket, Left
	N	44073-92A	Bracket, Right
23-2306	O	44061-83	Spring Clip
23-2307	P	44062-83	Retaining Pad
23-0512	Q	44063-83	Pad Set with B
23-1998	55A	42549-75	Operating Shaft 1977-79
23-3066	56	44264-54	Cam Brake 1954-78
23-0505	40	44432-54	Lining and Rivet Set 1954-78
37-9172	58	45052-75	Cable pin
23-0503	60	44401-49B	Brake Shoe Set

Chrome Caliper Kit

Features 4 piston chrome caliper and polished stainless steel Dura brake disc. Fits 1984-99.

VT No. 23-0649

Front Chrome Billet Calipers

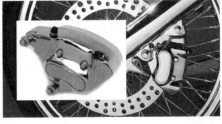

Feature 4-piston design with mount brackets included. Fits 1984-99.

VT No. 23-0279

Chrome Left Side 4-Piston Caliper

Features 2000-up styling to retro fit 1984-99 models.

VT No. 23-0555

Chrome Front Disc Caliper

Available right or left assemblies, or set for 11-1/2" brake discs. Includes all internal components and pads. Fits 1984-99.

23-2226
23-3082

VT No.	Item	VT No.	Item	VT No.	Item
23-2226	Pair	23-3085	Right Only	23-3082	Left Only

1984-99 Black Front Caliper include internal components. Replaces 046-84C, left.

VT No. 23-3061

Chrome Front Caliper Bolts

37-0800

VT No.	Years
37-0800	1993-99
37-8822	1984-92

Front GMA Billet Aluminum Brake Caliper

Machined from billet aluminum and clear anodized. Feature dual pistons which are internally connected, brake pads and brackets, when provided. Include spacers and hardware necessary for installation. Hoses and rotors not included.

VT No.	GMA	Fits	Bore
23-4508	400	77-83 XL Dual Kit, 8 Piston	3/4"
23-4513	200E	74-77 XL Single Disc	5/8"
23-4504	200F	84-99 Single Disc XL Kit, Left Only, 2 Piston	5/8"
Components			
23-4521	PA4	Caliper Piston Pair fits: 23-4508,23-9210,23-1793,23-9256	
23-4520	PA2	Caliper Piston Pair fits: 23-4513,23-4504	
23-4510	RB1	O-Ring Seal Kit fits: 23-4513,23-4504	
23-4522	RB4	O-Ring Seal Kit fits: 23-4508,23-9210,23-1793,23-9256	
23-4514	B Pad	SBS Brake Pad Set fits: 23-9513,23-4504	
23-9169	F Pad	SBS Brake Pad Set fits: 23-4508,23-9210	
23-0593	F Pad	Dura 4pc Set	

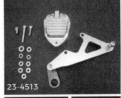
23-4513
23-4504
23-4508

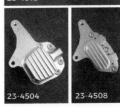
23-0865
23-1105

Edart Billet Front Caliper includes bracket for 1984-99 ST and XL models is one piece design.

VT No.	Piston
23-1105	2
23-0865	4

FRONT CALIPER

11.5" Chrome Front Caliper & Brake Disc Kit

23-0989

VT No.	Years
23-0649	1984-99
23-0562	2000-03
23-0989	2004- Up

Includes a complete chrome replica 4-piston caliper assembly with pads, polished stainless steel drilled rotor and chrome mount bolts.

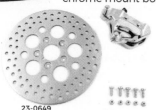

23-0649

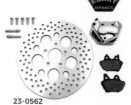

23-0562

1974-77 Clover Leaf 11-1/2" Brake Discs

23-0303

23-0302

23-0636

VT No.	Finish	Brand	VT No.	Finish	Brand
23-0303	Zinc	Dura	23-9042	SS Polished	Russell
23-0302	Zinc, Drilled	Dura	23-0636	SS Polished	Dura
23-0317	Stainless	Dura			

1974-1977 Single Caliper Pieces

1974-77 Front Caliper Service Fix Kit

Includes seal kit, spring, pins and bleeder screw.
VT No. 23-0148

VT No.	#	OEM	Item/Type
23-1723	K	44275-74	Piston
12-0943	L	44274-74	Piston, Friction Ring
23-0514	A&B	44281-74	Pad Set
23-0606	E&F	44277-74	Caliper Seal Kit
		44278-74	
23-0148	Kit		Service Kit includes C,D,E,F,G,N
23-1747	C&D	44280-74	Caliper Pin Set, two piece
		44283-74	Set
		43302-77	Spring, Service Fix
23-1995	H	44272-74	Anchor Arm
	I	44276-74	Plate, Floating Lining
23-0065			Anchor Arm Only
37-8996	M	Kit	Mount Bolt Kit Chrome
23-1730	J	Complete	Black Caliper Assembly with A-F+H,I
23-0711	N	41749-58	Bleeder Screw
8759-5	O	41191-74	Chrome Rotor Screw Set

23-0238

23-0240

23-0279

23-0884

1984-99 Chrome Billet Front Caliper Kit

Includes billet chrome front caliper and bracket with pads and polished 18 spoke stainless steel brake rotor with bolts. Kit includes hardware to fit 39 & 41mm forks FXST, FXD and FLST models.

VT No.	Item
23-0238	18 Spoke Kit
23-0240	Razor Kit
23-0279	Caliper & Bracket Only
23-0884	Caliper Rebuild for V-Twin Billet 4 Piston Calipers

Caliper Kit, Drilled

23-0564

Kit includes zinc or polished stainless steel brake discs. Fits 1974-77.

VT No.	Rotor	Type
23-0564	Steel	Zinc
23-0565	Stainless	Polished

Single Disc Front Caliper Assembly

23-1737

Features stock type construction in black or chrome with piston installed. Caliper units include zinc plated brackets and hardware. Fits 11 1/2" rotor on stock 35mm forks. Fits 1974-77.

VT No.	Finish	VT No.	Finish
23-1730	Black	23-1737	Chrome

23-0626

23-1100

1974-77 Single Disc Caliper Kit includes GMA Billet Caliper, 11.5" drilled zinc plated steel rotor and mount bolts.

VT No.	Item
23-0626	Kit
23-4513	Caliper Only (GMA)
23-1100	Edart Chrome Caliper Only

Front Caliper Assembly

23-2219

23-2237

Complete assembled with disc pads and all internals for 1973 only XL. Calipers accept 1/8" NPT line.

VT No.	Finish
23-2219	Black
23-2237	Chrome

2000-2003 Front Caliper

4 piston type including all internal components. 23-0554 features smooth face. Fits 2000-03.

VT No.	OEM	Side	Finish
23-0554	44046-00	Left	Chrome
23-0529	44046-00	Left	Black
23-0580	44025-00	Right	Chrome
23-0581		Set	Chrome

Left Chrome Front Caliper Cover

Includes chrome trim disc to conceal mount hardware. Fits 2000-2003.

VT No. 42-0844

23-2278   24-0602   24-0603   23-0523

1977-83 Dual Disc Caliper Hardware

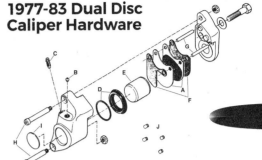

VT No.	#	OEM	Item
23-0509	A	44098-77	Pad Set (4)
23-9198	B	44141-77	Seat, brake hose
23-1731	C	44146-77	Bleeder Fitting
23-0607	D	44151-77	Seal, piston
		44153-77	
23-2278	E	44157-77	Piston
23-0523	F	44158-77	Plate, Outer
		44161-77	Plate, Inner
23-1734	G	44162-77	Pin
24-0602	H	44173-77	Screw
		44174-77	
37-8970	I		Chrome Insert, each
24-0603	J	46018-77	Mount Bushing Set
		46019-77	

Chrome Billet Front Caliper

For 2000-03 XL models.

VT No. 23-1039

Bolt Kit

37-0816/2080-4

Front disc brake caliper mount bolt kit fits 2000-Up models. Chrome.

Lower Slider

Chrome lower slider set fits 1977-82 dual disc 35mm forks.

VT No. 24-0541

Caliper Seal Kits

With seal & dust boot for year listed.

VT No.	OEM	Fit
23-2275	44047-83 44022-83	1984-99 XL
23-0533	44315-00	2000-03 All Front Only

Pistons

Pistons only, less seals. Sold each.

VT No.	OEM	Fit
23-2279	44020-83	1983-99 XL
23-0532	44313-00	2000-03 All, Front Only

Dual Disc Caliper and Rotor Set

23-0259

Includes two chrome calipers and 10" drilled rotors for 1977-83.

VT No.	Rotor
23-0250	Zinc Steel
23-0258	Polished Stainless
23-0259	Stainless Steel
8758-10	Bolt Set

23-0550 A 23-2220 B 23-1119

Dual Disc Front Disc Calipers

Includes body, piston, seals. Dual type fits 1977-83 FX-FXWG with 10' brake discs. Order mounting hardware separately.

VT No.	Side	Finish	Style
23-2221	Right	Black	A
23-1121	Right	Chrome	A
23-2238	Left	Black	A
23-1120	Left	Chrome	A
23-1119	Both	Black	A
23-1122	Both	Black, ET	B
23-2220	Both	Chrome, Daytona	B
23-0550	Both	Chrome, ET	A

2004-Up Front Caliper for XL

Feature 4 pistons design in chrome.

VT No.	OEM	Finish	Side	Model
23-0851	44121-04	Silver	Left	XLH
23-0852	44121-04	Chrome 2004-06	Left	XLH
23-0008	44546-04	Chrome 2004-06	Right	XLH
23-0286	44121-07A	Chrome 2007-up	Left	XLH
23-0821	24879-07	Chrome 2007-09	Left	"48"
23-0273	42822-04	Piston with seal	2004-06	
23-0274	43529-04	Seal Kit	2004-06	
23-0285	42028-07	Piston & Seal Kit	2007-13	
23-0292		Seal Kit	2007-13	
23-0827	41300006	Piston & Seat Kit	2014-up	
23-0294		Front Seal Kit	2014-up	

STAINLESS BRAKE DISC

Drilled Stainless Steel Rotors

Rotors feature rustless finish for appearance and long service life, in Russell or Dura Rotor brand. Available in standard or polished finish. Russell High Performance and Dura Stainless Steel Rotors are compatible with all disc pads including sintered metal and OEM.

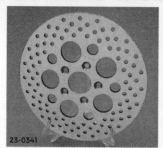
23-0341

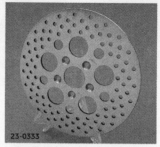
23-0333

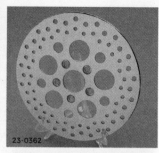
23-0362

23-0468

23-0469

23-0357

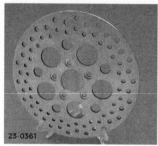
23-0361

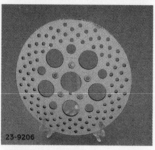
23-9206

23-0467

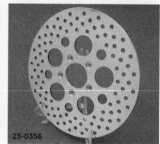
23-0356

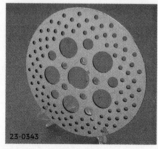
23-0343

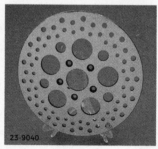
23-9040

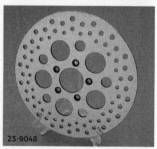
23-9048

REAR									
Dura Rotor		**Russell**		OEM	Dia.	Bolt Kit		Bolt Kit	Fits
Polished	**Standard**	**Polished**	**Standard**						
23-0341	23-0333	23-9044	23-0318	41791-79	11.5"	**8791-10** /Cast or wire		**8791-10T**	1979-92 Cast or Wire
23-0362	23-0361	23-9045	23-9926	41789-92	11.5"	**9807-10** /Cast or wire		**9807-10T**	1993-99 Cast or Wire
23-0468	23-0469			41789-92	11.5"	**9807-10** /Cast or wire		**9807-10T**	1993-99 Cast or Wire
23-0357	23-0387	23-9050	23-9051	41797-00	11.5"	**9807-10** /Wire **9793-5** /Cast		**9807-10T**	2000- Up Cast or Wire
23-9000	23-9001			41833-08	10.5"	**9807-10** /Wire **9818-5** /Cast		**9807-10T**	2011- Up Cast or Wire
FRONT									
Dura Rotor		**Russell**		OEM	Dia.	Bolt Kit		Bolt Kit	Fits
Polished	**Standard**	**Polished**	**Standard**						
23-0343	23-0334	23-9040	23-0319	44136-84	11.5"	**8793-5** /Cast	**8794-10** /Wire	**8793-5T** **8794-10T**	1984-91 Cast or Wire
23-9206	23-0368	23-9040	23-0319	44136-92	11.5"	**8793-5** /Cast	**8794-10** /Wire	**8793-5T** **8794-10T**	1992-99 Cast or Wire Wheel
23-0467				44136-92	11.5"	**8793-5** /Cast	**8794-10** /Wire	**8793-5T** **8794-10T**	1992-99 Cast or Wire Wheel
23-0356	23-0379	23-9048	23-9049	44156-00	11.5"	**8793-5** /Cast	**8794-10** /Wire	**8793-5T** **8794-10T**	2000- Up Cast or Wire Left Side Rotor
23-9002	23-9003			41500002	11.8"	**8793-5** /Cast	**8794-10** /Wire	**8793-5T** **8794-10T**	2014-Up Cast or Wire Left Side Rotor
23-6764	23-6765			41500002	11.8"	**8793-5** /Cast	**8794-10** /Wire	**8793-5T** **8794-10T**	2014-Up Cast or Wire Left Side Rotor

DISC BRAKE PAD

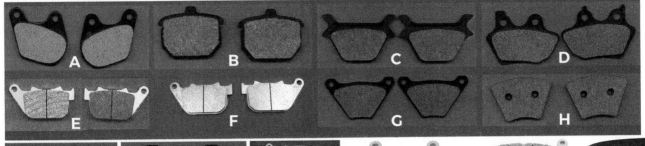

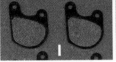    

DURA METALLIC | DURA CERAMIC | DURA SOFT | DURA SEMI

DURA KEVLAR | SBS SINTERED TECH | SBS CERAMIC | SBS CARBON

Disc Brake Pads are available in Dura, SBS, Dura Kevlar, Dura Semi-Metallic for excellent stopping on all types of disc rotors. Dura replacement pads are a soft compound designed to be compatible to all types of brake disc rotors. SBS brand is available in Sintered, Ceramic or Carbon Tech compounds. Sintered Metal Pads provides maximum stopping power but can never be used in calipers that were originally equipped with non-sintered pads. Works best with stainless steel disc rotors. Ceramic Pads are designed for general purpose use on carbon steel rotors and can be used on carbon steel rotors and can be used on calipers originally equipped with sintered metal brake pads. Carbon Tech Pads designed for use in all stock or aftermarket calipers. Works well with stainless steel or cast iron rotors.

Fits	OEM	Dura Metallic	Dura Ceramic	Dura Soft	Dura Semi	Dura Kevlar	SBS Sintered Tech	SBS Ceramic	SBS Carbon	#
Rear Disc Pad Sets for Stock Type Calipers										
1979-81 XL	43395-80		23-0999	23-0510	23-0640	23-0618		23-1766		A
1982- E 87 XL	44209-82		23-0912	23-0511	23-0641	23-0619		23-1764	23-1776	B
1987-99 XL	44213-87		23-0992	23-9163	23-0642	23-0620	23-1780		23-1779	C
2000-2003 XL	44082-00		23-0993	23-0526	23-0643	23-0546	23-4559	23-1781	23-1782	D
2004-06 XL	42836-04		23-0916		23-1950	23-1951	23-1952			E
2007-13 XL	42029-07	23-0183	23-0910			23-0184				F
2014- Up	XL	41300053	23-0185	23-0186				23-0187		L
Front Disc Pad Sets for Stock Type Calipers										
1973 XL	44131-73		23-0913	23-0513	23-0644	23-0621		23-1763	23-1775	G
1974-77 XL	44281-74		23-0915	23-0514	23-0645	23-0623	23-1767**	23-1786		H
1978-83 XL	44098-77		23-0911	23-0509*	23-0646	23-0624		23-1760*	23-1783*	I
1984-99 XL	44063-83		23-0996	23-0512	23-0647	23-0625	23-1784	23-1762	23-1785	J
2000-2003 XL	44082-00		23-0993	23-0526	23-0643	23-0546	23-4561	23-4560	23-1782	F
2004-13 XL	42831-04	23-1958	23-0914	23-1959	23-1955	23-1956	23-1960			K
2014 Up XL	41300004	23-0188	23-0189		23-0190	23-0191				M
* Set of Four	** Dura Brand									

V-Twin Mfg™ Brake Discs feature fine finish ground surface. Available with or without holes in steel with zinc finish unless as construction as noted as stainless. Exactly interchangeable with stock discs. Order bolt set separately.

23-0309

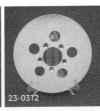

23-0312

Replica Steel Brake Disc

Drilled	Plain	OEM	Dia.	Bolt Kit	Fits	Type
Front						
23-0304	23-0305	41813-79	10"	8738-10	1972-84 FLH, 1973 FX	Steel
				8738-10T	Cast or Wire	
23-0309	23-0310	41806-72B	10"	8738-10	1972-84 FLH, 1973 Only FX	Steel
				8738-10T	Cast or Wire with built in offset	
23-0311	23-0312	44137-77A	10"	8758-10	1977-83 All, FX Cast or Wire 2-3/8" Inner Dia. Center Hole	Steel
Rear						
23-0307	23-0308	41791-79	11.5"	8791-10	1981-92 Cast or Wire	Steel
	23-0155	41791-79	11.5"	8791-10	1981-92 Cast or Wire	Stainless

BRAKE HOSE PARTS

Hoses Listed are of stock type rubber construction are D. O. T. approved.

VT No.	OEM	LN	Fits
Front			
23-0732	45521-74A	40"	1974-77 XL
23-0723	45121-77	19"	1977-79 XL Lower Only 1980-82 XL
23-0726	45121-77	19"	1977-79 XL Lower Only
Rear			
23-2310	44438-87B		L 1987-03 XL

Chrome Steel Brake Line Tees

VT No.	Type
23-0570	Center hole inverted flare 3/8"-24 UNF, side tubes 3/8" UNF, mounting hole 5/16" I.D.
23-0571	Center hole 1/8"-27 NPT, side tubes 3/8"-24 UNF, mounting hole 5/16" I.D.
23-0572	Center hole & side tubes 1/8"-27 NPT, mounting hole 5/16" I.D.

Billet Aluminum Brake Line Tees

VT No.	Type
23-9227	Front 3/8-24 inverted flare in all 3 holes
23-9228	Rear 3/8-24 inverted flare in 2 holes and 1/8 NPT in center hole

Front Replacement Brake Tees

For XL. Chrome finish.

VT No.	OEM	Fits
23-0706	43308-78	1978
23-0708	44311-80	1982
23-0705	43310-77	1979-81

Chrome Stock Billet Brake Clips.
VT No. 36-0351

Universal Straight Chrome Union

With bracket.

VT No.	Thread
23-0635	1/8 NPT
23-0688	3/8-24

Chrome Banjo Bolt Kits

Use with universal or stock lines, front and rear, washers included. The VT No. 37-8979 is to be used when a master cylinder or caliper uses a 3/8-24 banjo bolt and the line has a 12mm hole instead of 10mm.

VT No.	OEM	Line	Size/Item
23-0612	41747-82A	10mm	3/8-24
23-0613	41731-82	10mm	Washers
23-0614	41739-84	12mm	7/16-24
23-0615	45583-83	12mm	Washers
37-8979	Special Kit	12mm	3/8-24
14-0568	41731-88	10mm	Washer with O-Ring
14-0567	41733-88	12mm	Washer with O-Ring
23-0882	2004-Up XL	10mm	Hex
23-0883	2004-Up XL	12mm	Hex
2300-3	2004-Up XL	10mm	Dome Hex
2302-3	2000-Up XL	12mm	Dome Hex

Chrome Brake Hose Fittings

For front master cylinder.

VT No.	OEM	Type
26-0622	43307-78	Angle
23-0517	Converter	10mm late threads to 1/8" NPT w/ inverted flare, early thread hose type, straight.

Banjo Bolt

Banjo Bolt by Russell accepts brake light switch and eliminates the need for junction block. Replaces the standard 3/8 x 24 bolt. Sold each.

VT No. 23-0746

Allen Button Head Banjo Bolts with Washers

VT No.	Size	MM
37-8517	3/8-24	10
37-8518	7/16-24	12

Feature built in O-Rings.

Brake Banjo Seal Washers

VT No.	OEM	Type
14-0567	41733-88	7/8" 12mm fits handlebar cylinders. 1984-00, single disc
14-0568	41731-88	3/8" 10mm fits 1982-00 Dual Disc Brake Calipers
14-0578	41731-01	Fits 2001-Up Master Cylinder & Brake Calipers

BRAKE FITTING & BOLT

RUSSELL

10mm Russell Street Legal Universal Brake Lines

Build-it-yourself line assemblies ready for adapter fittings. Pre-assembled with high performance #3 stainless braided hose and rugged Teflon® inner, and crimp-on chrome plated female swivel hose ends. Clear coated for abrasion resistance. Meets guidelines of the D.O.T. MVSS-106 requirements and are 50-state legal. Compatible with all brake fluids.

VT No.	Length	VT No.	Length	VT No.	Length
23-8352	4"	23-8100	28"	23-8202	50"
23-8002	6"	23-8110	30"	23-8170	52"
23-8010	9"	23-8120	32"	23-8180	54"
23-8020	12"	23-8130	34"	23-8272	56"
23-8030	15"	23-8342	36"	23-8282	58"
23-8362	16"	23-8140	38"	23-8229	60"
23-8040	17"	23-8242	40"	23-8332	62"
23-8212	18"	23-8150	42"	23-8312	64"
23-8050	19"	23-8252	43"	23-8322	66"
23-8060	21"	23-8262	44"	23-5833	68"
23-8070	23"	23-8192	45"	23-5835	72"
23-8080	25"	23-8372	46"	23-5836	74"
23-8090	26"	23-8160	47"	23-5840	80"

32-0425 32-0426 32-0434 32-0435 32-0443

Hydraulic Brake Switch

Features heavy duty contacts & quality brass terminals. 1951-up.

32-0443

VT No.	Type	Brand
32-0425	Screw	V-Twin
32-0426	Flag	V-Twin
32-0434	Screw	Accel
32-0435	Flag	Accel
32-0443	Flag, Black	V-Twin

23-4306   23-4307

Banjo

23-4305   23-4303   23-4304

VT No.	Type
23-4306	Front Wide Glide Junction Block
23-4307	Front Narrow Glide
23-4305	90° long forward control banjo, 10mm
23-4303	35° short rear brake banjo, 10mm
23-4304	90° short rear brake banjo, 10mm

A

B

Front Brake Line Clamp

Chrome finish. Fits under triple tree to secure stainless brake line. 1/4 x 20 mount hole.

VT No.	Type
23-0675	A
23-0686	B

Chrome Adapter Fittings

23-4050   23-4047   23-4293   23-4279   23-4244 23-4281
23-4053   23-4052

23-4396   23-4298   23-4283   23-4380

23-4284   23-4282   23-4051/ 23-4054

23-0746   23-4059   23-4304   23-6033   23-4055

VT No.	Fitting Type Adapts To:	VT No.	Fitting Type Adapts To:
23-4047	10mm Banjo, straight	23-0746	3/8 x 24 Brake Switch Banjo Bolt
23-4050	10mm Banjo, 35°		
23-4055	10mm Banjo, 45°	23-6037	35° Rear Banjo, 10mm
23-4051	10mm Banjo, 90°	23-6038	90° Short Rear Banjo, 10mm
23-4052	7/16" Banjo, straight		
23-4053	7/16" Banjo, 35°	23-6039	90° Long Forward Control Banjo, 10mm
23-4056	7/16" Banjo, 45°		
23-4054	7/16" Banjo, 90°	23-4396	3/8-24 Male Inverted Flare, straight, 2 pack
23-4057	12mm Banjo, straight		
23-4058	12mm Banjo, 35°	23-4380	3/8-24 Male Inverted Flare, 90° & 120° *Junction block to master cylinder
23-4059	12mm Banjo, 90°		
23-4244	1/8" Male NPT, straight		
23-4279	1/8" Male NPT, 90°	23-4281	3/8-24 Male Inverted Flare, 45° *Rear Calipers
23-4293	1/8" Male NPT, 45°		
23-4298	Male "T"	23-4282	3/8-24 Male Inverted Flare, 90°, short *Junction Block to Front Caliper
23-6033	Flare Union		
23-6034	3/8 x 24 Banjo Bolt		
23-6035	7/16 x 24 Banjo Bolt	23-4283	3/8-24 Male Inverted Flare, 90°, long *Junction Block to Front Caliper
23-6040	10mm x 1.25" Banjo Bolt		
23-6041	12mm x 1.25" Banjo Bolt		
23-6036	3/8 x 24 Double Banjo Bolt		
23-6042	10mm x 1.25" Double Banjo Bolt	23-4284	3/8-24 Male Inverted Flare, 150° *Forward Controls

Sold as each, unless noted. *Note: Most common use.

23-0891

23-0688   23-0612

Double Banjo Brake Line

Use with 10mm bolt.

VT No.	Item
23-0891	Line
23-0612	Bolt
23-0688	Junction

STAINLESS BRAKE LINE

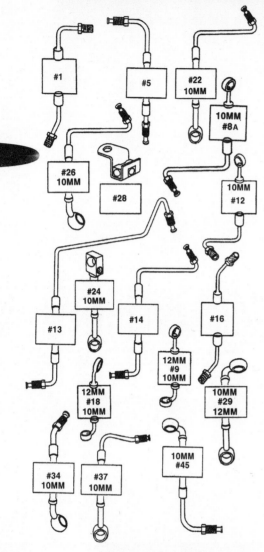

* Denotes D.O.T. approved.

Year	Model	Front	#	Rear	#
1974-77 +4" Ext		23-8901	1		
1974-77 +8" Ext		23-8902	1		
1978-79	XL, XLCH	23-8703	5	23-8800	20
1979	XLS	23-8704	5	23-8800	20
1980	XLS		5,14	23-8801	16
1980	XLH		5,14	23-8801	16
1981	XL, XLS		5,14	23-8801	16
1984-85	XLX	23-8729	18		
1984-85	XLH	23-8722*	9		
1984-85	XLS	23-8723*	9		
1984-85 +2" Ext		23-8943	9		
1984-85 +4" Ext		23-8944	9		
1984-85 +6" Ext		23-8945	9		
1987-99	XLH 883 Std (man. after 2/1/87)	23-8735*	29	23-8834*	
2000-03	XLH 883 Std	23-8735*	29	23-8835*	
2004-07	XLH 883 Std	23-8794*			
1987-98	XLH 883 DLX	23-8746*	9	23-8834*	
1987-98 +2" Ext			9	23-8834*	
1987-98 +4" Ext		23-8983	9	23-8834*	
1996-99	XLH 883 Hugger Custom				
2000-03	XLH 1200	23-8746		23-8834*	
1996-99	XLH 1200 Std	23-8753*		23-8834*	
2000-03	XLH 1200 Std	23-8753*		23-8834*	
1996-99	XL 1200S Sport	23-8754*		23-8834*	
2000-03	XL 1200S Sport	23-8754*		23-8835*	
1996-03	XLH 1200 Custom	23-8755*		23-8834*	
1997-98	XLH 1200	23-8755*		23-8835*	34, 37, 48
2004- Up	XL 1200C Cust.	23-8794			
2004- Up	XL 50th Anniv.	23-8794			
2004- Up	XL 1200R Roadster	23-8794			

10mm Stainless Steel Banjo End Dual Disc Upper Hose

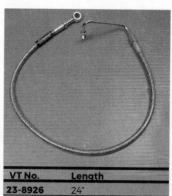

Fits 1982-up style master cylinders for single or dual disc application. Hose has nut with inverted flare at opposite end.

VT No.	Length
23-8926	24"
23-8928	28"

Front Lines / Dual Disc Upper Lines			sold each
VT No.	**Year/Model**	**LEN**	**#**
23-8908	1978-79 XLH/XLCH	Stock 19"	5
23-8909	1978-79 XLH/XLCH	+2"	5
23-8910	1978-79 XLH/XLCH	+4"	5
23-8911	1978-79 XLH/XLCH	+6"	5
23-8912	1978-79 XLH/XLCH	+8"	5
23-8906	1977-81 XL	Stock 14"	5
23-8926	1983 XLH	Stock 24"	12
23-8928	1983 XLH	+4"	12

Lower Lines / Dual Disc Lower Lines		2 required, sold each	
23-8908	1978-82 XLH/XLCH	Stock 19"	5
23-8909	1978-82 XLH/XLCH	+2"	5
23-8910	1978-82 XLH/XLCH	+4"	5
23-8911	1978-82 XLH/XLCH	+6"	5
23-8912	1978-82 XLH/XLCH	+8"	5
23-8909	1977-82 XL	Stock 21"	5
23-8910	1977-82 XL	+2"	5
23-8911	1977-82 XL	+4"	5
23-8942	1981 XL/XLS	+23"	14

41 MM GLIDE FORK

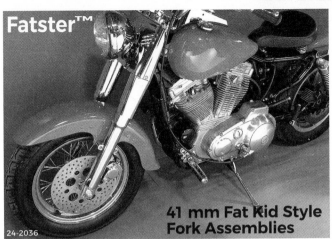

Fatster™

41 mm Fat Kid Style Fork Assemblies

24-2036

41mm Glide Fork assemblies for 1952-up XL models feature wide style with chrome triple trees, polished or chrome lower sliders, hard chrome fork tubes, axle, neck bearings, top cone and stem nut, pinch bolts and bearing dust covers. Fork is 31" overall length. Single disc units accept 11.5" brake discs, dual disc type uses two 10" brake discs. All units require Big Twin WG front wheels. Also available as complete kits with 21" wheels and black or chrome calipers, brake discs and brake disc bolts. Order neck cup set 24-0157 for 1952-78 models. Units do not include provision for fork lock. Single disc models accept 36-0803 speedo drive, dual disc models accept 36-0547 speedo drive kit.

FORK

8

Include chrome top tree, black lower tree with polished or chrome lower sliders assembled with hard chrome fork tubes and axle kit.

VT No.	Year	Sliders
24-0765	1982-2003	Polish
24-0766	1982-2003	Chrome
24-1457	Cone Nut	

Dual 10" Disc Style
24-2024,
24-2026

Single 11 1/2" Disc Style 24-
2023, 24-2025

FLST Style

Fat Kid Style

41mm FLST Style Complete Front End Assembly to fit XL models. Kits include the complete fork assembly kit, with the addition of the 5 piece chrome fork cover set, 7" headlamp and bracket, 16" chrome wheel, speedometer drive, chrome caliper, 11.5" drilled disc, and fat kid style or FLST style fender. Kits available with a chrome caliper and polished or chrome lower legs.

1982-2003 Fat Kid Style	
VT No.	**Type**
24-2036	Kit with Chrome lower slider
1982-2003 FLST Style	
24-2035	Kit with Chrome lower slider

The V-Twin™ Fork Assembly is shipped complete with axle, axle nut, spacer, top nut, bearings, cone nut, dust cover, triple trees and fork tubes & sliders. Fork tubes and sliders are fully assembled with internals. Final assembly of the remaining components is done by the dealer. Every leg assembly is shipped dry. We recommend use of the appropriate fork oil such as Type B. The amount of fork oil to add varies by model. A FX will need about 6 oz per leg. a FL will need about 8.5 oz per leg and a FXWG need about 10 oz per leg. Due to oil cling. dry for leg needs about 1 oz more to fill than a drained leg would require.

Fork Assemblies			
VT No.	**Type**	**Year**	**Slider**
24-0759	11.5" Single	1952-81	Polish
24-0760	11.5" Single	1952-81	Chrome
24-0758	10" Dual	1952-81	Polish
24-0761	10" Dual	1952-81	Chrome
24-0040	11.5" Single	1982-03	Polish
24-0041	11.5" Single	1982-03	Chrome
24-0042	10" Dual	1982-03	Polish
24-0043	10" Dual	1982-03	Chrome

Fork /Wheel Assemblies			
VT No.	**Type**	**Year**	**Slider**
24-2023	11.5" Single	1952-81	Polish
24-2024	10" Dual	1952-81	Chrome
24-2025	11.5" Single	1982-03	Chrome
24-2026	10" Dual	1982-03	Chrome

These fork/wheel assemblies include 21" chrome wheel, chrome caliper(s) drilled disc brake disc(s) and brake disc bolts.

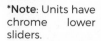

FORK ASSEMBLY

35mm 39mm Fork Assembly

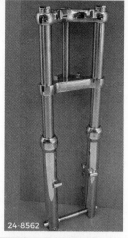

Complete narrow glide fork assemblies with polished lower sliders, unless noted with *.

FORK 8

*Note: Units have chrome lower sliders.

24-8562

Dual	Single	Fits	MM
24-8569		1977 Only	35 7/8" Neck Post
24-8570		1978-81	35 15/16" Neck Post
24-8571		1982-83, 1988-99 883, 1995-99 1200	35 1" Neck Post, 39, 39
	24-8559	1996- Up XLC	39
	24-8562*	1988-99	39
	24-8566*	2000-03 XL	39

39mm Chrome Fork Assembly

XL model Kits include:
- Chrome Triple Tree Set
- Chrome Fork Sliders
- Chrome Left Side Caliper
- 11.5" Polished Stainless Steel Brake Disc
- 19" or 21" Wheel Assembly
- Axle
- Fender
- Riser Bushings
- Bearing Set

24-0992

VT No.	Year	Wheel	VT No.	Year	Wheel
24-0991	1982-99	21"	24-1051	2000-03	19"
24-0992	1982-99	19"	24-1054	2004- Up	21"
24-1050	2000-03	21"	24-1053	2004- Up	19"

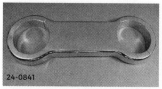

24-0841

Chrome Fork Brace

4-piece design fro easy installation on 41mm or 39mm forks.

VT No.	Size	Fits
24-0841	39mm	1985-05 FXR, FXD
24-1839	39mm	Custom

Steel Fork Brace

24-1041 24-1044 24-1042 24-1043

Black	Chrome	Fits
24-1041	24-1042	41mm - FXST
24-1043	24-1043	39mm - FXD
24-1076	24-1075	49mm - FXD
24-1044		1988-2005 FXD-FXDR

Fork Brace
Fits 2010-up XL 1200X.

24-1040

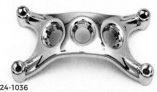
24-1036

50-1141

VT No.	Finish
24-1036	Chrome
24-1040	Black
50-1141	Fender

35mm Chrome Forged Aluminum Fork Brace

Add rigidity to forks by clamping to fork seal area of lower leg. Fits XL with Showa forks.

VT No. 24-0323

39mm Kwik-Klip

24-0497

Attaches brake line or speedo cable to fork leg.
VT No. 24-1023

39MM TRIPLE TREE

Chrome Triple Tree Sets

Include upper and lower trees to fit 39mm fork tubes as stock on 1990- Up.

FORK
8

VT No.	Years	VT No.	Years
24-0879	1990-03	2272-5	Screws
24-0936	2004- Up	24-1037	2011- Up "48"

Chrome Top Triple Tree

VT No.	Years	VT No.	Years
24-0865	1988-2003	24-1034	2010- Up "48"
24-0898	2004- Up		

39mm Lower Tree Applications

VT No.	Fits	Finish
24-0856	1988-03 XL 1200 1995-03 XL 883	Polish
24-1020	As Above	Chrome
24-0857	1996-2003 XLC	Polish
24-0665	As Above	Chrome
24-0858	1988-94 XL 883	Black
24-0897	2004- Up XL	Chrome

Lower Fork Stem Retaining Ring

Fits 1986-up all models. Replaces 45611-86.
VT No. 12-0979

Chrome Lower Triple Tree Cover

Fits 39mm forks 1987-Up. Designed for easy installation.

42-0342

Stop Plate

Mounts to custom triple trees under lower bearing for 39mm and 41 mm forks.
VT No. 24-0894

Upper Bracket Cover

Fits 1988-up XL-FXD 39mm forked models, when using a custom bottom mount headlamp.

VT No.	Item	VT No.	Item
42-0861	Cover	2272-5	Screw Set

Chrome Fork 39mm Stem Nut Cover

Fits over stock stem nut and held in place by set screws. Cover is one piece.1980- up, 39mm fork fitment.
VT No. 24-1336

Acorn Stud

For use on 1987- Up FXR-FXST. Order nut separately.

VT No.	Item
24-1209	Stud
37-0443	Acorn Nut

TOP STEM NUTS

39mm Chrome Fork Stem Nut Covers

Covers fit over stock stem nut and held in place by set screws. *Note: Includes (2) fork tube cap covers and (1) stem nut cover for 1988-up XL 883-1200.

VT No.	Pieces	Type
24-0637		Stem Only
37-9073*	3 pc	Flat
24-1278*	3 pc	Dome
24-1296*	3 pc	Pointed

FORK

Fork Cover Sets

Fit the space between the triple trees and cover the fork tube like the 1960's styling. Note: Will not fit "48" models, Required front fender removal 14" long.

1986-03	2004- Up	Finish
24-1316	24-1318	Black
24-1315	241317	Chrome

Steering Stabilizer

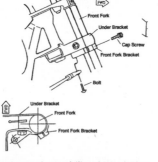

39mm steering stabilizer kit includes brackets and adjustable round body dampener piston. Fits 883-1200.

VT No.	Years
24-0171	1988-03
24-0172	2004-06
24-0664	2007- Up

Billet Fork Stop

Steering Damper is heavy alloy universal, multi-position, and adjustable, can be secured between the frame and most forks. Fork tube and frame clamps sold separately.
VT No. 24-0168

To be mounted to billet triple tree sets to allow for fork stops. Drilling of tree may be required.
VT No. 24-0749

Stainless Damper Fork Tube Clamp

Alloy finish-available in 2 piece design for attaching damper end to fork tube.

39mm	41mm
24-0657	24-0658

41mm Narrow Glide

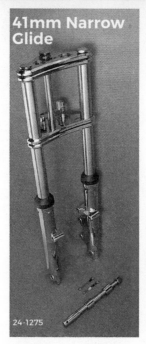

Will replace 39 mm assembly on XL models. Use with original wheel and brake assembly from 1984-03. Wheel not included

VT No.	Item	Type
24-1275	Fork Assembly	Dual
24-1276	Fork Assembly	Single
52-0170	19" Wheel	Single/Dual
52-0171	21" Wheel	Single/Dual
44-0852	Axle	Dual

39mm to 41mm Conversion Kit

24-0958   24-0958 Installed

For use with 1984-99 FXST/FXDWG 41mm fork leg assemblies and 1984-99 narrow glide 19" or 21" wheel assembly with aluminum hub and front fender. Utilizes the original FXD or XL 19" or 21" wheels as well as the caliper and brake disc from the original motorcycle. Shown with stock leg assembly 24-0510 FXST style. Accepts OEM 11.5" brake disc and caliper (custom brakes may cause interference with laced wheels). Measures $4^{15}/_{16}$" between fender mounts. For front wheel speedometer operation, replace left side axle spacer with speedometer drive unit.

KIT INCLUDES:
- UPPER AND LOWER TRIPLE TREES
- STEM
- STEM NUT
- FORK STOPS
- AXLE
- AXLE SPACERS
- FENDER SPACERS

VT No.	Item
24-0958	Kit
36-2450	Speedometer Drive

Chrome Steel Mount Clamp

3/8" mount hole. Use to mount damper body to frame tube. Sold as a pair.

VT No.	Inner Diameter
27-0057	1 in
27-0059	1-1/2 in

33MM, 35MM TRIPLE TREE

42-0308

42-0291

42-0290

Lower Fork Stem Covers

Chrome finish covers for 1957-85 with 35mm forks. VT No. 42-0290 can be installed without disassembling forks. VT No. 42-0308 replaces 45750-70 in one piece style.

VT No.	Type	Style
42-0308	1 piece	Smooth
42-0291	1 piece	XLCH
42-0290	3 piece	Smooth
8757-8	Allen Screws	

Chrome Fork Stem Nut Cover

Fits over stock stem nut and held in place by set screws. Cover is one piece.

VT No.	Fits
24-0636	1971-87 35mm fork

Top Triple Tree

for Sportsters

VT No.	OEM	Year	Finish
24-0801	45739-62B	1954-72	Cast
24-0802	45738-73	1973-87	Cast
42-0803	45738-73	1973-87	Polished
42-0826	45736-78B	1973-87	Chrome
28-1503	Bushings	1954-99	
37-0860	Screw Kit	1962-86	

Fork Stem Lock Tabs replace broken, bent or missing on stock lower triple trees, to be welded on. Fits 1981-83 XLH.

51-0099

Lower Stem Pinch Bolts

Allen   Hex

VT No.	Type	Finish
37-8834	Hex	Zinc
37-9220	Allen	Chrome

Chrome Dome Shaped Fork Stem Nuts

9978-2

VT No.	Fits	VT No.	Fits
7618-1	1952-77	7619-1	1978-87
7618-1T	1952-77	7619-1T	1978-87
37-0598	1952-77	9978-2	1988- Up

Chrome Flat Top Stem Nut

Replaces 45718-71 on 1978-87.

VT No.	Item
37-8137	Nut
9963-1	Washer
37-0988	Washer

Lower Trees

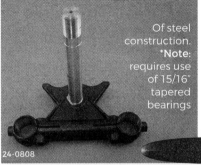

Of steel construction.
*Note: requires use of 15/16" tapered bearings

24-0808

24-0855

VT No.	OEM	Year	Tube Size
24-0807*	45703-71	1957-72	33.4 mm
24-0808	45703-73	1973-77	35 mm
24-0930	Chrome	1973-77	35 mm
24-0809	45703-78	1978-81	35 mm
24-0810	47693-81	1982-87	35 mm
24-0855	Chrome	1982-87	35 mm

Stem Bolt and Cover Kit

8809-6

Includes sleeve, stem bolt, dust shield, spacer rubber plug and chrome cover. Fits all 1957-78 without steering damper.

VT No.	OEM	Item
8809-6		Nut Kit, Cover
8810-2		Cover
24-0223	45752-52	Spacer
24-0224	45721-54	Sleeve

FORK
8

FORK TUBE

Fork Tubes are precision machined with ground finish for fit and quality. Available in chrome or hard chrome as stock. Sold in pairs.

FORK 8

33.4 mm

1954-72 XL

VT No.	Size	Type
24-0012	22 3/4" Stock 45953-71	Hard Chrome

35mm

1975-83 XLH, XLCH, XLCR   1983 XLX, XLS

VT No.	Size	Type
24-0013	23 1/4" Stock 45407-75	Hard Chrome
24-0425	2" OS 45644-77	
24-0426	4" OS	
24-0427	6" OS	
24-0428	8" OS	

1979-82 XLS, Showa Fork

VT No.	Size	Type
24-0425	25 1/4" Stock 45644-77	
24-0014	As above	Hard Chrome
24-0426	2" OS	
24-0427	4" OS	

1973-74 XL, Kayaba Fork

VT No.	Size	Type
24-0015	23 1/2" Stock 45977-73	Hard Chrome
24-0421	2" OS	
24-0422	4" OS	

1973-74 XL

VT No.	Size	Type
24-1073	23 1/2" Stock	

1984- E 86 XL, except Sport pkg

VT No.	Size	Type
24-0016	23 1/4" Stock 45407-83	Hard Chrome
24-0430	2" OS 45392-83	Hard Chrome

L 1986-87 XL

VT No.	Size	Type
24-0434	23 1/4" Stock 45407-86	
24-0435	2" OS	
24-0436	4" OS	

39mm

1988-08 XL - 883-1200, 39mm except Hugger

VT No.	Size	Type
24-0020	23 3/8"	Hard Chrome
24-0019	25 3/8"	Chrome
24-0434	23 3/8"	Chrome
24-0439	27 3/8" (+2")	Chrome
24-0442	29 3/8" (+4")	Chrome

2009- Up XL except 883L, 1200L, 883N, 1200N

VT No.	Size	Type
24-0390	Stock	Hard Chrome
24-0391	2" OS	
24-0392	4" OS	
24-0393	6" OS	

35mm, 39 mm Fork Tube and Slider Assembly

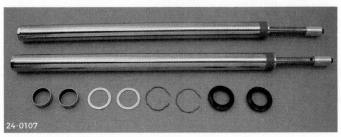

Available in right and left pairs, completely assembled. Units have hard chrome fork tubes, and chrome lower sliders, with springs and all internal components installed.

Dual	Single	Fits	MM
	24-0590	1994-99 XLH	39mm
	24-0984	2000-03 XL	39mm
	24-0384	2004- Up XL	39mm
24-0589		1977-84	35mm

24-0107

39 mm Fork Tube Assembly includes internals with springs, assembled for 1987-99. Tube length is 23 3/8".

VT No. 24-0107

24-0373   24-0079   24-0353

39mm Chrome Single Disc Lower Fork Sliders for XL

VT No.	Fits
24-0373	1988-99
24-0079	2000-07
24-0353	2008- Up
2273-7	Bolt Set

FORK PLUG & SPRING

Chrome Top Fork Tube Plug replaces 45756-59 on 1957-72 . Sold each.

VT No. 7621-1

Fork Tube Spring Retainers and Pin Wrench Kit includes 2 retainers for 1952-72 XL and pin wrench for installation removal of retainers.

VT No. 7700-3

Features a small oil fill cap built into fork tube top plug which will allow fork oil change/fill without removing top fork cap. Pairs.

E-Z Fill Fork Tube Top Plug

VT No.	Type	Fits
24-0862	35mm	1973-85
24-0863	39mm	1988- Up

FORK

8

Fork Tube Spring Sets

Feature high tensile strength wire construction with ground ends. Sold in pairs for OEM replacement per the factory number. For more fork spring applications check factory parts book

VT No.	OEM	Fits	MM
24-0822	46057-52	1952-70 XLH-XLCH	33.4
24-0900	46057-71	1971-72 XLH	33.4
24-0901	45984-73	1973-74 XL	35
24-0904	45408-75	1976-83 XLH-XLCH	35
24-0903	45987-77	1979 XLS	35
24-0905	45907-80	1980-83 XL	35
24-0906	46052-80	1980-82 XLS	35
24-0913	45376-87	1987-94 XL, Except Hugger	39
24-0933	45372-92	1992-96	39
24-0919	45376-97	1997-2003	39
24-0932	45376-04	2004-2008	39

Chrome 39mm Fork Plugs

Replace 45596-87.

VT No.	Year	Type	UM
9914-2	1988- Up	Domed	Ea
24-0335	1988- Up	Flat Top	Pair

Chrome 35mm Fork Plugs

*Note: 24-0166 is drilled and tapped to accept gauge mounts.

VT No.	#	OEM	Year
7622-1	A	45993-73	1973-85
7622-1T	A	45993-73	1973-85
37-8988	A	45993-73	Pair
24-0166*	B	45933-74	1974-85
8863-1	A	45993-86	L 1985- M 87

Progressive Suspension Fork Lowering Kit

Each kit comes with Progressive rate fork springs and spacers. Each kit can be installed at two different levels to lower fork 1" or 2".

VT No.	Fits
24-1560	1988- Up
24-1559	1984-87

Street Tough Fork Springs

By 20th Century Suspension. Progressively wound 39 mm springs are made using drawn spring wire. Eliminate front end sag, reduce nose dive under braking and improve stability. Fits 1988-91 Showa.

VT No. 24-0164

20th Century Fork Spring Lowering Kits

Kits for Showa forks are progressively wound springs that resist bottoming out. Installation requires minor disassembly to lower the front forks 1 1/4" or 2" depending on the spacer used. Kit includes springs, spacers and hardware. Easily converts back to stock by reinstalling stock fork springs.

VT No.	Size	Fits
24-0160	39mm	1987-95
24-0161	35mm	1975-87

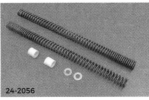 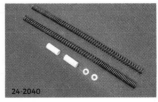

Progressive Suspension Fork Springs

Feature high quality, high performance replacement fork springs that eliminate front end sag, reduce nose dive under braking, improve cornering stability, increase ride comfort and allow forks to utilize full travel. Sold in pairs

VT No.	Size	Fits	VT No.	Size	Fits
24-0883	39	2004- Up XL	24-2040	35	1952-87 XL, XR
24-2056	39	1988- Up XL except Hugger	24-2045	39	1992- Up XL Hugger

FORK DAMPER TUBE

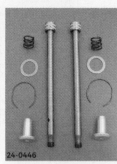

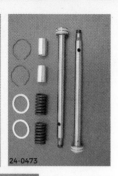

24-0454

24-0446

24-0473

Fork Damper Tube Kits

24-0475

Includes for 2 sides, damper tubes with rings, screws and washers, lower stops, slider seal washers and retaining rings.

VT No.	Type	Fits	MM
24-0454	Steel Leg	1971-72 XL	33.4
24-0457	Kayaba	1973-76 XL	35
24-0446	Showa	1976-83 Xl	35
24-0473	Showa	1988-93 XLH	39
24-0474	Showa	1994-96 XLH	39
24-0475	Showa	1997- Up XLH	39

1952-70 Internal Conversion

Send us your lower Sportster legs, we will update by drilling to accept later 24-0454 damper tube kit. New bushings can be added at the same time for an additional charge.

VT No. 60-0235

FORK DRAIN PLUG

9907-4

9910-4

24-0010

Fork Drain Screws are supplied with washers, sold pair.

VT No.	Use	Finish
9907-4	1952-72 XL, K	Chrome
9908-4	1952-72 XL, K	Cadmium
9910-4	1973- Up, Showa	Chrome
24-0010	1976- Up, Showa	Chrome

35mm, 39mm Fork Damper Tubes less hardware, sold as pairs.

VT No.	OEM	Fits	MM
24-0464	45925-88	1988-93 XL	39
24-0476	45925-94	1994-96 XL	39
24-0477	45925-97	1997-08 XL	39
24-0676	45462-87	1987- Up, Nylon Ring	39
24-0677	45460-90	1990- Up Dyna, Nylon Ring	39
24-0096	45409-75	1975-83 XL Showa	35
24-0675	45412-75	1975-86, Nylon Ring	35

Lower Damper Tube Springs

VT No.	OEM	Fits
13-9210	46062-71	1971-72, pair
13-9160	45382-83	1983-86, 10 pack
13-9258	45374-87	1987-up, pair

Lower Damper Tube Stop

VT No.	OEM	Fits
24-0459	45918-73	1973-77 XL Kayaba
24-0094	45402-75	1976-83 XL Showa
24-0460	45403-84	1984-87 XLH
24-0466	45463-87	1988-89 XL
24-0375	45361-90	1990-up XL

Sold pair.

Damper Tube Screw

VT No.	OEM	Fits
24-0188	45995-73	Kayaba, 1973-86
24-0787	45405-75A	Screw pair with washer, showa
24-0786	Showa	Screw only, 5 pack

Damper Tube Washers

10 pk.

VT No.	OEM	Fits
14-0017	45992-73	1973-74 XL Kayaba
	Fiber	Screw pair with washer, Showa
14-0018	45406-75	1975-up XL Showa
	Copper	

Chrome Fork Slider Axle Cap

For the left side. Cap is of alloy material with a chrome finish. Fits 1975-83 models with 35 and 39 mm fork tubes. Replaces 45410-75.

VT No. 24-0505

Drain Screw Fiber Washers

10 packs.

VT No.	OEM	Years	Use
14-0959	6218W	1952-72	Early XL
14-0019	45986-73	1973-75	Kayaba
14-0020	45403-75	1976- Up	Showa

FORK BOOT COVER & SEAL

24-9939

24-0090

14-0956

39mm Fork Boot Cover Dust Shield Kit fits 1988-up.

VT No.	Item
24-0090	Complete Kit
14-0956	Seals Only

Chrome Wiper Boot Covers

Die cast to fit over the stock rubber fork wiper boot.

VT No.	Type	Year	MM
24-0104	Kayaba	1973-74 XLH	35
24-0105	Showa	1975-87 Xl	35
24-9939	Showa	1988- Up XL	39

Black Rubber Fork Boots

Designed for a better fit and improved sealing and wiping action. Sold pairs.

VT No.	OEM	Fits	MM
28-0900	46001-71	1971-72	33
28-0902	45983-73	1973-74 Kayaba	35
28-0903	45404-75	1975-87 Showa	35
28-0905	White	1975-87 Showa	35

Two Piece Chrome Fork Boot Cover Sets install over stock rubber fork boot by the unique interlocking springs, supplied with the kit, to securely hold boot covers in place. 35 mm. Fits 1973-87. **VT No. 24-9992**

Gaiter Fork Boots are flexible type for 39mm forks. Rubber boots are 230 mm long, black, sold as a pair.
VT No. 28-0440

39mm Fork Gaiter for Nightster XL, FXD

28-0758   28-0885

VT No.	Type
28-0758	XLN
28-0885	V-Twin

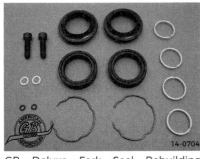
14-0704

GB Deluxe Fork Seal Rebuilding Kits include all pieces illustrated as appropriate for each application.

VT No.	Fits		MM
14-0702	1973-74	Kayaba	35 mm
14-0703	1975-84	Showa	35 mm
14-0704	1988-15	Showa	39 mm
14-0705	1984-87	Showa	35 mm

Leak Proof Fork Seals feature a Teflon coating to reduce drag and carry a manufacturer's lifetime guarantee, sold in pair.

VT No.	MM	Year
14-0250	35	1973-74 XLH-XL Kayaba
14-0251	35	1975-87 XL, Showa
14-0024	39	1988-up XL

Fork Seal Sets

Molded with factory part number, sold pairs for XL models.

VT No.	OEM	Fits	MM
14-0010	45975-71	1971-72	32.5
14-0013	45927-73	1973-74	35
14-0011	45400-75	1975-82	35
14-0016	45387-83	1982-87	39
14-0021	45378-87	1988-up	39
14-0956	45401-87	1988-up	Dust Seal

Zinc Plated Slider Seal Washers

VT No.	OEM	Year
24-0642	45928-73	1973-76
24-0091	45911-80	1980-83

Fork Seal Retaining Ring

VT No.	OEM	Year
24-0641	45931-73	1973-76 XL
24-0613	45401-75	1975-80 XLH
24-0614	45908-80	1980-87 XL
24-0623	45905-87	1988- Up XLH

V-Twin Deluxe Seal Kits

14-0942

14-0043

Include seals, gaskets, snap rings, washers and o-rings. James Kits include seals and o-rings only.

James	VT No.	MM	Year	Fits
	14-0043	33.4	1952-70	XL-XLH, Gasket only
14-0039	14-0940	33.4	1971-72	XLH-XL
14-0040	14-0941	35	1973-74	XLH, Kayaba
14-0041	14-0942	35	1975-84	XL Showa
14-0044	14-0998	35	1984-87	XL
14-0042	14-0943	39	1988-15	XL

Fork Seal Spacer
Fits 1986-87. Replaces 45386-83.
VT No. 24-0627

NECK CUP KIT

24-0225

Neck Cup Kits
for Sportster

24-1098

Convert 1952-77 ball bearing style cups to Timken tapered type. Complete conversion kit includes two (2) chrome cups, two (2) tapered bearings and dust shields, 1978-up types are for stock replacement.

*Note: unit does not include neck cups.

VT No.	OEM	Year	Item
24-0225	Kit	1952-77	Complete Kit
24-0232	Set	1952-77	Bearing Set
24-0233	Set	1952-77	Dust Covers
24-0157	Set	1952-77	Cups with Races
24-0338	48310-78	1978-81	Cups with Races
24-0101	45586-78	1978-81	Bearing Set
12-0354	As Above		Each
24-0221	45597-78	1978-81	Upper Dust Shield
24-0619	48370-78	1978-81	Lower Dust Shield
24-9935	All	1978-81	Kit with 2 Dust Shields
24-9936*	All	1982-up	Kit with 2 Dust Shields
24-0118	Set	1982-up	Bearings Only
24-1098	Set	1978-81	Cups without races

1957-81 Kit

Neck Cup Kit features solid internal fork stops that are built into the cups and hidden away. Fits stock and custom rigid frames that accept stock XL neck cups.

Kit includes cups, races, bearings and covers. Drilling and triple tree required at bearing area.

VT No. 24-0236

"Raked" Neck Cups

24-0294

24-0376

1982-up "Raked" Chrome Neck Cup Kit includes longer stem. Rake requires long fork tubes and neck lock cannot be retained.

VT No.	Stop	Year	Angle
24-0294	Tab	1988-03	3°
24-0376	Plate	1982-03	3°
24-1285	Plate	1982-03	5°
24-1267	Plate	1982-03	7°

24-0135

24-0195

24-0110

24-0157

Ball Bearing Neck Cups

Available in pairs as zinc cups only or chrome kit with races and balls. Fits 1952-77 Sportster.
Note: Sportsters use 28 ball bearings.

VT No.	OEM	Item/Finish
24-0110	48310-30	Zinc
24-0135	Kit	Chrome
24-0195*	Kit	Chrome *Note: Includes top nut, sleeve and dust cover.
12-0157	8860	5/16" Balls, 50 pc
12-0128	8860	5/16" Balls, 30 pc
24-0099	48346-39	Upper Race
24-0621	48347-52	Lower Race

Fork Stem Bearings /Races

Order separately as noted for 1982-up XL.

VT No.	OEM	Item	U/M
24-0118	48360-60	Bearings	Pair
12-0384	Peer	Bearings	Pair
12-0335	Timken	Bearing	Each
12-0348	48315-60	Race	Each
12-0383	Peer	Race	Each

Dust Shield

VT No.	Finish
24-0117	Zinc
24-0114	Chrome

Sets include upper and lower for 1982-up.

Zinc Plated

Zinc Plated			
VT No.	OEM	Fit	Model
24-0221	45597-78	Upper	1978-81
24-0618	48361-80	Upper	1982- Up
24-0112	48365-48A	Lower	1982- Up
24-0619	48370-78	Lower	1978-81
24-0111	48370-52	Upper	1952-78
14-0174	48184-01	Upper/Lower	2001- Up

"Raked" Chrome Neck Cup Kits provide 3° rake when installed.

Note: Rake Neck Kits are for Show Applications only and Require longer Fork Tube to be Installed.

24-0289

VT No.	Year
24-0289	1952-77
24-0291	1978-81

37-6370

50-0932

FRONT FENDERS
FOR 35MM & 39MM FORK

50-0120

Front Stock Type Fender, in raw steel finish, has chrome tubular type brackets riveted in place.

50-0118

50-0119 unassembled

50-0392

50-0789

VT No.	Year	Type	Cable Bracket
50-0120	1970-83	Assembled	Right
50-0392	1970-83	Assembled	Left
50-0188	1970-83	Unassembled	
50-0119	1970-83	Bobbed	
50-0932		Bracket Set	
50-0789	1984-91	Assembled	
37-6370		SS Rivets	25pc

Universal Sport Style

50-1586

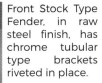

50-0133

Front Fender is rolled on edge and in front. The brackets are not included.

50-0196

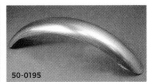

50-0195

VT No.	Type	VT No.	Type
50-0133	Chrome, Drilled	50-0196	Chrome
50-0195	Plain	50-1586	Rib, Raw
50-1141	Raw		

Chrome Stuff for Front Fender

50-0690 - Skull

Fit stock front fenders, rear tail.

50-0432 - Tips

Chrome Front Fender Allen Head Screws assemble brackets to stock front fender and attach fender to fork.

Screws
VT No.	Brand
37-6367	GW
2531-12	Colony

37-6367

50-0122

50-0164

50-0123

50-0889

FENDER
9

50-1140

50-0136

50-0191

50-0165

Narrow Type Front Fenders for 35 or 39mm forks feature a raw or chrome steel fender with brackets riveted on to fit 19" wheels. 50-0122 fits 19" wheels on 1973-90 XLX models, 50-0164 fits 1973-up models with 21" wheel and 1991-up with 19" or 21" wheel.

VT No.	Finish	Brackets	VT No.	Finish	Brackets
50-0122	Plain	Chrome	50-1140	Raw	Raw
50-0136	Plain	Raw	50-0270	Raw	Raw
50-0123	Chrome	Chrome	**Rib Style**		
50-0164	Raw	Chrome	VT No.	Finish	Brackets
50-0165	Raw	Raw	50-1583	Raw	Raw
50-0191	Chrome	Chrome	50-1584	Raw	Chrome
50-0889	Raw	Raw	50-1585	Raw	Chrome

Spring Fork Style

The classic shape and flare in 5" wide for 19" and 21" wheels. Includes chrome braces. Fits 1973-up.

VT No. 50-0116

Early Style

Front Fender for 1957-69 replacing 59007-52 stock fender, braces riveted on, raw finish.

VT No. 50-0129

Fender Trim

50-1055

50-1050

50-1049

50-0915

Chrome Front Fender Tips in stamped, includes screws. Fits fender width as noted.

VT No.	Style	Wid	Model	VT No.	Style	Wid	Model
50-1055	Eagle	4"	XLX	50-1049	Smooth	5"	XL
50-1050	Smooth	4"	XLX	50-0915	Eagle	5"	XL

STEEL FENDER   *ALL FENDERS ARE STEEL!*

EZ Bob Rear Fender Kit for Sportster models includes steel fender and chrome taillight bracket which includes cat eye 33-0306 taillight. Order chrome struts and covers separately.

FENDER 9

50-0787 Installed

50-0787

50-0799

50-0856 Installed

50-0856

50-0866

When installing 04-up rear fenders on 2007-up models it will be necessary to cut out opening to accommodate the ignition module.

VT No.	Item
50-0178	1979-81 Fender Kit
50-0787	1982-93 Fender Kit
50-0799	1994-03 Fender Kit
50-0856	2004-06 Fender Kit
50-0866*	2007-up Fender Kit

*Note: Order taillight bracket and cat eye taillight separately.

Related Parts VT No.	Item
50-0787A	1982-93 Fender
50-0881	Splash Insert (82-03)
31-0472	Taillight Bracket 1982-03
31-0991	Taillight Bracket 2004-up
33-0306	Cat eye Taillight

Related Parts VT No.	Item
50-1097	1979-81 Chrome Struts
50-0899	1982-89 Chrome Struts
50-1035	1990-93 Chrome Struts
50-1093	1994-03 Chrome Strut Covers

EZ Bob

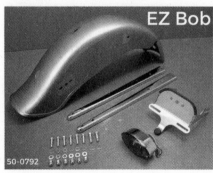

50-0792

EZ Bob Rear Fender Kit for 1952-78 Sportster model includes steel fender, cat eye taillight, chrome taillight, bracket and chrome struts. Order sissy bar components separately.

50-0810

VT No.	Item
50-0792	1952-78 Fender Kit
50-0929	Struts for Above
31-9030	Tail lamp Bracket for Above
50-0813	Lo Boy Sissy Top Bar for Above
50-0810	Side Straps

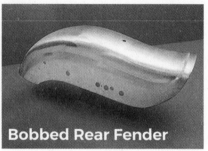

Bobbed Rear Fender

Mounts to stock strut bars. Fits 1994-03 with mounting holes. OEM 60025-01.

VT No. 50-0253

FL Style Rear Fender   Fits 1982-up models. Must be drilled for installation.

50-0942   50-0471   50-0860   50-1525

VT No.	Width	VT No.	Width
50-0942	6.5"	50-0860	8"
50-0471	7.5"	50-1525	9"

Bobbed Rear Fender for Rigids

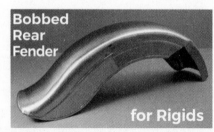

7 1/4" wide by 5 1/2" deep raw finish with right cutout, 50-0927 includes bracket to accept taillight plate.

VT No.	Item
50-0151	Right
50-0927	Right, with Bracket

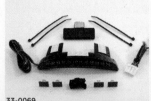

33-0069

33-0070

Fender Edge LED Lamp Kit

Fits 2004-2014 XLs with chopped rear fender.

VT No.	Color
33-0069	Red
33-0070	Smoke

XL, XLCH REPLICA REAR FENDER

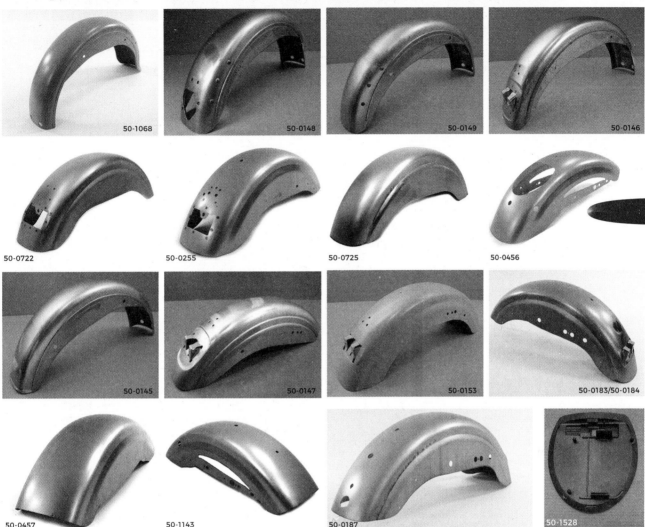

50-1068	50-0148	50-0149	50-0146	
50-0722	50-0255	50-0725	50-0456	**FENDER 9**
50-0145	50-0147	50-0153	50-0183/50-0184	
50-0457	50-1143	50-0187	50-1528	

Steel Rear Fenders mount to stock struts.

Note: VT No. 50-0146, 50-0147, 50-0153 accept VT No. 33-0301 (68008-73A) taillight. 50-0148 accepts 33-0300 early taillight (68006-64).

*Note: VT No. 50-1068 XLH and K Style Rear Fender features full length style with rear flare, without tail light cut out, but includes internal reinforcement to mount 1955-72 type light, tombstone or beehive light.

VT No.	OEM	Years	VT No.	OEM	Years	VT No.	OEM	Years
50-1068*	59609-52	1952-78	**50-0183**	59674-94A	1994-96	**50-0456**	59865-07	2004-2009 1200N Only
50-0148		1959-72	**50-0184**	59756-97	1997-98	**50-0457***	Bobbed	2004-up
50-0149		1952-78	**50-0187**	59674-99	1999-2003			2004-2009 (holes must be drilled for mounting)
50-0145	Flared	1952-78	**50-0722***	Undrilled	1982-2003	**50-1700**	Bobbed	
50-0146	59611-73A	1973-78	**50-0725***	Bobbed	1982-2003			
50-0147	59674-79A	1979-81	**50-0255**	59847-04	2004-2009	**50-1528**	Insert	2004- Up
50-0153	59674-81A	1982-93	**50-1701**	69847-04	2004-2009	**50-1143**	59865-10	2010- Up 883N, 1200N

When installing 04-up rear fenders on 2007-up XL 883N, XL 1200N models it will be necessary to cut out opening to accommodate the ignition module on 50-0255, 50-0456, 50-1701 & 50-1700. 50-1700 has no cutout.

Fender Extension Rubber Flap

Fits 1979-81.
VT No. 28-0745

Chrome Rear Fender Bracket

Fits 1954-78. Reduces vibration between fender and frame, includes foam pad, replaces 59795-52A.

VT No.	Item
50-0912	Bracket with Pad
28-2246	Foam Pad only

STRUT

XL Fender Struts
Chrome die cast alloy construction.

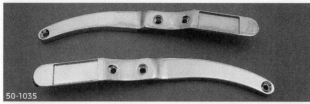

50-1035

33-0016

50-1097

FENDER
9

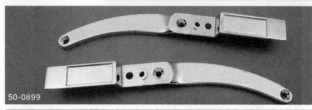
50-0899

VT No.	OEM	Year	Item
50-1035	59950-89 / 59951-89	1990-93	Set
50-1142		1990-93	Set
50-0899	59950-81B / 59951-81	1982-89	Set
50-1097	52754-79 / 52755-79	1979-81	Set
37-9084		1982- Up	Allen Bolts
33-0016	59259-90	1990-93	Reflector, Red

50-1034

50-0908

50-0904

Chrome Steel Fender Strut Sets available in smooth or stock style with or without turn signal holes.

Smooth	Stock	OEM	Year	Fits
50-0908	50-0904	59930-52B	1955-78 XL	W/O signals
	50-1034	59934-73	1973-78 XL	With signals

Sportster Fender Strut Covers
Chrome Strut Covers for Sportsters fit over existing stock struts.

50-1092

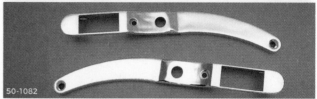
50-1082

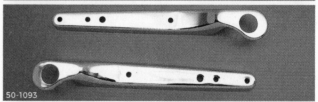
50-1093

50-0238

VT No.	OEM	Year
50-1092	59243-95	1982-89
50-1082	59541-95	1990-93
50-1093	59897-94	1994-2003
50-0238	59902-04 / 59903-04	2004-Up

50-1187   50-1188

Black Rear Fender Struts, Die Cast Alloy

VT No.	Fits	VT No.	Fits
50-1187	1982-89 XLH	50-1188	1990-93 XL

Fender Rail Bolt Kit
Attaches struts to the rear fender.

Stock	Acorn	Cap	Allen	Fits
8880-18			2529-6	1952-58 K, XLCH
2626-18				1952-58 XL, Cadmium
8881-18	7207-8	8462-8		1959-81
2665-18				1959-81, Cadmium
			37-9050	1957-78
			37-9084	1982-03
			2274-10	2004- Up

FRONT ENGINE BAR

Engine Bar Footpeg Mount Kit

27-0660 Installed

27-0654

27-0654

27-1788

Chrome Billet Engine Bar Footpeg Mount Kit fits on 1-1/4" front engine bars with male pegs.

VT No.	Item
27-0660	Kit
27-0654	Chrome, Mounts only
27-1788	Black, Mounts only

XLH - XLCH 1-1/4" Diameter

51-0886

51-0939

FENDER

9

Mega Footpeg Kit

27-0587

Features billet clamp set to attach to 1-1/4" engine bars.

VT No.	Item
27-0587	Footpeg Kit
27-0698	Bracket Set

51-0881

Chrome Footpeg Mount Kits

27-0032

Kits include clamp set and extension bars to accept male pegs.

VT No.	Size
27-0032	1"
27-0033	1-1/8"
27-0034	1-1/4"

51-0985 Installed

VT No.	OEM	Year
51-0886	49042-56A	1956-81
51-0881	49018-88C	1986-03
51-0888	With pads	1986-03
51-0939	49060-04	2004- Up
51-0985	With pads	2004- Up

Footpeg Mount Kit allows male-type pegs to be mounted to 1-1/4" diameter engine bar.
VT No. 27-0651

Bar Clamps

Bar Clamps fit 1-1/4" engine bars to mount male footpeg sets.
VT No. 27-0892

2004-Up XL Turn Signal Hi-Way Bar

VT No.	Finish
50-0021	Chrome
50-0022	Black

50-2078

VT No.	Year
50-2078	2011- Up
14-0977	Replacement O-Ring

Lindby Custom Highway Bars

Lindby custom front Highway Bars with footpegs feature 1 1/4" tubing and built in O-Ring pegs. Fits XL models without forward controls.

SHOCK STUD KIT

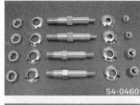

54-0460

54-0449

54-0448

54-0450

FENDER

9

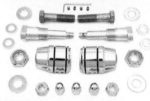

54-0451

Shock Stud Kits include all pieces for upper and lower positions. Including washers, nuts and lockwashers as necessary. Studs and bolts are zinc plated. Outer nuts and washers are chrome.

VT No.	Year	VT No.	Year
54-0460	1956-74	54-0449	1982-85
54-0448	1979-81	54-0450	1986-90
		54-0451	1991-2001

Shock Covers

1950's style chrome top cover. Fit all models of swing arm with stock shocks including 1952-78 Sportster. Some seats may cause interference.
VT No. 54-0154

Lower Shock Covers

Give the Big Twin look on XL models 1979-up with Showa shocks. Covers install easily without dismantling the shock.
VT No. 54-0206

Kit updates 1954-74 to late model bushing diameter of 1/2". Kit includes 4 studs, 4 nuts and 8 washers and top covers. Use with VT No. 54-0106 with 1/2" holes.

Shock Stud Conversion

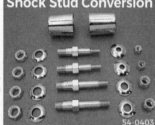

54-0403

VT No.	Item
54-0403	Kit
28-0231	Bushings, 1" Inner Dia.

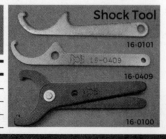

16-0954

Shock Tool

16-0101

16-0409

16-0100

VT No.	Years
16-0101	1975-78
16-0409	1979- Up
16-0100	1952-74
16-0954	1979- Up

54-0152

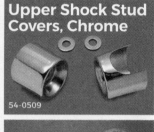

Upper Shock Stud Covers, Chrome

54-0509

54-0153

54-0532

54-0514

54-0124

VT No.	Years	VT No.	Years
54-0152	1965-74	54-0509	1991-99
54-0153	1975-78	54-0532	1991-2003
54-0514	1982-90	54-0124	2004- Up

54-0417

2406-10

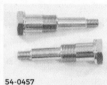

54-0457

Chrome or Zinc Plated Rear Shock Studs

With cup washers. Each kit includes two (2) studs and four (4) chrome cup washers. Cup washers and lock nuts may be purchased separately.

Upper			Lower		
Chrome	Zinc	Fits	Chrome	Zinc	Fits
54-0443	54-0414	1956-75	54-0444	54-0415	1956-74
	54-0417	1975-78		54-0405	1975-78
	54-0455	1991-93, 2 studs	54-0430		1982-91

Upper-Lower		
Chrome	Zinc	Fits
54-0457	1994- Up, 2 studs	
2406-10		2000-03
2405-10		2004- Up

Shock Stud Washer
10 pack.

VT No.	Type	Finish
54-0418	5/8" hole cup	Chrome
54-0419	3/8" hole cup	Chrome
54-0420	1/2" hole cup	Chrome
54-0421	1/2" hole x 1" flat	Chrome
54-0424	5/8" hole x 1.3" flat	Zinc
54-0432	3/8" hole 1.25" flat	Zinc

Nylock Shock Stud Nut

VT No.	Finish	QTY
54-0422	Zinc	10
54-0447	Chrome	4

5/8-18, replaces 7993.

SHOCK SET

All shocks are measured eyelet to center of eyelet.

AEE Series Chrome Shocks

Feature an adjustable spring pre-load nitrogen charged with multi-stage automatic damping in a black body with chrome spring and end caps. Note: When installing replacement shocks on 1978-00 XL models, it may be necessary to modify or space the chain guard/belt guard to allow proper shock clearance.

Year	Model	11"	11.5"	12.5"	13	13.5"	14.25
1980-06	XLH 1200,	54-0020	54-0021	54-0022	54-0023	54-0024*	54-0025
	XLH 883 Hugger	54-0020	54-0021	54-0022*	54-0023	54-0024	54-0025
1988-03	XLH 883	54-0020	54-0021	54-0022	54-0023	54-0024*	54-0025
1979-87	XLX-XLH-XLS	54-0020	54-0021	54-0022*	54-0023	54-0024	54-0025
1954-78	XL					54-0027	

54-0021

*Note: Denotes stock length shock. When installing other than stock length shocks, tire to fender clearances must be checked.

FENDER

9

Progressive Suspension 412 Series Chrome Shocks

Manufactured from the finest material available. Magnum 412 Series shocks are nitrogen charged with six-stage automatic damping and an adjustable spring pre-load. Available with chrome spring and end caps, shock cartridge is not chrome. All shocks are measured eyelet to center of eyelet.

Note: When installing replacement shocks on 1978-00 XL models, it may be necessary to modify or space the chain guard/belt guard to allow proper shock clearance.

Year	Model	11"	11.5"	12.5"	13	13.5"	14.25
1988-03	XLH 1200	54-0093	54-0033	54-2000	54-2001	54-2002*	54-0059
1988-03	XLH 883 Hugger	54-0093	54-0033	54-2000*	54-2001	54-2002	54-0059
1988-03	XLH 883	54-0093	54-0033	54-2000	54-2001	54-2002*	54-0059
1979-87	XLX-XLH-XLS	54-0093	54-0033	54-2000*	54-2001	54-2002	54-0059
1953-78	XLH, XLCH					54-2009	54-2003

*Note: Denotes stock length shock. When installing other than stock length shocks, tire to fender clearances must be checked.

Progressive Suspension 440 Series Chrome Shocks

Progressive Suspension 440 Series Chrome Shocks feature two rebound damping circuits and are available in standard for the average single rider, heavy duty for touring or carrying passengers. Fit 1977-02.

Standard	Heavy	Size
54-4005	54-4022	11"
54-4006	54-4011	11.5"
	54-4050	12"
	54-4001	12.5"
54-4009	54-4003	13.5"

54-0128 Installed

Mount Studs not included with shock sets.

Warning: Installing a lowering kit or shorter shocks will decrease initial ground clearance. The motorcycle will be lower to the ground and care should be taken to avoid bottoming, especially over bumps or in turns.

1" Rear Shock Lowering Kits

54-0510

54-0523

54-0542

54-0541

54-0127

54-0128

VT No.	Fits	Finish	VT No.	Fits	Finish
54-0510	1989-99	Black	54-0541	2000-03	Chrome
54-0523	2000-03	Black	54-0542	1989-99	Chrome
54-0511	1982-85	Black	54-0127	2005-Up	Black
			54-0128	2005-Up	Chrome

SHOCK SET

54-0671

54-0143

54-0516

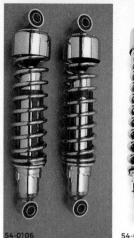

54-0106

54-0098

54-0099

FENDER 9

Shorter Length Shocks

Shorter Length Shocks lower the seat height by amount listed. 54-0143 shocks feature chrome-plated springs and body caps with suspension pre-load.

VT No.	Fits	Finish	Lowers	Len.
54-0143	1991-2005 XL 883, 883DLX, 1200 1992-2005 XL 883R	Chrome	1"	
54-0516	All XL models, 1991-03	Chrome	1"	11.75"
54-0671	2006-10 883XL, 2009- Up 1200XL			11.75"
54-0191	As Above	Chrome	2-1/4"	10.5"
54-0192	As Above	Black	2-1/4"	10.5"

1 or 2-1/4" Lower Shocks!

54-0143 Installed

Warning: Installing a lowering kit or shorter shocks will decrease initial ground clearance. The motorcycle will be lower to the ground and care should be taken to avoid bottoming, especially over bumps or in turns.

24-2140

28-0231

28-0220

Shock Bushings

VT No.	Year
28-0220	1954-73
28-0231	1982-84
28-2140	1985- Up

Shock Sets for Sportster

Includes chrome springs.

VT No.	OEM	Length	Fits
54-0106*	54490-78	14.5"	1975-78 XLH, XLCH
54-0099	54568-79B	13"	L 1979-81 Xl, XLS
54-0098	54568-82	12.5"	1982-87 XL, XLS, XLX 1988-90 XLH 883 Hugger
54-0501	54566-91	13.375"	1991-93 XLH 883 STD/Deluxe 1991-93 XLH 1200
54-0503	54568-92	11.75"	1993-03 XLH 883 Hugger
54-0144	54568-04	13.38"	2004-08 XL 1200

*Note: Use 54-0403 stud kit for installation on 1952-74 models.

Shock Absorbers for Lowering Sportster

*Note: A - Lowers seat height 1" B- Lowers seat height 2"

VT No.	OEM	Length	Fits
54-0098	54568-82	A 12.50"	88-90 XL 883 Std Deluxe XL 1200
54-0503	54568-92	B 11.75"	91-03 XL 883 Std Deluxe XL 1200
54-0503	54568-92	A 11.75"	91 XL Hugger, Stock on 92-03 Hugger
54-0516	54568-92	As Above, V-Twin	

Shock Absorbers for Raising Sportster

*Note: A - Raises seat height 1" B- Raises seat height 2"

VT No.	OEM	Length	Fits
54-0501	54566-91	A 13.375"	1991 XL Hugger
		B 13.375:"	1992-03 Hugger

Mount Studs not included with shock sets.

54-0100

54-0101

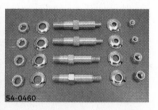

54-0460

14" Replica Shock Sets for 1952-78 Sportster

Include bushings with 5/8" hole use with 54-0460 stud kit.

VT No.	OEM	Type
54-0100	54504-73	Chrome Springs
54-0101	54500-56A	Full Covered
54-0460	Mounting Kit for above	

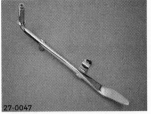
27-0047

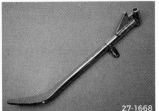
27-1668

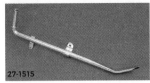
27-1515

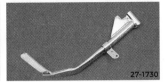
27-1730

27-1672

27-0520

27-1516

27-0048

KICKSTAND

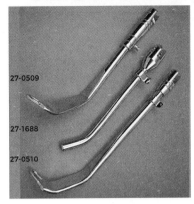
27-0509
27-1688
27-0510

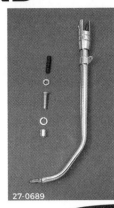
27-0689

FENDER
9

27-1688

27-0806

27-1733

1984-Up Kickstands
27-0946

13-9162   37-9153

VT No.	Year	Item	VT No.	Year	Item
27-0520*	1990-03	Short Stand	27-0946	2008-Up	Stock
27-0047	1984-88	Stock Stand	27-0823	2011-Up	Stock
27-1515	1984-88	Extended Stand	27-0492	2011-Up	Stock
27-0048	1984-88	Catch	27-0019	2004-Up	Stock, Gloss Black
13-9159	1984-88	Spring			
27-1668	1989-03	Stock Stand	27-0020	2004-Up	1" Lower, Gloss Black
37-9153	1989-Up	Pin	27-0828	2004-Up	Chrome Kit
13-9162	1989-Up	Spring	27-1516	1989-03	Bushing Set
27-1672	2004-Up	Stock Stand	37-9153	1989-Up	Pin
27-1730	2004-Up	1" Lower	13-9162	1989-Up	Spring

*Note: Hugger type for lower shocks.

Weld-On Kickstand Assembly

VT No.	Item
27-0257	Kit
27-0795	Bushing

Includes weld on type heavy duty mount, chrome spring and chrome kick stand with forged flat end.

27-0257

27-0257 Assembled

Kickstand Tab and Pin

27-1500

51-0515

VT No.	Item
51-0515	Repair Tab
27-1500	Pin Kit

For 1952-83. Tab is for weld on repair. Pin includes screw.

Kickstand Extension Kits

With chrome mounting hardware, rubber extended peg for easier operation of kickstand.

VT No.	Fits
27-0093	2004-06 XL
27-0094	2007-Up XL

Center Stand

Constructed of cast aluminum, and includes spring and hardware for mounting to stock swing arm frames. Replaces 49701-57 for 1952-81 K/XL

VT No. 27-0548

Chrome Finish Forged End Kickstands

VT No.	OEM	Fits	Length
27-0806		1952-83	Stock
27-0509	50006-80	1952-83	Stock
27-0689		1957-83	Stock
27-1688	50062-52A	1952-79	Stock
27-1733			2" Short
27-0510*	Extended	1952-83	11.5"
37-9117			Pin, fits 27-0509, 27-0510
27-1500			Pin, fits 27-1688

*Note: For use with +2" or +4" forks.

Chrome Kickstand Springs

13-0154

13-0545

13-9162

13-9159

28-2234

VT No.	Fits	VT No.	Fits
13-0154	1952-85	13-9159	1984-88
13-9162	1989-06	13-0545	2007-Up
28-2234	1990-07	Bumper Stop	

27-0522

27-0025

Kickstand Extensions

Kickstand extensions allow rider to more readily access side stand. Replaces 50212-98 and fits 1984-up.

VT No.	OEM	Model	Finish
27-0522	50212-98	1984-2003 XL	Chrome
27-0025	50250-04	2004-Up XL	Chrome
27-0801		2007-Up XL	Black

FOOTPEG

27-1624

27-1735

Driver Peg Support Bars

Splined type, less pegs. Fit 1952-74. Replaces 50948-71 left, 50949-67 right. Use with large female type driver pegs.

VT No.	Finish
27-1624	Zinc
27-1735	Chrome

Chrome Forward Control Footrest Support fits XLC models with forward controls.

VT No. 27-0010

Rear Peg Mounts

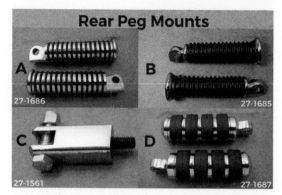

A 27-1686

B 27-1685

C 27-1561

D 27-1687

Rear passenger peg mounts (D) replace 50610-86 on 1986-2003 models, to mount rear passenger pegs to swing arm. Choose pegs to complete or order kit.

VT No.	#	Item	VT No.	#	Item
27-1686	C-A	Kit	27-1687	C-D	Kit
27-1685	C-B	Kit	27-1561	C	Mounts Only

Passenger Peg Mount Bracket Sets

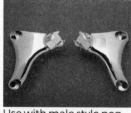

Chrome	Black	Years
27-1564		2004-13
27-0825	27-0271	2014-Up

Use with male style peg.

Rear Passenger Peg Relocation Bracket Set

Fits 2004-13 XL with 30-0300 pipe set. Black finish. Order chrome footrest for support bracket separately.

VT No. 31-0766

27-0044

23-3079

23-3024

27-1577

12-2117

23-1728

27-1556

27-1638

23-1728

12-0552

23-3080

23-3015

Foot Rest Supports

VT No.	OEM	Years	Item
Left Side			
27-1556	50948-75	1977-85	Support
12-0552	24752-75	1977-85	Stud
27-1638	50951-90	1991-03	Support
27-0817	42972-04	2004- Up	Support
Right Side			
23-3024	34886-86A	1986-90	Stud
27-1577	50949-75	1977-79	Support
12-2117	247751-75	1977-79	Stud
23-3079	42441-90A	1991-03	Peg Clevis
23-3015*	42441-80	1980-90	Pivot-Stud *Acts as foot support brake pivot
23-0780	42971-04	2004-Up	Support
23-1728	34909-90	1991-03	MC Support Bracket

27-0633

27-0631

27-0634 Installed

Chrome Rear Footpeg Brackets

Bolts to rear motor mount bolts, for use on Rigid or Swing Arm frames

VT No.	Fits
27-0633	1957-78 Sportster Use large female Driver pegs 27-1215, 27-1220 and 27-1581
27-0634	1982-90 XL use 27-1227 Small Male Pegs
27-0631	1957-81 except 1979 Use 27-1227 Small Male Pegs

27-0634

HI-WAY BAR

Hi-Way bars for Evolution Sportster mounts to front motor mount, factory style. Includes O-Ring pegs. Fits 1985-2003 883-1100-1200.

VT No.	Style
27-0611	O-Ring
27-1630	Cats Paw

27-0611

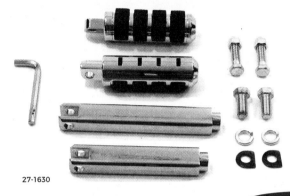

27-1630

Adjustable Hi-Way Footpeg

Fits XL models with mid mount brake and shifter controls. Adjusts quickly into 3" height positions and can be used with engine guard. Order soft pegs separately. *(27-1582).*

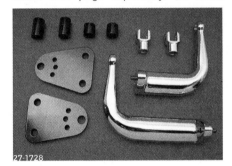

27-1728

27-1712

27-1582

VT No.	Fits
27-1712	1984-2003
27-1728	2004- Up

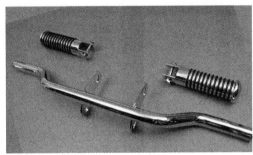

1984-2003 Forward Footpegs for Sportster

Chrome one-piece design that bolts to motor mount. Bolts on for firm mounting, features O-Ring pegs for all 883-1100-1200 models.

VT No. 27-1572

Include chrome mount plates, peg extension bars, and O-Ring peg set.

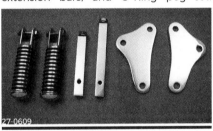

27-0609

VT No.	Fits
27-0609	1952-81
27-0610	1982-84

Hi-Way Bar Kits

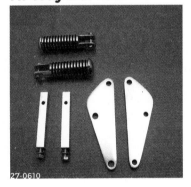

27-0610

2004- Up XL Turn Signal Hi-Way Bar

Chrome	Black
50-0021	50-0022

Chrome Footrest Support Bar Sets

Right and left support bar set for use on all XL models with welded square insert on motor mount plate, which has a filter for 1983-E 84. A set of 2 for Hi-way bars on FX, FXRS, 1977-Up. Heavy duty and chrome, measures 3-1/4" long.

27-0635

27-1227

27-0604

40-0301

VT No.	Item	VT No.	Item
27-0604	Support Bar Set	8851-4	Bolt Set
27-0635	Bar Set	13-9185	Spring Washer
27-1227	Peg Set	40-0301	Engine Mount W/ Filter

BELT GUARD

27-1667

27-0123

27-1745

27-0862

VT No.	Year	VT No.	Year
27-1667	1991-1999	27-0123	2000-2003
27-1745	2004- Up	27-0862	2004- Up

FENDER 9

20-0784

Lower Belt Guard

For XL. Chrome .

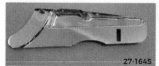

27-1645

27-0788 Installed

27-0788

VT No.	Year
27-1645	1991-2003
27-0788	2004- Up
20-0784	2004- Up

Belt Guard with Holes

27-1443

27-1445

Upper	Lower
27-1443	27-1445

Chrome Chain Guard with Spatter Apron

1983-87

27-0112

1988-92

27-1573

Rigid Frame Chain Guard for Sportster

VT No.	Item
27-0128	Guard, Chrome
31-0710	Strap

27-0101

25" length.

Universal Right Side Guard

Chrome Rear Pulley Cover

42-0670

42-0934

42-7512

42-1132

Order VT No. 37-8671 chrome torx bolt set separately.

VT No.	Year	Tooth	VT No.	Year	Tooth
42-0670	1991-2003	61	42-7512	2004- Up	68
42-0934	2004- Up	68	42-1132	2004- Up	68

Dress Up Kits

27-0619

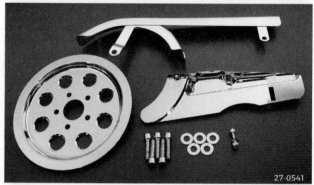

27-0541

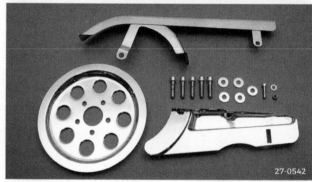

27-0542

Chrome Guard / Rear Pulley / Dress Up Kit includes belt guards, upper and lower, and 61T rear pulley cover for 5-Speed belt drive models with hardware.

VT No.	Year
27-0541	1991-1999
27-0542	2000-2003
27-0619	2004- Up

Chrome Chain Guards for Sportster

27-0102

27-0103

27-0401

27-0400

27-0106

27-0107

VT No.	Year	VT No.	Year
27-0102	1954-71 XLH	27-0103	1954-71 XLCH
27-0401	1972-78 XLCH	27-0400	1972-78 XLH
27-0106	1979-81 XLCH, XLH	27-0107	1982 XL

RIGID FRAME

Custom Rigid Frames to fit XL models. Available without Fat Bob mounts. These frames can only be used with custom oil tank and battery tray, ordered separately. VT No. 51-2174 use VT No. 24-0225 neck cup kit. VT No. 51-2176 and 51-2175 frames include kickstand tab which must be welded on by customer. All frames use a 140 rear tire except 51-0107 which will accept a 180 tire with chain drive.

VT No.	Year	Stretch	Rake	Brake	Tire
51-2174*	1957-76	1"	40°	Drum	140
51-2176	1986-03	Stock	Stock	Disc	140
51-0107	1986-03	2-1/2"	40°	Disc	180

*Note: Stock neck rake is 28°

51-2176

FRAME

10

7704-2

40-0437

40-0416

Related Parts	
VT No.	**Item**
40-0416	Custom Oil Tank (180 & 200 Tire)
40-0437	Battery Tray w/ strap & top. Uses 12N16-4B battery.
23-0370	1987- Up Rear Caliper Kit
44-0221	10-1/2" Chrome Axle Kit
7704-2	Chrome Rear Chain Adjuster
27-0047	1986-03 Stock Kickstand
27-0128	Chain Guard for above

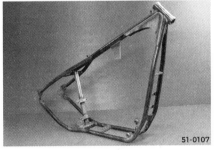

51-0107

50-2174

Rear Axle Cover for XL

Customizes the rear axle and swingarm end. Fits 2004.
VT No. 42-0945

1972-78 Neck fits XL model to be welded in place on stock or custom frames. Accepts 24-0225. Neck cups, 7/8" size.
VT No. 51-0524

1972-78 XL Neck

Chrome Swingarm

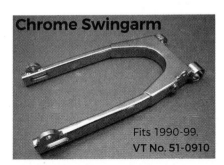

Fits 1990-99.
VT No. 51-0910

51-2053

51-2053

51-2053

31-0224

44-0540

SWINGARM FRAME

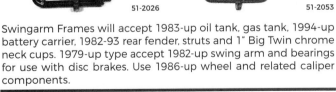

51-2026

51-2053

Swingarm Frames will accept 1983-up oil tank, gas tank, 1994-up battery carrier, 1982-93 rear fender, struts and 1" Big Twin chrome neck cups. 1979-up type accept 1982-up swing arm and bearings for use with disc brakes. Use 1986-up wheel and related caliper components.

VT No.	Year	Type	VT No.	Year	Type
51-2053	1986-1990	Belt/Chain	51-2028	1982-03	Disc
51-2054	1991-2003	Belt/Chain	51-2026	1979-81	Disc Belt/Chain

Related Parts		Related Parts	
VT No.	**Item**	**VT No.**	**Item**
40-0397	Oil Tank	54-0516	Shock Set, (11.75")
23-9209	Caliper	24-0253	Neck Cup Set w/ Bearings
44-0566	Axle Kit	54-0449	Shock Mount Kit
44-0540	Swing Arm Bearing Kit	50-0899	Strut Set
28-0410	Battery Pad	31-3978	Front Mount Set, 1979-85
28-0409	Bumper	31-2137	Front Mount Set, 1986-up
40-0391	Oil Tank, 1997-up	31-0224	Rear Mount, 1979-81

SWINGARM BEARING

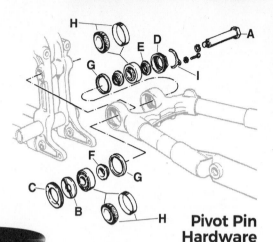

FRAME 10

Pivot Pin Hardware

VT No.	#	Year	Item
44-0107	A	1952-81	Pivot Bolt, Chrome
44-0098	B	1952-73	Nut
44-0097	B	1974-81	Nut
44-0096	C	1952-73	Locknut
44-0095	C	1974-81	Locknut
44-0088	D	1954-73	Locknut, Right
44-0087	D	1974-81	Locknut, Right
44-0094	E	1952-73	Outer Spacer
44-0093	E	1974-81	Inner Spacer
44-0367	F	1952-81	Spacer, pair
44-0110	G	1952-81	Shield, pair
44-0108	H	1952-73	Bearing Set
44-0109	H	1974-81	Bearing Set
17-0920	I	1952-81	Locktab

44-0540 · 44-0714 · 44-0709 · 44-0092 · 44-0872 · 12-0362 · 44-0875 · 12-0360 · 12-0127 · 44-0091 · 44-0626 · 44-0151

Pivot Bolt Kit
Includes black pin, screw, spacer, bushing, bearing and dust covers.

VT No.	Item	VT No.	Item
44-0540	1982-03 Kit	44-0709	2004-Up Kit
44-0714	2004- Up Kit, Chrome	44-0875	2004-Up, Kit
44-0872	2004-Up Pivot Shaft, Zinc	44-0092	1982-03 Bolt
44-0151	2004-Up Bolt/Nut	44-0091	1982- Up Dust Cover (2)
12-0362	1982-03 Bushing, Left	12-0127	2004-Up Bearing, Right
12-0360	1981-99 Bearing, Right	44-0626	2004-Up Pivot Retaining Ring

Swingarm Bearing Assembly Kit

Contains parts pictured for 1952-81.

VT No.	Fits
44-0539	1952-73
44-0538	1974-81

Covers Set covers end of pin.

VT No.	Fits
37-1206	2004- UP
37-9522	2004- Up

Smooth Swingarm Pivot Covers

Swingarm Pivot Kit
Includes all parts shown for 1952-80 XLH-XLCH Sportster models.

VT No.	Fits	VT No.	Fits
44-1959	1952-73	44-1960	1974-80

XL-XLH Swingarm Bearings and Kits

VT No.	Years	Item	U/M
44-0108	1952-73	Kit	4pc
12-0332	1952-73	Bearing	Pair
12-1100	1952-73	Race Set	Pair
44-0109	1974-81	Set	4pc
12-0333	1974-81	Bearing Set	Pair
12-1101	1974-81	Race Set	Pair

Rigid Frames for XL

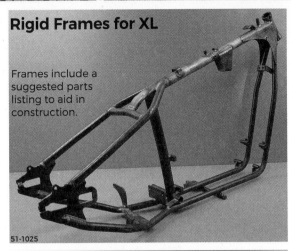

Frames include a suggested parts listing to aid in construction.

51-1025

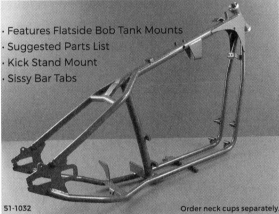

- Features Flatside Bob Tank Mounts
- Suggested Parts List
- Kick Stand Mount
- Sissy Bar Tabs

51-1032   Order neck cups separately.

Rigid frames for XL models will accept 1" neck cups, VT No. 24-0119 and include mounts for flat side fat bob tanks or stock tank. Frames with cross shafts include bushings. Order oil tank and battery box separately. Disc brake models accept 1987-99 caliper assembly VT No. 22-0370 and a 140 tire. All frames have 40° rake and 1" stretch. 1975-76 models require use of forward controls. *Note: 1957-79 application requires modification of rear motor mount to accept kick shaft.*

VT No.	Years	Engine	Brake Type
51-1025	1957-76	Ironhead	Mechanical
51-1028	1977-78	Ironhead	Mechanical
51-1031	1952-78	Ironhead	Disc
51-1032	1979-81	Ironhead	Disc
51-1027	1986-2003	Evolution	Disc, Belt, Chain (140)
51-3525	1986-2003	Evolution	Belt (200)

Chrome 5.5" Round Oil Tank for XL

40-0474 Installed

40-0474

40-0742

Fits XL with Rigid frame mounts by clamping to center tube or top mount center fill.

31-1755

VT No.	Type	Finish	Brackets
40-0474	Clamp	Chrome	
40-1476	Clamp	Raw	
40-0741	Top Mount	Chrome	31-1755
40-0742	Top Mount	Raw	31-1755

RIGID FRAME

Wyatt Gatling — Styled in Steel

Wyatt Gatling Rigid Frame

51-3525   51-3575

Rigid Frame by Wyatt Gatling features 40 degree rake, 3" stretch in front legs, to accept 1.125" belt with 200 series tire. Frame has kick stand tab and battery box mount welded in place.

Related Components for 200 1986-2003 XL Frame	
VT No.	**Item**
44-0148	Axle, 14.5"
44-0545	Adjuster Kit
20-4001	Belt, 133T x 1.125"
20-0512	Offset Pulley
31-0953	Front Top Mount
24-0253	Neck Cup Set, 1"
44-0786	Right Hand Rear Axle Spacer
40-0404	Oil Tank, Round
40-0474	Round Oil Tank
42-9912	Battery Box
22-0370	Caliper Kit
37-0889	Axle Nut Set

VT No.	Year
51-3525	1986-2003
51-3575	1957-85

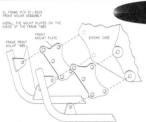

Note: On 51-3525 motor mount plates fit inside of frame mount tabs as shown.

- FRAME   51-3525
- FORK   24-0938
- PIPES   30-0300
- OIL TANK   40-0474
- GAS TANK   38-0196
- FWD CONTROL 22-0731

V-Twin Rolling Chassis

Bobber

Chassis includes rigid frame, single disc glide fork assembly, 16" chrome rear wheel, 21" chrome front wheel, 3-1/2 gallon bobbed tank set, cast dash kit, axles, Avon rear tire as noted, oil tank and kick stand. Disc brake models will accept 1987-99 GMA Rear Caliper VT No. 23-9209.

VT No.	Year	Engine Type	Brake Type	Tire	Type
51-1030	1952-76	Ironhead	Mechanical	130	Bobber
51-1033	1977-78	Ironhead	Mechanical	130	Bobber
51-1034	1979-81	Ironhead	Disc	130	Bobber
51-1035	1982-03	Ironhead/Evo	Disc(Belt/Chain)	130 Belt	Bobber
51-5002	1982-03	Ironhead/Evo	Disc	150	Chopper
51-1260	1982-03	Evolution	Disc	180	Chopper
51-1265	1982-03	Evolution	Disc	180	Bobber

Weld-On Caliper Bracket Set

Fits Rigid XL frame for left side use.
VT No. 51-0630

"200" XLST FRAME ASSEMBLY

Complete Kit

51-1038

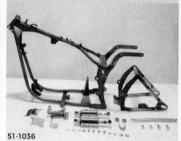

51-1036

51-1037

Softail Frame for Sportster Models

VT No.	Fits	Engine
51-1036	1957-85	Ironhead
51-1037	1986-2003	Evolution
51-1038	1986-2003	Evolution

Features 40° rake with 1" stretch and includes the rear section, including pivot bolt kit. Frame accepts readily available components for ST, which are available separately including neck cups, flat side gas tanks, oil tank, 23-0587 caliper, rear fender, fender struts and fork assembly as noted.

KIT INCLUDES CHROME SHOCKS, RAW REAR SECTION AND MOUNT BOLTS.

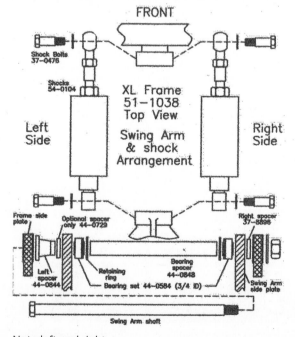

51-1037

Related Components for 1986-2003 XLST Frame		Related Components for 1986-2003 XLST Frame	
VT No.	Item	VT No.	Item
40-0393	Oil Tank, Raw	52-2033	17" Rear Wheel
40-0394	Oil Tank, Chrome	50-0112	9" Rear Fender
44-0638	Rear Axle	50-1069	Struts, Smooth
44-0545	Adjuster Kit	31-0713	Top Mount
24-0322	Neck Cup Set	31-4004	Front Mount
23-0587	Rear caliper	20-4004	Pulley, Offset
31-0221	Oil Tank Mount	23-8834	Rear Brake Line
31-2137	Front Mount Set		

Pivot Pin Spacer Assembly Placement

FRONT

Shock Bolts 37-0476

Shocks 54-0104

Left Side

Right Side

XL Frame 51-1038 Top View Swing Arm & shock Arrangement

Frame side plate

Optional spacer only 44-0729

Right spacer 37-8896

Left spacer 44-0844

Retaining ring

Bearing spacer 44-0848

Swing Arm side plate

Bearing set 44-0584 (3/4 ID)

Swing Arm shaft

Note left and right.

52-2033

40-0394

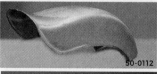

50-0112

23-0587

50-1069

31-2137

31-0713

44-0545

20-0512

HARDTAIL

Hardtails fit to stock frames for years listed.

51-0984 Installed

VT No.	Fits	Type	Style
51-0723	1952-81	Weld-On	Drum
51-0921	1952-72	Weld-On	Drum
51-0922	1952-78	Bolt-On	Drum
51-0981	1973-78	Weld-On	Drum
51-0982	1979-81	Weld-On	Disc
51-0984	1982-2003	Weld-On	Disc
51-0996	2004- Up	Weld-On	Disc

Chrome 5.5" Round Oil Tank

Fits XL with rigid frame mounts by clamping to center tube or top mount side fill. 31-1755 clamp set will mount 40-0742/40-0741 in 1957-78, 1979-81 and 1982-03 stock frames with hardtails installed.

40-0474 Installed

40-0741

40-1476

40-0742

40-0474

31-1755

VT No.	Type	Finish	Brackets
40-0474	Clamp	Chrome	
40-1476	Clamp	Raw	
40-0741	Top Mount	Chrome	31-1755
40-0742	Top Mount	Raw	31-1755

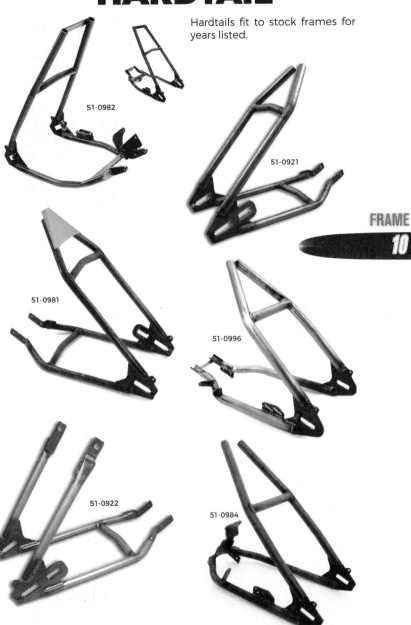

FRAME 10

Notes: VT No. 51-0921 eliminates seat casting area and accepts stock drum brakes. VT No. 51-0922 is bolt on top and bottom, 51-0921, 51-0981, 51-0982 and 51-0984 with 3/4" axle slots is weld on top and bolt on bottom for alignment. Seat plate must be welded in place.

MOTOR MOUNT

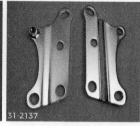

31-0629   31-0591   31-2137

Chrome Top Motor Mount

Fits 1986-2003 XLH.

VT No.	Fits	OEM
31-0591	1986-94	16278-86A
31-0629	1995-03	16278-95B
42-0027	1986-94	Top Center Mount Cover

Chrome Filled Coil Cover

Fits coils on top motor mount, as on FXR or custom applications.
VT No. 42-0962

31-0410   9967-4

VT No.	Item
31-0410	Mount
9967-4	Bolt Kit

Chrome Top Motor Mount

Replaces OEM 16214-86 on 1986-2003 Evolution XL 883-1100-1200 models.

1986-03 Acorn Bolt Sets	
8871-13	Center
9773-8	Cyl. Head

Chrome Teardrop Coil Cover

Fits top motor mounts with 2 holes such as 31-0664. Includes key switch hole.
VT No. 42-0926

Billet Top Motor Mount

For 1986-2003 XL. Accepts coil bracket, horn. Chrome finish.
VT No. 31-0713

Chrome Motor Mounts

Fit Late 1984-2003 Evolution XL.

VT No.	Item
31-2137	Front Mount Set
3772-22	Allen, as above

31-0715   31-0882   31-0887

31-0863

31-0862

31-0884

2004-up Motor Mounts

VT No.	Item
31-0715	Mount
31-0863	Tie Rod
31-1273	Tie Rod, Chrome
31-0862	Center Mount
31-0881	Tie Link Mount Bracket
31-0882	Rear Iso
31-0883	Pivot
31-0884	Rear Mount
31-0887	Front Iso
31-1280	Front Mount

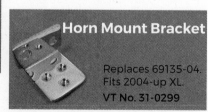

Horn Mount Bracket

Replaces 69135-04. Fits 2004-up XL.
VT No. 31-0299

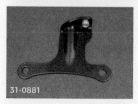

31-0881   31-1280   31-1273

Chrome Allen Bolt Set fits 2004-up motor mounts.
VT No. 2228-16

Top Motor Mount Kits

31-0115   31-0116

1957-76 Sportster models. Chrome finish.

VT No.	Item
31-0115	2 pc
31-0116	3 pc

1957-77 Chrome Top Motor Mount

31-0113   31-0114

Accepts molded coil. Available with or without hole to mount universal key switch.

VT No.	Type
31-0113	Key Hole
31-0114	No Key

1979-81 Top Mount

31-0135   31-0242

VT No.	Item
31-0135	Upper Front
31-0242	1982-85 XL Upper Front Motor Mount

Top Motor Mounts

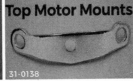

1957-76.

31-0137   31-0138

VT No.	OEM	Item
31-0138	16250-57	Cylinder Head
31-0137	16251-58	Cylinder Head to Frame

Rear Engine Case Studs

1952-81: 24817-52.
1982-90: 24825-82.

VT No.	Item
12-1151	1952-81
12-1150	1982-90

Ignition and Horn Brackets

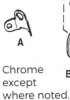

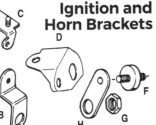

Chrome except where noted.

VT No.	#	OEM	Years	Type
31-0133	A	69041-73	1973-85	Horn Bumper, Black
31-0134	B	69117-71A	1971-85	Horn Mount, Zinc
31-0122	C	69129-72A	1972-85	Upper Horn & Choke
42-0330	D	71510-72A	1972-up	Switch Cover
28-2247	F	69125-65	1965-up	Iso Mount
12-0550	G	69149-65		Nut, 10pk
31-0129	H	69117-65	1965-70	Mount, Zinc

Chrome Front Lower Motor Mount Plates

31-3978   31-0120

*Note: Does not have oil filter provision.
**Note: Includes oil filter.

VT No.	Years	Item
31-0120	1952-81	
31-3978*	1982-E84	
40-0301**	1982-E84	
7141-18	1952-84	Acorn Bolt Kit

4pc Top Motor Mount Kit

31-0117

Replaces the following 69129-72 zinc, 16250-57 chrome, 16266-76 zinc, 16265-76 chrome. Fits 1977-81.

VT No.	Item
31-0117	Kit
37-0848	Allen Bolt Set

FRAME 10

9798-20   7141-18

Front Lower Motor Mount Bolt Kits 1957-84

VT No.	Item
7141-18	Acorn, Stock with Spacer and Washer
7408-10	Extra length for forward pegs, Acorn. Order Spacers separately.
9797-20	Allen Type, Complete
9798-20	Stock Hex Type, Chrome, Complete
9799-20	Stock Hex Type, Cadmium, Complete
37-9207	Stock Hex, Chrome, Bolts only
37-9086	Spacer Set, Chrome
37-9158	5 Locating Washers

XL Rear Motor Mount Cast Replacement

31-0111   31-0224

Top 2 bolt style. Order studs separately.

VT No.	OEM	Fitment
31-0111	16203-67	1967-81 XLH, 1970-81 XLCH
31-0224	16203-82A	1982-90 XLH
3035-2		Nut Insert
3058-10		Mount Kit, 1983-85 XL

Front Isolator Mount Kit

31-0848   31-0849   31-0850

VT No.	Fitment	VT No.	Fitment
31-0848	2004-16	3035-2	Nut Insert
31-0849	2004-2013	3058-10	Mount Kit
31-0850	2014-2016	31-0850	2014-2016

 2004-UP EXHAUST PIPE

Heat Wrapped Drag Pipe Set for XL

1986-03, black wrap.
VT No. 30-4049

Oxygen Sensor Units

Sold each. Fits 2007-up.

VT No.	Fits
30-0434	2007-13
30-0490	2014-Up, front

Namz O2 Enrichment Device. Recommended for bikes with high flow air cleaner performance exhaust systems. Reduces engine operating temperature between 20 to 30 degrees. Simply plug in between oxygen sensors and wiring harness. Works with stock ECM. Fits 2007-up XL. Sold in sets.
VT No. 32-6556

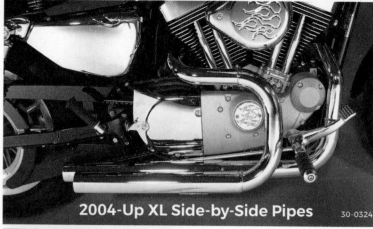

2004-Up XL Side-by-Side Pipes 30-0324

30-0327

Pipes fit XL and XLC models with forward controls. Pipes are 1-3/4" at head and 2-1/4" at end and includes brackets and baffle set. 2007-up has provisions for oxygen sensors. Sensors may be capped by 30-0423 if desired.

VT No.	Type	Fits
30-0477	Straight	2007-up
30-0324	Straight	2004-06
30-0327	Slash	2004-06
30-0380	Slash	2007-up
30-0423	Oxygen Sensor Plugs	2007-up

2-1/2" Drag Pipe Set

Features built in mount tabs to bolt to stock bracket. Chrome replacement bracket and baffle set available separately. Fits 1986-2003 XL models.

VT No.	Item	Type
30-0342	Pipe	Down Slash
30-0385	Pipes	Side Slash
31-0418	Bracket	
30-0050	Baffle Ring	

30-0796   30-0797

Billet End Tips

Tips fit 1-3/4" straight cut drags.

VT No.	Finish	VT No.	Finish
30-0796	Chrome	30-0797	Black

30-0050

31-0418

STOP ✋

Caution: These exhaust products are not legal for sale or use in California on pollution controlled vehicles. These products are intended for the experienced rider only.

Straight Pipe Set

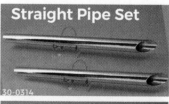

30-0314

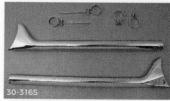

30-3165

Fit over 1-3/4" exhaust pipes. 1-7/8" outside diameter allows pipes to be cut down and still slide over pipes. 30" long.

VT No.	Type	VT No.	Type
30-0314	Slash	30-3165	Fish Tail

EXHAUST

2" Curvado Pipe Set for XL

Include removable oxygen sensor plugs to fit 2007-up models.

VT No.	Item	Fits
30-0387	Pipe Set	2004-13
30-0384	Pipe Set	1986-03
31-0988	Mount Bracket	1986-03
31-0989	Mount Bracket	2004-13

Wyatt Gatling 2-into-1 Exhaust Header

1986-03	2004-Up	Finish
29-0932	29-0934	Chrome
29-0933	29-0935	Black

One piece design featuring turn out mufflers. Fits 1986-2003 XL with stock foot controls.

EXHAUST

11

1979 Only Drag Pipe Sets

Drag Pipe Sets by Cycle Shack are 40" in length.

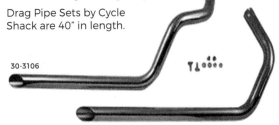

VT No.	Size	Fits	Bracket
30-3106	1-3/4 in	1979 Only	31-9994
30-3132	1-3/4 in	1979 Only	
		Black Bracket	31-4052
		Chrome Bracket	31-4057

Note: Drag Pipes do not include brackets. VT No. 30-3132 uses 31-2101 mounting clamps. VT No. 31-3106 uses 31-9994 mounting bracket.

Magnum Exhaust Drag Pipe Set

Constructed of steel featuring heat shields. For 2004-2013 XL.

VT No.	Finish
30-1286	Black
30-1285	Chrome

Cycle Shack 2004-2013 XL Pipe Sets

Fit all 883 and 1200 models. 1-3/4" header set accept factory heat shields. 2" headers are supplied with heat shield Both 1-3/4" and 2" type mount to factory support bracket. Muffler pipe sets feature one piece construction and high flow rate baffles.

2007-2014	2004-2006	Style
	30-0077	Straight
29-0192		Taper
	29-0186	Turnout
	30-0075	1-3/4" Slash Cut Ends
	30-0356	Heat Shields

STOP Caution: These exhaust products are not legal for sale or use in California on pollution controlled vehicles. These products are intended for the experienced rider only.

DRAG PIPE

1-3/4" Drag Pipe Sets available in black or chrome finish with formed heat shields (as noted) and either slash cut or straight ends. 38" length. Pipes mount by stock brackets except where noted. 2007-up style have oxygen sensor ports.

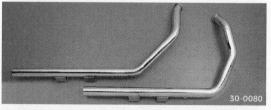
30-0080

30-0081

EXHAUST

11

30-3022

30-0070

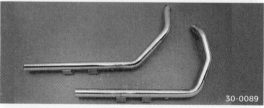
30-0089

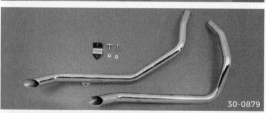
30-0879

30-3011

30-3012

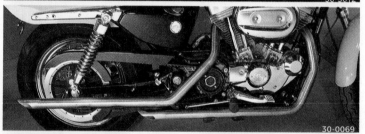
30-0069

30-3009

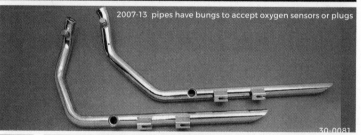
2007-13 pipes have bungs to accept oxygen sensors or plugs
30-0081

Chrome		Black	Fits
Heat shield	No Heat shield	No Heat shield	Notes
	30-3012	30-3020	1986-2003 Use with or without forward controls
29-0192	30-0879**		
	30-0070**		
	30-0071		
	30-0069*		2004-2006
	30-0080*		
	30-0075		
	30-0077*		

Chrome		Black	Fits
Heat shield	No Heat shield	No Heat shield	Notes
	30-0081	30-3021	
	30-0089*		2007-2013
	30-0071		
30-3006	30-3010	30-3022	1957-1978, 1980-1984 These pipes require mounting bracket
	30-3018***	30-3420	

*Note: With straight ends
**Note: Without O2 ports
***Note: Goose style

 Caution: These exhaust products are not legal for sale or use in California on pollution controlled vehicles. These products are intended for the experienced rider only.

Limited Warranty. Exhaust Products distributed by Tedd Cycle Inc. are warrantied against defects in material and workmanship, which include fitting and finish quality at the time of installation only. Claims regarding discoloration, peeling blistering or blued chrome will not be considered as defective material or workmanship and cannot be returned as such as per manufacturers warranty.

EXHAUST

Goose Style Drags

30-3353

30-3372 Installed

Retro chopper styling in 1-3/4" diameter and slash cut ends, 34" long on all models except VT No. 30-3353 at 40". Note: Order mount bracket as noted. Bracket not required on stock type.

VT No.	Mount Bracket	Year
30-3132	31-2101	1979 Only
30-3355	Stock	1985-2003 883,1100,1200
30-3372	Stock	2004-06
30-3353	Stock	1986-03

29-0180 Installed

Shot Gun 1-3/4" Drag Pipe Set

Fits rigid frames only and requires bracket for mounting. Slash cut ends.

VT No.	Year
29-0179	1957-84
29-0180	1986-2003
29-0200	Rigid
29-0201	Swing Arm

Stainless Exhaust Head Clamp

Stock type construction, sold as a pair. Replaces 65519-52. Fits 1952-71.

VT No.	Item
31-0226	Clamps
27-8684	Bolt Set

Upswept Drag Pipe Header Set for 1957-03 XL

UPSWEEP

29-0157

Available with slash or straight cut ends and rigid swing arm models.

29-0087

30-0118

VT No.	Years	Type	End
29-0087	1957-85	Rigid	Straight
29-0084	1986-03	Rigid	Straight
29-0114	1957-85	Rigid	Slash
29-0157	1986-03	Rigid Swing Arm	Slash
29-0188	1986-03	Rigid	Slash
30-0118			Heat Shield, Flame design
31-0064	1959-79 XLCH	Exhaust Clamp Kit	7pc
31-0066	1957-70 XLH	Exhaust Clamp Kit	5pc

Chrome Muffler End Clamp

Clamps mufflers to pipes.

1-3/4"	1-7/8"
31-2103	31-0318

Vance & Hines Super Radius 2-into-1

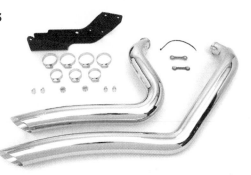

2 into 2 Pipe Set. Super radius brings a deeper richer tone to the custom styled exhaust and is engineered for today's larger capacity engine to get solid performance and just the right sound. Features include deeper tone, full coverage heat shields and available in chrome. Fits 2014-up XL.

VT No. 30-1656

EXHAUST
11

UNIVERSAL MUFFLER

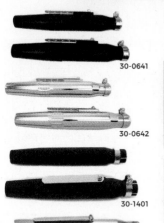

30-0641

30-0642

30-1401

30-0147

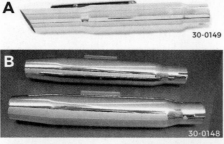

A 30-0149

B 30-0148

C 30-0348

D 30-0150

E 30-0296

30-0794

F 30-2105

EXHAUST

11

Slip On Chrome Mufflers

VT No.	#	Type	Len.	Dia.	Mount	Removable Baffle	U/M
30-0149	A	Slash	16"	2-1/2"	Stud	No	Each
30-0148	B	Tapered	16-1/2"	2-1/4"	Channel	Yes	Pair
30-1401		Tapered	11"	11"	Black	Yes	Set
30-0641		Tapered, Black	11"	2-1/2"	Channel		Set
30-0642		Tapered, Chrome	11"	2-1/2"	Channel		Set
30-0147	C	Baloney Slice	16-1/2"	2-1/2"	Stud	Yes	Each
30-0348	C	Baloney Slice	16-1/2"	2-1/2"	Channel	Yes	Pair
30-0150*	D	Shorty	12"	2-1/4"	Stud	Yes	Each
30-0296	E	Megaphone	19"		Channel	Yes	Each
30-0794		Megaphone	19"		Channel	Yes	Pair
30-2105	F	Megaphone Upsweep			Channel	Yes	Pair

Steel baffled with 1-3/4" inlet. *Note: Fits 13/4" or 1-1/2" diameter.

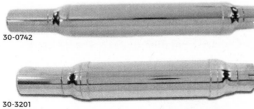

30-0742

30-3201

30-0986

30-0212

30-3221

30-3222

30-1109

31-0318

31-0303

31-0319

65231--65A

31-0301

Original Seamed Type!

30-0795

31-0231

VT No.	OEM	Fits	Type
30-0742	Replica	1952-56 K-KH	2-1/2" Long
30-3201	65231-58	1959-61 XLCH	Channel
30-0986	Replica	1962-64 XLCH	Slash
30-1109	Replica	Pair	Slash
30-0212	65230-65	1965-73 XLCH	Taper
30-0795	65231-65A	1965-70 XLCH	Replica, Embossed
30-3221	65281-77	1977-78 XLCR	Left, Black
30-3222	65286-77	1977-78 XLCR	Right, Black
31-0301	65275-57	1-7/8" I.D.	End Clamp
31-0318	Chrome		End Clamp
31-0303	65412-75	1975-80 XL	Cover Clamps
31-0231	65279-57	1952-59	Body Clamp
31-0319	Stainless	1952-59	Body Clamp

K+ Early XLCH Mufflers have 2-3/8" body diameter, and 1-3/4" inlet.

 Caution: These exhaust products are not legal for sale or use in California on pollution controlled vehicles. These products are intended for the experienced rider only.

XL EXHAUST

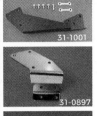

31-1001

31-0897

30-0103

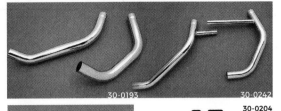

30-0193   30-0242

30-0204

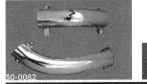 30-0082

30-0795

Radii Exhaust Sets feature the "Quad Finishing" which includes triple dura nickel and chrome as the final finish. After chrome plating, pipes are normalized and dried @ 572° F for the final finish process.

30-0383

For 2004-2006 models you must purchase 30-0423 plug set. For 1986-2003 models you must purchase 30-0423 plug set and 31-0897 bracket. Order baffle style as desired for required back pressure.

VT No.	Fits	VT No.	Item
30-0987	2004-13	31-0897	1986-03 Bracket
30-0383*	1986-03	31-1001	2004-13 Bracket
		31-0103	Baffles
		30-0423	Plug Set

*Note: Must be used with a forward control kit.

1957-74		1975-84	
VT No.	Item	VT No.	Item
30-0193	Header Set	30-0242	Header Set
30-0795	Muffler Set	30-0204	Black Cover
30-0082	Heat shield Set		
31-0064	7pc Clamps		
31-0066	5pc Clamps		

EXHAUST

11

Dual Straight Stagger Shots

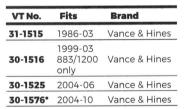

30-1515

30-1516

30-1525

Feature full length, full coverage heat shields, 1-3/4" header pipes with 2-1/4" bodies, removable baffles, and mounting hardware.

VT No.	Fits	Brand
31-1515	1986-03	Vance & Hines
30-1516	1999-03 883/1200 only	Vance & Hines
30-1525	2004-06	Vance & Hines
30-1576*	2004-10	Vance & Hines

*Note: Pre2007 models require O2 Sensor Plugs VT No. 30-0423

Vance & Hines 3" Round Slip-on Mufflers

3" Round Twin Slash Slip-On Mufflers fit 2004-10 XL. Feature :

- Muffler bodies shielded by full-coverage heat shields for blue-proof look
- Increased performance with a throaty growl
- Louvered core baffles

VT No. 30-1584

Exhaust System Clamp Kit

7 piece clamp kit is for use with dual exhaust applications. Kit includes exhaust port, stainless steel muffler & clamps and front chrome pipe clamp.

XLCH 1959-79	XLH 1957-79
31-0064	31-0066

Chrome Stock Rear Exhaust Bracket

Fits 1980-2003 XL.

VT No. 31-0418

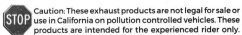 Caution: These exhaust products are not legal for sale or use in California on pollution controlled vehicles. These products are intended for the experienced rider only.

XL EXHAUST

SAMSON EXHAUST **BIG GUNS**

30-0414

30-0407

30-0406

Big Guns Exhaust System mounts using stock bracket unless noted. Drag pipes feature 1-3/4" head port end with 2-1/4" diameter body. Heat shields sold separately. All pipes fit with XLC forward controls except 30-3303. Fits 2004-2006 Big Slash

VT No. 30-0414

Big Guns II

Samson Big Guns II feature 1-3/4" head pipes with 2-3/4" full coverage heat shields. All Big Guns II come complete with mounting bracket and hardware. Fit 2004-06 XL.

VT No.	Style
30-0406	Cannons w/ Forward Controls
30-0407	Classics

Rinehart
Staggered Style Racing Crossback 2-into-1 Exhaust

The crossover three step header design with 2-1/2" chrome torque and horsepower across the RPM range. Crossback systems are available 220° full coverage heat shields that merge flush to the muffler bodies, custom baffles (2" outside diameter for engines up to 96CI and 2-1/4" outside diameter for large high performance engines). All system includes two oxygen sensor parts. Fits 2004-13 XL.

VT No. 30-1553

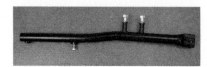

Black Support Tube to mount drag pipes or stock muffler system for 1958-79 XL-XLH models. Replaces 65316-65B.
VT No. 31-4029

Brake Pedal Stop required on 1980-85 XL models when fitted with drag or custom pipe sets, to act as pedal stop which was originally welded on stock header pipes have a combination mounting bracket/brake pedal stop welded to stock header pipes.

VT No. 31-2124

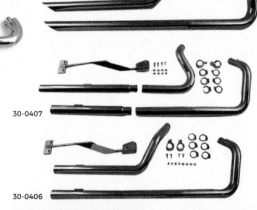

Vance & Hines Big Radius System

Virtually blue-proof. Scalloped end caps for a unique look. Removable baffles and mounting hardware included. Include mounts for factory O2 sensors as required Pre 2007 models require O2 sensor plugs VT No. 30-0423. Fits 2004-2012 XL.

VT No. 30-1575

 **O2 Sensor Sealing Washer**

VT No.	Fits	Size
15-0081	2006-10	18mm
15-0012	2011- Up	12mm

  **Exhaust O2 Sensor Plugs**

Replacing your oxygen sensor? Use this threaded plug in its place.

VT No.	Size
30-0423	18mm
30-0448	12mm

 31-4057

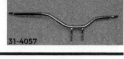 31-4057

VT No.	Item
30-0082	Heat shield Set
31-4052	BK-4 Cycle Shack PHD-112 series and PHD-117 series muffler pipes & PHD-110 & PHD-210 drag pipes for Sportster produced with adjustable channel mount
31-4057	BK-4 Chrome

 STOP Caution: These exhaust products are not legal for sale or use in California on pollution controlled vehicles. These products are intended for the experienced rider only.

EXHAUST

30-0300

30-0300

30-0319 Installed on Ironhead Models. Brackets must be fabricated for installation

30-0319

EXHAUST

11

Wyatt Gatling Drag Pipe Sets Down Type

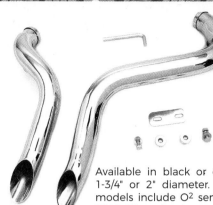

Wyatt Gatling Styled in Steel

30-0460

Available in black or chrome finish, and 1-3/4" or 2" diameter. Pipes for 2004-up models include O^2 sensor bung plugs for 2004-07 applications.

30-0722

30-0727

30-0728

30-0728

Chrome	Black	O.Dia.
2004- Up		
30-0722	30-0735	1-3/4"
30-0460	34-0464	2"
1957-85 Ironhead		
30-0727	30-0728	1-3/4"

Staggered Short Shots

Feature 1-3/4" headpipes with 220° coverage heat shields and slash cut ends. Includes baffles and mounting hardware. Chrome finish, fits 2004-13.

VT No. 30-0952

*Note: Pre 07 Models require O2 sensors port plug set.

Radii™ Curved Exhaust Headers

Headers feature 2" diameter. Note: For 2004-up models order additional bracket separately. 1957-85 Iron Heads require fabrication of rear bracket and will not work with XLH (Side Mount) oil tank.

VT No.	Years
30-0319	1957-85
30-0300	1986-07
31-0765	2004-07 Bracket

Vance & Hines Side Shots

Feature power chamber design 220° full length heat shield, 2-1/2" header pipe, and removable baffles mounting hardware included. Fits 2007-13.

30-1536

2-Stage Torque Kit fit 2-1/2" inner diameter exhaust pipes, reduces noise and increases back pressure.

VT No. 30-0617

Passenger Peg Mount Bracket Sets Only. Use with male style peg.

Chrome	Black	Years
27-1564		2004-13
27-0825	**27-0271**	2014-Up

Rear Passenger Peg Relocation Bracket fits 2004-13 XL with 30-0300 pipe. Black finish. Order footrest for support bracket separately.

VT No. 31-0766

Wyatt Gatling Slip-on Mufflers

Fit 2004-2013 XL models. Chrome finish unless noted.

2" Slip-On Drag Pipe Extensions

Feature removable baffles and cross tube nipples to connect to OE bracket. Removable baffle style.

30-1278 30-0463 30-1277

30-1280 30-0462

30-1279

VT No.	Style	VT No.	Style
30-0875	Slash Cut	30-0463	3" Tapered End
30-1277	Barrel End	30-0462	Slash
30-1278	Tapered End	30-1279	Black 3" Tapered End
		30-1280	Black End

EXHAUST 11

30-0444

2" Slip On Slash Cut Muffler Sets

Available with black or chrome finish. Featuring removable baffles and mount to stock brackets.

VT No.	Type	Finish
2004-2013		
30-0743	Side Slash	Black
30-0444	Side Slash	Chrome
30-0326	Down Slash	Chrome
2014- Up		
30-0446	Down Slash	Black
30-0447	Down Slash	Chrome
30-0874		Chrome
30-1407	Baffle Set	Replacement

3" Slash Cut Muffler Set

VT No.	Finish
30-0767	Black
30-0766	Chrome

Fit 2014- up XL models. Feature removable baffles.

30-0767 Installed

30-0743 Installed

30-0444 Installed

30-0446 Installed

30-0447 Installed

RMB BAFFLES 30 SECOND REMOVAL!

Motorcycles modified with some aftermarket parts, accessories and performance engine parts may be restricted from use on public roads and/or limited to closed courses. Please see United States E.P.A. and your respective state regulations.

STOP Caution: These exhaust products are not legal for sale or use in California on pollution controlled vehicles. These products are intended for the experienced rider only.

Limited Warranty. Exhaust Products distributed by Tedd Cycle Inc. are warrantied against defects in material and workmanship, which include fitting and finish quality at the time of installation only. Claims regarding discoloration, peeling blistering or blued chrome will not be considered as defective material or workmanship and cannot be returned as such as per manufacturers warranty.

SLIP ON MUFFLERS

Slip-On Muffler Sets with Removable Baffles

30-0239

30-0359

30-0934

30-0935

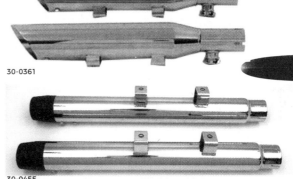

30-0361

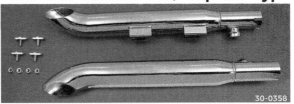

30-0455

EXHAUST 11

30-0821

Chrome	Black	Style	Year	Type
30-0239		Slash	1980-03	Side
30-0644	30-0649	Taper	1980-03	Tapered
30-0359*		Slash	2004-13	Side
30-0361*		Slash	2004-13	Down
30-0934	30-0935	Slash	2004-13	Down
30-0821	30-0843	Taper	2004-13	Replica, Embossed
30-0455	30-0456	Straight	2014-up	Straight
30-0568	30-0569	Slash	2014-up	Down
30-0874		Slash	2014-up	Side

Note: Slash style includes RMB removable baffle set.

Connector Tube Gasket Set.

VT No. 15-1533

V-Slots Torque Tube Set

Features improved baffling and back pressure for XL. Slash type mufflers with removable baffles. Use with slip on mufflers with 3" inner diameter.

VT No. 30-0633

Turn Out Muffler Set, Slip-On Type

30-0358

Baffles not removable.

30-0240

VT No.	Year
30-0240	1980-03
30-0358	2004-13

STOP Caution: These exhaust products are not legal for sale or use in California on pollution controlled vehicles. These products are intended for the experienced rider only.

HEAT SHIELD

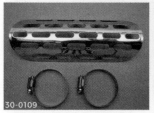

Universal Heat Shields include clamps for installation.

VT No.	#	Type	Dia.	Length
30-0109	A	Perforated	1-3/4"	9"
30-0106	B	Smooth	1-3/4"	7"

EXHAUST
11

Flame Design Shield

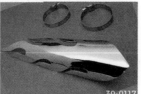

Chrome	Black	Diameter	Length
30-0118		1-3/4"	8"
30-0117		1-3/4"	11"
30-0481	30-0483	1-3/4"	9"
30-0482	30-0484	1-3/4"	12"
30-0473	30-0479	2-1/4"	9"
30-0478	30-0480	2-1/4"	12"

Skull Shield

Chrome	Black	Diameter	Length
30-3385	30-0466	2-1/4"	9"
30-3386	30-0467	2-1/4"	12"
30-0468	30-0471	1-3/4"	9"
30-0470	30-0472	1-3/4"	12

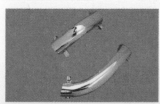

Heat Shield Set

Heat Shield Set fits 1-3/4" stock or drag pipe sets, fits 1957-84 XL except 1979.

30-0082

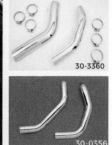

30-3360 Installed

30-3360

30-0356

Chrome Finish Exhaust Pipe Heat Shields

1957-84			1986-2003		
VT No.	Type	Style	VT No.	Type	Style
30-0099	Front	Stock/Drags	30-3360	Set	Drag
30-0100	Rear	Stock/Drags	30-0356	Set	Drag
30-3218	Rear	Stock/Drags			

Chrome Front Muffler Pipe Junction Shield

Fits 1984-2003 XL.
VT No. 42-0523

Chrome Pipe Shield

For 1983-85 XL-XLS.
VT No. 42-0521

Universal Straight Heat Shield

Available for 1-3/4" or 2-1/4" pipes. Includes mounting clamps.

2-1/4"		1-3/4"	
VT No.	Size	VT No.	Size
30-0120	4"	30-0122	10"
30-0121	10"	30-0123	12"
		30-0124	18"

30-0120

Sold individually.

Chrome Heat Shield

Includes 2 clamps.

VT No.	Len
30-0221	5-1/2"
30-0245	9"

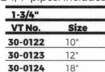

30-0221

30-0245

Chrome Heat Shield Set

Fits 2004-2013.

VT No.	Type
30-1167	Holes
30-0356	Smooth

30-1167

30-0356

HEADER CLAMPS

EXHAUST CLAMP

Chrome Allen Exhaust Clamps

Feature a unique design which allows the bolt to be nearer the exhaust pipe for positive clamping strength which permits easy access with hex wrench. Available in wide or extra wide. Fit 1957-85.

VT No.	#	Type
31-2112	A	Standard Wide
31-3942	B	Extra Wide

Stainless Exhaust Head Clamp

Stock type construction for 1952-85 sold in pairs.

VT No.	Item
31-0226	Clamps
37-8684	Bolts

2004-Up Chrome Exhaust Flange Set

Replaces 65184-02.   VT No. 30-0368

Finned Exhaust Flange

Fits 1986-up XL models, chrome finish.
VT No. 30-0857

Super Manifold Clamps

Stainless steel aircraft clamps. Designed with a heat treated 'T' bolt and self-locking nut. Fits 1957-85.
VT No. 31-2110

1957-84

Chrome Allen Exhaust Clamps

With allen cap screws securing 2 barrel swivels.
VT No. 31-4038

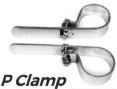

Exhaust Mount Clamps

2 inches and under.

P Clamp

Hanger Clamp

VT No.	ID Size	Style
31-3947	1"	P Clamp - Long
31-2100	1-1/2"	Hanger - Long
31-2101	1-3/4"	Hanger - Long
31-2146	1-3/4"	P Clamp - Short
31-1011	1-3/4"	P Clamp - Long
31-0816	1-7/8"	P Clamp - Short
31-2105	1-7/8"	Hanger - Long
31-2102	2"	P Clamp - Short

Muffler Mount Clamps		
VT No.	ID Size	Style
31-2120	2-1/2"	Hanger - Long
31-2106	2-1/2"	P Clamp - Short
31-2119	2-1/4"	P Clamp - Short
31-2108	3"	Hanger - Short
31-1977	3-1/2"	Hanger - Short
31-2107	2-3/4"	Hanger - Short

31-0273   31-2131

Frame Mounting Clamp

VT No.	Finish
31-2131	Chrome
31-0273	Black P Clamp

1" clamp for mounting exhaust pipes or footpegs. Sold in pairs. Order bolts and nuts separately.

31-2134   31-2115

Chrome Exhaust Strap Brackets

VT No.	Type
31-2134	Straight
31-2115	Offset

Straight strap, 6" long. Offset 2" between 3/8" holes. Made from 1/8" steel.

31-2134

Universal Chrome Straps

Sold in pairs.

VT No.	Length
31-2133	3"
31-2134	6"
31-2135	8"

31-0270   31-1007

31-2103   31-0301

1-5/8" for use when attaching muffler to 1-1/2" tubing.

VT No.	ID Size
31-0270	1-5/8"
31-2132	1-3/4"
31-2103	1-7/8"
31-2144	1-7/8" Heavy
31-1007	1-7/8" Super
31-9914	2"
31-0283	2-1/4" Narrow
31-2099	2-7/8"
31-2141	3"
31-1977	3-1/2"
31-2109	3-1/4"
31-4016*	3-1/4"
37-8683	Bolt Set

Chrome Muffler End Clamps

EXHAUST
11

*Note:
Stainless steel sold each

1958-85 XL.
VT No. 31-2104

Chrome Front Pipe Clamp

31-9971   31-9973

1" Wide Exhaust Brackets

VT No.	Type
31-9971	3" - Short
31-9972	4-3/4" - Long
31-9973	"L" Bend - 1x3-3/4

1" wide x 1/8" thick for mounting goodies. Sold as pairs.

A   B

Chrome Bracket Pairs

VT No.	#	Type
31-0676	A	3/8" holes
31-0677	B	1/2" holes

31-0783

7" Chrome Angle Bracket

EXHAUST FLANGE

Stainless Steel Taper Valve Kit

Includes two pure stainless extruded sleeves that fit between pipe and exhaust port to aid in back pressure when drag pipes are used. Kit includes solid copper machined exhaust seals which will not restrict flow. VT No. 30-0312

Stainless Exhaust Taper Valves

Fit into exhaust between pipe and head to put back the low end torque which is lost when large diameter or straight pipes are used. Fit Evolution w/ factory or aftermarket pipes. Pair.

VT No.	Type	VT No.	Type
30-0113	Machined	30-0355	Extruded

Stainless Steel Taper Valve Exhaust Kit

Fits into the header at the flange area to compensate for exhaust velocity when large diameter pipes installed. Fits Evolution and XL models 1986-up with large outside diameter aftermarket pipes. Kit includes two valves with gaskets.
VT No. 30-0119

Exhaust Port Gasket

Knitted stainless steel. Evolution engines.

VT No.	Type	Qty
15-0227	Tapered	2
15-0267	Mesh Gasket	5
15-0712	Tapered, James	5
15-0732	Tapered	10

Exhaust Port Gasket Kit

Includes two stainless steel knitted gaskets, two snap rings and four heavy duty flange nuts. Fits all 1985-up Twins.

VT No.	Brand	VT No.	Brand
15-1285	Radii	15-1274	James

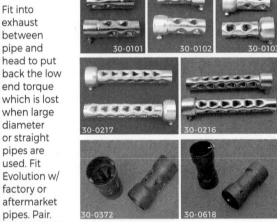

Pipe Baffles

Fit inside straight pipes, sold in pairs. Note: Baffle size denotes size of pipe into which it fits.

VT No.	Size	Len.
30-0101	1.5"	4"
30-0102	1.75"	4"
30-0103	2"	4"
30-0216	1.75"	8"
30-0217	2"	8"
30-0372	2.25"	4.5"
30-0618	2.25"	4.5"

*Note: Fits Cycle Shack stainless steel pipes, sold each.

Jims Exhaust Gasket Installer Tool

Correctly installs exhaust port gaskets into cylinder heads, minimizes gasket distortion. Helps heads flow better.
VT No. 16-2112

1986-Up Exhaust Gasket Set

Includes 2 snap rings.

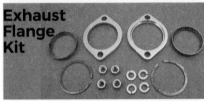

Exhaust Flange Kit

Fits 1986-up Sportster models. Kit includes snap rings and mesh gaskets.

VT No.	Item	U/M
30-0205	Kit	ea.
12-0942	Snap Ring	10
15-0227	Gasket	2
15-0732	Gasket	10
15-0451	Gasket & Snap Ring Kit	Kit
12-1187	Exhaust Stud - 16715-83	5
30-0257	Chrome Flange Only	2
30-0724	Drilled Flange	

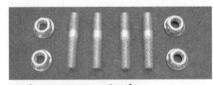

Exhaust Stud Kit

Includes four studs and four stainless flanged nuts. Fits 1986-up Sportster.

VT No.	Item	VT No.	Item
12-2125	Kit	12-1187	Studs Only

Solid Copper Exhaust Gaskets

Fit Evolution models.
VT No. 15-0777

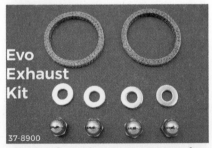

Evo Exhaust Kit

Includes four chrome cap nuts, four washers and two mesh gaskets. For 1984-up 883-1100-1200 1340 Evolution model.

VT No.	Mfg.	VT No.	Mfg.
37-8900	V-Twin	15-0726	James

IMPORTANT INFORMATION:
EMISSIONS AND NOISE REGULATIONS

NOTE: The California Air Resources Board ("CARB") and/or the Environmental Protection Agency ("EPA") do not permit the use of aftermarket emissions-related part(s) that alter the performance of OEM emissions-related devices unless CARB has issued and Executive Order, other than on racing vehicles on closed courses. Check your local laws and manufacturer's information. More California exhaust information is available at www.arb.ca.gov/.

NOTE: Aftermarket products, including by not limited to exhausts, catalytic converters, oxygen sensors, fuel/air controller modules, air filter kits, camshafts, O2 eliminators, and carburetors and jet kits which alter, modify, or replace emission control devices or systems of an originally compliant highway motorcycle, are not legal for sale or street use in California unless they have been issued a CARB Executive Order. Aftermarket emissions-related products which have not been issued an Executive Order, or which are not aftermarket Replacement Parts, as defined in Title 13, California Code of Regulations, Section 1900(b)(2), are authorized for closed circuit race use only. Products shown may be designed, manufactured, intended and sold for closed circuit race use only, and use of the same on public roads or lands may be a violation of local, state, and/or federal laws. See manufacturer's information and state and local laws to determine what is authorized for your use on your vehicle.

THE FOLLOWING EMISSIONS-RELATED DEFINED TERMS ARE USED IN THIS CATALOG
PARTS WITH THE FOLLOWING DESIGNATIONS ARE NOT ILLEGAL FOR SALE IN CALIFORNIA UNDER CARB REGULATIONS:

• **"CARB E.O."** means the specified Executive Order issued by CARB. An Executive order constitutes an exemption by CARB from CA Vehicle Code 27156 and 38391, for sale of the part number for the make/model/year fitment(s) specified in the Executive Order.

• **"Replacement Part"** means any aftermarket part intended to replace an original equipment emissions-related part and which is functionally identical to the original equipment part in all respects which in any way affect emissions (including durability), or a consolidated part.

• **"Qualified Manufacturer Declared Replacement Part"** means any aftermarket part intended to replace an original equipment emissions-related part and which is functionally identical to the original equipment part in all respects which in any way affect emissions (including durability), or a consolidated part that has been evaluated and declared by the manufacturer to meet this definition and carry this categorization and designation label. This manufacturer has declared in writing that it has documentation, based upon sound engineering judgement, indicating the replacement part does not reduct the effectiveness of any required emission control device and it does not cause the modified vehicle/engine/equipment to exceed applicable emissions standards for that make/model/year fitment(s) advertised.

NOTE: Products shown may not conform to federal, state, or local emissions and/or noise regulations.

WARRANTY: There is no warranty on exhaust pipes and mufflers with regard to any discoloration. Discoloration (blueing) is caused by tuning characteristics, i.e., cam timing, carburetor, etc., and is not caused by defective manufacturing. Look for Chemicals and Lubes that will help prevent or remove blueing. Check your applicable laws and manufacturer's publication(s) and/or website(s) for manufacturer's warranty, maintenance, safety, mounting, and any regulatory compliance/cono-compliance information.

XL TOOLS

Transmission Door Puller Tool

Fits 1957-90 XL and 1952-56 K.

16-0139

Primary Plug Wrenches for Sportster

VT No.	OEM	Fits
16-0158		1971-84
16-0985*	33186	1971-Up
8862-1	Evolution	1986-Up
8862-1T	Evolution	1986-Up

*Note: Uses 3/8 socket handle

Jims Sportster Crankshaft Locking Tool

Use on Pinion side of all 1991-up XL to keep crankshaft assembly from rotating during assembly on valve train repair.

VT No.	Fits	VT No.	Fits
16-1666	1991-2002	16-1665	2003-Up

Clutch Adjusting Gauges

Used to find correct distance between outer drive plate and outer releasing disc for 1971-83 Sportsters, 1936-67 early and 1968-84 late Big Twins. Set of 3 tools

16-1807

Sprocket Shaft Timken Bearing Installer Tool

16-0149

VT No.	Jims	OEM	Fitment
16-0149		97081-54	1954-76 XL
	16-1837	As Above	Jims
	16-1760*	2.500 Long	1977-up XL
	16-1761*	2.060 Long	1977-up XL

*Note: Sold separately for 1977-up use with 16-0149 and 16-1837.

Evolution XL Cam Relief Tool allows the installation of high lift cams in 5-Speed XL models by removing some of case material at the base of the lifter bores and around the pinion bearing for lobe swing clearance. This tool cuts clearance quickly and can be performed on an assembled engine in the frame.

VT No. 16-0353

Sprocket Shaft Timken Bearing Inner Race Puller

Fits 1952-76 XL.

16-1758

Timken Bearing Removers

16-0667   16-1883

Outer Primary Cover Starter Bearing Removal Tool

16-0717

Removes 9063 Torrington Needle Bearing for XL covers. This tool will also fit 4-Speed Sportster Clutch Gear.

Shaft Turning Tool

Fits spline on assembled motor and allows engine to be turned over by 1/2" ratchet or impact driver. Sifton unless noted. Fits 1957-up XL.

VT No. 16-1852

16-1514

Clutch Compression Tool

1990-up BT and 1991-up XL models.

16-1805   16-1849

1990-up BT Clutch Compressor

Tool features access windows to ease the removal and installation of snap ring, by Jims.

VT No.	Fits
16-1805	Big Twin
16-1849	Adapter to fit 1991-up XL

16-0127   16-1857

Cam Shaft Needle Bearing Installer

VT No.	Jims	OEM
16-0127	16-1857	97273-60

Pinion Shaft Race Installer

Fits 1977-E81 Sportster models. Replaces 97080-77A.

VT No. 16-0965

Bearing Race Press Plug

Used to remove and install Timken bearing outer race.

16-0045   16-0046

VT No.	Fits
16-0045	1957-76 XL
16-0046	1977-Up XL

Remove bearing from shaft without removing shaft from flywheels.

VT No.	Fits
16-0667	1957-76 XL
16-1833	1977-Up XL

Clutch Drum Locking Tools

16-0159

16-0992

16-0125

Countershaft Support Plate

Tool fits 1991-up 5-speed Sportster.

VT No. 16-1756

Drive Bearing Press

Tool fits 1991-up XL. 37842.

VT No. 16-1767

Motor Stand

Fits 1952-03 XL

VT No. 16-0507

Main Bearing End Plug

Tool allows the setting of proper end play in Big Twin Timken Bearing Assemblies by selection of proper spacer from the catalog. Use when refitting bearings or bearing sets on late models when spacers are not included. Not needed for our VT No. 12-0309 or 12-0310 Timken sets, these are pre-spaced from the factory. Fits 1977-up XL.

VT No. 16-1796

Final Drive Tool

Fits final drive pulley, so the nut can be properly set to torque specifications. Fits XL.

VT No. 16-0588

Ratchet Plate Riveting Fixture

Securely aligns plate to drum while setting rivets on 1971-79 XL model clutch drum.

VT No. 16-0165

Bushing Reaming Tool

16-0980

Fit pinion bushing in cam cover

VT No.	OEM	Year	Model
16-0981	94812-37A	1954-76	XL and 45"
16-0980	94812-80A	1977-85	Sportster
16-0962	94812-89	1986-Up	Sportster
16-1791		1957-Up	Sportster

1-3-4 Cam Cover Bushing

Clutch Compressor Tools for XL

16-0156

16-0059   16-1769

VT No.	Year
16-1769*	1991-Up
16-0156	1971-84
16-0059	1985-90

Allows disassembly of clutch pack.

*Note: Adapts 16-0967 to fit 1991-up XL.

Used to remove clutch hub and motor nuts.

VT No.	Fits
16-0125	1952-70
16-0159	1956-84
16-0992	1971-84

Sifton Pinion Gear Puller

Used to install and remove the pinion gear. Fits 1957-76 XL.

16-1060

TOOLS

COLI

32-7572

32-7573

32-0511

32-0743

32-0771

12-0856

Volt Tech Black Molded Coil

Features black late shape with bobbin type windings. 32-0511 features side terminals for 1983-99.

VT No.	OEM	Year
32-7572		1965-79
32-7573		1980-82
32-0511	31614-83A	1983-03
32-0743	31655-99	2000-06
32-0771	31656-07A	2007- Up
12-0586	7638	All

80 KV Coil

For 1965-99 mounts to stock locations.

VT No. 32-0095

32-0709   32-0712

Andrews Coils

Black coil fits through 1980 with point type ignition sets. Rust colored coils are for 1981 and later with electronic ignition systems. Both coils produce more voltage than stock coils.

VT No.	Color	OHMs	Year
32-7079	Black	4.8	Pre 1980
32-0712	Red	2.8	1980-1999

ACCEL

Accel H.V. Super Coil

High performance bolt on for points or electronic ignition systems. High-tech molding for exact fit on 1965-99.

32-7771

32-7800

VT No.	Ignition	OHMs
32-7771	Points	4.7
32-7800	Points, Chrome	4.7
32-7772	Electronic	2.3
32-7801	Electronic, Chrome	2.3

Accel Single Fire Super Coil

Features ultra fast coil rise time with voltage output 45% higher than stock and 3.0 ohms of primary resistance. Mounts to stock coil bracket and fits under stock coil covers.

VT No.	Finish
32-0090	Yellow
32-7802	Chrome

Accel Power Pulse Coil

Provides longer spark duration with a greater KV rating and faster rise time than stock coil. Molded in bright yellow epoxy. 12 Volt 1965-83 Twins.

VT No. 32-0130

Coil Mount Studs replace 64611-55, 64612-55 models, pairs. Fits 1955-67 XLH. VT No. 37-9156

32-0474

V-Tech™ Single Fire Coil

Gives 1 spark for each cylinder as fired and will mount to stock bracket and accept stock coil cover.

VT No.	Finish
32-0467	Black
32-0474	Chrome

32-0467

Volt Tech™ Stock Coils

Factory quality to fit stock brackets.

VT No.	OEM	Year
32-0711	6V	Pre 1965
32-0128	12V	1965-79
32-0129	12V 2.8 OHM	1980-83
32-1268	12V, Red	1965-79

Note: VT No. 32-0129 for electronic ignition, top terminal mounting.

32-0128   32-0711

32-1268

Chrome Stock Coils

Bolt to original brackets for exact fit.

VT No.	OEM	Year
32-0513	31609-65A	1965-79
32-0514	31609-80	1980-83
32-0512	31614-83	1984-99

Blue Streak 45,000 Volt Coils

45,000 Volt Coils provide more spark and energy than stock coil and the higher voltage eliminates spark deterioration at peak RPM

32-0171   32-0172

VT No.	Ignition	OHMs	Years
32-0171	Electronic	2.7	1980-99
32-0172	Points	4.6	1965-79

31-0131   31-0321   31-0758

Chrome Coil Mount Bracket Kit

VT No.	Year	VT No.	Year	VT No.	Year
31-0131	1971-94	31-0321	1995- Up	31-0758	2004- Up

42-0839

42-0039

42-0418

Coil Cover

Available in polished stainless or chrome.

VT No.	Fits	Finish
42-0839	1983-03	Chrome
42-0039	1985-03	Stainless
42-0418	1971-78	Chrome

TUNE UP KIT

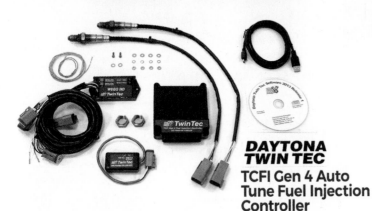

DAYTONA TWIN TEC
TCFI Gen 4 Auto Tune Fuel Injection Controller

Fully programmable plug in replacement for the 36 pin Delphi controller with J1850 data bus.

- Quickly auto-tune fuel curves for front and rear cylinder on a dyno or on-road with new WEGO IID dual channel wide band oxygen sensor interface.
- Fully programmable plug-in for 36 pin Delphi® controller with J1850 data bus.
- Powerful Windows software for custom programming and data analysis
- Full support J1850 data bus used for communications with turn signal/security module (TSM/TSSM) and instrument cluster
- Support for new 6th gear indicator.
- Extended data logging and diagnostics. DataFLASH memory stores full 60 minutes of operating data at 10 samples/second.
- Programmable user input and output.
- Billet aluminum housing with black anodized finish
- Easy plug-in installation
- Supports all sensors including theft/security module

Includes TCFI Gen 4 plug-in fuel injection controller with billet aluminum housing with black finish, dual channel wide band exhaust gas oxygen sensor interface, two Bosch LSU 4.2 wide band exhaust gas oxygen sensors, and two 18 x 1.5mm weld nuts for exhaust pipes. Quickly auto-tune fuel curves for front and rear cylinders on a dyno or on-road. The robust alpha-N fuel control eliminates problems with long duration/high overlap camshafts. Windows software provides custom programming and data analysis. Its full support for J1850 data bus used for communications with turn signal/security module and instrument cluster.

NOTE: Not legal for sale or use on pollution controlled vehicles.

Fits 2007-up Sportster

VT No. 32-7401

Dynatek Fusion EFI Ignition Module

VT No.	Sportster	Years
32-1178	883	2010-13
32-1179	883	2014-Up
32-1180	1200	2007-09
32-1181	1200	2010-13
32-1182	1200	2014-Up

Dyna Ignition Booster for single point systems only transforms inconsistent electrical surges into controlled bursts of energy to the coil, power is not wasted.
VT No. 32-7787

32-1115

32-0116

V-Twin Tune-Up Kits

Include plugs, points and condenser. Also available as points and condenser kit only.

W/Plugs	W/O Plugs	Years	Fitment
32-1114	32-0114	1957-70	XLH
32-1115	32-0115	1970-74	XLH
32-1116	32-0116	1958-69	XLCH Magneto
	32-0115	1975-78	XL
32-1232		1957-70	XLCH Kit

Accel Performance Tune-Up Kits

Include replacement spark plugs, matched crown contact points, condenser, gap settings and point cam lube. Kits available without spark plugs.

VT No.	Fits
32-0109	1957-69 XLCH with Magneto
32-0107	1957-70 XLH, 1969 XLCH
32-0106	1970-78 XL

32-0156

32-0157

Blue Streak Premium Parts 1970-78

VT No.	OEM	Item
32-0156	32661-70	Points
32-0157	32726-30A	Condenser

32-0117

32-0118

Points Sets

VT No.	OEM	Item	U/M
32-0117	309605-48	1957-70 XLH, 1970 XLCH	Each
32-0118	32661-70	1970-E 78 XLH, XLCH	Each
32-0119	29533-55A	1958-69 XLCH Magneto	Each

32-0121

32-1244

Condensers

VT No.	OEM	Year/Model
32-0121	32726-30A	1957-70 XLH, 1970 XLCH 1971- E 78 XLH, XLCH
32-1316		As Above, 5pk.
32-1244		1957-70 XLCH, 1957-78 XLCH
32-0122	29534-55A	1958-69 XLCH Magneto

SPARK PLUG

V-Twin Performance Spark Plugs

Feature copper core electrode for a longer service life, nickel plated housing, 95% pure alumina insulator and a heat crimping process to ensure a leak free seal.

VT No.	#	Applications
32-6691	6R12	1986- Up Evolution
32-6696	4R5	1979-85
32-6697	4R	1971-85
32-6698	3	1957-78

Blue Lightning Bug Spark Plug Ends

Neon gas filled plugs glow as strobe lights. Fit plugs with screw terminal fittings only, pair.
VT No. 32-1552

1986- Up Head Bolt & Spark Plug Covers

Die cast and chrome plated to cover entire head bolt area and spark plug base. Held in place by rubber boots on spark plug wires. Fits 883-1200 XL models.
VT No. 42-0741

Autolite Platinum Plugs

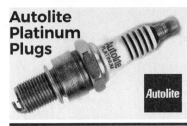

VT No.	Autolite#	H-D #	Model	U/M
32-9232	AP4164DP2	1986-Up	V-2 Evolution	Pair
Standard				
32-9293	4316	4	1954-79 Hotter Plug	10
32-9294	4123	4R5	1980-85	10
32-9295	4164	6R12	1986-up Evolution XL	10

OE Factory Spark Plug

Spark plug set have copper coated electrodes for foul resistance. Sold as a pair. Fits 1971-85 XL. Replaces OEM# 32301-80. Mfg # 4R5.
VT No. 32-8903

ELECTRIC
12

Sparkies

Chrome plated die cast covers fit perfectly on a spark hex for Evolution XL 883-1200 models, pair.
VT No. 37-8953

Champion Spark Plug

Available in Copper Plus styles.

Engine	Fits	H-D #	Gap	Copper Plus #	QTY	Copper Plus VT No.
1200 V2	1988- Up XL	6R12	.040	RA8HC	4	**32-7547**
1100 V2	1985-87 XL	6R12	.040	RA8HC	4	**32-7547**
883 V2	1985- Up XL	6R12	.040	RA8HC	4	**32-7547**
1000	1979-85 XL	4-RS	.040	RL82YC	4	**32-7545**
	1972-78 XL	4	.030	H8C	4	**32-7544**
	1972-78 XL	4	.030	H10C	4	**32-8073***
900	1957-71 XL	4	.030	H8C	4	**32-7544**
	1957-71 XL	4	.030	H10C	4	**32-8073***

*RN13LYC may also be used

Bosch Spark Plugs

Sold in pairs. Available in silver type with hard silver center electrode and extended service life.
VT No. 32-1223

Engine	Fits	H-D #
1200 V2	1988- Up XL	6R12
1100 V2	1985-87 XL	6R12
883 V2	1985- Up XL	6R12

Spark Plug Wire Clamp Set

37-9062

37-2911 Installed

VT No.	Size	Finish
37-9062	7mm	Chrome
37-2911	8mm	Chrome

WIRE SETS

Universal 7mm Wire Sets

40" long with double 90° spark boots. Simply cut to the desired length and install coil terminal clips supplied. Available in copper or suppression core.

32-0648

32-0696

VT No.	Color	Type
32-0647	Yellow	Suppression
32-0648	Yellow	Copper
32-0650	Orange	Copper
32-0651	Black	Suppression
32-0696	Black	Copper
32-1123	Red	Copper

Sumax by Taylor Colored 8mm Plug Wires

Wires are pre-cut and have the plug/coil boots and terminals already installed. Designed for electronic ignition, but work great on point types.

32-7233

32-2004

32-2044

32-2024

32-2064

32-2034

Color	1986-2003	2004-Up	Color	1986-2003	2004-Up
Red	32-7233	32-2024	Black	32-7033	32-2004
Purple		32-2034	Yellow		32-2044
Blue		32-2064			

8mm Pro Spark Plug Kit

Universal 8mm kits feature 24" wire leads with either 90° or 180° molded plug boots and straight coil boots with brass terminals. Wires feature the Spiro-Pro design which provides 10x the firepower of carbon core wires and heat protection to 600°F. Works with electronic or points style ignition. All wires have a resistance factor of 350 ohm/ft. Great for magnetos, distributors, or dual plug heads.

90° Kits	Color	90° Kits	Color
32-6081	Black	32-6681	Blue
32-6181	White	32-6381	Purple
32-6281	Red	32-6085	Black (180° Kit)
32-6481	Yellow		

Splitfire 7mm

Splitfire Dual Mag Black 7mm wire set incorporates two premium magnetic suppression core conductors, which are protected by a layer of braided fiberglass and a 100% pure silicone outer jacket. Fits 1985-98.

VT No. 32-2086

ACCEL

32-9248

Ends are terminated with either 90° or variangle boot and comes with a hardware kit which includes terminals, boots, and instructions.

42" Accel 8.8 Wire Sets

VT No.	Color	Type
Variangle		
32-9248	Black	Suppression
32-9252	Yellow	Suppression
32-9253	Yellow	Copper
90°		
32-9250	Black	Suppression
32-9254	Yellow	Suppression
32-7536	Yellow	Copper

Accel 8.8 Ignition Wire Set

32-7535

Available in 300+ or custom fit.

8mm V-Twin Wire Set fits 1971-83 XL, XLCH.

VT No. 32-0661

300+	Custom Fit			
Black	Yellow	Black	Year	Model
32-9101	32-0656	32-8044	L 1979-85	XL, XLCH, XLX
			L 1979-82	XLS
32-9101	32-0655	32-8046	1971- E 78	XLH, XLCH
32-9102	32-0659	32-8047	1958-69	XL, XLCH w. Magneto
32-9105	32-7535	32-8050	1986- Up	All XL

Sumax Thunder Volt 50 Black Wire Sets

Feature a ferrite spiral wound coated core that is a blend of copper/nickel alloy bonded by a conductive acrylic latex cover. This process is designed to reinforce and assist in holding core resistance to 50 ohms. The fat 10.4 mm (.409") wires also feature three layers of pure zimplex silicone, 600 degrees of heat protection, 102,000 volts dielectric strength with a tightly woven heat treated fiberglass braid and black pro boots bonded to the black with gold lettering wires. Available in 8.2mm or 10.4 mm.

8.2mm	10.4mm	Fits
32-5026	32-0033	1986-2003 XL
32-5204	32-2032	2004- Up XL
32-5208	32-5608	24" Universal, 90° boots (2pc)
32-5202	32-0031	1971-85 XL

Blue Streak Wire Set

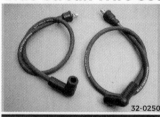

32-0250

Blue Streak XXX silicone 8mm wire sets offer maximum RFI suppression. Copper core wire sets are for point type ignition systems only and feature a copper core wire to allow for special improved electrical conductivity and mechanical strength. All wire sets are supplied with electrical boots and OEM style terminals that lock onto the spark plug.

Copper Core Sets		
VT No.	Year	Model
32-0250	1958-69	XL/XLCH w/Magneto
32-0251	1971-78	XLH/XLCH

XXX Silicone Sets		
VT No.	Year	OEM
32-0253	Universal Application Self Make Kit	32095-98
32-0257	1986-05 XL	32092-98
32-0261	1998-up 4 Plug XL 1200S	32054-98
32-0270	2004-06 XL	31958-04A
32-0271	2007-up XL	31901-08

IGNITION ADVANCE UNIT

Stainless Advance Unit

Features stainless base, heat treated weights & cam center screw for 1970-up mechanical advance ignition.

VT No.	Item	Brand
32-0178	Set	Sifton
32-0168	Set	V-Tech, without bolt
32-0055	Bolt	V-Twin

1970-Up Advance Weight Springs

VT No.	Fits
13-9247	Severe Duty Advance Weight Springs for all Hi-compression and heavily modified engines. Also useful for applications experiencing detonation (pinging) or very erratic idle. Pair.
13-9246	Heavy Advance Weight Springs for slightly modified stock, low compression, or mild stroker application. Helps cure minor idle problems. Pair.
13-0121	Original type replacement. Uses Premium grade spring steel. 10pk.

Tuneable Advance Unit

Features stainless base, heat treated weights cam bolt and 3 different color coded spring sets which allows full advance at 1400, 2000, and 2600 RPM depending on which springs are selected. Can be used with all ignitions, points, single or dual fire types which utilize an advance unit. Springs also available separately.

VT No.	Type	Item
32-9920	Stock	Kit
32-9261	Needle Bearing	Kit
32-7510	Stock	Base Only
32-0055	Bolt	

Competition Advance Unit

Features machined stainless steel shaft and plate, metallic coated weights and special wound springs for exact advance. Replaces 32505-78A for 1970-up, mechanical advance applications. Center screw included.

VT No.	Item	Brand
32-9037	Competition Unit	Rivera
32-9220	Complete with tuneable springs	V-Twin

Blue Streak Sifton "Tuneable" Ignition Advance Assembly

Includes stainless advance base, points plate with "Blue Streak" points and condenser with hardware and 3 pairs of color coated springs which allow full advance at 1400, 2000 and 2600 RPM depending on which spring is selected.

VT No. 32-0713

Mallory Ignition Plate

Fits all 1971-78 XL models.

VT No. 32-5129

Advance Units

Feature heat treated weights. Order center bolt separately.

VT No.	Type
32-7510	With Steel Base
32-0055	Center Bolt

Automatic Advance Rebuild Kit

Kit includes 2 of the following: springs, weights, and 4 roll pins. For all 1970-78 Twins.

VT No. 32-0140

Points Plate Screws

VT No.	Year	Type
32-0049	1982- Up	Steel
32-0760	1982- Up	Stainless
32-0051	1970-81	Steel

Points Plate Assembly

Available as stock point and condenser replacement or Accel Super plate with micro chip condenser and 32 oz. spring points. Both for 1970-78.

VT No.	OEM	Item
32-0549	32577-70	Point Plate Assembly
32-0042	32618-70A	Mount Plate Only
37-8809	1047	Point Mount Plate Screws
	7115.6189W	Washer Assortment

Points Conversion Kit

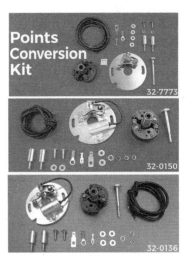

Includes everything necessary for direct replacement on 1971-78 Sportsters or for converting late model electronic-type back to points. Accel™ available with microchip points, which require domed shaped points cover *such as VT No. 42-0299* to fit taller points. V-Twin™ unit includes stock style points and condenser. Available with stock needle bearing weights.

VT No.	Item	Type
32-7773	Accel Microchip	Stock
32-0136	V-Twin Points	Stock
32-0150	V-Twin Points	Needle

XL IGNITION AND POINTS COVER

Chrome Points Covers

42-0090

42-0106

42-0087

42-0088

Vertical application for 1971-2003 and horizontal for 2004-up use.

VT No.	Style	Year	Type
42-0090	Live to Ride	1971-2003	Chrome
42-0106	Live to Ride	2004-up	Chrome
42-0087	Live to Ride	1971-2003	Gold
42-0088	Live to Ride	2004-up	Gold
42-0035	V-tech	1971-2003	Both
42-0299	Domed	1971-2003	All, 2-hole
42-0662	Flat	1971-2003	Chrome
42-1535	Flame		Mesh
42-0638	Finned	1971-2003	Chrome
42-0084	Skull	1971-2003	
42-0081	Skull	2004- Up	
42-0582	Skull	1991- Up	
42-1261	Skull	2004- Up	
42-1262	Skull	2004- Up	
42-0960	Maltese	2-hole	Flat
42-6100	Maltese	2-hole	Raised
42-0561	Chrome/Black	1971-03	
42-0560	Chrome/Black	2004- Up	
42-1383	Air Flow	2004- Up	Chrome
42-1384	Air Flow	2004- Up	Black
42-1524	Skull	1971-05	Black Mesh
42-0464	Skull	2004- Up	Black Mesh
42-1146	Grooved	1971-2003	Chrome
42-1148	Grooved	2004- Up	Chrome
42-1147	Grooved	1971-2003	Black
42-1166	Grooved	2004- Up	Black
42-1197	AMF	1971-84	
42-0748	Flame	2004- Up	Chrome
42-5522	Flame	2004- Up	Chrome
42-0065	Flame/Skull	2004- Up	Chrome
42-1078	Skull	2004- Up	Chrome
42-1110	Perforated	1971- Up	Chrome
42-1115	Ball Milled	2004- Up	Black
42-0155	Smooth	1971- Up	Chrome
42-1058	Milled Skull	2004- Up	Chrome
42-1116	Smooth	1971- Up	Black
42-1125	Perforated	1971- Up	Black
42-1122	Black/Alloy	2004- Up	
42-1095	Ball Milled	2004- Up	Chrome
42-0581	Chrome Skull	2004- Up	Black
42-0474	Flame	2004- Up	Chrome
42-0475	Flame	2004- Up	Black
42-0189	Smooth	2004- Up	Black
42-0198	Smooth	2004- Up	Chrome
42-0465	Flames/Mesh	2004- Up	Chrome
15-1032	Points Cover	1971-2003	
15-1033	Gasket	1980- Up	

42-0638   42-0960   42-6100   42-0035

42-1384

42-1383

42-0662

42-0299

42-1524

42-1261

42-0084

42-0582

42-1262

42-0464

42-1176

Smoothie Hidden Points Cover Kit

Features an inner mount system in which the outer cover screws on. No visible mount screws. Fits 1971-02.

VT No. 42-0956

Screws

VT No.	Item	Year	Type
8764-2	Screws	1970-78	Allen
8765-2	Screws	1978- Up	Allen
8402-2	Screws, Chrome	1978- Up	Acorn
2219-2	Torx	2004- Up	Gold

Chrome Maltese Cross Spinner Points Covers

Feature iron cross design that spins when engine is running. Can only be used with mechanical type advance assembly. As a drive shaft bolts to the camshaft and turns

VT No. 42-0162

Clear Timing Plugs

16-1731   16-0829   16-0160

Available as a long optically clear type or a short standard version with or without internal hex.

VT No.	Item
16-1731	Long Type
16-0829	Hex Type
16-0099	Standard, 10pk
16-0160	Standard, ea.

CONTROLS BY: Wyatt Gatling

Button Switches

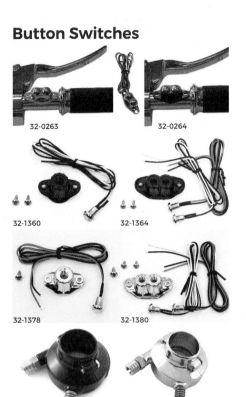

32-0263   32-0264

32-1360   32-1364

32-1378   32-1380

35-0856   35-0857

VT No.	#	Finish
32-0263	2	Chrome
32-0264	2	Black
32-1360	1	Black
32-1364	2	Black
32-1378	1	Chrome
32-1380	2	Chrome
35-0856		Black Throttle Housing
35-0857		Chrome Throttle Housing

GMA Master Cylinders

With switch housing for acceptance of stock switches. Order matching clutch lever assembly and left side switch housing separately. All 3/4" bore.

VT No.	Year
26-0638	1996-Up
26-0639	1996-Up
23-1716	Rebuild Kit
Lever Assembly	
26-0641	1996-Up

Vintage Style Control Kit

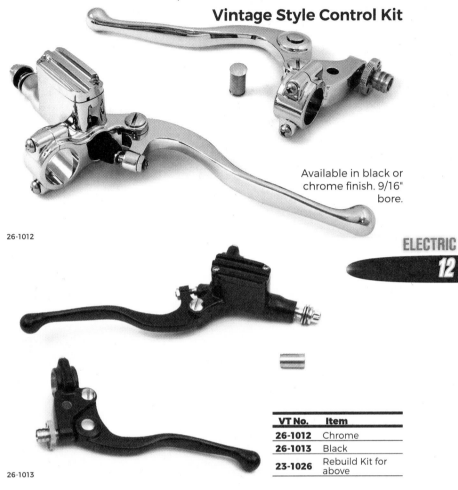

Available in black or chrome finish. 9/16" bore.

26-1012

26-1013

VT No.	Item
26-1012	Chrome
26-1013	Black
23-1026	Rebuild Kit for above

ELECTRIC
12

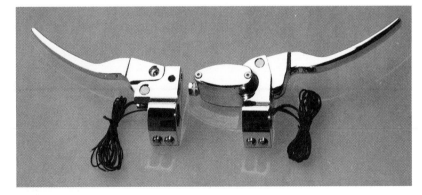

Chrome Handlebar Control Kit

Includes 5/8" brake master cylinder and micro switches on right and left sides. VT No. 26-2210

IGNITION

DYNA

Dyna 2000 Digital Ignition Systems

Systems include Dyna 2000 HD-1 Ignition Module and a matched Dyna Twin Fire Coil for each application.

VT No.	#	Fits
32-0802	SFK-3	1994-up XL
32-0804	SFK-1	Pre 1994 XL
32-9118		Programming Software for 32-0802
32-9117		Programming Software for 32-0804

Dyna 2000I Digital Ignition

Available in module only or complete kits that include correct coil as listed. Features include single or dual fire operation, 8 advance curves, built in tach driver, adjustable RPM limit from 6000 to 7500 and easy static timing with built in timing indicator. Fits all 1970-98 carbureted models and requires 1983-up sensor cup for 1982 and earlier applications. Advanced Programming Software allows mechanic or tuner the ability to fine tune 2000i ignition but requires adapter harness

VT No.	Item
32-9151	Kit Single Plug/Single Fire with DC3-1
32-9152	Kit Dual Plug/Single Fire with DC1-1
32-9153	Kit Dual Plug/Dual Fire with DC2-1
32-9155	Kit Single Plug/Single Fire with DC6-5 miniature coil
32-9159	Module Only
32-9087	Sensor Cup, 1983-94
32-9124	Sensor Cup, 1995-up
32-9052	Cup Screw, 10 pk
32-9120	Advanced Programming Software for Above Ignitions
32-9121	Software Adapter Harness for Above Ignitions

Power Commander V Fuel Ignition and Timing Control

Power Commander V Fuel and Ignition Timing Control for each cylinder in a new smaller enclosure. Rev Xtend feature increases stock rev limiter. Switch between two maps "on the fly" maps can be adjusted on a "per gear" basis. Allows for one map per cylinder per gear if required. Adjustment of fuel and timing based on engine temperature is provided by the cold start feature. Will power up with USB cable only for programming. Note: not legal for use on pollution controlled vehicle

VT No.	Fits	VT No.	Fits
32-0844	2007-2009 XL 883	32-1031	2010-12 XL 883
32-0846	2007-2009 XL 1200	32-1032	2010-12 XL 1200
		32-1051	2013-up XL 883

Dyna Twin Fire Ignition Coils

Designed to work with Dyna 2000 HD-I ignition modules. Twin fire coils are slightly larger than stock coils, fit the stock mounting bracket. Twin fire coils can be used with any electric advance ignition system that incorporates dwell control except Dyna DS6-2 or similar type ignitions.

VT No.	Dyna	Ohm	Type
32-9285	DC6-5	3	Twin Fire II Miniature Dual Output Towers. Replaces DC6-3 on all FXR, FXST, and Dyna.
32-9264	DC6-4	3	4 Output Towers. Fits Dual Spark Plug

Daytona Twin Tec

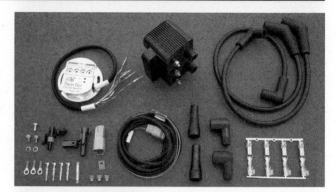

Daytona Twin Tec Internal Ignition Kit for 1998-03 Sportster models (except 1200S). Kit includes matching Deutsch plug and harness for single fire conversion, coil and spark plug wire set.

VT No. 32-3016

Internal Ignition - 1970-99 BT/1971-97 XL

Twin Tec internal ignition is for 1970-99 Big Twin models and 1971-1997 XL. Two advance curve families with adjustable advance slope accommodate stock to highly modified engines. Digitally set RPM Limit (100 RPM Steps). Selectable single or dual fire mode. Coil outputs protected against short circuits. Optional PC link cable and software for programming custom advance curve

VT No. 32-1005

Daytona Twin Tec External Ignition Kit

Includes module, coil and spark plug wire set.

VT No.	Fits
32-3017	1990-93 Sportster
32-3018	1994-99 Sportster

Daytona Twin Tec Internal Ignition Kit

1971-97 Sportster models. Kit includes ignition, coil and spark plug wire set.

Sensor Cup Kit includes special screw to fit all "Sensor" type ignition kits. Fits 1995-99.

VT No. 32-9124

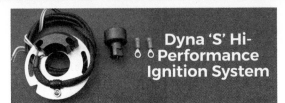

Dyna 'S' Hi-Performance Ignition System

Completely self contained, it fits behind ignition cover, uses magnetic rotor with the original spark advancer. Factory advance curve is maintained. Improves performance, extends spark plug life, eliminates points and condensers. Great for dual plugged heads, on 1980-up use advance mechanism VT No. 32-7510. DS6-1.

VT No. 32-7778

Dyna 'S' Single Fire Ignition

Has the features of the Dyna 'S', but fires front and rear cylinders independently of each other, allowing accurate timing of each cylinder. This eliminates the inherent problem of stock ignition fire both cylinders at the same time, with the wasted sparks on the exhaust stroke. For use with either dual or single plug heads. On 1980-up models, use VT No. 32-7510 Advance assembly. DS6-2.

VT No. 32-7777

Ignition Sensor Plate Assembly

VT No.	OEM	Fits
32-9020	32400-80A	1980-94 XL
32-0519	32400-94	1995-97 XL

Replacement Rotor for Dyna Ignitions

VT No.	Fits	VT No.	Fits
32-9300	DS-6-1	32-9301	DS-6-2

Dyna Electric Tach Adapter Kit must be used with Dyna 'S' single fire ignition is installed on any twins when electric tach is used.
VT No. 32-7799

K. V. Recommends the following coils for Dyna Ignitions:
DS6-1 Ignition VT No. 32-7778
Street, Single plugs use DC-7 or DC-8
Race, Single plugs use DC-1 or DC-6
Street/Race Dual plugs use 2 DC-2 or DC-5, wired in series
DS6-2 Ignition VT No. 32-7777
Race, Single plugs use 2 DC-3
Street, Dual plugs use 2 DC-7 or DC-8
Race, Dual plugs use 2 DC-1 or 2 DC-6
Street, Single plug uses 2 DC10-1

'S' IGNITION

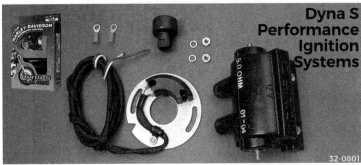

Dyna S Performance Ignition Systems

Dual or single fire for street applications only. Each kit includes sensor plate assembly and correct coil for each application. Single plug only. 1980-up applications require 32-7510 advance mechanism.

VT No.	#	Type
32-0800	DSK6-2	Single Fire
32-0801	DSK6-1	Dual Fire

Crane H1-4N Multi Function Performance Ignition

1-piece machined aluminum housing, BCD switches with solid detent and legible markings, allows for easy adjustment of mode. Advance rate and rev limit, single or dual fire operation and initial timing marks that allows precise adjustment. Fits 1970-97 XL. Also available as ignition kit including HI-4N ignition, single fire coil and 8.5 mm plug wire set.

VT No.	Item
32-1731	HI-4N Ignition
32-1732	HI-4N Kit

A

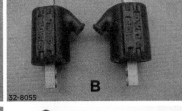
B

C

C

Dyna Coil

35,000 volts! Works with all points ignitions, aftermarket or factory electronic ignitions.

VT No.	Volt	Ohm	#	Dyna	Type	U/M
32-7789	12V	3	A	DC-1	Angle, Dual	Pair
32-7790	6V	1-1/2	A	DC-2	Angle, Dual	Pair (need 2 for dual plug heads)
32-7792	12V	3	C	DC-6	Stock, Dual	Each (Electro)
32-7793*	12V	5	C	DC-7	Stock, Dual	Each (Points)
32-8055	12V	3	B	DC-3	Angle, Single	Pair
32-8086	12V	5	A	DC-8	Angle, Dual	Pair
32-9035	12V	5	B	DC-10-1	Angle, Single	Pair

*Note: Use 2 for single fire ignition.

ELECTRIC 12

Single Fire: Just the spark plug for the piston that is in its compression stroke will be fired. The other piston, being in its overlap position will not be ignited. **Dual Fire**: Both spark plugs are fired simultaneously at the time only one piston is in its compression stroke. This is the way the stock motor works. **Single Plug**: One spark plug in each head. Total of 2 spark plugs in one engine. **Dual Plug**: Two spark plugs in each head. Total of 4 spark plugs in one engine.

MODULE FOR XL

Power Commander III

Power Commander III Engine Management System is for fuel injected models and allows for both fuel and ignition adjustments. USB cable and 9 volt battery power adapter are included. The Power Commander includes an link cable and software package which allows you to fully map the fuel ignition curves on a computer. If a computer is not available, the fuel curves can be adjusted by using three touch buttons on the face plate. This unit includes a specific map, designed to improve performance over stock. Fits 2007-2008 XL 883, EFI model.

VT No. 32-3029

42-0399   42-0399 Installed

Bolt-On Replacement Ignition Modules

Harness 32-9014 required as noted.

VT No.	OEM	Fits
42-0399		Cover
32-2218	32466-95A	1995-97 XLH 883

S&S Spark Technology Ignition System Installation Kit

32-1053   32-7806

VT No.	Fits
32-1049	1986-03
32-7806	2004-Up

Compu-Fire Plug In Performance Ignition

Features programmable advance curve, RPM limit, Single Fire or Dual Fire operation, Accu-Ray Timing light which simplifies installation, and 2 selectable levels of VOES control. Fits 1996-97 8 pin Deutsch style. Note: Each module has 2 pigtails and plug connector. White lead goes to tach, red lead goes to the second coil for single fire operation.

32-2503

Power Commander V

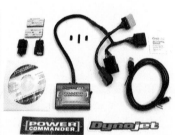

32-1053   32-1060

Features 2 position map switching function, gear and analog input. Power commander also allows each cylinder to be mapped individually and for each gear. This has 10 throttle position columns, and enhanced accel pump utility. Unit has a -100/+250 percent fuel change range and is compatible with 2009 and newer models.

VT No.	Fits
32-1053	2014- Up 883
32-1060	2014- Up 1200

32-9079   32-9080

Vacuum Switch Assembly

VT No.	OEM	Fits
32-9079	26557-83	1983-85 XL,XLS,XLX
32-9080	26558-84	1986-93 all XL

Self Learning Module by Accel

Helps regain control of fuel injected bike. Improves mileage-while increasing power and reducing emissions, works on all stock and mildly modified. Automatic recalibration-optimizing modifications gains expected from performance exhausts, air cleaners and camshafts. Easy installation-direct plug-in connections to factory throttle position, crank shaft position, and oxygen sensors. Self learning-module seamlessly compensates for changing loads, weather conditions and altitude while you ride; no need dyno tuning sessions or downloading new calibration maps to a laptop computer. Smoother running engine-eliminates to pop and bang associated with a mis-programmed ECU due to intake or exhaust modifications, the need to re flash the factory ECU has been eliminated, truly a plug and play proposition. ACCEL NO. SLM03 07-11 Sportster utilizes factory installed O2 sensors

VT No. 32-1702

Dyna Tek FL Controller

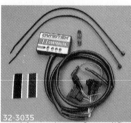

32-3035

A plug module that offers 3 user selectable base fuel curves that are designed to improve engine operation and can be modified to suit a wide variety of modifications. Fuel mixture can be enriched or leaned as required. The Dyna FI controller uses the factory connectors for easy installation and there is no PC required for tuning or adjusting the fuel curves. There are no modifications required to the stock ECU and removing the Dyna FI controller returns the vehicle to the factory configuration.

VT No.	Fits	VT No.	Fits
32-3035	2007-09 XL 883	32-3036	2007-09 XL 1200

For late model Twins with carb, by Accel. Features faster rise time, higher voltage, maximum spark and energy to spark plugs for quicker starting, improved idle and crisper throttle response. Fits in OEM location. Black finish. Fits 2005-06 All XL models.

Late Model Super Coil

VT No. 32-1810

Dyna 2000 Ignition Modules

32-9123   32-1067   32-1068

For 2000- up Sportster models. Featuring programmable advance curves, rev limiter and LED diagnostic lamp for easy static timing. Plugs into stock harness and bolts to stock module location.

VT No.	Fits
32-9123	2004-07 w/ Carb
32-1067	2007- Up 883 w/ EFI
32-1068	2007- Up 1200 w/ EFI

CHARGING SYSTEM

Alternator Rotor by Volt Tech

32-9099

Features vibration proof magnet construction, as magnets are held in place by a stainless steel non-magnetic insert for durability. Unit includes sprocket. OE type has stock type magnets.

VT No.	Fits	Teeth
32-9099	1991-2003	35
32-0024	2004-Up	38
32-0030	2004-Up	34

Alternator Rotor Clutch Shell Assembly

Feature vibration proof magnet construction, as magnets are held in place by stainless steel non-magnetic insert for durability. Replaces 36791-84. Fits 1984-90. Bearing and ring gear included.

VT No. 18-8324

Stators

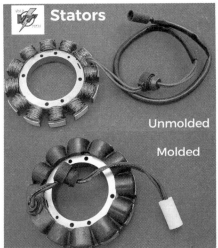

Unmolded

Molded

Stators replace stock units for models listed in molded or unmolded type. 32-0965 features heavy duty copper windings

32-0965

VT No.	Brand	Type
1985-89 XL, Replaces 29967-84A, 19 Amp		
32-7566	Volt Tech	Unmolded.
32-9043	Accel	Unmolded
32-9044	Accel	Molded
1990-06 XL, Replaces 29967-89A, 22 Amp		
32-9230	Volt Tech	Unmolded
32-0965	Volt Tech	Unmolded
32-9046	Accel	Unmolded
2007-up XL, Replaces 29997-07A		
32-0958	Volt Tech	Unmolded

32-0472

Volt Tech 1991 - Up XL Charging System

Charging System for XL models. Complete kits include rotor, stator, regulator and all hardware necessary for complete installation.

VT No.	Fits	Teeth
32-0471	1991-93	35
32-0472	1994-03	35
32-0023	2004-Up	38
32-0025	2004-U	34

ELECTRIC 12

1984-90 XL Charging System

32-0473

Fits 1984-90 XL models with alternator in clutch drum. Kit includes alternator rotor clutch shell assembly with bearing and ring gear installed, which features vibration proof magnet construction, as magnets are held in place by stainless steel non-magnetic insert, stator and chrome regulator.

VT No. 32-0473

Charging System Kit for XL developed by V-Twin in 1995

Warranty

All Electrical Components sold as individual pieces or in kits are covered under our warranty "Replacement Only" Provision. All electrical related item part numbers begin with a 32 prefix. No credit will be issued for these items as they are exchange only.

REGULATOR

 A  B C D E

32-0684

32-0809

32-0989

32-0778

Volt Tech™ and Accel Solid State Regulators feature rugged aluminum alloy construction. Accel Brand available in chrome, alloy or black stock finish with polished top fins or Volt Tech's black or chrome finish. Provides more accurately regulated voltage under all electrical loads. All units listed carry the full replacement warranty by Accel or Volt Tech.

Accel Black	Accel Alloy	Accel Chrome	Volt Tech Black	Volt Tech Chrome	Dome Chrome	OEM	Lead	#	Fits
			32-0618	32-1532		All 6V	N/A	D	1958-64 XL-XLH-XLCH, Replaces Mechanical Regulator
32-8064	32-0607	32-0857	32-0619	32-0989		All 12V	N/A	D	1965-77 XL-XLH-XLCH,1958-69 FL-FLH replaces Mechanical Regulator
		32-0851	32-0617		32-0684	74504-78	5"	A	1977 XLCH, 78-81 XLH-XLCH-XLS 12V Gen.
		32-0853	32-0620	32-0032		74504-82	5"	B	1982-84 XL-XLS-XLX with 12V Gen., 1982-E84 uses 12V Gen., L1984 uses 12V Alt.and 74523-84A Reg.
32-8068		32-0854	32-7570	32-0782		74523-84A	29"	C	1984-90 XL 19 Amp. Alt.
32-8170		32-0855	32-9002	32-0798		74523-91/92	9"	C	1991-93 XL 22 Amp. Alt.
32-8171		32-1856	32-7530	32-0779		74523-92A			1992-93 XL
32-8172		32-1857	32-0669	32-0777		74523-94		C	1994-03 XL
		32-1858	32-0811	32-0809		74523-04		C	2004-06 XL 22 Amp
			32-0981	32-0982		74546-07A		E	2007 XL
			32-0980	32-0984		74711-08		E	2009-up XL

32-0623   32-0621   32-0626

Replica Mechanical Regulators

Replica mechanical regulators for generator systems. Each unit features heavy duty shock mounted steel bases, vibration resistant internal wire connections, fiber and mylar insulated pads and large diameter contact surfaces.

Note: A. Fits 1952-65 XLH
   B. Fits 1965-78 XLCH Kick Start
   C. Fits XLH 1967-78

VT No.	Chrome	OEM	Brand	Type	Note
	32-0763		Accel	6V 2 Brush	A
32-0623	32-0624	74510-47A	VT	6V 2 Brush	A
32-1209			Delco		
32-0626	32-0627	74511-65	Accel	12V Bosch	B
32-0625		74511-65	Bosch	12V Bosch Zinc	B
32-0621	32-0622	74510-64	Accel	12V Delco	C
32-0995			Delco	12V Delco	

Rectifier-Regulator Mount

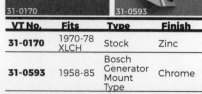
31-0170   31-0593

VT No.	Fits	Type	Finish
31-0170	1970-78 XLCH	Stock	Zinc
31-0593	1958-85	Bosch Generator Mount Type	Chrome

Chrome Solid State Regulator Mount bolts directly to 2 brush generator housings on BT and Sportsters. Fits Accel and V-Twin finned regulators.
VT No. 31-0207

42-0399

42-0402

42-0403

42-0442

Chrome Regulator Covers

VT No.	Type	Fits	Volt
42-0399	Module	1980-03	12
42-0403	Delco	Large	12
42-0402	Bosch	Center screw	12
42-0442	Delco	3 Brush	6
42-1047	Delco	Black	6

Chrome Voltage Regulator Cover

Features open center grill to allow for cooling of regulator. Fits 1985-03 XL.

VT No. 42-0453

32-0067   32-0071

"Look-a-Like" Relay

Exact shape and size of earlier 6V relay and mounts the same. Electronic design will function with 2 brush generators.

VT No.	Type	VT No.	Type
32-0071	12V	32-0067	6V

Solid State Generator Regulator

Features die-cast chrome end cover which mounts to all 1965-77, 12 Volt, 2 brush generators. Small solid state regulators fits behind cover for a clean look.

VT No. 32-7757

Mallory Unilite Distributor

Includes gear. Features 12V electronic performance dual fire type. No external box required. Electronic ignition module fits inside distributor. Adjustable advance limit, using spring kit pre 1970. Use with low resistance coils as low as 2 ohms for greater spark energy. No points to adjust or replace. Use larger spark plug gaps up to .040. Billet aluminum housing. Top may be removed without removal of front cylinder head.

VT No.	Item	Year
32-0174	Mallory Distributor XL	1952-70
32-5119	Mallory Ignition Plate	1971-84
32-7792	Dyna Coil	3 OHM
42-0442	Delco	3 Brush
42-1047	Delco	Black

Distributor Hold Down Clamp
31-3966

Replica Generator Armatures
32-0222
32-0224

Replica Generator Armatures feature heavy copper windings on precision shafts with solid copper commutator.

VT No.	OEM	Volt	Fits	Brand
32-0224	30851-65A	12V	1965-80	Accel
32-0226	30851-58	6V	1958-60	VT
32-0222	30851-65A	12V	1965-80	VT

Replica 2 Brush Field Coils

Feature warp-free laminates and heavy copper core winding. Matched pair with lead.

VT No.	OEM	Type	Volt
32-0229	30201-58A	58/61	6V
32-7599	30201-65	65	12V

Generator End Brush Band

VT No.	Finish	
32-0199	Chrome	For 1966-80 2-brush
32-0200	Black	generators replaces 30475-66 with bolt.

Generator Terminal Nuts

Replace 7634, on all generators 1930-up, 10 pack.

VT No.	Type
12-0572	Brass
12-0581	Steel with star washer

2-Brush Generator Components

VT No.	OEM	Item
32-0164	30012-58	Bolt (2)
32-0234	30426-58	Brush Set
32-0231	29913-82	Brush Set, Hitachi
12-0581	7634	Terminal Nut
12-2120	30280-58	Pole Screw
32-0209	30350-58	6 Volt Brush Holder
32-0210	30450-66	12 Volt Brush Holder
13-0117	30453-58	Brush Spring, 10 pack
12-0302	9005	Brush End Bearing
12-0303	9007	Gear End Bearing
12-0304	9007	As Above (Open)
10-2553	30148-58	Comm End Cover Bushing
12-0319	9064	End Cover Bearing
12-0902	11004	Front Retaining Ring
14-0112	30145-46A	1958-69 Large Seal

Generator Rebuild Kit

Complete as shown, all small parts necessary for rebuilding a 6 or 12 Volt, 2-Brush Generator.

VT No. 32-0431

DISTRIBUTOR

Chrome Auto Advance Distributors

Completely assembled with gear and all internal parts. The XLH type fits 1952-70 Sportster models and requires VT No. 31-3966 hold down.

VT No.	OEM	Years	Type
32-7558	32506-70	1952-70 XLH	Complete
42-0300	32589-65	1965-70	Top Only
31-3966	32515-66	1952-70 XL	Clamp

32-7558

Mallory Electronic Advance Distributor

Rev limiting for 1952-70 Sportster models. Adjustable electronic advance curves, single on dual fire modes and CNC machined billet housing. Use with 3 ohm coil.

32-7804

ELECTRIC 12

2-Brush 1958-69

Generator terminal kits include nuts and insulators.

VT No. 2127-11

2-Brush Hardware

2 Brush Generator Hardware Kits include gaskets and replacement hardware as shown.

VT No. 32-0227

32-0217   32-0219

Generator Parts

VT No.	OEM	Item	Year
32-0217	31035-58	Oil Deflector	1958-81
32-0219	31067-63	Washer	1958-69

Brush Sets

32-0234

VT No.	OEM	Fits	Model
32-0234	30426-58	1958-80	2Brush
32-0231*	29913-82	1981-84	Hitachi

*Note: V-Twin Replica

Generator Mount Gaskets

VT No.	Fits	U/M
15-0150	1958-69	10pk
15-0565	1958-69	Gary Bang, pr.

Hitachi Style Generator Parts

Parts for 1977-E84 models as a high output unit.

VT No.	OEM	Item
N/A	29978-77A	Generator Complete
N/A	29920-82	Armature
N/A	29922-82	Field Coils
10-8542	29907-82	Thrust Washer .004
10-8543	29908-82	Thrust Washer .010
10-8544	29909-82	Thrust Washer .020
10-8545	29910-82	Thrust Washer .039
14-0627	29911-82	Oil Seal
32-0231	29913-82	Brush Set
15-1023	30143-58	Gasket
32-0221	31073-63A	Drive Gear, 14T
42-0522	31599-82	Chrome End Cover

GENERATOR

2-Brush Generators

By Cycle Electric or Volt Tech brand with built in regulators. All styles fit 1952-81 XL. Order gear kits separately. VT No.s 32-9000, 32-0788 and 32-0789 in addition to models noted above will also replace Hitachi generator on 1981-E85 XL models. Order VT No. 32-0983 for gear kit to complete the installation. Units noted as low output for use with VT No. 53-0505 mini 12V battery.

32-0787

32-0790

VT No.	Volt	Type	Finish	Brand
32-0212	12V	Low Output	Black	CE
32-0790	12V	Low Output	Black	VT
32-0787	12V	Low Output	Chrome	VT
32-9000	12V	High Output	Black	CE
32-0788	12V	High Output	Black	VT
32-0789	12V	High Output	Chrome	VT
32-9001	6V	Standard	Black	CE
32-0983	XL	Gear Kit 14T		

Generator Screws

VT No.	Year	Finish	Type
8877-2	1957-70	Chrome	Stock
8878-2	1957-70	Cadmium	Stock
9457-2	1957-70	Chrome	Allen
7154-2	1971-84	Chrome	Allen
8787-2	1971-84	Chrome	Allen
9880-2	1971-84	Chrome	Stock
9881-2	1971-84	Zinc	Stock

Stock

Generator Gear Kit

Available as complete installation kit. Kits include gear, deflector nuts and proper pieces for each application. Fits 1959-81. 14 Teeth.

VT No.	Item	VT No.	Item
32-0983	Kit	32-0221	Gear Only

32-0983

ALTERNATOR CONVERSION KIT

32-0371

32-0390

32-0372

Alternator conversion kit replaces original generator and regulator. Compact high output alternator 3-1/4" long, weighs only 3lbs. Features include high power output, 17 amp@1000RPM, billet housing for strength and accurate alignment, and stress proof shaft is stronger than stock. Includes alternator unit in chrome or black, black voltage regulator and instructions. Fits 12V 1965-83 XL, pre 1965 which have been converted to 12V electric. May be used on earlier models if generator bolt holes are drilled out to 5/16". Cannot be used with mini (12N55A-3B) battery.

VT No.	Item	VT No.	Item
32-7528	Complete Kit, Black Alt/ Black Reg	32-0372	Chrome Alternator
32-0390	Complete Kit, Chrome Alt/ Black Reg	32-0667	Replacement Black Regulator
32-0371	Black Alternator	31-0172	Regulator Mount Bracket

32-0207

32-0967

2-Brush Generator by Cycle Electric or Volt Tech

All styles fit 1952-81. Order gear kit separately.

VT No.	OEM	Volts	Type	Finish
32-8999		12V	VT	Black
32-8998		12V	VT	Chrome
32-7526	29975-65A	12V	CE	Black
32-0967	29975-65A	12V	VT	Black
32-0207	29975-65A	12V	VT	Chrome
32-1530	With gear	12V	VT	Chrome
32-0213	29975-61A	6V	CE	Black
32-0214	29975-61A	6V	VT	Black

Regulator End Cover

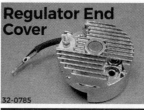

32-0785

Features solid state components in generator end cover. Cover with needle bearing installed black with fins for all 29975-65A 12 volt and 29975-61A generators.

VT No.	Volt	Finish	Brand
32-7768	12V	Black	CE
32-0795	12V	Black	VT
32-0785	12V	Chrome	VT
32-0969	12V	Built in Indicator	VT
32-0970	12V	Built in indicator	VT

VT No.	Type
32-7762	12V Low Output
32-7758	12V High Output

Regulator End Cover by Cycle Electric. Replacement units for generators VT No. 32-9000 12 Volt High Output, VT No. 32-9001 6 Volt and VT No. 32-0212.

Warranty Information

Volt Tech Brand Electrical Products Warranty claims are serviced through our Missouri Facility. Cycle Electric warranty claims are returned to Cycle Electric Co in Ohio. Allow extra time for these claims. All electric items will be repaired & replaced at manufacturer's discretion, no credit will be issued for these returns.

Alternator Conversion for Sportsters

32-1671

32-1673

32-1674

32-1676

VT No.	Item	Year	VT No.	Item	Year
32-1671	Black	1971-83	32-1674	Chrome	1971-83
32-1673	Chrome	1958-70	32-1676	Black	1958-70

MAGNETO

32-1311

32-1314
32-1801

32-7784

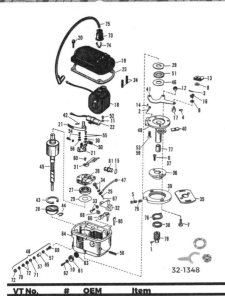

32-1765

32-1807

32-0976

32-1348
32-1229

32-0971

32-1045

VT No.	#	OEM	Item
32-0029	1	255	Pin, Drive Gear
12-1112	2	491	Pin, Tachometer Plug
37-8660	3	510	Cotter Pin 1/16" x 1/2"
32-1027	5	1074W	Screw, No. 8-32 x 7/8" Fillister
32-1029	7	3791	Bolt, 1/4-28 x 3/4 Hex Head (2)
37-1020	8	6107B	Washer, 5/16 x 11/16 x 1/8
37-1021	9	6165	Washer, 3/16 x 3/8 x 1/32
37-1022	10	7010	Lockwasher, No. 6
37-8917			Lockwasher, No. 8, & Screws, 25pk
37-1024	12	7683	Nut, 1/4-28 (2)
31-1031	13	9958	Clamp, on tappet guide
31-1030		9994	Clamp, on crankcase stud
31-1032	14	11024	Spring Clip, tachometer plug pin
14-0506	15	11110	O-ring, tachometer plug
13-0157	16	27291-32	Spring, wire block
2658-5	17	27450-36	Wire Block, magneto control
32-0716	18	29524-55A	Coil
32-0645	19	29530-55A	Cover, Black, each
32-0644		29530-55A	Cover, Clear, each
32-1564		29530-55A	Cover, Red, each
37-1025	20	29531-55	Screw, magneto cover (4)
32-0119	21	29533-55A	Circuit Breaker Points Set
32-0122	22	29534-55A	Condenser Only
15-0149	23	29550-55	Magneto Cover Gasket
32-0266	26		Bearing Support Kit
32-1800	26	29561-55	Bearing Support, right hand
32-0026	27	29562-55	Rotor Cam End Bearing
32-0027	28	29563-55	Bearing, rotor shaft end
37-1026	29	29564-55A	Washer
37-1027	30	29565-55	Contact Screw Washer (2)
32-0028	32	29590-62	Primary Insulator Block Kit for ground
37-1028	33	29591-62	Insulating Block Screw and Washer Set
37-1029	34	29593-62	Ground Wire to Block Screw and Washer
32-1292	35	29600-48	Magneto Base Adapter Plate
32-0646	35	29600-62	Magneto Base Adapter Plate
32-0515	36	29600-65C	Magneto Base Adapter Plate
37-1030	37	29601-48	Magneto Adapter Screw (2)
14-0528	38	29603-48	Timer Seal Ring Housing (5)
32-0516	39	29604-65	Magneto Advance Lower Adapter Plate
37-1031	40	29607-62	Washer, magneto adapter (2)
36-0514			Tach Cable Driven Gear
31-0485	41	29607-65	Magneto Control Arm
31-1033	42	29620-55	Breaker Spring Clip
12-1113	43	29621-55	Rotor shaft end Shaft End Snap Ring
31-1034	44	29622-55A	Rotor shaft end Spring Clip
32-2110	45	29623-55A	Magneto Rotor Assembly with Hex drive
37-1032	46	29624-55	Washer, rotor shaft end
32-0079	47	29625-55	Ground Terminal Wire
32-0080		29625-62	Ground Terminal Wire
32-0081	48	29626-55	Ground Terminal Assembly
32-0082	49	29626-62	Drive Housing and Screws
32-0036	50	29628-55	Wick and Holder
32-0037		29629-55	Breaker Arm Wick
14-0166	51	29630-55	Rotor Shaft End Seal
15-1539		29631-55	Magneto Gasket Kit
37-1033	52	29632-55	Condenser Mount Screw
2884-6	53	29632-66	Magneto Adapter Plate Screw Kit
37-1035	54	29633-55	Breaker Arm Screw and Washer (2)
37-1036		29633-62	Breaker Arm Screw and Washer (2)
37-1037	55	29634-55	Breaker Arm Contact Screw and Washer
37-1038	56	29635-55	Breaker Arm Washer
37-1039	57	29635-62	Ground Terminal Washer (2)
37-1040	58	29636-55	Coil Set Screw (2)
37-1041	59	29632-62	Taper Screw Set (4)

VT No.	#	OEM	Item
37-1042	60	29638-55	Safety Gap Plate Screw
32-1002	61	29639-55	Vent Cover
37-1043	62	29640-55	Vent Cover Screw
32-1018	63	29641-55	Vent Screen
32-1229			Mount Kit
32-1801		29642-62	Magneto Housing w/o Keylock Provision
32-1805		29642-62	Magneto Housing w/ Keylock Provision
32-1022	65	29645-62	Ground Terminal Bushing
32-0073	66	29646-62	Ignition Ground Lock & Keys Kit
32-1037	67	29647-62	Ground Switch Ball
32-1033	68	29648-62	Ground Lock Retainer Clip
37-1046	69	29657-62	Ground Terminal Screw
37-1047	70	29658-62	Ground Terminal Lockwasher
37-1048	71	29659-62	Lockwasher, ground terminal, int. tooth
37-1044	72	29660-62	Nut, ground terminal (3)
15-0154	76	32522-37	Adapter Plate Gasket
15-1031	76	32522-37	Adapter Plate Gasket
10-0717	77	32525-36A	Bushing, drive housing
32-0198	78	32531-36	Drive Gear
32-0077	80	71626-62	Ground Switch Lock Key
32-1034	81	92077-62	Tach Plug and O-Ring
36-0513		92077-62	Tach Cable 1965-1969
32-1348			Adapter Plate Set (3 pc)
14-0107		12023	Magneto Base Plate Seal
32-0976			Magneto Rebuild Kit
32-1045			Tag, Points, Condenser Kit
32-1346			Magneto Base and Gear
32-1807			Magneto Tach Plug Kit
32-0971			Drive Kit
32-1057		29534-55A	Condenser
12-0181		29562-55, 29563-55	Bearing Set
12-1114			Race
13-9208			Coil Springs, 10 pack
32-7784			Lighting Capacitor
32-0116			Points and Condenser Kit
15-1020			Top Gasket
15-0972			Magneto Neoprene Cap Gasket
32-0064			Screw Kit
32-1038			Metal Morse Tag
32-1081			Kill Button
32-1563			Kill Button Kit, 1959-70
32-1082			Bearing Kit
32-1102			Drive 1971-80
32-1247			Rotor and Magneto Shaft Assembly
32-1255			Angle Drive
32-1347			Base 1971-80
32-1490			Magneto Base
32-1664			Adapter Plate
32-0823			Cast Base
32-1284			Terminal Kit
32-1293			Magneto Base Mount Kit
32-1345			Magneto Base Kit
32-1298			Magneto Body
37-1030			Magneto Advance Screw
32-1425			Magneto Name Tag
32-1314			Insulator Block
32-0269			Rotor Kit
32-1146			Kill Switch Kit
32-1232			Magneto Ignition Points and Condenser Kit
32-1453			Kill Switch Kit
32-1563			Kill Switch Kit
32-1766			Vent Cap Kit (2)

32-1788

32-1298

32-0644

32-0645

32-0269

32-1346

32-0116

MAGNETOS

Burkhardt Magneto Head with Key Lock

With right hand rotation features internal female hex drive on rotors to fit all Joe Hunt, Morris and Fairbanks Morse drive units. This complete head is with key lock, ready to spark and start! OE look and construction. Magneto grounding stud for kill switch is located on the left side when facing the two spark wire terminals. The die cast magneto body comes with magnetic laminates cast in place as original. Order drive assembly separately. Fits XL 1957-1970.

32-1309

32-1302

32-0285

32-1305

32-1863

32-1358

32-1345

32-1276

For Sportsters.

Magneto Assembly

With right hand rotation features internal female hex drive on rotors to fit all Joe Hunt, Morris and Fairbanks Morse drive units.

VT No. 32-1311

VT No.	Year	Brand
32-1678	1957-1964	Base Drive Assembly Kit
32-1276	1957-64	Direct Drive
32-0285	1965-70	Direct Drive
32-1869	1957-70	Burkhardt
32-1302	1971-80	Joe Hunt
32-1305	1971-80	Burkhardt
32-1863	1971-80	Burkhardt
32-1346	1957-70	Shaft Assembly
32-1680	1957-70	Shaft Assembly, cad
32-1358	1971-80	Shaft Assembly

Shaft Assembly		
VT No.	Year	Item
32-1490	1957-70	Base

MAGNETO REBUILDS

Got a Good Body with Good Magnets...? We Can Rebuild!

Our Motor Shop will completely rebuild Joe Hunt, Fairbanks Morse or Morris Magnetos. We stock the most complete selection of replacement components.

VT No. 60-1957

Magneto Cloth Patches

48-1603

48-2292

48-0472

48-1772

Can be sewn or ironed on. Sold as a pair.

VT No.	Design	VT No.	Design
48-2292	Vertical	48-1772	Vintage Hunt
48-0472	Rectangular Hunt	48-1603	Burkhardt

Forged Aluminum Magneto Cap

Features a recessed design to hold gasket in place and features a natural finish with Burkhardt logo.

VT No. 32-0284

MAGNETO FOR XL

32-1788

32-1297

32-1490

32-1276

VT No.	Item
32-1788	Burkhardt
32-1276	Burkhardt
32-1297	Hunt
32-1490	Base Drive Assembly
32-1783	Base Kit

36-0873   36-0514   36-2549

VT No.	OEM	Item	Years	Type
36-0873	Set	Gear and Cable		
36-0514	92063-63	Gear	1962-70	Magneto
36-0513	92065-67A	Cable	1965-69	Magneto
36-2575	92062-65A	Cable	1965-69	XLH Dist.
36-0990	92065-70	Cable	1970-73	XLH-XLCH
36-2549	92097-71	Drive	1971-80	XLH-XLCH
12-1400	25517-71	Drive Gear for Cam	1971-80	XLH-XLCH
36-0991	92065-74	Cable	1974-80	XLH-XLCH
36-2573	As Above	Cable	Stainless	XLH-XLCH
36-0999	+6"	Cable	1974-80	XLH-XLCH

Magneto Drive and Base Kit

Use on 1957-70 XL. Kit will accept hex drive Magneto. Includes cast base, gear, pin, shaft, mount plate, tachometer drive plug, shouldered mount bolts, seal and gasket.
VT No. 32-1293

Magneto Drive and Gear Kit

Use on 1957-70 XL. Magneto kit features a drive shaft with hex end and spiral grooves for tachometer drive. Also includes drive gear and pin. Kit is for use with Fairbanks Morse type case base.

VT No.	VT No.
32-0584	32-1566

TACHOMETER

Stock Genuine Early Tachometer

39-0321   39-0762

Use on 1965-73 XLH-XCH 0-8,000 RPM. Mounts in 3-1/4" dia. hole. Replaces 92051-65. Use cable VT No. 36-0990, which will connect this tach for use on all model XL, 1971-80 with mechanical tach drive.

VT No.	Fits	Item
39-0321	1965-73	OE Tachometer
39-0762	1971-72	Tach Kit 2:1 ratio for cable drive off cam cover
39-0763	1971-73	Kit
36-0990	1971-80	29-1/2" Distributor Drive Tach Cable
36-0980	1965-69	29-1/2" Magneto Black Tach Cable

STARTER MOTOR & RELAY

MOTOR

32-7760

32-7761

Hitachi Type Starters

Replicas for 1974-76. Parts interchange with original. 5" overall body length.

VT No.	Fits	Brand
32-7760	31570-73	Complete, Black
32-1307		Complete, Black
32-7761	31570-73	Complete, Chrome
32-0306	31580-73	Armature
32-7769	31575-81	Brush Set, 1981-90 XL
32-0307	31582-73	Brush Set
32-0308	31579-73	Field Coils
32-0059	31576-73	Thru Bolts
12-0347	31583-73	Bearing, Drive End

1.4 KW

32-5123

32-5121

High Torque Starter Motor

Features 1.4 kw design that generates more power and shaft speed than original type .8 kw starter.

VT No.	Finish	Type	VT No.	Finish	Type
32-5122	Black	Hitachi	32-5120	Black	Prestolite
32-5123	Chrome	Hitachi	32-5121	Chrome	Prestolite
			32-1634	Black	V-Twin

32-7524

32-7525

32-1308

32-0303

Prestolite Type Starter Motor

Replaces Prestolite starter used on 1967-73 XL, 1977-80 XL models. Chromed unit is completely chromed. 6" overall body length.

VT No.	OEM	Item	VT No.	OEM	Item
32-7524	31458-66A	Complete, Chrome	32-0680	31540-66	Field Coil Set
32-7525	31458-66A	Complete, Black	32-0592	31535-66	Thru Bolts
32-1308		Complete, Black	12-0325	31539-66	Bearing
32-0303	31542-66	Armature			

RELAY

A	B	C	D
32-0640	32-0641	32-0642	32-0738

E	F		G
32-9076	32-7783	32-0185	32-0737

32-8036	32-8041	32-0740	32-8042	32-0643

VT No.	#	OEM	Fits	Brand
32-0640	A	71463-73A	1975-79 XL	Accel
32-0641	B	71463-73A	1975-79 XL	VT, Replica
32-0642	C	31506-79	1980-90 All	
32-0738	D		1980-90 All	w/ weatherproof skirt
32-9076	E	31504-91A	1991-04 XL	
32-0643		71455-67	1967- E 68, L 1971-74 XL	
32-0185	F	71455-67	1967- E 68	
32-0768	G	31601-04	2005-Up XL	

Starter Relay Connectors

VT No.	OEM	Fits
32-8036	72046-79C	1979- Up, all Twins
32-8041	4-Lug	1973-78 all Twins, when using 1979-90 type starter relay.
32-8042	5-Lug	1973-78 all Twins, when using 1979-90 type starter relay.

Note: 32-8036 includes crimp style connector ends and 32-8041 and 32-8042 includes pigtail harness.

Start Boost Relay

Reduces 12v voltage drop in single fire ignition applications during cranking. Will allow full battery voltage to the module and coil.

VT No. 32-3000

Starter Brush Spring,1973-Up Hitachi Starter Motors

VT No.	OEM	Years
13-0223	31593-73	1973-80
13-9157	31557-81	1981-up, Compression
13-9220	31600-90	1990-up, Starter Clutch Assy

13-0223

Starter Motor Clamp

31-0099

Fits 1973-80. Replaces 31473-67 in stainless.

Hitachi Starter Hardware

Brushes, holder, springs, thru bolts and insulator commutator end bushing for 1973-80.
VT No. 32-0553

Starter Solenoid

Replaces 71469-65 on 1967-80.

32-0633   32-0699   32-0632

VT No.	Brand	Finish	VT No.	Brand	Finish
32-0699	Volt Tech	Zinc	32-0632	Accel	Chrome
32-0633	Accel	Zinc	32-1021	Volt Tech	Chrome

32-0698

Fits 1967-80. Kit includes chrome or zinc solenoid, outer & inner rubber boot, foam gasket, bolts & spacer.

Starter Solenoid Kit

VT No.	Finish
32-0697	Zinc
32-0698	Chrome

42-1034   28-0117

Chrome Solenoid End Cover

Order roller boots separately.

VT No.	Item
42-1034	Cover
28-0117	Boot
42-0400	Cover

Solenoid Plunger Hardware

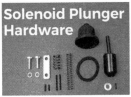

Fits 1967-80 solenoids.
VT No. 32-7571

Starter Block Plate fits 1970-78 XLCH, 1970-78 XLH when starter assembly is removed. Replaces 31460-70.

VT No. 31-0126

42-0413   42-0412   42-0410

Chrome Starter Motor Covers

VT No.	OEM	Type	Model
42-0413	31565-67	End	Prestolite 1967-80 XL, FL Hitachi 1973-80 XL
42-0412	31350-83T	Wrap Long	Prestolite 1966-82 FL, 1967-80 XLH
42-0410	31351-83T	Wrap Short	Hitachi 1974-E 76 XLH

Starter Housing

VT No.	Type
43-9132	1967-72 Prestolite
43-9133	1973-78 Hitachi
12-0317	Needle Bearing
15-0152	Gasket

Needle bearing sold separately.

Starter Ring Gears

18-3640   18-3645

VT No.	Fits	Teeth
18-3640	1967-80	62
18-3645	1981-E84	78
18-3646	1984 1/2 - 1990	78
18-3647	1991- Up	78

Replacement on stock clutch drums only. Must be welded on. Note: Bevel edge is for welding (outside) teeth side.

1967-80 XL Starter Shaft Assembly.
Order starter drive separately.
VT No. 17-0243

STARTER

XLH Starter Parts

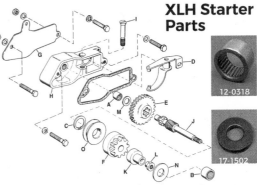

12-0318

17-1502

Parts listed fit 1967-80 XLH electric start Sportsters.

17-0083

17-1504

43-9155

VT No.	#	OEM	Item
43-9155	Kit	Prestolite	A-O, except G
43-9154	Kit	Hitachi	A-O, except G
12-0317	A	9062	Bearing
12-0318	B	9063	Bearing
17-1501	D	31424-67	Lever
14-0080	E	31429-67	Gear
32-0639	F	31443-65A	Bendix Drive
31-0126	G	31460-70	Block Off Plate
43-9132	H	31462-67	Housing, Prestolite
43-9133	H	31462-74	Housing, Hitachi
17-1500	I	31478-67	Bolt
17-0083	J	31483-67	Shaft
17-0082	K	31490-67	Spacer
17-0081	L	31493-67	Nut
17-0093	L,K	Kit	Nut, Spacer
17-1503	M	31501-65	Washer
17-1504	N	31502-65	Washer
17-1502	O	31503-65	Collar
17-1512	Kit		C,K,L,M,N

Starter Gaskets

15-0215   15-0181

15-0243

GB No.	James	OEM	Fits
15-0151	15-1026	31461-70	1970-E79 XLCH Starter Housing to Primary Mount
15-0152	15-1027	31471-67A	1967-80 Starter Housing to Primary Mount
15-0215	15-1028	31488-77	1967-80 Starter Body to Housing Mount
15-0243	15-1029	31488-81	1981-2000 Starter Mounting
15-0181	15-0917	60645-65	1967-80 Solenoid

1967-80 XL ELECTRIC START

XLH Electric Start Kits include parts pictured to fit 1967-80 XL. Your existing clutch drum must have starter ring gear attached. Side mount electric start oil tank 40-0400 must be purchased when fitted to 1971-80 models. Kick and electric start sprocket cover must be used if kick start is to be retained. Battery, top cover and strap not included. Also available with chrome starter motor.

V-Twin Developed Starter Kits for XL in 1981.

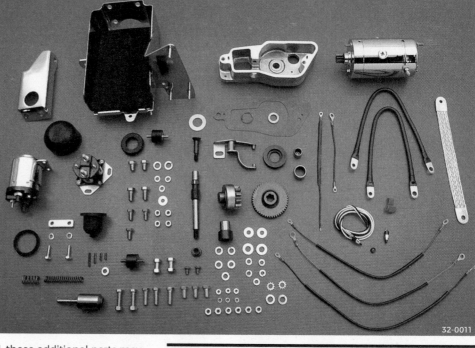

32-0011

For XLH Electric Start Kits listed, these additional parts may be required. Note: 28-2217 is rubber strap only.

Year	Battery Side Cover	Sprocket Cover Chrome	Sprocket Cover Polished	Battery Top and Strap
1967-70	42-0509		43-0114	42-5514
1971-76	42-0509	43-0180	43-0118	42-5514
1977-78	42-0509	43-0144	43-0112	42-5514
1979	42-0504	43-0177	43-0119	28-2217
1980	42-0503	43-0152	43-0120	28-2217

Black	Chrome	Model	Type
32-0002*	32-0010*	Prestolite	1971-78 XLH
32-0003*	32-0011*	Hitachi	1971-78 XLH
32-0006	32-0012	Hitachi	1979-80 XLH

*Note: Can also be used 1967-70 models but engine cases must be electric start type as kits can be used for replacement only for these years.

STARTER DRIVES

32-0638

32-9032

32-2506

32-9031

32-0639

Starter drive features high strength five roller clutch, stainless steel springs, hardened ramped clutch receivers, premium bronze bushing, and factory pre-lubing.

VT No.	Item	Fits	Brand
32-0638	31443-65A	1967-80 All	Accel Heavy
32-0639	31443-65A	1967-80 All	Volt Tech
32-2506	31443-65A	1967-80 All	Volt Tech Heavy Duty
32-9032*	31567-81	1981-90	OE
32-9031	31663-90	1991-up 1200	With bearing

*Note: Drive Assemblies

32-0964

Starter Clutch Drive Kit

Includes clutch drive, O-ring, lock tab, seals, spring and cable boot. Fits 1991-up.

VT No. 32-0964

Starter Motor Replacement Parts		
VT No.	OEM	Fits
12-9994	8882	1989-90 Commutator End
12-9996	8883	1991- Up Commutator End
12-9995	8871	1991- Up Gear End
13-9220	31600-90	1991- Up Plunger Spring
13-9219	31692-90	1991- Up Clutch

12-9994

12-9995

13-9220

Chrome Starter Cover

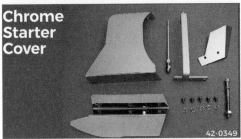

Completely cover the top of the right side of starter motor. 42-0347 covers the end of starter and solenoid only.

VT No.	Fits	Type
42-0347	1981-90	1-piece
42-0349	1991-2003	3-piece

Chrome Generator Covers

VT No.	Fits	Type
42-0414	2 Brush, End	1958-81
42-0522	Hitachi, End	1982-84
42-0406	2 Brush, Body Wrap	1958-81

Push Button Starter End Cap

VT No.	Finish	VT No.	Finish
32-0742	Chrome	32-1195	Black

Chrome Starter Solenoid Plate
Replaces 31688-90. Fits 1994-up XL models.
VT No. 32-7798

1991-UP STARTER

Chrome Starter Assembly

Features built in button for remote starting. Unit has polished aluminum parts and chrome steel parts. Fits 1981-07 XL.
VT No. 32-5127

ELECTRIC
12

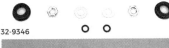

32-9346

32-9347

32-5124

32-5125

1981-Up High Torque Starter Motor by Volt Tech

Available with 1.4 kw field wound. Stock starter motor is 1.2 kw field wound type. Chrome units have all aluminum parts, polished and all steel parts chrome plated. All units are supplied with jackshaft bolt.

VT No.	Finish	VT No.	Finish
32-5124	Black	32-5125	Chrome

*Note: Provides 15% greater torque over stock starter motor.

Stock Black Starter Motor and Parts

VT No.	OEM	Fits	Item
32-9072	31390-91B	1991-Up XL	Motor, Complete
32-9075	31546-81	1981-94 883 1981-90 1100 1981-90 1200	Solenoid Assembly
32-9346	31605-90	1981-94 883 1981-90 1200	Solenoid Repair Kit
32-9347	31603-91	1991-Up 1200	Solenoid Repair Kit
32-7769	31575-81	1981-90 XL	Brush Set

IGNITION

32-0161   32-1100   32-1267

32-0175   32-1099   32-0416

Chrome Stock Key Switch for ignition and light switch for Sportster, replaces 71425-77 & 70124-75. Includes two keys and mounting ring.

VT No.	Type	Year
32-0161	Replica	1977-98
32-0416	Stock Type	1977-98
32-1099	As Above Cam Lock	
32-0175	Replica	1973-76
32-1100	As Above Cam Lock	
32-1267	Off/On	Start

Chrome Switch Cover

Fits 1972-87 models.

VT No. 42-0330

42-0648   42-0935

Ignition Switch Covers

Chrome finish. Fits 1995-up models. Includes decal.

VT No.	Years
42-0648	1995-2003
42-0935	2004-2013

Universal Key Switch

Includes mounting ring and two keys.

32-0415

32-0478

32-0479

VT No.	Type
32-0415	On-Off-On
32-0478	Off-On-Start
32-0479	Off-On-On
32-0420	Off-On-On
32-1236	Lock/Key

Barrel Key Ignition Switch

Features round style keys. Two position activation with positive detent to retain key in the off position. Fits 1973-94. Run position with lights off.

VT No. 32-9053

Universal Toggle Switch

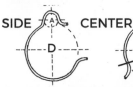

32-0423   32-9030

VT No.	Type
32-0423	On/Off with leads
32-9030	Spotlamp On/Off w/o leads

Shrink Wrap Tubing

Easy to use. Cut to length, thread the wires, carefully apply heat and watch the insulation shrink to a perfect fit.

VT No.	Inner Dia.	Length
32-0124	1/4"	4 ft.
32-0125	3/8"	4 ft.
32-8039	5/8"	4 ft.

SIDE   CENTER

Control Cable/Wire Clamps

Zinc plated spring steel, 10pk.
"D" is the diameter of the tube it fits.
"A" is the size wire/loom that is secures.

VT No.	D-Tube Size	A-Wire Size
37-8677	1" Side	3/16" - 7/32"
37-8678	1-1/4" Side	3/16" - 7/32"
37-8679	1" Center	3/16" - 7/32"
37-8680	1" Center	5/16"
37-8681	1-1/8" Center	5/16"

Chrome Handlebar Wiring Clips

36-0614

Snap into handlebars with holes at bends, 10 pk.

VT No.	OEM	Size. Inner Dia.
36-0613	56073-83	3/8"
36-0614	70345-84	1/2"

Circuit Breaker
Stock replacements.

32-0412

32-0414   32-0436

32-8921

37-9069   31-9964   12-0581

31-9952   32-8922   32-8945

32-0413

VT No.	#	OEM	Amp	Fits
32-0414	A	74589-73	15	1973-up
32-0413	A	74599-77B	30	1978-up
32-0412	B	74594-71	20	1971-72 XL
32-0436	H	74587-94	15	1994-96
32-9207	A	74600-94	50	1994-up
32-8921	C	74598-73		Connector Bar, each
32-8922		69999-77		Connector Bar, each
32-8945		7/8" C/C		Connector Bar, pair
37-9069	D	7602		Nylon Nut, 10/32", 25 pack,
12-0581	E	7629		Nut, 10 pack
31-9952	F	9952		Mount Clip, 10 pack secures breaker or flasher to fender
31-9964	G	8672		Rivet for Above

32-8946   32-0410

In-Line Fuse Holder

With 6" long wire leads.

VT No.	Type
32-0410	Fuse
32-8946	ATC Type

WIRING

Wiring Kits feature plastic covered wires. All 1970-99 harness are available as complete "builders kit" with main harness, handlebar, tail lamp and starter wires, or as main harness.

XLH Electric Start 1970-1999

Complete Kit	Main Harness	OEM	Application
	32-9206	Starter	1967-80 XLH
32-7617	32-9010	70151-70	1970-72 XLH
32-7618	32-9059	70151-73	1973-74 XLH
32-7619	32-7554	70006-75	1975-76 XLH
32-7620	32-9304	70006-76	1977-Early 1978 XLH
32-7621	32-9209	70006-79	Late 1978-79 XL-XLS
32-7622	32-9210	70006-80	1980 XL-XLS
32-7623	32-9211	70006-81	1981 XL-XLS
32-7624	32-9212	70006-82	1982-E84 XL-XLS
32-7625	32-0721	70135-84	1984-85 XL-XLS
32-7626	32-0722	70135-86	1986-90 XL-XLS
	32-8929	70135-92A	1992-93 XLH
	32-8937	70135-97	1997 Standard, Hugger
	32-8939	70135-98	1998-99 Standard, Hugger

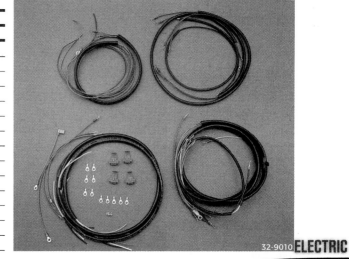

32-9010 **ELECTRIC**

12

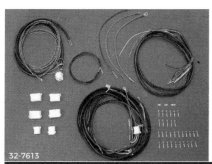

32-7613

XLCH Kickstart 1970-79

Note: Order the appropriate factory service manual to facilitate wire harness installation.

Auxiliary Harness for 1967-80, starter wire set.
VT No. 32-9206

Complete Kit	Main Harness	OEM	Application
32-7610	32-9283	70153-70	1970-E71 XLCH
32-7611	32-7577	70153-71	L1971-72 XLCH
32-7612	32-7578	70153-73	1973-74 XLCH
32-7613	32-0671	70001-75	1975-76 XLCH
32-7614	32-9305	70001-76	1977 XLCH
32-7615	32-7579	70001-78	1978 XLCH
32-7616	32-7580	70001-79	1979 XLCH

32-8011

1952-69 Wire Harness Kits

Feature cloth covered color-coded wire as original.

XLH Battery Type 1952-67

VT No.	OEM	Application
32-8011	70320-59	1959-64 XLH, 6V
32-7556	70320-65	1965-66 XLH, 12V
32-7557	70320-67	1967 Only XLH, Electric Start
32-7559	70320-68	1968-69 XLH, Electric Start

XLCH Magneto Type 1958-69

VT No.	OEM	Application
32-9057	70320-58	1958-64 XLCH
32-9058		1965-69 XLCH

PVC Covered Tail Light Wires

VT No.	Fits
32-9309	1970-72 XL-XLCH
32-9312	1973-77 XL, XLCH, 1982-84 XL
32-9313	1978 XL-XLCH
32-9314	1979-81 XL

Accessory Kits

VT No.	OEM	Type
32-9206		1967-80 XLH- Small Starter Wire Set, PVC
32-0323	70018-77	Relay to Solenoid Wire
32-0158	70169-70	Relay to Ground Wire
32-0163	70165-58	Battery Box to Ground 1965-69 BT

Electrical Terminal Plates

Pre-assembled for main junction which includes studs for mounting coil and auxiliary junction for headlamp wiring on 1970-74 XL headlamp. Replaces 72303-70.
VT No. 9817-15

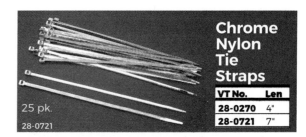

25 pk.

28-0721

Chrome Nylon Tie Straps

VT No.	Len
28-0270	4"
28-0721	7"

BATTERY

53-0547 53-0585

· LOCK BONDED PLATES
· STAINLESS STEEL TERMINAL BOLTS
· EXACT FIT

Sealed AGM Battery

Notes: AGM Batteries require charging prior to installation. 1998 and earlier XL models require battery side cover VT No. 42-0770 and top cover VT No. 42-0786.

"Absorbed Glass Mat" Technology provides higher cold cranking amps, better rechargeablity with longer overall life. Batteries are fully sealed for trouble free service in a black case.

VT No.	OEM	Fits
53-0547	65991-75C	1977-78 XLCR, 1979-96 XL
53-0585	65991-75	1973-84 FXE
53-0789	Dry	1997-2003 XL
53-0548	65958-04	2004-up XL

42-5515
42-9914
42-9951

Battery Carrier Kits

Fit stock frames with bracket & Iso-Mounts included as required. All units are chrome plated except where noted. Order battery top cover and strap kit as noted separately.

VT No.	Year	Model	Finish	Cover Kit
42-9951	1970-78	XLCH	Zinc	42-5515
42-9914	1967-78	XLH	Chrome	42-5514
	1994-03	XL	Black	42-5519

Chrome Battery Carrier Bracket

Fits 1967-78 XLH. Replaces 66480-67.
VT No. 31-0130

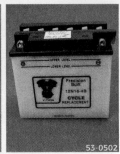

53-0501 53-0518 53-0502

1970-78 XLCH Kickstart Models (5-13/32" x 3" x 5-5/16")

VT No.	OEM	Type	Brand
53-0504	66006-70	12N7-4A	V-Twin
53-0515	66006-70		Yuasa Yumicron

1967-78 XLH Electric Start Models (8-1/8" x 5-1/4" x 6-1/2")

VT No.	OEM	Type	Brand
53-0501	66006-65A	H-12	V-Twin
53-0516			Yuasa
53-0532			Champion/Super Crank

1979-96 All XL, 1977-78 XLCR (7" x 4" x 6-1/4")

VT No.	OEM	Type	Brand
53-0502	65991-75C	12N16-4B	V-Twin, 16 amp
53-0517			Yuasa, Yumicron
53-0518			Yuasa, CX 19 amp

VT No.	OEM	Fits	Brand
53-0530	65989-97A	1997-03 All XL	V-Twin
53-0557	65958-04	2004- Up XL	V-Twin

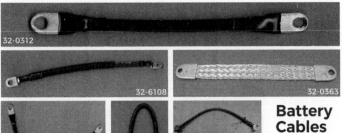

32-0312

32-6108 32-0363

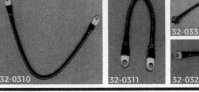

32-0310 32-0311 32-0325 32-0332

Battery Cables

Replacements of the originals with heat shielded terminal ends.

Negative

VT No.	OEM	Len	Application
32-0325	70011-81	8"	1981-85 All XL
32-0311	70097-75A	10-3/4"	1986-96 XL (POS.) 1975-79 XLH, 1979 XL
32-0324	70235-67A	9"	1967-72 XLH, Braided
32-0363	70235-67A	8.5"	1967-72 XLH, Braided
32-0312	70295-70	6-3/4"	1970-78 XLCH

Positive

VT No.	OEM	Len	Application
32-0315	70083-82A	15-3/4"	Pos. to solenoid, 1982-88 XL
32-0332	70076-89A	14-3/4"	Pos. to solenoid, 1989-96 XL

Miscellaneous

VT No.	OEM	Len	Application
32-0310	70069-65B	15-1/2"	Solenoid to Battery and Starter, 1967-75 XLH, 1982 XL

2 Gauge Cables

VT No.	Len	Application
32-2011	11" & 16"	1981-2003, Set
32-2012	12" & 13"	2004- Up, Set

BATTERY COVER KITS

 42-0504
 42-0770
 42-0714
 42-0503
 42-0542

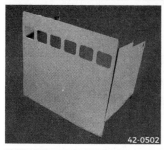 42-0502
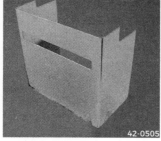 42-0505
 42-0509
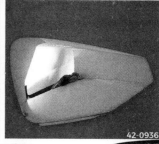 42-0936

 42-0511
 42-0513
 42-0936
 42-0512

Battery Covers
*Note: Fits AGM Battery.

Side Chrome	Top Chrome	Year/Model
42-0505	42-0512	1970-78 XLCH
42-0509	42-0513	1967-78 XLH
42-0504	42-0511	1979 XLH
42-0503	42-0511	1980-81 XLH

Side Chrome	Top Chrome	Year/Model
		1980-96 XLH
42-0502	42-0511	1982-up XLH
42-0714	42-0786	1997-up XLH
42-0770*	42-0786	1998-2003 XLH
42-0936		2004-13 XL

 A
 B
 C
 D
 A-1 28-0658   A-2 28-0636
 28-0749

Iso Mounting Rubber Studs
All types UNC threads 1/4" used on XL battery box and oil tank, 28-0619 used on FX dash

VT No.	OEM	#	Size	Type	QTY
28-0749	Hex	A-1	1/4"	Male-Male	2
28-0546	62563-65	A	1/4"	Male-Male	5
28-0549	62563-65T	A	1/4"	Male-Male	5
28-0418	w/ spring	A	1/4"	Male-Male	5
28-0636	Lord	A-2	1/4"	Male-Male	2
28-0547	62563-66	B	5/16"	Male-Male	Each
28-0402	62569-94	B	5/16 x 1/4"	XL Oil Tank	Each
28-0619	50235-63	C	5/16"	Male-Female	Each
28-2247	69125-65	D	5/16"	Male-Male, Horn	Each

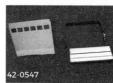 42-0547

2004- Up Left Side Battery Cover

VT No.	Fits
42-0936	2004-13 XLH
42-1041	2008-up XR

Chrome Battery Cover Kit
Includes both top and side covers with correct stainless steel strap. Note style of side cover.

*Note: Battery strap not included, top and side cover only.

VT No.	Fits	Style
42-0576	1998-03 XL	Slotted
42-0547	1991-97 XL	Slotted
42-0548	1982-90 XL	Slotted
42-0575	1979 Only XL	Smooth (Rubber)
42-0575	1980-81 XL	Smooth Note: Strap not included
42-0542*	1970-78 XLCH	Slotted
42-0557	1967-78 XLH	Ribbed

 Chrome XLH & K Battery Top replaces 66375-52 on 1952-64, 6-volt models. VT No. 42-0732

 Battery Top Cover and Strap Kit. Help save time by ordering the proper cover and hold down strap.

VT No.	Fits
42-5514	1967-78 XLH
42-5515	1970-84 XL Kick Only
42-5519	1997-03 XL

Replacement Battery Straps
 42-1211

VT No.	OEM	Application
28-2217	66105-77	1979 XL (Rubber)
42-0514	66470-67	1967-78 XLH
42-0515	66470-70	1970-78 XLCH
42-0524	66476-73A	1986-97 XL, XLS, XLX
42-0798	66476-98	1998-2003 XL
42-1211	66476-04A	2004-up XL

AIR CLEANER

Hi-Flow Air Cleaners

34-1280   34-1066

34-1374

34-1374 Installed

For 1988-up XL models. Cover not included.

VT No.	Item	Brand	Year
34-1077	Kit	OE	1988-2003
34-0734	Kit	K&N	2004-2006
34-1066	Element	OE	1988-2003
34-1187	Element	K&N	2004-2009
34-0559	Cover	VT	2004-Up
34-1374	Kit	VT	1988-2006
34-1464	Kit (Black)	VT	2007-Up
34-1304	Kit (Chrome)	VT	2007-Up

INTAKE 13

Complete Maltese Carburetor Cover Kit

34-0610

Includes brackets or breather kit as required. Order filter separately.

VT No.	Fits
34-1141	1991-Up
34-1142	1988-90
34-1143	1985-87
34-0608	1967-84
34-0160	S&S E
34-1168	Filter

Polished Maltese Air Cleaners

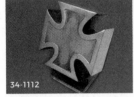

34-1112

Include backing plate as noted. Order filter and brackets separately.

VT No.	Type	VT No.	Type
34-1168	Filter	34-1112	Cover Only

Wyatt Gatling Air Cleaner

Includes bracket, filter element, breather bolts, and hardware. Fits 1991-Up XL.

VT No. 34-0491

Siren

Siren Air Cleaner Assembly fits 1991-up XL models. Includes chrome cover, backing plate and mounting hardware.

VT No. 34-1529

S&S Super E Complete Carburetor Kit

Fits 1979-1985 XL.

VT No. 35-0007

Chrome Velocity Stack

Kits include 2.5" chrome stack, chrome support bracket and breather kit with black or stainless hose kit as listed for stock Keihin or CV carburetors.

With Breather		Without Breather Kit		
Black Hose	SS Hose	Black Hose	SS Hose	Fits
34-1134	34-1124			1991-Up
		34-1119		1988-90
		34-1120		1985-87
		34-1126		S&S E + G
		34-1127		4" S&S E + G

V-Charger™ Chrome Air Cleaner

34-0582

Features air scoop "blower" design with built-in chrome screen and filter. Kits include brackets and/or breather kits as required.

VT No.	Type	Fits	VT No.	Type	Fits
34-0583	CV	1991-Up	34-0586	CV	1988-90
34-0589	Keihin	1986-87	34-0588	Keihin-Bendix	1957-85
34-0616	S&S	E	34-1070	Filter	All

Chrome Teardrop Air Cleaner

Kit includes backing plate, filter, breather brackets and teardrop cover.

VT No. 34-0938

Early Style Carburetor Breather Snoots

34-1081

Feature chrome cover without filter. Bendix Keihin & CV is 3 bolt pattern. CV requires use of 35-0121 for 1991-up XL.

VT No.	Type
34-1046	Bendix-Keihin
34-1081	CV
34-0659	Cover Only

34-1046

Axel's Chrome Billet Air Cleaner

34-0831   34-0821

34-0668

Fit to CV carburetors. Order mount kits separately. Bracket listed features built in breather passage and includes bolts for Evolution and TC-88 models.

VT No.	Style	Model
34-0668	Sweeper	CV
34-0821	Diamond	CV
34-0831	Skull	CV
34-0826	Diamond	Keihin
34-0837	Diamond	S&S
34-0694	Bracket	1991-Up XL

34-0545   34-0710   34-0707

Chrome Air Cleaner Covers

Fit S&S carburetor stock backing plate and filter, "bolt on" style.

Super E	Super B	Style
	34-0545	Eagle Spirit Chrome
34-0978		Smooth (S&S)
34-0707		Skull
34-0709		Maltese
34-0710		Flame

Big Sucker Air Cleaner Assembly

Bolts on to 1991-up XL with internal breather bolts included.

VT No. 34-0101

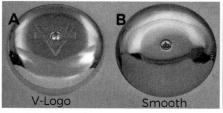

A — V-Logo

B — Smooth

C — LIVE TO RIDE · RIDE TO LIVE · EAGLE SPIRIT · 34-0524

7" Air Cleaner

7" Air Cleaner with center screw available with cover to fit Bendix, Tillotson, Keihin & CV carburetors, features breather tube, backing plate and foam element, 3" thick.

Bendix-Keihin	CV Type	#	Item
34-0524		C	Eagle Spirit
34-0505		A	V-Logo
34-0547		B	Smooth
34-0408			Bobber, black
	34-0554	B	1988-90 XL, with mt brackets
	34-1032	B	1988-up XL, Ev without Mount Brackets
34-1043	34-1044		Plate Only
34-0905			Unifilter foam filter
34-0916			V-Twin Foam Filter
34-1041			7" Smooth Air Cleaner Cover
34-1042			7" V-Logo Air Cleaner Cover
9916-2			Mount Kit
	34-1032		Smooth, chrome
	34-0406		Smooth, black
	34-0550	C	Cover Only, Eagle Spirit
	34-0555	A	Cover Only, Smooth

34-0526

34-0900

34-0432

Original Style Oval Chrome Air Cleaner

Includes element, cover, screws and backing plate, fits 1965-up Bendix and Keihin carburetors only.

VT No.	Item	VT No.	Item
34-0526	Complete Assembly, Bendix	34-0930	Backing Plate only, Keihin, Bendix
34-0924	Complete Assembly, Keihin	34-1248	Filter Element
		34-1350	Backing Plate only, CV
34-0475	Complete Assembly, CV	8212-3	Cover Screws, Chrome
34-0900	Element	34-0560	Mount Kit
34-0559	Cover only	34-0432	Insert Oval, Black

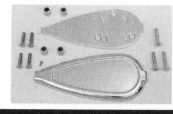

Tear Drop Deflector

Fits Bendix Keihin.

VT No. 34-1301

AIR CLEANER

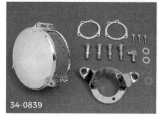

34-0839

34-0803

New Era Air Cleaner Assembly Kits

Include complete chrome air cleaner, mounting bracket and breather kit to fit stock Keihin carburetors.

Black	Chrome	Fits	Carburetor Type
34-1314	34-0839	1991-up XL	CV Integral/Breather
	34-0803	1991-up XL	CV External/Breather
	34-0814	1985-87 XL	Butterfly Keihin External/Breather
	34-0835	1988-90 XL	Butterfly CV External/Breather
34-0977	34-0977		Element

Air Cleaners

34-0977 · 34-1318 · 34-1318 Assembled

34-1095 Installed · 34-1095

New Era, B, C, and Round A styles. Includes cover, element and backing plate. Round type is 7" with center screw. Order the brackets separately.

Bendix Keihin Pre 1988	CV Type 1988-Up	Finish
34-1008		Chrome, Smooth
34-1292	34-1095	Chrome, Smooth
34-1322	34-1318	Black, Smooth
34-0977	34-0977	Element Only
34-0905	34-0905	Element Only, fits 34-0904
	34-0937	Screen

34-0665

35-0652

Teardrop Air Cleaner Kits

Include chrome air cleaner assembly with smooth, finned or flame teardrop cover, chrome mount bracket and a breather kit with a black hose and breather unit or bracket only as required.

Finned	Smooth	Flame	Year
34-1701	34-1700	34-1702	1991-up
34-0665	34-0658	34-0652	1991-up
34-0881	34-0882	34-0883	1988-90
34-0688	34-0689	34-0690	1985-87
34-0685	34-0686	34-0687	1957-84

WYATT GATLING AIR CLEANER

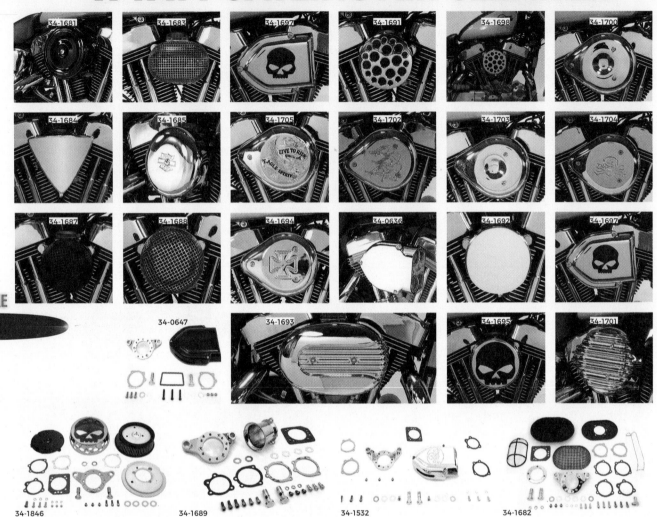

Wyatt Gatling Air Cleaners include integral breather system with bracket, mounting kit and air cleaner. Includes air filter element. DIY easy install bolt-on assembly has no hoses to connect! Fit 1991-up XL.

VT No.	w/Air Cleaner	Shape	Style	VT No.	w/Air Cleaner	Shape	Style
34-1681	34-0406	Round	Black, 7"	34-1699*	34-1081	Breather Snoot	Chrome
34-1859		Round	Chrome	34-1699		Snoot Assembly	Chrome
34-1860		Round		34-1700	34-1022	Teardrop	Chrome, Smooth
34-1861		Round		34-1701	34-0530	Teardrop	Chrome, Finner
34-1709		Round	Chrome, 7"	34-1702	34-0511	Teardrop	Chrome, Flame
34-1846		Round	Chrome, Smooth	34-1703	34-0630	Teardrop	Chrome, Slotted
34-1706		Round	Chrome	34-1704	34-0629	Teardrop	Chrome, Skull
34-1682	34-0764	Oval	Black, Mesh	34-1705	34-1020	Teardrop	Chrome, Live to Ride
34-1683	34-0746	Oval	Chrome, Mesh	34-0636	34-0620	WG Chrome	
34-1684	34-1206	Diamond	Billet	34-0647	34-1430	WG Black	
34-1849		Diamond	Chrome	34-1697	34-1429	WG Skull	
34-1850		Diamond	Chrome	34-1532	34-1129	WG Skull	
34-1685	34-1373	Round	Chrome, 7"	34-1366	34-1334	WG Inverted	
34-1686	34-0475	Oval	Chrome	34-0636		WG Smooth	
34-1687	34-0742	Round	Black, Mesh	34-0647		WG Black Smooth	
34-1688	34-0732	Round	Chrome, Mesh	34-1244		WG Skull	
34-1689*	34-1119	Velocity Stack	Chrome	34-1847		WG Swiss Cheese	
34-1691	34-0762	Round	Chrome, Drilled	34-1845		WG Skull	
34-1692	34-0763	Round	Chrome, Baby Moon	34-1707		Skull	Chrome
34-1693	34-1374	Oval	Chrome, Late Style	34-1708		Skull	Black
34-1694	34-0628	Teardrop	Chrome, Maltese	34-1857		Scoop	Chrome
34-1695	34-1735	Round	Chrome, Skull Mesh	34-1848		Sweeper	Chrome
34-1698	34-1742	Round	Chrome, Hole Pattern	34-1856		Dish	Chrome

*Note: Does not require filter element

Oval Air Cleaner Assemblies

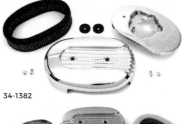

34-1382

34-1374

With backing plate, filter and chrome cover.

	Bendix	CV
Assembly	34-1382	34-1374
Backing Plate	34-0930	34-1350

Bendix-Keihin Carburetor Cover

Installed   Installed

34-1293

34-1295

3 bolt style and made of alloy.

VT No.	Style	VT No.	Style
34-1293	Finned	34-1295	Rocket

5-3/4" Chrome Air Cleaner

34-0512

34-0510

For Bendix and Keihin 3 bolt carburetors. Includes foam washable element, 2-1/4" thick.

Bendix	CV	Item
34-0510	34-0762	Drilled
34-0512	34-0763	Smooth
34-0915	34-0915	Element Only

34-0501   34-0040   34-0506

34-0501 Installed

34-0732

34-0746

34-0906

Air Cleaners

Cleaners include element.

Chrome	Black	Fits
34-0501	34-1325	Bendix-Keihin, Round
34-0733		
34-0040	34-1370	Bendix-Keihin, Turbo Oval
34-0078	34-0078	Filter Only Above
34-0506		Bendix-Keihin, Flat with Mesh
CV Type		
34-0746	34-0764	CV Turbo
34-0732	34-0742	CV Round
34-0079	34-0079	Filter Only for Above
34-0906		Foam Element for VT No. 34-0506
34-0711		Foam Element for VT No. 34-0501, 34-0733

34-0634

34-0987

34-0634 Installed

34-0641 Installed

Air Cleaner Inserts

34-0557

34-0558

Fit recessed area of round center screw type units.

*Note: Full outer cover replaces stock 8" type. Does not have lower cut out for Late 1989-up applications.

Chrome	Gold Inlay	Fitment	Chrome	Gold Inlay	Fitment
34-0557	34-0558	Evolution 8"	34-0986	34-0987	Oval
			34-0641	34-0634	2004- Up

Chrome Smooth Teardrop Air Cleaner

Fits 1988 - Up XL.
VT No. 34-1501

INTAKE
13

Chrome S&S Super E & G Air Cleaners

Available as complete units or replacement covers only. Complete assemblies include backing plate with built-in brackets to mount to Evolution heads.

VT No.	Item / Fitment
34-1015	Complete Assembly
34-0981	Chrome Cover All Super 'E'
34-1063	As Above with Notched Cover for 5 Gallon Tanks
34-0984	Uni Filter Super 'E' Foam Type
9980-3	Chrome Allen Screw Set for S&S Covers

34-1354

34-1355

34-1379

34-1380

Air Cleaner Cover Only

Chrome	Black	Diameter
34-1354	34-1355	8"
34-1379	34-1380	7"

38mm

38mm Air Cleaner Adapter Plate will adapt any CV style 3-Bolt Air Cleaner to Keihin/Bendix carburetor.
VT No. 34-0619

Adapter Plate

Allows installation of CV air cleaner to S&S E carburetors and vertical or horizontal mounting of 34-0670 tapered cone air cleaner.
VT No. 34-0673

BREATHER AND BRACKET

34-1429 · 34-1303 · 34-0638

V-Charger Air Cleaner Units Only
Include element. Order brackets and breather kits as required. Use filter 34-1070. Fits 1988- up.

Chrome	Black	Style
34-0638	34-1430	Smooth, with raised bevel center
34-0087		Replacement cover for 34-0638
34-1429	34-1456	Raised Skull
34-0620		Smooth
34-1303		Engraved Skull
34-1244		Replacement cover for 34-1303
34-0640		Engraved Flames

34-0283

6" Moon Air Cleaners

VT No.	Fits
34-0481	CV Backing Plate
34-0283	Air Cleaner Kit, Keihin

Sifton™ Braided Hose Crankcase Breather Kit

35-0123 · 40-0570 · 35-0126

Features 3/8" inner diameter stainless steel braided hose attached. Includes breather filter (with mounting stud), 24" hose, hardware and instructions. Air cleaner and carburetor support bracket must be purchased separately. Fits 1991-up XL custom applications only.

VT No.	Item	VT No.	Item
35-0123	Kit	35-0126	Bolt Kit
40-0570	Breather	31-0751	Support Bracket

31-4042 · 31-0751 · 31-3961

Chrome Air Cleaner Bracket for Evo
Mounts to boss on engine heads to support custom air cleaners. *Note: to be used with breather kit or breather buttons 40-0453.

VT No.	Fits
31-4042	1985-87
31-3961	1988-90
31-0751*	1991- Up

Cleaner Mount Gaskets, 10pk

James	VT No.	OEM	Fits
15-1146	15-0148	29058-77	1977-89
15-1016		As Above	.062 Thick
15-1017	15-0285	29059-88	1988- Up CV Type
15-1147		As Above	Steel Core
15-1148		As Above	Adhesive Coated
15-0596		29095-95	1995-2000 EFI
	15-1527	28583-01A	2001- Up EFI
15-1199		29062-95B	1995- Up Carb
15-1149		29313-95	1995- Up Air Cleaner

15-0285

34-0631 · 34-0528 · 34-0511 · 34-1022

34-0544 · 34-1020 · 34-0628 · 34-0629

34-0515 · 34-0520

Teardrop Air Cleaners
Order appropriate bracket set separately.

1987 and Earlier VT No.	Style
34-0532	Eagle Spirit, Bendix Keihin
34-0544	Eagle Spirit Gold
34-0516	Smooth
34-0515	Smooth Polished
34-0520	Smooth Steel
34-0528	Finned
34-0631	Slotted
34-0527	Smooth with Flames

1988-Up - CV Type VT No.	Style
34-1020	Eagle Spirit
34-1022	Smooth
34-0511	Flames
34-0530	Finned
34-0630	Slotted
34-0628	Maltese
34-0629	Skull
34-0560	Screws

Individual Parts for Units VT No.	Style
34-0517	Polished Cover only
34-0518	Chrome Cover only
34-0519	Bendix Keihin Backing Plate
34-1054	CV Back Plate only, Alloy
34-1080	CV Back Plate only, Steel
34-1389	CV Back Plate only, Chrome
37-8556	Chrome 3 piece screw kit
34-0545	Eagle Spirit Chrome Cover
34-0905	Uni-filter Element
34-0916	Foam Filter Element
34-0434	Backing Plate

Brackets For Teardrop Air Cleaners	
34-0201	1957-85 XL
31-3941	1985-90 XL Evolution
31-0431	1991-up XL Evolution

Air Cleaner Brackets
Chrome finished brackets are used to install custom round or teardrop air cleaners.

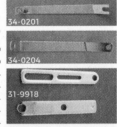 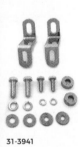

34-0201 · 34-0204 · 31-9918 · 31-3941

VT No.	Fits
34-0204	1966-85 S&S XL
34-0201	1957-85 Sportster
31-3941	1985-90 Evolution XL
34-0204*	1975-85 XL
31-9918*	All Adjustable type

*Note: these support brackets fit S&S 1-7/8" Super 'B' Carburetors.

Hi-Flow Air Cleaner Back Plate Kit
Includes filter and brackets with integral breather passages.

34-1257 · 34-1281 Installed

7" w/o cover

VT No.	Size	Cover	VT No.	Size	Cover
34-1257	7"	No	34-1281	8"	Yes

Air Cleaner Adapter Ring
Adapts Linkert 4 bolt air cleaner to CV carbs.
VT No. 34-1302

REPLICA™ AIR FILTERS

34-0934

34-0734

34-1176

34-0948

34-1067

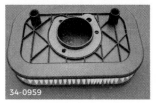
34-0959

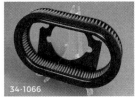
34-1066

34-0935

34-1040

34-1248

Washable Paper Air Filters

Feature original shape and styling for exact fit.

VT No.	Fits	VT No.	Fits	VT No.	Fits
34-0934	1988-2003 XL	34-0064	2014-up XL, filter	34-1248	1973-76 XL
34-0935	S&S "B"	34-1040	Screamin' Eagle Round	34-1334	Inverted Type
34-1176	S&S, "E" and "G"	**VT No.**	**Fits**	34-0734	K&N
34-0948	Tapered, Velo Type	34-1298	Eagle Round	34-0277	Mount Set
34-1067	Sifton Air Power™	34-1158	Eagle Round Foam 1972-78		
34-0959	2004-13 XL	34-1066	Oblong		

INTAKE 13

34-0903   34-0900

34-0913

34-1048

34-0957

34-0957

34-0916

34-0966

Air Filters

Available in 4 types, K&N paper, Uni Filter foam, Accel 2-stage foam and V-Twin foam.

K&N	Accel	Uni Foam	Fits	K&N	Accel	Uni Foam	Fits (Aftermarket Models)
34-1329			2014-up XL	34-0960	34-0975	34-0905	S&S Super "B"
34-1191			2004-13 XL			34-0916	S&S Super "B" (VTwin) Round Style
34-1048		34-0913*	1988-2003 XL	34-1010		34-0984	S&S Super "E" & "G"
34-0957	34-0966	34-0909	1986-87 XL			34-0906	34-0506, 34-0508
34-0951		34-0900	1983-85 1000			34-0915	34-0510
34-0954	34-0970	34-0903	1979-82 1000			34-0977	New Era
34-0953		34-0902	L1975-78 1000	34-1009			Mikuni HSR-40 smooth bore
34-0952	34-0967	34-0901	L1973-E75 1000	34-1078			Mikuni HSR 42/45 smooth bore
34-1248			1968-75 FL, FX	34-1070			Hyper Charger
34-0951		34-0900	1967-75 900/1000	34-1187			Screamin' Eagle 2004-up

Air Cleaner Cover Allen Mounting Kit
VT No. 9916-2

S&S Chrome Air Cleaner Cover Screws

Countersunk allen screws mount cover on S&S air cleaners. Three screws per kit.

VT No. 9980-3

Chrome Air Cleaner Screws

VT No.	#	Size	Style	U/M
37-8556	B	1/4 - 20	S&S	3 pack
8212-3	C	5/16 - 24	Early Stock	Kit
7206-2	A	5/16 - 24	1957-77 Acorn	2 pack
8461-2			As Above Cap	2 pack
7806-3	A	5/16 - 18	1978-84 Acorn	3 pack
9916-2	B	5/16 - 18	Chrome Flat Allen	Kit
37-2096	C	5/16 - 24	Early Stock	4 pack
37-8750		8mm - 5/8		4 pack

Wyatt Gatling Billet Air Cleaner Kits

34-0249 34-0248

For 1991-up XL CV models.

34-0250 34-0241

Black	Chrome	Style
34-0239	34-0248	Spoke
34-0240	34-0249	Skull
34-0241	340-250	Flame

2007-2015 XL Air Cleaner Mount Kit
VT No. 34-0468

Skull Style Air Cleaner Intake
Kit fits both carbureted and fuel injected models. Fits 2004-up XL.
VT No. 34-1671

FOR CV & EFI APPLICATIONS!

Easy and Secure Mounting!

No Hoses Required!

34-0694

XL Billet Chrome Integral Breather/ Carburetor Mount Bracket

Includes mount bolts for installation of any 3 bolt CV type air cleaner or velocity stack to be installed in vertical or horizontal position.

VT No.	Year
34-0694	1991-Up
35-0791	Bolt Set

Carburetor Support Bracket

Replaces 27433-57. Zinc plated. Fits 1957-67.
VT No. 31-0463

Air Cleaner Breather Manifold

Kits fit custom air cleaners to motors with internal breathing system. Includes chrome breather manifold, chrome banjo bolts, chrome air cleaner support brackets, gaskets and instructions. Fits 1991-up air cleaner noted.

31-0431

VT No.	OEM	Air Cleaner
31-0431	29281-91T	Teardrop
35-0671		Tube Only

Billet Air Cleaner Mount Set

Mounts air cleaners with flat backing plates to Evolution and TC-88 models. Offset Billet mounts feature built in breather passage that feeds inside air cleaner housing. Can be rotated to proper position, then drilling the back plate. Threaded breather nipples fasten back plate to brackets. Fits 1991-Up XL.
VT No. 34-0750

Sifton

Sifton Dual Canister Set includes hardware for 1991-up XL.
VT No. 40-0452

Sifton Dual Breather Kit includes 2 canisters and banjo tubes with hardware for 1991-up XL.
VT No. 40-0451

Sifton Dual Breather Kit Includes 2 canisters, banjo tubes and bolts for 1991-up XL.
VT No. 40-0436

Crankcase Breather and Bracket Kit

Fits CV Carburetors to allow use of aftermarket air cleaners on models with cylinder head/ crankcase breather systems. Order air cleaner separately.

VT No.	Fits	VT No.	Fits
35-0121	1992-06	35-0697	2007-Up

Sifton Mini-Breather Bolt Kit has built in mount bolt. Chrome finish. Use with carburetor mount bracket 31-0751 on 1991-up models.
VT No. 40-0453

Sifton Breather Canister

40-0446

40-0450 40-0449

Features enclosed breather filter and tube for attaching to breather cross over lines, which is held in place by set screws. Bottom cover is removable for cleaning for 1991-Up.

VT No.	Item
40-0446	Canister
40-0449	Breather Tube Kit
40-0450	Tube Only

Sifton Dual Vent Kit includes 2 vent canisters, banjo bolts for 1991-up with necessary fittings. Use 35-0126 Bolt Kit.
VT No. 35-0441

Breather Bolt and Banjo

34-0500

34-0808

Includes bolts for XL applications and 2 banjos to accept 5/16" hose.

VT No.	Item
34-0500	Without tee
34-0808	With tee
37-0985	Evolution Nylon Washers
37-0986	TC-88 Nylon Washers

Chrome Vented Breather Canister accepts 5/16" or 3/8" hose.
VT No. 40-0457

Chrome Billet Canister

Set includes bolts for 1991-up XL applications.
VT No. 40-0346

INTAKE MANIFOLDS

35-8021   35-0161   35-8033

Manifold for Evolution Models

Converts stock rubber compliance fittings to a more rigid mount system. This manifold is included in super kit for Evolution. Order flange kit separately.

VT No.	Item	Brand
35-8021	Manifold	S&S
35-8033	Manifold	Sifton
35-0161	Flange Kit	
35-9150	Flange Adapter	Use on 1990- Up XL to attach CV carburetor
37-0410	Spacer	

S&S Manifolds

35-0101   35-0102

Replacement for all S&S 1-7/8" Super carburetors or can be used as stock replacements

VT No.	Type	Model
35-0101	O-Ring	1957-77 Models
35-0109	O-Ring	As above w/ .200 longer cylinder
35-0102	Flat Seal	1978-84
35-9184	Flat Seal	As above w/ .200 longer cylinder
35-8021	Flat Seal	1986- Up XL EVO

Carburetor Spacers

Spacers for S&S are available in 1" or 3/8" thickness for spacing out 1-7/8" carburetors on models with 5 gallon tanks.

VT No.	Size
35-0105	1"
35-0086	3/8"
14-0957	Super 'E' Carburetor Base, O-Ring

Intake Manifold Mount Screws, Allen Style

VT No.	Year	Style
9932-8-P	1995- Up	Polished
9933-12	1986-87	XL, Knurled
9933-12-P	1986-87	XL, Polished

35-0411

1966-77 Intake Manifold Rings

Use to update early style O-Ring intake manifolds or cylinder heads to late style flat band type seals. Available for stock or stroker .200 taller cylinders. Set includes 4 standard and 2 stroker rings.

VT No.	Type	QTY
35-0411	Adapter Rings, Stock	10
35-0412	Stroker Rings	10
35-0429	Set	

35-0085   35-0084

Shock Intake Manifolds

35-9188   35-9195

Cast alloy, as original. Fits XL models.

VT No.	OEM	Fits	Type
35-0805	27021-71A	1966-77	O-Ring
35-0084	27021-78	1978-84	Flat Seal
35-9188	27004-88A	1988-03	Spigot
35-9195	27024-04	2004-06	Spigot

CV Carburetor Adapter

35-9150

Adapts HSR-42 Mikuni or CV carburetor to 2 bolt manifold. Use spigot seal VT No. 14-0180.

VT No. 35-9150

Manifold Spacer

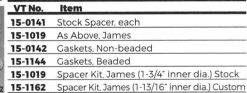

15-0142

Replaces 29250-78 on 1971-88 models. 3/8" thick.

VT No.	Item
15-0141	Stock Spacer, each
15-1019	As Above, James
15-0142	Gaskets, Non-beaded
15-1144	Gaskets, Beaded
15-1019	Spacer Kit, James (1-3/4" inner dia.) Stock
15-1162	Spacer Kit, James (1-13/16" inner dia.) Custom

35-9136   35-0117   35-0194   35-4574   35-9162

35-9340   35-9341   35-0098   35-0088

Carburetor Adapters

VT No.	Size (mm)	Type	VT No.	Size (mm)	Type
35-9136	30-45	Spigot Rubber	35-9340	42	Flange Adapter
35-0117	42-42	Spigot Rubber	35-9341	46	Flange Adapter
35-0194	44-44	Spigot Rubber	35-0098	38	2 Bolt Adapter w/rubber
35-4574	36-38	Flange Adapter	35-0088	38	Flange
35-9162	40	Flange Adapter	28-0981	38	Rubber Sleeve for Flatside

For EFI

Chrome Manifold Cover

Fits 2007-up XL.

VT No.	Item
34-0100	Kit
15-1527	Gasket

INTAKE CLAMPS

V-Twin's 360° Power Intake Clamp

Full stainless steel which features a "floating bridge." Closes the gap under the "T" bolt for total 360° wrap around seal. The best available sold as a set with O-Rings or seals.

VT No.		Type	U/M	
35-0415	35-0449	1955-77	O-Ring	Kit
35-0409	35-0448	1978-84	Flat Seal	Kit
14-0519		1957-77	O-Rings	10 pk
14-0113		1978-85	Flat Seals	10 pk

Intake Clamp Update Kit

For 1967-77 models. Kit includes manifold rings, Silicone seals and stainless clamps. Use to update early intakes to late style seals or when intake flanges are damaged on early heads.

VT No. 35-0436

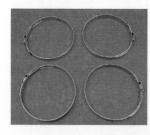

1978-84 Intake Clamp

Set includes 4 pieces of single use clamp, installed by VT No. 16-0050 tool.

VT No. 35-0419

Replica Intake Clamp Set

Fillister head screws, pair.

VT No.	Year	Finish
35-0417	1955-56	Cadmium
35-0439	1957-76	Cadmium
35-0440	1977-84	Zinc

Stock Style Intake Clamp Sets

Include O-ring or seals for proper year, feature Fillister or allen screws as factory. Available in chrome or stainless.

VT No.	Year	Finish	Screw	VT No.	Year	Finish	Screw
35-0408	1955-77	Chrome	Allen	35-0410	1978-84	Chrome	Allen
35-9177	1955-77	Stainless	Fillister	35-0418	1978-84	Stainless	Fillister

Polished Intake Manifold Clamps

Strong yet easy to install. For Big Twin, 1955-Early78, Sportster 1957-Early78 with O-rings.

VT No.	Item	VT No.	Item
35-0407	Clamp Kit	14-0519	O-Rings, 10 pk

V-Twin Style Intake Clamps

2-pc polished brass or chrome. Seals included in 1978-84.

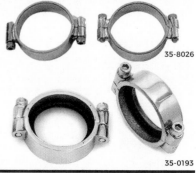

VT No.	Years	Type	Finish	Note
35-0406	1955-77	O-Ring	Chrome	No Seals
35-8026	1978-84	Flat Seal	Chrome	No Seals
35-0193	1957-77	O-Ring	Brass	Seal
35-0192	1978-84	Flat Seal	Brass	Seal

Intake Manifold O-Rings and Seals

James	VT No.	OEM	Type
	14-0519	27060-55	1955-77, O-Ring
14-0626	14-0113	27062-78	1978-85 Flat Seal
	14-0924	As Above	Red Silicone
14-0624	14-0165	26995-86A	1986-up
14-0573		As Above	Blue Silicone
14-0678		As Above	Oversize
14-0689		As Above	Rubber with metal element, Std.
14-0708		As Above	Rubber with Extra Thick, Metal Insert Standard Size
14-0625*	14-0180*	27002-89	1990-up

*Note: Seal for carburetor to intake manifold.

BENDIX CARBURETOR

Bendix Carburetor Kit

Fits 1957-85 XL. Kit includes 38mm Bendix Carburetor with adjustable main jet, throttle handle with grips, cable and cable bracket and 7" round logo air cleaner with support. Kit includes seal adapters to use on pre-1978 O-Ring heads.
VT No. 35-0118

Bendix Repair Kit

35-4570

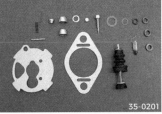

35-0201

Includes accelerator-pump for all 38 and 40mm, stock or adjustable jet carburetors. Replaces 27132-71.

VT No.	MM	Brand
35-4570	38	Facet
35-0201	38	V-Twin
35-9164	40	Facet

INTAKE 13

Bendix Carburetor

35-0021 · 35-0060 · 35-0022

Has 38mm Venturi and 42mm throat. Complete with choke, accelerator pump, and built-in return spring. This complete unit bolts onto all Big Twins from 1971-75 as stock replacement.

VT No.	MM	Type	Cable	Finish	VT No.	MM	Type	Cable	Finish
35-0021	38	Fixed	Single	Cast	35-0022	40	Adjustable	Dual	Cast
35-0060	38	Adjustable	Single	Cast					

Bendix Main Jets

VT No.	OEM	Size
35-9143	27651-75	.095
35-9144	27652 75	1.00
35-9145	27653-75	1.05
35-0198	27654-75	1.10
35-9146	27655-75	1.15
35-9147	27656-75	1.20
14-0520	O-Ring	10 pk

Adjustable Main Jet Conversion Kit

Fits all Bendix carburetors.

VT No.	Item
35-0202	Jet Kit
16-0865	Jet Tap 9/32" x 32 Some early carbs require drilling and tapping for jet installation.

Idle Adjusting Screw

Allows ease of adjustment with "T" handle design. A single idle "T" screw is available for Bendix.

VT No.	Finish
35-0221	Stainless Steel
35-0931	Brass

35-0203 · 15-0147

Bendix Carburetor Replacement Parts

VT No.	OEM	Item	Brand/Finish
35-0507	27630-71	Float	Facet
35-4577	27645-71	38mm Float bowl	Facet, Plain
35-9250		40mm Float bowl	Facet, Plain
15-0147	27646-71	Bowl gasket	10 pack
35-0203	27762-71A	Pump	V-Twin
35-9132	27389-71	Pump boot	Accel
13-9242	27659-71	Float Pin Spring	10 pack
35-0424		Float Needle	38mm
35-0425		Float Needle	40mm
35-0533		Idle Jet Tube	
12-2557		Throttle Stop Screw with Spring	
13-9223	27613-71	Throttle Stop Screw Spring	

DELL'ORTO

Flat Adapter

Dell'Orto Pumper Air Cleaner allows use of Bendix, air cleaners.
VT No. 34-1060

Dell'Orto Spigot Carburetor Adapters
O-Ring seal with steel flange for 38 mm carburetors.
VT No. 35-9076

36-2550

Dell'Orto Pumper features adjustable accelerator pump and choke. Kit includes throttle assembly, cable, grips, air cleaner adapter and carburetor adapter to fit stock two bolt XL manifolds on pre1985 models.

VT No.	Item
35-0030	38mm Complete Kit
35-0031	40mm Complete Kit
36-2550	Replacement Throttle Cable for 38 & 40mm
35-0238	38mm Carburetor Only
35-0239	40mm Carburetor Only

VT No.	OEM	Years	Size
12-2099	33298-65	1965-77	5/16 - 1-1/2
12-2126	24824-67	1967-70	3/8 - 2
12-2110	29254-78	1978-89	5/16 - 1-1/4

Mount Studs

1976-87 KEIHIN

Installed

Keihin Carburetor Rebuilds

Contains needle, proper o-rings and diaphragm.

VT No.	Year	Brand
35-0200	1976-78	GB
35-0240	1976-86	Keihin
35-0196	1983-89	GB
35-0219	1976-86	James
35-0416	1989-up CV	GB
35-0422	1988-up CV	James
35-0444	1988-up CV	VT

Enricher for CV Carburetors

Eliminates choke cable. Unit has three positions.
VT No. 35-0447

CV Hot Rod Kit

Includes enhancement items and rebuild components.
VT No. 35-0612

Keihin Low Speed Jets

Fit 1976-89 Keihin carburetors, except CV.

VT No.	OEM	MM
35-0297	27896-79	.65
35-0294	27894-78	.68
35-0296	27897-78	.72
35-0295	27382-77	.75
35-0299	27348-77	.88
35-0298	27348-76	1.00

Keihin Main Jets

VT No.	OEM	MM
35-0357	27419-76	1.65
35-0358	27418-76	1.70
35-0359	27417-76	1.75
35-0361	27416-76	1.80

44mm 2-Bolt Turbulator

Turns the intake manifold into a violent mixing chamber. The heavier fuel particles are directed away from the sides of the intake manifold back to the center of air flow. The fixed valve turbulator then tumbles the mixture resulting in higher horsepower.
VT No. 35-9264

Boyesen Power X-Wing The Power X-Wing

A cost effective, bolt on upgrade that will eliminate sluggish throttle response. Dyno test shows up to 4 hp and 5 ft lbs of torque gained compliments air filter system upgrades and requires no re-jetting.

VT No.	Type	Fits
35-0904	HSR-42/45	With 1-3/4" ID Adapter
35-0906	HSR 48	With 2" ID Adapter

CV Main Jets for Keihin

MAIN SLOW Sold as 5 pk.

CV Main Jets	
VT No.	Size
35-0451	1.40
35-0452	1.45
35-0453	1.50
35-0454	1.55
35-0375	1.60
35-0376	1.65
35-0377	1.70
35-0378	1.75
35-0334	1.80
35-0379	1.85
35-0335	1.90
35-0336	1.95
35-0337	2.00
35-0455	2.05

CV Slow Jets	
VT No.	Size
35-0380	.040
35-0381	.042
35-0338	.044
35-0382	.045
35-0339	.046
35-0383	.048
35-0456	.050
35-0457	.052
35-0458	.054

1967-70 Tillotson Carburetor Gasket and Hardware Kit

Includes 27806-66 gasket, 27816-66 diaphragm, (2) 27689-61 idle and intermediate adjuster screw springs, 27706-66 throttle shaft spring, 27691-66 throttle lever stop screw spring, and (6) diaphragm cover screws.

VT No.	Item	VT No.	Item
35-0223	Kit	13-9217	Throttle Lever Stop Screw Spring
35-0229	Kit w/ Accelerator Pump, Intermediate Adjuster Screw, Needle & Seat	13-0230	Throttle Shaft Spring
		35-0262	Adjustable Jet Kit
35-0226	Needle and Seat	35-0225	Pump Assembly Kit
35-0224	Intermediate Adjuster Screw	35-1258	Adjustable Knob
		35-1259	Fuel Fitting
13-9215	Inlet Valve Lever Spring	35-0264	Carb Gasket/Hardware
35-0272	Jet/Ticker Assembly	35-0265	Carb Gasket/Hardware
13-9216	Idle Adjuster Spring	35-0365	Tracker

Facilitates removal of Keihin slow jets with no damage to jet.
VT No. 16-0546

Slow Jet Screw Driver

For CV carburetors. Kit includes brass jets and instructions designed for specifically for each model listed. These kits feature no drilling installation and will work on stock to heavily modified engines.

35-0765

EZ Quick Tuner Kits

VT No.	Fits
35-0765	1988-03 Sportster 883
35-0760	1988-03 Sportster 1200
35-0761	2004-06 Sportster

CV KEIHIN REBUILD KITS

CV Carburetor Rebuild Kit

Includes seals, O-Rings, diaphragm and vacuum piston.
VT No. 35-0465

35-0416

35-0444

CV Carburetor Rebuild Kit - 1989-Up

VT No.	Brand
35-0416	GB
35-0422	James
35-0444	Deluxe

Keihin Screw Kit

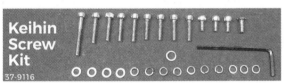

37-9116

Includes chrome screws where required.

VT No.	Years	Type
35-0206	1976-89	Allen
37-9116	CV	Allen
2596-13	CV	Allen
35-0259		Hex

Deluxe Carburetor Kits

35-9172

Includes pieces shown for 1976-89 Keihin carburetors.

VT No.	Type
35-9172	Stock
35-9176	Viton
35-9279	Replica

35-9279

CV Tuner Kits

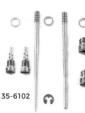

35-6102

VT No.	Fits
35-6102	1988-03 XL
35-6103	2004-06 XL

40mm CV Carburetor

Accurate reproduction of Keihin CV Carb. Fits 1986-2006 Sportster models.
VT No. 35-0569

35-8029

35-8032

35-8025

Chrome CV Carburetor Top

35-9107

VT No.	Type
35-8025	Smooth
35-8029	Eagle Spirit
35-8032	Ball Milled
35-9107	Perforated

Replaces black plastic cover on 1988-up XL.

Extended Float Bowl Kit

Fits CV carburetors for extra capacity, includes Hi-Flow inlet fitting.
VT No. 35-0135

CV Carburetor Main Jet Assortment

For all CV carbs and 35-9075 kit.

35-9099

INTAKE
13

CV Tuners Kit by Kinetic-Karb - 1989-99 Keihin

Constant velocity carburetors to permit easy tuning after installation of custom air cleaners, cams and exhaust. Includes instructions, 3 main jets, needle jet, adjustable needle with spacers and circlips, a spring and drill bits. This dual purpose kit fits 1989 models without accelerator pump 1990-99 with accelerator pump. Jet assortment includes #140-205, 70 piece main jet assortment.

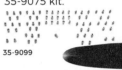
35-9075

VT No.	Item
35-9075	Kit
35-9099	Jet Assortment

CV JET KITS 1988-UP MODELS

DynoJet stock carburetors work with mild cams, stock, or aftermarket exhaust and stock or aftermarket air cleaner.

35-0527

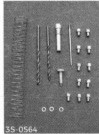
35-0564

35-0530

VT No.	Fits	DynoJet #
35-0527	1989-96 883 w/accelerator pump disabled. Race only	8703
35-0564	2004-up 883	8134
35-0530	1989-03 1200 XL Thunderslide Kit	8109

Carburetor Choke Cable Bracket

Stainless Steel carburetor choke knob bracket will mount the knob assembly on top of CV carburetors for use with all air cleaners.
VT No. 35-0681

KEIHIN

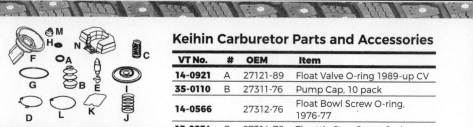

Accelerator Pump Kit

Improves throttle response on 1979-88 type Keihin carburetor models with a greater volume of fuel from the pump circuit.

VT No. 35-9050

35-0220 Installed

Idle Screw

Keihin and CV Idle Screw allows for easier adjustment by hand.

VT No. 35-0220

Keihin Adjustable Main Jet
Fully adjustable for maximum tuning efficiency. Sold as pictured.
VT No. 35-0369

High Flow Fuel Inlet replaces broken fuel inlet to the carburetor bowl for modified motors. Fits all Keihin carburetors (Butterfly and CV) 1976-up XL.
VT No. 35-0134

35-0230

Keihin Carburetor Fitting
Replaces 27371-76, 90°, plastic, sold ea.
VT No. 40-0534

Keihin Carburetor Parts and Accessories

VT No.	#	OEM	Item
14-0921	A	27121-89	Float Valve O-ring 1989-up CV
35-0110	B	27311-76	Pump Cap, 10 pack
14-0566		27312-76	Float Bowl Screw O-ring, 1976-77
13-9234	C	27314-76	Throttle Stop Screw Spring
14-0560	D	27324-83	Float Bowl O-ring 1983-91 CV, 5pk
35-9067	E	27337-76 27338-76	Float Valve with clip
35-0230	F	27585-88	Vacuum Piston
14-0559	G	27358-76	Float Bowl O-ring 1976-78
35-9066	I	27361-76	Pump Diaphragm
13-9168		27362-76	Diaphragm Spring
14-0564	K	27577-88	Float Bowl O-ring 1989-91 CV
14-0937	K	27577-92	Float Bowl O-ring 1992-up CV
14-0557	L	27889-78	Float Bowl O-ring 1978-82
14-0679	M	27385-76	Low Speed Jet Plug 1976-up
13-9212		27123-89	Accelerator Rod Spring 1989-up
13-9169		27136-81	Throttle & Idle Adj. Screw Spring, 1981-up
13-9213		27162-89	Vacuum Piston Spring, 1989-up
13-9179		27315-88	Primary Starter Spring, 1988-up
13-9181		27319-76	Low Speed Adjuster Screw Spring,1981-up
13-9183		27322-76	Throttle Lever Spring, 1981-up
13-9178		27584-88	Primary Vacuum Spring, 1988-up
35-9196	N	27576-92	Float 40 mm CV 1992-up

MIKUNI

35-9320

Mikuni HSR 42 Easy Kits

These kits are designed to work with stock intake manifold, choke cable, air cleaner and throttle cables.

VT No.	Fits	VT No.	Fits
35-9320	1994-2006	35-9115	1971-1985

Mikuni Carburetor Kits

38mm for all XL. Includes air cleaner, carburetor, manifold adapter, hose clamps, main and pilot jet assortment and throttle cable. Fits 1957-up.

VT No.	Item	VT No.	Item
35-0100	Complete Kit	34-0567	Air Cleaner
36-0105	Cable	35-0071	Throttle Handle

Mikuni Carburetor Parts and Information Manual
VT No. 48-0671

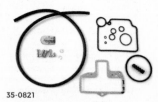

35-0821

Carburetor Rebuild Kit

For Mikuni carburetor includes flow fuel hose, throttle valve seal, float bowl seal o-ring, and carburetor top gasket. Custom application for HSR-42/HSR-45 carburetors.

VT No. 35-0821

Mikuni HS and HSR Jets

Pilot Jets		Main Jets		Main Jets	
VT No.	Size	VT No.	Size	VT No.	Size
35-0800	22.5	35-0806	150.0	35-0812	165.0
35-0801	25.0	35-0807	152.5	35-0814	170.0
35-0802	27.5	35-0808	155.0		
35-0803	30.0	35-0809	157.5		
		35-0810	160.0		
35-0805	35.0	35-0811	162.5		

Jet Needles

HSR-42		HSR-45	
VT No.	Size	VT No.	Size
35-0815	95	35-0818	95
35-0816	96	35-0819	96
35-0817	97	35-0820	97

35-0806

35-0800

35-0815

35-0818

1-7/8" "E" Black Carburetor

35-1050

Sifton Enricher

For S&S, fits Super E&G and B carburetors, includes chrome knob.

VT No. 35-0466

Jet Assortment

For S&S Super 'E', 'G' and 'B' carburetors. Complete kit includes 7 intermediate jets from .025" to .033" and a main jet only which includes 14 main jets from .062" to .084".

VT No.	Item
35-0995	Complete
35-0287	Main Only

Chrome Choke Knob

For Super E&G. Allows use of the stock plunger and spring. Kit includes brass plunger nut and chrome knob.

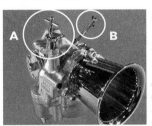

VT No.	#	Item
35-0132	A	Choke Knob
35-0217	B	Idle Screw Set

Long Float Bowl Screws

Fit S&S E carburetors, to facilitate easy removal of bowl.

VT No.	Item	VT No.	Item
35-0025	Brass	35-0029	Chrome

Hi-Flow Air Cleaner Element

Fits S&S E Air Cleaners. Kit includes washable 3.5" high filter and mount studs. Mount studs available separately.

VT No.	Item
34-0653	Kit
37-0055	Mount Studs

Replica Air Filter Elements

Fit S&S models. Washable.

34-1176   34-0935

VT No.	Model
34-1175	E&G
34-0935	B
34-0251	E&G

1-7/8" Bore "R" Carburetor

VT No.	Item
35-0992	Carburetor
35-8035	Manifold, BT
35-8033	Manifold, XL

35-0992

Air Cleaner Support Brackets

Fit S&S Super 'E' and 'G' for 1957-85 XL

VT No. 34-0337

ThunderPro ThunderJet

Fits S&S 'G' & 'D' Series carburetors. Increases fuel delivery. Black finish.

VT No. 35-0179

S&S Air Cleaners for stock carburetors. Chrome plated S&S tear drop air cleaners to fit all Tillotson, Bendix or Keihin carburetors. Complete with cover, backing plate, element and all hardware needed for installation.

34-0199

VT No.	Fits	VT No.	Fits
34-0199	1966-84	34-0108	1986-87

All Carburetors sold as individual pieces or in kits are covered under our warranty "Replacement Only" Provision. All Carburetor related item part numbers begin with a 35 prefix. No credit will be issued for these items as they are exchange only.

SUPER 'E' & 'G'

Tedd Cycle, Inc. original S&S Distributor since 1981!

35-0009

S&S 1-7/8" & 2-1/16" Super 'G'

Feature adjustable volume pump, enrichment device for ease of starting and a throttle spool assembly designed for late 2 cable operation. Supplied with tear drop air cleaner, mounting bracket and black fuel line. Super 'E' Carburetor is approximately 1-7/16" shorter than the Super 'B' carburetor, making installation length of the Super 'E' the same as stock. The 1-7/8"is for street stock applications, 21/16" for big bore and race use. Intake manifold clamps or flanges must be purchased separately when they are required.

1-7/8" 'E'	2-1/16" 'G'	Fits
35-0005		Pre1978 XL
35-0008	35-9207	1986-90 XL Evolution
35-0009	35-9208	1991-03 XL Evolution
35-9368		2004-up XL Evolution
	35-0470	Carburetor only
2596-13		Screw Kit
35-0970		Float Needle and Seat Set
35-0850		S&S Super "E" Rebuild Carb Kit
35-0849		90° Elbow Tube
35-0966		Accelerator Pump Kit
35-0355		Carb Intermediate Jet

Sifton Carburetor Hop Up Kit

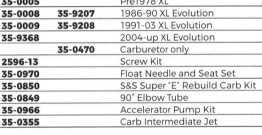

Includes emulsion tube and bomb sight annular booster tube for all S&S E carburetors.

35-0026 Installed

VT No.	Item
35-0133	Kit
35-0026	Idle Mixture Screw

Accelerator Pump Adjusting Screws

35-0830

Allow adjustment of idle and accelerator pumps by these 'T' bar style screws for ease of adjustment.

VT No.	Item	VT No.	Item
35-0217	T Screw	35-0931	Idle Adjuster Screw Set
35-0830	Brass Knurl Screw Set		

S&S Air Cleaner Breather Bolt Kit

1993-up Super E & G Air Cleaner Assemblies features two piece breather bolt with rubber coated washers. Fits 1990-up.

VT No. 35-1705

Throttle Cable Adapter Block

Allows use of stock 1996-up throttle cables on S&S E carburetors.

VT No. 36-0546

"L" SERIES

35-0980

35-0977

35-0980

35-0762

35-0977

INTAKE 13

35-1673

35-0981 35-0663

35-0287 35-0303

VT No.	Item	VT No.	Item
13-0932	Idle Screw	35-0287	Jet Kit
35-0656	Throttle Shaft	35-0657	Throttle Door
35-0658	Spring	35-0659	Kit
35-0660	Screw	32-0980	Bowl
35-0752	Arm	35-0762	Dual Bowl Mount
35-0664	Throttle Arm	35-0788	Bowl Dual Kit
35-0840	Sub Assembly Kit	35-0977	Body
35-0663	Main Nozzle Discharge Tube	35-0981	Carb Throttle Return Spring Kit
35-0998	Throttle Arm & Door	35-1673	Choke Door Kit
35-1703	Fixed Jet	35-0965	Air Bleed Jet Kit
35-1280	Complete Carb "L"	35-0939	Shaft

38mm OKO Flatside Carburetor Kit

Has built-in choke activator, throttle cable, manifold, air cleaner, twist grip set and carburetor spigot adapter.

Fits 1957-84 Ironheads.

35-0695

35-0696

VT No.	Fitment	VT No.	Fitment
35-0695	1971-85 XL	35-0696	1986- Up XL

V-Twin Flatside Carburetor Patch

Embroidered patch can be ironed or sewn on.

VT No. 48-1676

38 mm & 40mm Dell'Orto Spigot Carburetor

Features adjustable accelerator pump and choke. Kit includes throttle assembly, cable, grips, air cleaner adapter, and carburetor adapter to fit stock two-bolt XL manifolds on pre-1985 models.

VT No.	Item
35-0030	38mm Complete Kit
35-0031	40mm Complete Kit
36-2550	Replacement Throttle Cable for 38mm & 40mm
35-0238	38mm Carburetor Only
35-0239	40mm Carburetor Only

35-0238

35-0030

DELLORTO

36-2550

1954-76 XL-XLCH OIL PUMP

Small parts are available in packs of 10. The major parts are sold each. Fits 1952-76 all XLH-XLCH Sportster models.

*Note: 1972-76 body may be fitted on earlier models if later gears are substituted.

**Note: GB Brand.

12-0421

12-1377

XL Oil Pump, Complete

1957-76 XL Oil Pump Complete includes all parts assembled. Hardware is sold minus gears and body.

VT No.	OEM	Years
12-9979	26217-56	1957-66
12-9930	26204-67	1967-76
12-0177	Hardware	1957-76

XL Oil Pump Drive Gears.

VT No.	OEM	Fits
12-0421	26318-37	1957-76
12-1380	26318-75	1977-87
12-1377	26318-88A	1988-up

Oil Pump Gasket Kits for Sportster

James	VT No.	Years
15-0849	15-0311	1952-76

Machined Oil Pump Body replaces 26214-72 for 1972-76 XL models, accepts later gears as listed below. Includes gear dowel pressed.
VT No. 12-1410

VT No.	OEM	#	Years	Item
12-9930	26204-67		1967-76	Complete Pump
12-1524	240	A	1961-71	Feed Pin
12-1160	603	A	1972-76	Roll Pin
12-0158	8873	B	1954-76	Check Ball
N/A	9095	C	1961-76	Dowel
12-0901	11002	D	1955-62, 1972-76	Retainer
8814-15	24819-52	E,F	1952-E 71	Stud and Nuts
8815-15	24819-52	E,F	As Above	Cadmium
9614-10		L	1971-76	Stud and Nuts
12-0154	25276-52	G	1954-73	Screen
12-1410*	26214-72	H	1972-76	Body
14-0114	26227-58	I	1958-76	Seal
12-9904	26241-52	J	1954-76	Cover
12-9946	26250-56	K	1956-76	Plate
12-8950**	26331-52	L	1952-55	Breather Valve Gear
12-8951**	26331-56	L	1956-59	Breather Valve Gear
12-8952**	26331-60	L	1960-71	Breather Valve Gear
12-8953**	26331-72	L	1972-76	Breather Valve Gear
12-9947	26331-72	L	1972-76	Breather Valve Gear
12-9948	26315-72A	M	1972-76	Scavenger Gear
12-9949	26317-72A	N	1972-76	Scavenger Idle Gear
12-9950	26322-52A	O	1954-62, 1972-76	Idler Gear
12-9951	26323-52A	P	1954-62, 1972-76	Gear, Feed
15-0942	26256-52	Q	1954-76	Gasket, Case
15-0945	26258-52	R	1954-62, 1972-76	Outer Gasket
15-0946	26258-62	R	L 1962-71	Outer Gasket
15-0950	26259-52	S	1954-62, 1972-76	Inner Gasket
15-0951	26259-62	S	L 1962-71	Inner Gasket
12-0800	26327-52	T	1954-76	Idler Shaft
12-0204	26340-36	U	1960-71	Key
12-0205	26348-15	U	1972-76	Key
12-0214	26341-37	V	L 1962-71	Retainer Half
13-0115	26364-57	W	1957-72	Check Spring
13-0116	26364-72	W	L 1972-76	Check Spring
N/A	26420-57	X	1957-76	Fitting
32-0427	26552-72	Y	1954-76	Switch
37-8777	45830-48	Z	1958-76	Plug
40-0566	63533-41	AA	1967-76	Feed Fitting
8816-10	Chrome		1954-76	Allen Bolts
8817-10	Chrome		1977-90	Allen Bolts
9806-8	Chrome		1977-90	Acorn Kit

32-0428

32-0427

Precision Calibrated Oil Pressure Switches

VT No.	OEM	Fits
32-0427	26552-72	1954-76 900-1000
32-0428	26554-77	1977- Up XL
12-1488	26420-57	Fitting
32-1159		1955-70 900

VT No.	OEM	Type
12-9948	26315-72A	Scavenger
12-9949	26317-72A	Scavenger Idle
12-9950	26322-52A	Idle
12-9951	26323-52A	Feed

1972-76 XL Pump Gears

12-9948   12-9949   12-9950   12-9951

Oil Pump Breather Parts

12-1541

VT No.	OEM	Item
12-1541		Breather Kit
12-1542		Oil Strainer Kit
12-1290	25265-63	Deflector
12-1512	24975-37	Oil Strainer 1954-76 XL
12-1173	333	Pin, 10 pack
15-0214	24978-57	Gasket, 10 pack
12-1511	25075-55	Oil Transfer Valve, 1957-76 XL
40-0121	24912-52	Breather Pipe, 1954-78 XLH-XLCH Chrome with fitting nut
40-0546	24918-52	Nut only for Above

12-1511

12-1512

12-1290

OIL PUMP ASSEMBLY 1977-UP

XL Oil Pump Mounting Kits

ACORN SCREW

ALLEN SCREW

Hex Chrome	Hex Cadmium	Allen	Acorn	Years
8814-15	8815-15	8816-10		1952- E 71
9614-10		8816-10		L 1971-76
		8817-10	9806-8	1977-90
		9774-8	9775-8	1991- Up

Complete Oil Pumps

12-9929

Oil Pump Seals

James	GB No.	OEM	Fits
14-0611	14-0109	12036A	1977-90
14-0623	14-0114	26227-58	1958-90

Shims for XL Models

12-0704

VT No.	OEM	Use
12-0711	6732B	Pushrod
12-0704	.005	Rocker Arm
12-0710	.007	Rocker Arm
12-0715	.015	Rocker Arm
12-0705	6769	.007 Cam (1, 3, 4)
12-0706	6770	.005 Cam (1, 3, 4)
12-0716	6771	.015 Cam (1, 3, 4)
12-0717	6773	.005 Cam (#2)
12-0718	6775	.010 Cam (#2)
12-1258	6778	.015 Cam (#2)
12-0709	6802	Starter Crank
12-0713	.003	Sprocket Shaft 1952-76
12-0714	.003	Sprocket Shaft 1976-up

12-1562   12-1563

VT No.	OEM	Years	Type
12-1562	26197-83 26204-75	1977-85 1000cc	Complete
12-1563	26204-86	1986-90	Complete
12-9980	26488-75	1977-90	Shaft w/Gear only
12-0957	26497-75	1977-90	Retaining Ring
12-0055	26204-91A	1991-up	1991-up Complete
12-9929	26204-91A	1991-up	Complete
12-9981	26488-91	1991-up	Shaft w/Gear only
10-0749	26431-76	1977-90	Cover Bushing
10-0750	26489-75	1975-90	Body Bushing

OIL LINES

Breather Pipe

Replaces 24912-52A on 1954-78 XLH-XLCH, chrome with fitting nut.

40-0121

Stainless Braided Overhead Rocker Arm Oil Lines

Fit 1957-84 Sportster.
VT No.
40-0242

Chrome Oil Line Sets

40-0115   40-0116

VT No.	Fits	Type
40-0115	1957-84	Coil
40-0116	1957-70	Magneto
40-9986	Fittings for above, 4pk	
14-0147	63529-57	Seals 100pk
14-0930	63529-57	Red Silicone 50pk

Oil Pump Drive Gears, XL

James	VT No.	Years
12-1380	26318-75	1977-87
12-1377	26318-88A	1988- Up

Oil Pump Gasket Kits for Sportsters

James	VT No.	Years
15-0850	15-0613	1977-90
15-1225		1991- Up
15-1372		1991-Up w/ DL type gasket

15-0613

For Sportster rocker boxes which include fittings and seals.

Pressure Switch is precision calibrated. OEM 26554-77. 1977- up.

VT No. 32-0428

Oil Pump Gaskets			
GB No.	James	OEM	Fits
15-0129	15-0942	26256-52	1957-76 Body to Crankcase
15-0945	15-0945	26258-52	1957-E62;1972-76 Outer Cover to body
15-0133	15-0946	26258-62	1962-71 Outer Cover to Body
15-0135	15-0950	26259-52	1957-E62; 1972-76 Body to Inner Cover
15-0136	15-0951	25259-62	1962-71 Body to Inner Cover
15-0199	15-0961	26435-75	1977-90 Pump Mounting
	15-1436		As Above, Foamet®
15-0684	15-0962	26495-89A	1991-up Pump Mounting
	15-1437		As Above, Foamet®

DIPSTICK & TEMP

LCD Dipstick

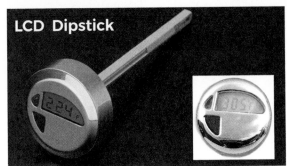

40-0361

40-0667

40-0667

40-0495

40-0360

40-0463

LCD Dipstick with temperature read-out. Fits 1984-2003 XL models.

VT No. 40-0658

28-0219

40-0227

40-0227

Oil Tank Dipstick / Temp Gauge Plug

Stock dip stick also available, replaces rubber plug in caps.

Oil Temperature Dipstick

- Lighted LCD readout
- Fahrenheit or Celsius operation
- Replaceable battery
- Fits 1984-2003

VT No. 40-0602

VT No.	Years	Type
40-0361	1979-2003	Temperature Gauge
40-0667	2004 - Up	Temperature Gauge
40-1526	2008 - UP XR	Dipstick
28-0219	1970-78	Oil Tank Cap
40-0227	1970-78	Oil Tank Cap, Maltese
40-0495	1970-78	Dipstick
40-0360	1979-2003	Dipstick
40-0463	1979-2003	Dipstick, Maltese

OIL COOLER

31-1177

31-0722

Dual Cool Chrome Oil Cooler

Includes stainless steel hose and adapter fitting for engine to allow use of oil filter which is included on 40-0270 and 40-0272. 1971-81 models may require bracket modification. Note: Brackets included also sold separately.

VT No.	Year	Brackets
40-0272	2004-up	31-1177
40-0270	1979-2003	31-0722
40-0271	1957-78	31-0722

40-0305

40-0306

Sifton Oil Cooler

31-1758

Replica style in black or chrome. Order bracket separately.

VT No.	Finish
40-0305	Black
40-0306	Chrome
31-1758	1982- Up Bracket

40-1510

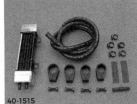
40-1515

Sifton Oil Coolers for XL

These are mounted vertically.

Deluxe	Slim Line	Chrome	Years
40-1525	40-1516	40-1518	1957-2003
Jagg			
40-1510		40-1512	1957- Up

Billet Twin-Cooler Set

VT No.	Length	Finish
40-0339	9"	Chrome
40-0805	7"	Black
40-0806	11 1/2"	Black
Clamp	**Size**	
40-0342	1.125"	
40-0590	1.0"	

Feature two independent 1" diameter cooler canisters with four billet clamps for mounting to 11/8" front frame tubes.

OIL TANK

XLH Chrome Side Oil Tank

Fits electric start Sportster 1954- E 78. Cap not included.

VT No.	Item	VT No.	Item
40-0400	Chrome Tank	37-0827	Mount Bolt Kit
40-1254	Black Tank	15-0200	Cap Gasket (1952-65)
40-0504	Cap Assembly	15-0201	Cap Gasket (1966-78)
40-0845	Cap Kit		

Chrome Electric Start Oil Tank fits electric or kick starter models 1967-78. Tank utilizes stock mounts for installation. Measures 12" x 6" x 6". Some 1973-78 models may require strut brace modification. Battery compartment measures 7 1/2 long x 4 1/4" wide.

VT No. 40-0403

XLCH Front Oil Tank Mount. Zinc plated, fits 1953-65.
VT No. 31-0426

CAPS

Oil Tank Plug is constructed of rubber with chrome cap for tanks which accept a push in plug.
VT No. 28-0219

Chrome Oil Tank Cap

Fits the stock oil tank on 1952-78 XLH. Replaces 62610-52A

VT No.	Item
40-0504	Cap
15-0329	Cap Gasket
15-0341	Cap Washer
40-9955	Dipstick
12-0970	Retaining Ring

Magnetic Drain Plug

Prevents metal particles from circulating through oil tank and time hole. Plug is 5/6 -18. OEM#720, 706A.
VT No. 37-0098

XLH Chrome Oil Tank

Fits 1970-78 with kick start in rigid or stock frame. Includes chrome fill plug. Top mount and lower mount available separately.

VT No.	Item	Finish
40-0425	Tank	Chrome
40-0612	Tank	Black
40-0324	Tank	Black, Early
31-3975	Lower Bracket	Chrome
31-3965	Upper Bracket	Zinc
37-0826	Mount Bolt Kit	Zinc

Chrome 5.5" Round Oil Tank

Fits XL with Rigid frame mounts by clamping to center tube or top mount center fill.

VT No.	Type	Finish	Brackets
40-0474	Clamp	Chrome	
40-1476	Clamp	Raw	
40-0741	Top Mount	Chrome	31-1755
40-0742	Top Mount	Raw	31-1755

Chrome Magneto Horseshoe Oil Tank

Horseshoe Tank for Sportster features side fill spout with a capacity of 3 3/4 quarts. Fits 1957-78 kick starter applications. No provision for a battery. Use mount kit to attach 40-0404 to single tube XL rigid frame. Includes cap.

VT No.	Item	Type
40-0404	Tank	Swingarm, stock
37-0098	Drain Plug	

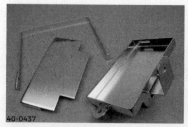

Chrome Rigid Oil Tanks

VT No.	Item
40-0416	Oil Tank
40-0437	Battery Tray w/ strap and top

Tanks fit V-Twin frame nos 51-2174 through 51-2177. Battery tray accepts 12N164B battery, VT No. 53-0518.

1979- UP OIL TANK AND COVER

OIL TANK COVER "INSTANT" INSTALLATION

40-0001 Installed

40-0000

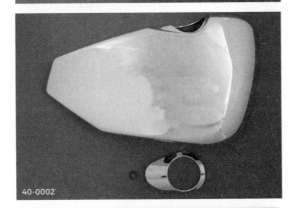

40-0002

Oil Tank for XL

40-0397

40-0399

40-0391

40-0401

40-0397

40-0390

FUEL
14

Chrome	Black	OEM	Year
40-0399	40-0390	62475-83	1983-93
40-0391	40-0401	62475-94	1994-96
40-0397	40-0257	62475-97	1997-2003
	40-0274	62888-04	2004-2009
28-0546		62563-65	Iso-mounting studs for above tanks

VT No.	OEM	Year	Item
28-0409	60429-97	1997-2003	Bumper
28-0410	66214-97	1997-2003	Pad

VT No.	Year
40-0000	1983-93
40-0001	1994-2003
40-0002	2004 Up

Chrome Oil Tank Covers are of one piece form fitting design to fully cover the outer surface of the tank. Cover is easily installed without removal of tank. It is attached to the rear oil tank fittings by springs supplied on 1983-93 model and by clips on 1994-up models.

V-TWIN DEVELOPED THE FIRST FORM FIT OIL TANK COVERS IN 1978 FOR THE SPORTSTER ELECTRIC START OIL TANK.

42-9973

42-9974

42-0310

Ignition Module Cover, 1982-2003

VT No.	Style	Item	VT No.	Style	Item
42-9973	Chrome Eagle Spirit	Cover	37-0824	Chrome Screw Set	1982-97
42-9974	Gold Inlay Eagle Spirit	Cover	37-0893	Chrome Screw Set	1998-2003
42-0310	Smooth Chrome	Cover	37-8348	Insert for Above	

Chrome Right Side Oil Tank Cover

VT No.	OEM	Year
40-4005	66415-79	1979
40-4006	66601-80	1980-81
28-0158	11406	Mounting Grommet, 1980-81, pair

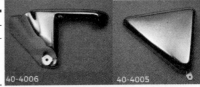

40-4006   40-4005

173

OIL FILTER KIT

Universal Oil Cooler Filter Kit

Includes chrome spin on filter, finned aluminum mount flange with hose and clamps.

40-0098

VT No.	Item
40-0098	Alloy Kit
40-0952	Chrome Kit
40-0709	Filter Only, Chrome
31-2131	1" Frame Clamps

Sifton Oil Pre-Filters

40-0388, Exploded View

Spring   Magnet   Screen

40-0388

Constructed of machined alloy with a #40 mesh screen installed to trap large debris and a circular magnetic collar to collect the ultra fine ferrous particles before they reach the engine. Unit can be installed in the following locations for 3/8" inner diameter oil line: Supply line before the engine, all models. Return line to oil tank on XLCH and models without a factory filter, External oil return on high performance heads. Any pressure supply or return (use the prelifter with the 1/8" NPT threaded body).

VT No.	Type	Hose
40-0388	1/8" NPT Body	3/8"
40-0387	Barbed End	3/8"
40-0389	Barbed End	1/2"
31-2131	1" Frame Clamps	

40-0097

Pura-Flow Oil Filter Kit

Fits 1957-77. Kit includes left side motor mount plate, chrome filter and hose with clamps.

VT No.	Item
40-0097	Kit
40-0709	Replacement Filter

Pura-Flow Universal Clamp-on Oil Filter Kit

Kit includes filter and hose.
VT No. 40-0850

Sifton Oil Filter Adapter

Adapter for 1986-90.   VT No. 40-0540

Oil Filter Adapter

Use with 40-0709 filter. For 1986-2003 XL .
VT No. 40-0273

XLH XLS Oil Filter Kit

Installs as engine mount plates and oil filter unit on all 1982-84 except Evolution. Accepts late peg assembly. Includes chrome filter, hose, clamps and chrome motor mount plates 16210-81 and 16213-81.

VT No.	Item
40-0301	Complete Kit
40-0711	Replacement Filter
27-0635	Late type Foot Rest Support

Oil Filter Adapter

40-0315

40-0315 Installed

40-0709

For 1984-up XL alternator models, use 40-0709 filter.

VT No.	Item	Finish
40-0315	Adapter	Alloy
40-0316	Adapter	Chrome
40-0709	Filter	Chrome

1986-99 Oil Filter Hardware.		
VT No.	OEM	Item
37-9195	6016	Washer
14-0556	11148	Quad Seal
13-9182	26002-86	Spring
14-0517	26433-77	O-Ring for Check Valve
13-9180	26436-86	Spring
32-0428	26554-77	Oil Pressure Switch

Allen   Acorn

9752-4   8864-4

Oil Filter Adapter Screw Kit for 1986-92 models.

OIL FILTER

Magnetek™ Oil Filter

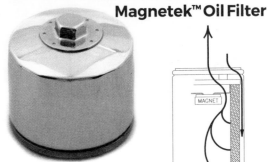

40-0865 with nut

Oil is drawn around the outer diameter, through the filter media, then dispelled, passing by the magnet. The magnetic ring captures particles less than 10 microns, which could have escaped through the filter wall.

Hex	VT No.	OEM	Fits	Length
40-0865	40-0851	63782-80	1980 E 84	2.5"
40-0864	40-0852	63796-77 5 Speed XL	1984 - Up	3.75"

K&N Spin-On Filter

Available in chrome or black. Feature hex nut end for easy removal and installation. Improved pressure and relief valve and anti-drain back valve.

VT No.	Finish	Fits	Length
40-1720	Chrome	1980-E84	2.5"
40-1710	Chrome	1984-Up	3.75"
40-1711	Black	1984-Up	3.75"

Fram Spin-On Filter

Chrome Fram Spin-On Oil Filter replaces 63782-80. Fits 1980-E84. 2.5" in length.
VT No. 40-0725

Drop In Filter Unit includes spring, O-ring and one piece filter.
VT No. 40-0172

Oil Filter Wrench

Fits all spin on filters 3/8" drive.
VT No. 16-0743

Spin-On Oil Filters replaces stock units in chrome or black, Perf-form or V-Twin Brand in stock or with hex nut style. Perf-form Tall Chrome Filter is 3/4" longer than stock and will not fit fuel injected models. All filters listed are low restriction type.

Note: Chrome and Black Spin On Filters are 3" outer diameter.

40-0363

40-0857

40-0709

Hex	VT No.	Per-Form	OEM	Finish	Length	Year
40-0857	40-0711	40-0363	63782-80T	Chrome	2.5"	1980 - E 84
40-0871	40-0710	40-0379	63810-80T	Black	2.5"	1980 - E 84
40-0860	40-0708	40-0378	63805-80T	Black	3.75"	1984 1/2 - Up
40-0872	40-0709		63796-77T	Chrome	3.75"	1984 1/2 - Up

Perf-Form Filter Unit

A complete drop-in replacement. 1954-78 XLH. Spring included.
VT No. 40-0380

40-0504

40-0700

40-0705

Oil Filter Elements

Original style. Fit 54-78 XLH models. Replaces 63888-53.

VT No.	Type
40-0700	Felt
40-0705	Metal Perforated
40-0720	Fram

Oil Filter Hardware for 1954-78 XL

VT No.	#	OEM	Item
40-0714	A-H (no G)		Kit
40-9953	A-H		Kit, with G.
40-9954	G	63839-53	Cup
40-0700	B	63839-53	Filter Element, 12pc
40-0122	E	63846-67	Lower Washer
13-0207	D	63831-67	Spring, 10pk
40-0125	A, C	63881-67 63882-67	Upper Seal Kit Lower Seal
14-0526	F	63879-53	O-Ring, 10pk
12-0940	H	63878-53	Clip, 10pk
40-9955	I	63885-65	Dipstick
40-0504	J	62610-52A	Chrome Cap Assembly

40-9953

40-0714

40-0125

40-9988   40-9988   40-9987

Nugget Oil Gauge Kit

40-0010   40-0358

Original hex design places oil gauge at rocker box level on 1957-85 Sportster. Sold as kit with 60 lb. Liquid filled gauge. Hex dome matches our rocker shaft end plugs early 7142-4, late 7143-4.

VT No.	Item
40-9987	1957-70 Complete Kit, White Face
40-9988	1971-85 Complete Kit, Black Face
40-0359	1957-70 Fitting Only
40-0358	1971-85 Fitting Only
40-0010	1971-85 Fitting Only, Knuckle Nut Style
40-0500	60lb Gauge only, liquid, whiteface

1" OD Mini Oil Gauge

Sold with 1/8" pipe fitting.

VT No.	Year	Type
40-0878	1971-84	FX, FL
40-0589	1/8" NPT	Gauge Only

40-0878   40-0589

Oil Pressure Gauge

40-9906   40-0382   40-0386

40-0385   40-0569   40-0571   40-0500

Has a stainless steel case and rim house. Available with liquid filled housing with 1-1/2" face, 1/8" NPT male rear fitting.

VT No.	Pounds	Face	Brands
40-9906	0-30	Black	V-Twin
40-0500	0-60	White	AEE
40-0569	0-60	Silver	Sifton
40-0571	0-60	Blue	Sifton
40-0382	0-60	Black	Accel
40-0386	0-60	Black	V-Twin
40-9907	0-100	Black	Accel
40-0385	0-100	Black	V-Twin

OIL GAUGE

All gauges measure 1.5" diameter.

Sifton™ Rocker Box Oil Pressure Gauge Kits

Feature 0-60lb liquid filled pressure gauge with case fitting which allows retention of oil pressure switch for indicator lamp with chrome bracket and screw to mount to head. Stainless steel line included.

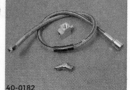

40-9966   40-0182

VT No.	Item	Year	VT No.	Item	Year
40-9966	Kit	1991-03	40-0632	Kit	2004-up
40-0182	Line		40-0841	Hardware	

1-1/2" Deluxe Liquid Filled Oil Gauge Kit

40-0515

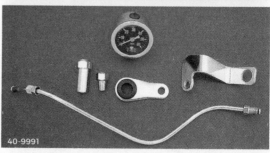

40-9991

Liquid filled face eliminates needle bounce, giving a constant reading. Gauge features weather resistant sealed lens with chrome rim and extra-heavy mechanism in stainless steel case. Includes necessary chrome fittings for bolt-on installation.

VT No.	Fits
40-0515	1957-1984 All XL
40-9991	1985-1990 Evolution XL Head Mount

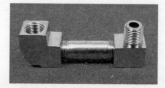

Oil Gauge Fitting Kit accept standard oil gauge with 1/8" NPT. 1957-84 XLH. 3 piece kit.

VT No. 12-1415

TANK FOR 2004-UP XL

Bobber Gas Tank

38-7079

38-7080

For XL. Tanks have a 2.3 gallon capacity and left side petcock.

VT No.	Year	VT No.	Year
38-7079	2007- Up	38-7080	2004-06

King Tanks

38-0283

38-0295

Available with pop up gas cap. Capacity is approximately 3.3 gallons. 38-0283 purchase gas cap 38-0352 separately.

VT No.	Style	Year
38-0295	Pop Up	2004-06
38-0283	Aircraft	2004-06
38-0296	Cap Only	

3.2 Gallon Bobber Tanks

38-0026

Fit 2004-06 models. 38-0026 accepts dash kit.

VT No.	Type	Cap
38-0025	Smooth	2
38-0065	Smooth	1
38-0026	Accepts Dash	2
37-0350	Bolt Set	

38-0025

38-0065

Chrome Right and Left Gas Tank Cover

Fits 2004-up XL.
VT No. 38-0933

35-0748

35-0750

Adapter Bushing

Allows use of carb type petcock on electronic fuel injection models

VT No.	Model
35-0748	FX, FL
35-0750	XL

Replica Tank

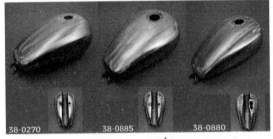

Stock or aero filler neck.

38-0877

38-0270   38-0885   38-0880

38-0951

38-0853

Replica	Aero	Year	Type
38-0270*	38-0885*	2004-06	Carburetor
38-0553		2004-Up	2" Raised
38-0877*	38-0880	2007-Up	Electronic Fuel Injection
38-0853		2007-Up	Electronic Fuel Injection
38-0544		2007-Up	2" Raised
38-0951		2011-Up	2.4 Gallon 1200X
28-0928		2007-Up	EFI Plug

*Note: Order cap separately.

Note: 2007-up XL models are fuel injected and require a fuel tank that accepts the Electronic Fuel Injection unit.

2" Stretch Tank

38-0030

38-0030 Installed

Shown on 2004 XL Sportster, to fit 2004-06 models, 4.0 gallons.

VT No.	Type	Cap Type
38-0030	Smooth	Screw In
38-0425	Smooth	Pop-up
38-0296	Cap Only	

4.0 Gallon One Piece Bobbed Tank

Fits 2004-06 XL and includes bolt in locking aircraft style gas caps and full rubber mount system.

VT No. 38-0299

1982-03 TANK

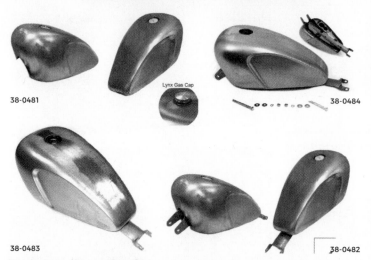

38-0481

Lynx Gas Cap

38-0484

38-0483

38-0482

Legacy Gas Tanks
Use stock bung cap for Sportsters.

VT No.	Year	VT No.	Year
38-0481	1983-03	38-0483	2004-10
38-0482	Custom	38-0484	2007-up EFI

King Tanks

38-0281

Available with air craft or pop up gas cap. Feature smooth radius edge profiles. Capacity is approximately 3.3 gallons.

Air Craft	Pop Up	Year
38-0281*		1982-1995
38-0426	38-0296	Cap Only

*Note: Does not include cap must be purchased separately.

One Piece Bobber Tank

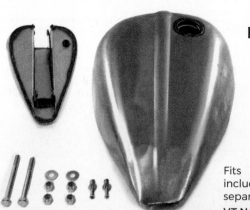

Fits 1982-03 brackets included. Order cap separately.
VT No. 38-0639

Seamless Side Panel

38-0260

38-0262

Indented Sides

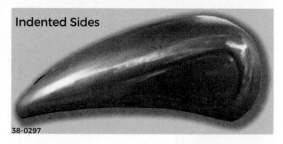

38-0297

38-0930   38-0931

2" Stretch Tanks

Tank fits 1982-2003 XLS. One piece curved design with full rubber mounting. Order coil and switch location kit for 1995-2003 models. Dash type accepts 2, 3 or cast dash assemblies.

VT No.	Type	Year	Type
38-0260	Dash Type	1982-2003	Smooth
38-0262	Single Cap	1982-2003	Smooth
38-0297	Single Cap	1982-2003	Indent
38-0930	Single Cap	2007-up	Smooth (No Cap)
38-0931	Single Cap	2007-up	Indented

3.2 GALLON E-Z BOB TANK

Bobbed Tank Kit with Dash

38-0191

Kit features one piece 3.2 gallon design, which includes chrome bung style late caps, and all necessary mount hardware for installation. Kit also includes a chrome cast dash kit.

VT No.	Years
38-0179	1982-94
38-0177	1995-03
38-0191	2004-06

*NOTE: THE ABOVE TANK KITS INCLUDE A DASH KIT WHICH INCLUDES A PLAIN DASH BASE WITHOUT WIRING, 2:1 RATIO BOB STYLE SPEEDO, A 43" SPEEDO CABLE FOR FRONT WHEEL DRIVE APPLICATION AND A LATE BOB TYPE 6 POST CHROME KEY SWITCH. UNITS FOR 1995-UP DO NOT INCLUDE SPEEDO OR CABLE, THESE KITS DO INCLUDE BRACKET TO MOUNT STOCK ELECTRONIC SPEEDO FROM MOTORCYCLE AND A COIL RELOCATION KIT. TANK IS 21-3/4" LONG AND 12-3/4" WIDE. MOUNT HOLE TO MOUNT HOLE IS 15-1/4". PETCOCK ON LEFT. TANK ASSEMBLIES ARE SOLD WITH "PLAIN DASH BASE" AND ARE NOT DESIGNED TO BE WIRED FOR INSTRUMENT LIGHTING. DASH BASES VT NO. 39-0959 FOR 3-LIGHT AND VT NO. 39-0960 FOR CAST DASH ARE AVAILABLE SEPARATELY FOR BUILDER REQUIRING DASH LIGHTING.

Bobbed Tanks -One Piece

38-0076

38-0075

For all Sportster models. Bolts to existing mounting holes.

Kit	Tank Only	Years
38-0075	38-0097	1952-78
38-0076	38-0094	1979-81
38-0077	38-0096	1982-94
38-0067*		1995-03
	38-0026	2004-06

*Note: Does not include speedometer cover

Includes hardware. Available as tank only which will accept 2, 3 or cast type dash kits which includes 3 lite dash, plain unwired dash base, 2:1 ratio speedometer, key switch(for cosmetic looks only) gas cap set, gas tank and mounting hardware. 1982-up models must use XLS or shorter seat. All tanks use 38-0321 gas cap set and are 3.2 gallon capacity. Tank measure 21-3/4" long and 12-3/4" wide and is 15-1/4" from mount hole to mount hole with petcock location on left hand side. 1995-up kits include coil relocation kit VT No. 38-0218 and speedometer adapter ring that allows use of stock speedometer in dash cover.

Smooth Top Bobbed Tanks

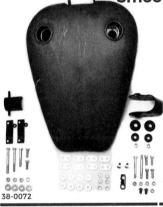

Featuring a smooth top that does not accept dash panel or speedometer. 3.2 gallon capacity. Includes necessary hardware for installation. Order cap set VT No. 38-0321 late bung style caps separately.1995-up kits include coil/ignition switch kit. Tank width is 14-1/2" tapering to 9", overall length is 19", tunnel height is 7-1/2" and width is 2-1/2".

*Note: Mount hardware not included.

38-0072

VT No.	Years
38-0090	1957-78
38-0072	1979-81
38-0091*	1982-94
38-0071*	1995-03

VT No.	Years
38-0025	2004-06
38-0321	Chrome Two Cap Set
31-0321	Coil Mount and Switch Cover Kit

Bobbed Gas Tank Kit

38-0082

Kit includes a 3.2 gallon one piece tank, chrome dash without key switch hole, plain dash base, and mounting hardware. All kits can be used with a solo seat or custom seat with a shorter nose, such as our XLS types. Dash will not accept a speedo with a built in tachometer. Order speedo separately. Tank is 21-3/4" long and 12-3/4" wide. Mount hole to mount hole is 15-1/4" petcock on left. 1995-up Kits include coil relocation kit.

VT No.	Year	Cap
38-0082	1982-94	Bung

Bobbed Tank for XL

3 gallon tank features bolt in locking aircraft style gas caps and full rubber mount system for 1982-03 XL models.
VT No. 38-0033

Cap Only with 2 Keys

Fits above tank, for 1982-03 XL.
VT No. 38-0426

REPLICA GAS TANK & CAP

38-0104

38-0024

38-0117 38-0743

38-0039

38-0085

Replica Gas Tanks for Sportster are stock styled high-tunnel Tanks that feature stock mounts and filler neck. Fits 1955-up, 2.4 gallon capacity. Tanks use a 1975-up petcock.

VT No.	OEM	Fits	Side
38-0095*	61000-54C	1952-70 includes vent tube & accepts early petcock 35-0400	Right
38-0024*	61023-83	1982-93 Rubber Mount	Right
38-0104*	61044-75	1958-78	Right
38-0743		1958-78	Right
38-0105*	61097-79	1979-81	Right
38-0117**	61023-83	1982-92	Right
38-0085**	61023-93	1993-2003	Right
38-0039**	61023-93	1993-2003	Left

*Note: Uses early cap 38-0310   **Note: Uses cap 38-0317

38-0757 38-0361

38-0391

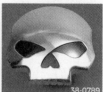

38-0405

38-0423

38-0789

38-7001

38-0541

Gas Caps for screw in bung style gas tanks. Vented type fits 1983-up single cap XLH tanks. Sold each.

VT No.	Style	VT No.	Style
38-0787	Pop-Up	38-0361	Pop-Up
38-0391	Cross	38-0405	Flame
38-0423	Maltese	38-7001	Eagle
38-0789	Skull	38-0541	Flame
38-0539	Smooth Black	38-1132	Skull, Black
38-6719	Wings		

Chrome Spinner Gas Cap

VT No.	Fits
38-0409	1983-95
38-0429	1983-95 Set

Fits bung style tanks with vent.

38-0207

38-0216

38-0217

XLCH Gas Tank Mounting Hardware Kit

Includes nuts, washers and spacers for mounting stock gas tank.

VT No.	Fits	VT No.	Fits
38-0207	1958-85	38-0217	1993-2003
38-0216	1986-92		

38-0224

31-0321

38-0219

Iso-Mount Kit

38-0218

VT No.	Fits
38-0224	1957-78
38-0225	1979-81
38-0219	1982-2003
38-0218	1995-98 Coil and Switch Mount Relocation Kit
31-0321	Coil Mount and Ignition Switch Cover with Hardware, 1995-up

Gas Tank Mounting Kit

Includes chrome custom acorn nuts, washers, studs, spacers and grommets.

2107-16

2265-6

VT No.	Fits
2107-16	1996-03
2265-6	2004- Up

Hardware for above available separately.

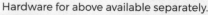

VT No.	OEM	Year	Item
37-9209	42500-80	1980-up	Spacer
37-9208	5787	1993-up	Spacer
37-9211	61135-57	1952-81	Spacer

KING GAS TANK

V-Twin™ Replica King Tanks

38-0132

38-0133 Installed/ Painted

38-0799

38-0032

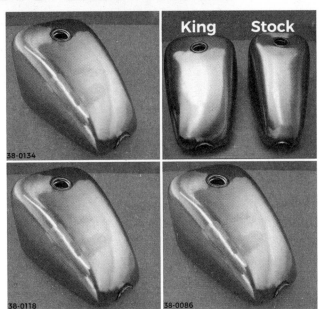

King   Stock

38-0134

38-0118   38-0086

'King' Gas Tanks are made 2" wider than stock and include stock style mounts, 3.1 gallon capacity. King Tank is 17-1/2" long, 10-3/4" wide. 38-0106 accepts 3/8" NPT petcock. Petcock side as noted.

VT No.	Fits	Side	
38-0106*	1958-78	Right	
38-0107*	1979-81	Right	
38-0118**	1982-92	Right	*Note: Uses Early Cap 38-0310.
38-0086**	1982-94	Right	
38-0965	1982-94	Left	**Note: Uses Cap 38-0317
38-0134**	1982-94	Left	

38-0485

38-0274

Feature an updated design shape that rolls the bottom edge under, to give flowing lines, while still retaining the classic shape. These are replicas of the 1996-up stock versions which are stock on all 1997-up models. King Tank is 20" long 10" wide.

VT No.	Year	Gallon	Petcock	Type
38-0133	1982-94	3.2	Right	Carburetor
38-0132	1995-03	3.2	Left	Carburetor
38-0274	1982-03	3.2	Left	Carburetor
38-0032	2004-06	3.2	Left	Carburetor
38-0485	2007-up	3.2	Left	Electronic Fuel Injection
38-0799	2007-up	3.2	Left	Electronic Fuel Injection, Aero
38-0845	2007-up	3.2	Left	Electronic Fuel Injection, Pop-up
38-0951	2007-up	2.4	Left	Electronic Fuel Injection, 1200 X
28-0923				Rubber Insert

38-0019

38-0021

38-0066

38-0098

Universal Gas Tanks   3.1 or 2.5 gallon capacity.

VT No.	Type	Size	Tabs
38-0019	2.5	Stock, Forward, Bayonet	Side
38-0021	2.5	Stock, Forward	Side
38-0023	2.4	Stock, Right	Side
38-0544	2.4	2" Raised	Side
38-0066	2.5	Stock	F & R
38-0098	3.1	King	F & R
38-0685		XR 750	

Allen Tank Mount Kits

VT No.	Year
37-9302	1972-79
37-9303	1986-95

Tank Riser Kit

Gives a 2" rise to the front tank on 1995-2010 Sportster models.

VT No. 38-0857

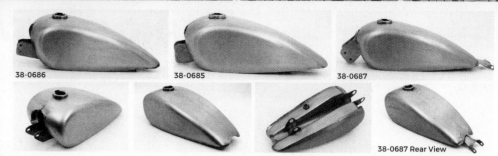

XR Style Gas Tank

Original shape for the "750" look.

VT No.	Year
38-0686	1957-78
38-0685	1982-03
38-0687	2004-06
38-0688	2007-up
38-0636	XR 750 1957-78 w/o brackets, universal

38-0686   38-0685   38-0687

38-0687 Rear View

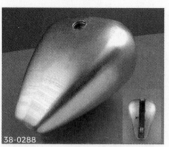

38-0288

38-0065

VT No.	Year	Cap
38-0288	1982-03	Bung
38-0065	2004-06	Bung

Chopper Tanks

Axed style tank with single center bung. 38-0288 is rubber mounted.

V-Race Patch

An authentic V-Twin racing patch that represents the WR, KR and XL speed products.

VT No. 48-1641

SPEEDSTER V-TWIN 750 WR • KR • XR

38-0037

38-0038

Porkster Tank™

38-0079

38-0069

38-0027

Replica Style 3.5 Gallon Tank

38-0037 Installed

VT No.	Year	Petcock
38-0038	1952-78	Right
38-0037	1982-2003	Left
38-0329	Cap	

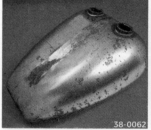

38-0062

38-0028

Porkster Tank is 4.2 gallon axed style large tank to bolt on Sportsters models, use 38-0310 cap for single and dual cap styles and stock petcocks. Available in single or dual caps. Tank is 13-1/2" wide, 15-3/4" long, 8-3/4" deep. Tunnel is 2-1/4" wide, 2-1/4" deep.

Replacement Fuel Pump Kit for EFI

OEM Style fits 2007- Up 883 and 1200cc Sportster models.

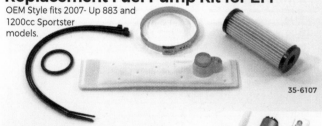

35-6107

Single	Dual	Years	Petcock Side
	38-0079*	1979-81	Right
	38-0069	1995-2003	Left
38-0027	38-0028	2004-2006	Left
	38-0062**	1982-94	Left

*Note: Uses early style pre-1975 type petcock all other numbers use 1975-up type petcock.

** Rubber Mounted Style.

VT No.	Item
35-1079	EFI Pump
35-6107	Filter Kit
35-0189	Petcock Adapter Fitting

35-1079

BILLET PETCOCK

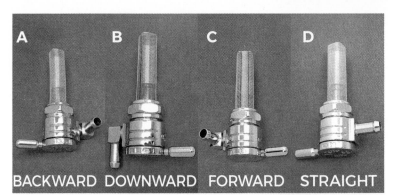

A B C D

BACKWARD DOWNWARD FORWARD STRAIGHT

Sifton Chrome Ball Petcocks

Feature stainless steel ball bearing mechanism that provides a secure on/off seal and prevents valve from freezing in open or closed position. Available with 3/8" NPT (pre 1975) on 22mm nut for 1975-94, and 4 outlet positions for any application. Also available with 6AN threaded fitting for fuel line hookup using stainless steel hose fittings. For use with 5/16" fuel line.

VT No.	#	Type
35-0590	A	NPT
35-0591	A	Nut
35-0592	B	NPT
35-0593	B	Nut
35-0594	C	NPT
35-0595	C	Nut
35-0596	D	NPT
35-0597	D	Nut
35-0598		Nut/6AN

1/4" Chrome Petcocks

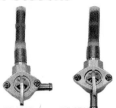

35-0396   35-0397
Use with 5/16" fuel line.

VT No.	Type
35-0396	90°
35-0397	Straight

Brass Petcock for S&S "E" Carb

Bolts directly to bowl. For use with 5/16" fuel line.

VT No. 35-0935

Petcock Left Outlet w/ Nut

Alloy with 90° left outlet and nut. Includes nylon filter screen, washer, and reserve position.

VT No. 35-9167

FUEL
14

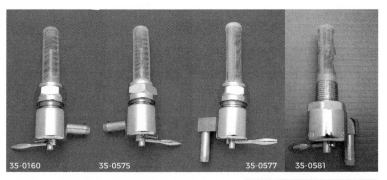

35-0160   35-0575   35-0577   35-0581

Sifton Chrome Billet Petcocks

Feature solid brass construction and on/off and reserve positions, screen, and a 3/8" fitting. For use with 5/16" fuel line.

W/Nut	3/8" NPT	Outlet
35-0160	35-0579	Rear
35-0575	35-0580	Forward
35-0577	35-0581	Down

Mini Petcocks

1/4" NPT w/ ball shut off for use with 5/16" fuel line.

35-9071   35-9072

VT No.	Reserve	Type	VT No.	Reserve	Type
35-9071	With	Straight	35-9072	Without	90°

Accel Hi-Flow 360° Swivel Petcock

Chrome plated, high volume and includes nut. The 90° fitting is a 360° swivel type. Petcock accepts a 5/16" fuel line. Designs are made for a seated position on the motorcycle with the hose outlet facing a direction to ease fuel line hookup. Fits 1975-95.

VT No. 35-9074

Wyatt's Billet Petcock Grooved Chrome

Fits 1975-94 applications with side exit. Nut Included. For use with 5/16" fuel line.

VT No. 35-0951

PETCOCK (FUEL VALVE) DIRECTION IS DETERMINED BY DIRECTION HOSE COMES OFF VALVE WHEN SITTING ON MOTORCYCLE.

Right: Left side mounted, hose outlet facing back, or right side mounted, hose outlet facing forward.

Under: Left side mounted, hose outlet facing right or right side mounting hose outlet facing left.

Left: Left side mounted, hose outlet facing forward or right side mounted hose outlet facing back.

Down: Right or left side hose outlet facing down.

OFF RES ON

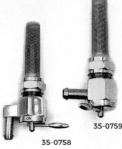

35-0757 35-0756 35-0758 35-0759 35-0685 35-0686 35-0687

35-0688 35-0689 35-0690

Sifton Hex Petcock

Constructed of forged brass with screen and brass hose spigot. For use with 5/16" fuel line.

Down	Rear	Forward	Type
Chrome			
35-0685	35-0687	35-0689	NPT
35-0686	35-0688	35-0690	Nut
Brass			
	35-0756	35-0757	NPT
35-0758	35-0759		Nut

Accel Hi-Flow Fuel Valve

35-9171   35-9074

Chrome plated, high-volume - includes nut. For 1975-94 models. The 90° type has 360° swivel fitting. For use with 5/16" fuel line.

VT No.	Type	VT No.	Type
35-9171	Straight	35-9074	90°

Pingel R In-Line Fuel Valve

Chrome plated fuel valve for in line use features simple on/off operation without reserve capacity and no filter. For use with 5/16" fuel line.

VT No. 35-0040

Petcock with Nut and Screen

For use with stock fuel line in 1995-up XL.

VT No. 35-0058

PINGEL

Pingel R Fuel Valve Rebuild Kit

Designed to work with single of dual outlet Pingel R reserve valves. Rebuild kit includes rebuilding parts for three fuel valves plus all tools, photos and instructions.

VT No.	Item
35-9290	Complete Rebuild Kit
35-9291*	Fuel Valve Rebuild Components (Rebuilds 5 valves)

Pingel R Fuel Valve ### PINGEL

Valve with nut fits 1975-94. Without nut is 3/8" NPT for 1975 and down. Unit features a metric nut utilizing right and left hand thread, so once installed adapter nut can be loosened, valve put in the desired position, and nut re-tightened. No need to use Teflon tapes, meaning less chance of leakage!

NOTE: for use with 5/16" fuel line. All descriptions and designs are made for a seated position on the motorcycle with the hose outlet facing a direction to ease fuel line hookup.

A   **B**

35-9083

A- Hex		B-Smooth		
Chrome	**Polished**	**Chrome**	**Tank Spigot**	**Type**
35-9083	35-9082	35-9309	Left	Nut
35-9090	35-9091	35-9310	Left	NPT
35-9085	35-9084	35-9311	Right	Nut
35-9092	35-9093	35-9312	Right	NPT
35-9088	35-9089	35-9313	Under	Nut
35-9178	35-0398	35-9314	Under	NPT
35-9087	35-9086		Down	Nut
35-9094	35-9095		Down	NPT
35-0218	35-0218	35-0218	Adapter, Nut Kit	
14-0571	14-0571	14-0571	Nylon Washer	

REPLICA PETCOCK

35-0400   35-9247

Wing Type Petcock

Includes screen and 2 handles, sliding valve control with reserve. Replaces 62125-55B. For use with 5/16" fuel line.

VT No.	Type	Finish
35-0400	1955-74	Chrome
35-9247	1955-74	Zinc
35-9248	Screen	Plastic

COMPONENTS

Inner Petcock Seal

Constructed for other custom style petcocks.

VT No.	Hole	Type
14-0909	4	OE
14-0007	3	V-T

Screens Only

35-0835   35-0834

VT No.	Type
35-0835	For use with 3/8" NPT Petcocks
35-0834	For use with 13/16" Nut Petcocks

Adapter Bushings

VT No.	Model
35-0748	FX, FL
35-0750	XL

35-0748   35-0750

Allow for use of carb type petcock on electronic fuel injection models.

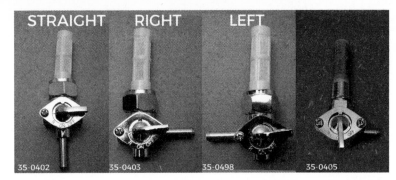

STRAIGHT   RIGHT   LEFT

35-0402   35-0403   35-0498   35-0405

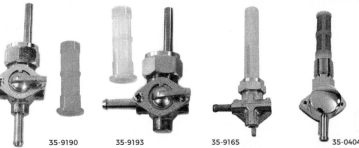

35-9190   35-9193   35-9165   35-0404

Replica Fuel Petcocks

35-0095   15-0265

Feature nylon filter screen, washer, and reserve position. Available in chrome or natural alloy finish. For use with 5/16" fuel line.

Alloy	Chrome	Black	Outlet	Type
35-9190	35-0402	35-0186	Straight	Nut
35-9165	35-0403	35-0188	Right	Nut
35-9193	35-0498	35-0187	Left	Nut
35-9167			Left	Nut
	35-0405	35-0570	1955-74 Right 3/8	NPT
	35-0404	35-0549	1955-74 Straight 3/8	NPT
	15-0265		Gasket, 10pk	1984- Up
	35-0095		Nut, each	

PETCOCK (FUEL VALVE) DIRECTION IS DETERMINED BY DIRECTION HOSE COMES OFF VALVE WHEN SITTING ON MOTORCYCLE.

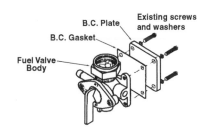

B.C. Plate
Existing screws and washers
B.C. Gasket
Fuel Valve Body

Fuel Valve Body Vacuum Bypass Kit

Includes plate, gasket, vacuum hose plug and instructions.
VT No. 35-0426

FUEL LINE & CLAMP

Fuel & Oil Line 25 Foot Rolls

Black	Clear	Size
40-0999		1/8" - 10 Foot Roll
40-0117	40-1250	3/16"
40-0118		1/4"
40-0119	40-1252	5/16"
40-0120		3/8"
40-0253		3/8" - 6 Foot Roll
40-0126		1/2"

40-0223 40-0214

Chrome Econo-Seal Hose Ends

Act as clamp and finished end when stainless jacket rubber hose is cut. Micro clamp is hidden under chrome end.

Smooth	Hex	Fits	Qty
40-0222	40-0213	1/4"	6
40-0248		5/16"	6
40-0223	40-0214	3/8"	6
40-0224	40-0218	1/4"	2
40-0249		5/16"	2
40-0225	40-0219	3/8"	2
	40-0220	13/16" Inner Diameter	1
	40-0591	15mm	2
	40-0592	17mm	2

Radii Polished Stainless Steel Hose Lock

Compression fitting that replaces conventional hose clamps. Feature a cleaner appearance and superior sealing performance. *Note:* Fits S&S Super "E" carburetor fitting.

Pair	Each	Size	Pair	Each	Size
35-0180	35-0175	1/4"	35-0183*		5/16"
35-0181		5/16"	35-0182		3/8"

Oil & Gas Hose Pliers

16-0000

Snip Hose Cutter

Hand held device quickly cuts any size rubber or nylon hose up to 3/4" diameter. Leaves hose perfectly clean and square.

VT No. 16-0049

Oil Fuel Line Clamp Assortment

Includes pliers. Refill for clamps as noted by Oetiker #.

16-0083

16-0080

VT No.	Oetiker No.	VT No.	Oetiker No.
16-0080	Service Kit	16-0081	15500003
16-0083	Pliers only	16-0085	15500009
16-0062	16700995	16-0053	16701009
16-0084	16700999		

Chrome Hose Cover

Flexible, spring loaded metal covering. To install, cut to same length as hose. Cover will compress under tension to allow installation of hose clamps for snug fit. 3 feet length.

40-0216

VT No.	Type	VT No.	Type
40-0215	1/4" Fuel	40-0216	3/8" Oil

Stainless Oil Line Kit

Includes 10 foot roll of 3/8" braided hose, and 6 chrome econo-seal hose ends.

VT No. 40-0418

Braided Stainless Hose

Bulk lengths cut to length as needed. Use Econo-seal ends or hose clamps to attach to fitting. **Warning:** Not for use in brake systems.

VT No.	Size	Feet	Type
40-0202	1/4"	10	V-Twin
40-0200	5/16"	5	V-Twin
40-0245	5/16"	25	V-Twin
40-1282	5/16"	25	Fuel
40-0210	3/8"	10	V-Twin
40-0244	3/8"	25	V-Twin

Flex Chrome Hose Covering

VT No.	Size
36-0552	1/4"
36-0553	3/8"
36-0554	1/2"

Features heavy gauge mylar construction with chrome finish, 25 foot length.

35-0442

35-8036

35-0413

35-0434

Stainless Hose Clamps

Available in Worm Gear type, Nickel Spring type, Torro drive type. Torro drive clamps feature pressed tooth and raised band edges to prevent damage to hose. Available in two sizes and sold in packs.

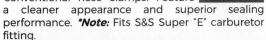

Stainless Worm Gear	Nickel Spring	Size	Line
35-0442	35-0836	1/2"	Fuel
35-0413		7/32" - 5/8"	Fuel
35-8031		5/8"	Oil
	35-8037	3/8"	
	35-8038	5/16"	

AXLE AND HUB

Rear Chrome Axle Nut Caps Set

Caps for both axle nut and axle head where required. Each cap has an internal hex to allow more thickness for set screws thread to eliminate thread stripping. Note: These axle caps will not work on late model rear axles with cotter key locking devices.

VT No.	OEM	Fitment
37-0041	44256-01	2000-07
37-8885		1982-87
37-8884		1973-80
37-8886		1971-72
44-0845	42034-07	2006-07
44-0742	41705-09	2008- Up

Front Axle Cap Cover Sets include right and left caps with set screws for glide type forks. Fits XL with 39mm forks.
VT No. 37-0036

Maltese Style Rear Axle Nut Caps for 1987-2006 FXST, FLST. Complete coverage for axle ends and cotter key area.
VT No. 37-9007

Front Wheel Spacers
Sold each for left side.

VT No.	Fitment	VT No.	Fitment
44-0391	1973 XLH, XLCH	44-0306	1978-95 XL, XLS
44-0305	1974-77 XLH, XLCH	44-0296	1986-99 All XL

Chrome Front Axle Spacer, Washer and Nut

Kit for XL models with 39mm forks. Smooth chrome finish. Fits 2000- Up.
VT No. 2028-5

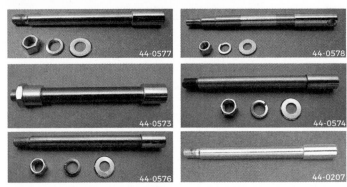
44-0577 · 44-0578 · 44-0573 · 44-0574 · 44-0576 · 44-0207

Chrome Front Axle Kits

Include plated axle, nuts, spacer, and hardware. *Note: Zinc Finish.

Year	Kit	Nut Kit	Axle	Axle OEM
1952-72	44-0573*	44-0308	44-0204*	43871-52
1973-77	44-0574	8768-3	44-0205	43871-73
1978-83	44-0576	8768-3	44-0206	43883-77
1986-87	44-0577	8768-3	44-0207	43883-84
1988-99	44-0578	8769-3	44-0086	43895-87
2000-07	44-0614	2028-5	44-0257	43895-08
2008-up		2509-6		
2010-up	44-0747			Model "48"

Pike Front Axle Cover Sets

Fits 1988-03 39mm forks.
VT No. 2263-2

Chrome Flush Mount Axle Fits 1988-99 XL models with 39 mm forks.
VT No. 44-0003

45-0671

45-0333 · 45-0792 · 45-0292

All Hubs include bearings, races, seals, seal spacers and are assembled and chromed except where noted.

Rear Hubs			
VT No.	#	OEM	Fits
45-0301	A	41017-55	1955-78 K-XL-XLH-XLCH
45-0668	B	43457-79	1979-81 All XL
45-0670	B	40952-82A	1982-85 XL
45-0671	B	40976-86A	1986-99 XL
45-0332	E	40976-00	2000-2004 XL
45-0333	E	41053-02	2005-2007 XL
45-0792	E		2008- Up without ABS
45-0810	E		2015- Up with ABS
Front Hubs			
45-0297	C	43600-73	1973 only XL
45-0307	D	43600-74	1974-77 XL, Single Disc
45-0310	C	43600-78	1978-83 XL-XLS
45-0311*	C		As above, Satin
45-0298	C	43619-84	1984-99 XL-XLS
45-0292	C		As above but Dual Disc
45-0532	C	43619-00	2000-07 XL Hugger, Dual Disc
45-0641	C	43610-00	2000-07 XL Custom 883/1200 Chrome Single Disc
45-0793	E		2008-Up Single Disc without ABS
45-0811	E		2015- Up Single Disc with ABS
45-0958			2010-Up "Model 48" without ABS

*Note: Internals not included, order separately

REAR AXLE

44-0643

44-0644

Rear Axle Kits include chrome axle, nuts, sleeves and spacers for each application.

Kit Cpt	Spacer	Collar	Axle Only	Nut Kit	Model
44-0565	44-0324	44-0317	44-0217	44-0326	1952-78
			44-0089	44-0326	1977-78, Zinc
44-0566			44-0220	8715-4	1979-85
44-0643	9997-3		44-0220	9997-3	1986-99
44-0644	2040-4		44-0220	37-9032	2000-03
44-0126	2258-5		44-0127	2258-5	2004
44-0125	2257-4		44-0128	2257-4	2005-07
44-0801	2510-5T		44-0248		2008-Up

WHEEL 15

Chrome Axle Kits

Include pike or acorn nuts. 3/4" diameter to fit 1979-2004 models.

Acorn 44-0665 / Pike 44-0664

9996-3 / 9997-3 / 2040-4

Chrome Rear Axle Spacer Kits

Include castle nut for axle and adjuster collars

Stock	Grooved	Years	Stock	Grooved	Years
2040-4		2000-03	2257-4		2005
9997-3	9996-3	1986-99		2483-4	2006-07
2258-5		2004	2510-5		2008-Up

Rear Axle Nut and Washers

Fit 1952-79 models.

VT No.	Item	Finish	U/M
44-0326	Nut with washer	Chrome	Kit
37-8127	Nyloc-Nut		10 pack
44-0317	41598-52, Sportster 1952-77	Zinc	Each
44-0500	As Above	Chrome	Each

44-0565

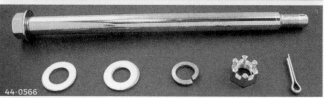
44-0566

Rear Pike Axle Nut Cover Set

Fits 1993-2003.
VT No. 2261-2

Chrome Rear Axle Spring Clip

Replaces 510 spring clip used on all 1991-Up, 5pk.
VT No. 2042-5

Chrome Rear Axle Nut Kit

5/8" x 18 thread nut kit includes washer and cotter pin for rear axles on 1989-up models, replaces 7987, 511.
VT No. 37-9032

Chrome Rear Axle Nut Kit

Custom hardware kit with installation instructions. Fits 1979-up.

VT No.	Type	VT No.	Type
8606-6	Acorn	8607-6	Cap

Chrome Rear Axle Nut and Washer Kit

Includes two extra thick washers, nut and lock washers for 1973-up, on square swing arms.

VT No.	Brand	VT No.	Brand
8715-4	Colony	44-0520	V-Twin

44-0421 / 44-0427 / 44-0422 / 44-0424 / 44-0324

Rear Axle Spacers for XL

VT No.	Year	Side	VT No.	Year	Side
44-0324	1955-78	Left	44-0422	1979-81	Left
44-0421	1982-85	Left (Pair)	44-0424	1979	Right
44-0427	1986-99	Both	44-0810	2004-07	Right and Left

DIY Universal Axle Spacer

Constructed of stainless steel 6" long with 3/4" inner diameter are 1-1/8" outside diameter, to be cut to length.
VT No. 44-0670

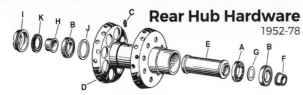

Rear Hub Hardware
1952-78

VT No.	OEM	#	Item
44-0404	Kit	All	Complete Hub Rebuild
45-0401	Cap		Chrome Hub Cap
12-0305	9008	A	Bearing without shield
12-0374	9009	B	Bearing with shield
44-0533	9851	C	Grease Fitting, 10 pack
45-0301	41017-55C	D	Complete Chrome Hub
44-0315	41185-63	E	Hub Spacer, each
44-1999	41195-52	F	Brake side Washer 1954-62
44-0395	41195-63	G	Brake side Washer 54-62, 10 pack
44-0392	41196-55	H	Seal Spacer, each
44-0529	41201-55	I	Locknut, Right Hand
44-0396	41205-52	J	Bearing Washer, 10 pack
14-0131	41210-55	K	Seal, 5 pack

HUB REBUILD

Front Internal Hub Kit

Includes all internal parts for complete rebuilding of all alloy front hubs. Includes inner spacer, bearings, races seals and seal spacer matched for each year group. Hub is not included.

VT No.	Type	Fits
44-0403	Drum	1964-72 XL, XLH
44-0311	Drum	Tube Spacer
44-0556	Drum	Dust Shield
12-0906	Drum	Snap Ring for Above
44-0402	10" Disc	1973 XL
44-0401	11" Disc	1974-77 XL
44-0400	Dual Disc	1977-83 XL
44-0537	11" Disc	1984-91 XL
44-0611	11" Disc	2000-07 XL

Rear Double Row Retro

Fit wheel bearing kits for models with bearings. Double row wheel bearings eliminate wheel play, have a longer wear life, require no adjustment. Kit includes two bearings, center spacer and spacers.

VT No.	Year
44-2295	1991-99
44-0921	Bearing Set Only
Replica Type	
44-0991	2000-04
44-0992	2005-07
44-0994	2008- Up

1955-78 XLH-XLCH Hub Rebuild

Use on all model steel hubs 1955-78, complete with all parts Illustrated. Everything necessary to install in a bare hub!

VT No. 44-0404

Hub Lock Nut Kit

Includes correct locknut spacer and seal for rear. Fits 1955-78.

VT No. 44-0412

Fits front and rear.

2000-Up Wheel Bearing

VT No.	OEM	U/M	Size
12-0592	9267	Each	3/4"
44-0993	9267	Pair	3/4"
12-0390	9247	Pair	1"
12-0631	9276	Pair	25mm

Rear Axle Adjuster Sets

VT No.	Years
44-0334	1979-84, with Chrome End Caps
44-0434	2005-08
44-0234	2009- Up

Rear Hub Rebuild Kits

Include all parts pictured less hub and internal bearing spacer. Fits 1979-Up.

VT No.	Fits	Wheel Type
44-0460	1979-81	Cast or Wire
44-0461	1982-83	Cast only
44-0462	1982-85	Wire only
44-0453	1986-99	Cast or Wire

Rear Chain Adjuster

Available in pairs with nuts. Fits 1952-78.

VT No.	Finish
7703-2	Chrome
9020-2	Cadmium

Chrome finish.
Includes nuts.

Pyramid Axle Adjusters

VT No.	Years	Item
44-0251	1997-03	Blocks Only
44-0365	1979-96	Complete Kit
44-0366	1979-96	Blocks Only

Chrome Calibrated Rear Wheel Adjuster

Features pyramid blocks with sight indicator to view calibrated adjuster bolt, for accurate and easy wheel alignment. Adjuster bolt is 1/2" rod with micrometer markings. Fits 1979-96.

VT No. 44-2011

WHEEL
15

FRONT WHEEL ASSEMBLY

Front Wheels on this page feature a chrome hub, unless noted as satin, with all internal bearings installed, choice of chrome or stainless spokes and chrome rim completely laced and trued.

52-1212
52-1088
52-0165
52-0151
52-1086

Front Wheels for Sportsters

WHEEL BUILDERS

SINCE 1969

52-1247

52-1290

WHEEL 15

Chrome Spokes	Stainless Spokes	Rim Dia.	Rim Wid.
1973 Only, XL - *Single Disc, 35mm Forks*			
52-0158		19" Drop Center	2.5"
52-0174		21"	1.85"
1974-77 XL Clover Type- *Single Disc, 35mm Forks*			
52-0165	52-0817	19" Drop Center	2.5"
52-0161		21"	1.85"
1974-77 XL Clover Type- *Single Disc, Satin Hub, 35mm Forks*			
52-0187	20-0188	19" Drop Center	2.5"
52-0189		21"	1.85"
1978-83 XL- *Dual Disc, 35mm Forks*			
52-0155	52-0818	19" Drop Center	2.5"
52-0151	52-0819	21"	2.15"
52-1025		23"	3"
1984-99 XLH, XL- *Single/Dual Disc, 35mm & 39mm Forks*			
52-0170	52-0827	19" Drop Center	2.5"
52-0171	52-0828	21"	2.15"
52-1024		23"	3"
1984-99 XLH, XL- *Single Disc, 35mm & 39mm Forks*			
52-0190	52-0192	19" Drop Center	2.5"
52-0191	52-0193	21"	2.15"
52-1024		23"	3"
2000-07 XL- *39mm Forks, 3/4" Axle, XL Standard Hugger*			
52-1086	52-1087	19" Drop Center	2.5"
52-1088	52-1089	21"	2.15"
52-2023	52-2024	21" Dual Disc	2.15"
52-1212		23"	3"
2008- Up XL - *39mm Forks without ABS*			
52-2035		19" Drop Center	2.5"
52-2036		21"	2.15"
52-1030		23"	3"
2010- Up - Model "48" without ABS			
52-1247		16"	3"
52-1290 (Black)		16"	3"
52-1031		23"	3"
2015- Up XL - *with ABS*			
52-2051		19" Drop Center	2.5"
52-2052		21"	2.15"

Twirled Spoke Wheels

Twirl Detail

52-0845

Wheels with Twirled Spokes include a chrome hub with internals, rim and twirled chrome spokes assembled.

VT No.	Fits	Type	Width
Front			
52-0845	1984-99	19" Dual	2.50"
52-0973	2000-up	19" Dual/Single	2.50"
52-0943	1984-99	21" Dual/Single	2.15"
52-0974	2000-up	21" Dual/Single	2.15"
52-0860	1974-77	19" Single	2.50"
52-0846	1977-83	19" Dual/Single	2.50"
52-0944	1977-83	21" Dual/Single	2.15"
Rear			
52-0177	1982-85	16"	3.00"
52-0865	1954-78	16"	3.00"
52-0883	1979-81	16"	3.00"
52-0842	1986-99	16"	3.00"
52-0851	As Above	16"	4.00"
52-0976	2000-2004	16"	3.00"
52-2018	2005-up	16"	3.00"
52-0978	2000-2004	16"	4.00"

Model "48" Components

Will install 16" wheel on XLH.

VT No.	Item
24-1037	Tree Set
44-0747	Axle
52-1247	Wheel
50-1215	Raw Fender

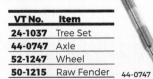

44-0747
24-1037
52-1247

16" Rear Chrome Profile Laced Wheel

Fits 2005-07 XL 883C and XL 1200C models.

VT No. 52-0665

16" Rear Chrome 3-Spoke Cast Wheel

Include bearings and spacers. Fits 2000-2004.

VT No. 52-1015

REAR WHEEL ASSEMBLY

WHEEL BUILDERS

SINCE 1969

Rim and Spoke

52-0700

52-0707

52-0700   52-0707

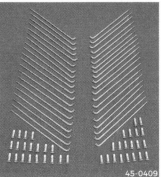
45-0409

1964-72 FX-XL ALLOY DRUM FRONT BRAKE HUB

1952-63 K AND XL 1/2 DRUM FRONT HUB

Above Hubs are shown for reference only.

1986-99 Sportster

52-0176

1954-78 Style

52-0172

Wheels for Sportster models are laced, trued and include bearings installed. 3.0 rims accept 130-140 tire, 4.0" and 4.5" accept 150-180 tires

Wheels for Sportster

52-0665 Profile Style

V-Twin	Year/ Model	Size	Type/Finish	Chrome	Stainless
Front Rims					
52-0946	52-56 K	18"	Steel/Chrome		45-0708
52-1018	52-56K 57-59 XL	18"	Steel/Chrome		
52-0969	52-56 XL	19"	Steel/Chrome		45-0707
52-0977	64-72 XL	19"	Drop Center/Chrome	45-0622	45-0657
52-0965	64-72 XL	19"	Steel/Chrome	45-0604	45-0658
52-0700	73- Up XL	19"	Drop Center/Chrome	45-0631	45-0714
Rear Rims					
52-0707	65-78 XL	18"	Drop Center/Chrome	45-0610	45-0656
Front or Rear Rims					
52-1023	10- Up	16"	Drop Center/Black	45-0722	

Spokes		Rims	
Chrome	Stainless	Diameter	Width
1954-78			
52-0172	52-0807	16"	3.0"
52-0142*		16"	4.0"
52-0884	52-0885	18"	2.15"
52-0890	52-0891	18"	2.5" Drop Center
1979-81			
52-0167	52-0808	16"	3.0"
1982-85			
52-0168	52-0809	16"	3.0"
1986-99			
52-0176	52-0810	16"	3.0"
52-0861**	52-0862*	16"	3.0"
52-0935**	52-0936*	16"	4.0"
52-0775		18"	4.50"
2000-2004			
52-1080	52-1082	16"	3.0"
52-1081	52-1083	16"	4.0"
52-0777		18"	4.5"
2005-2007			
52-1099	52-1098	16"	3.0"
52-0665		16"	3.0"
52-0913	52-0912	16"	4.0"
52-0779		18"	4.5"
52-0372		16"	5.0"
52-0373		16"	5.0"
2008-Up - *Without ABS*			
52-0789		16"	3.0"
52-1246		16" Black Rim	3.0"
2015- Up - *With ABS*			
52-2053		16"	3.0"

*Note: For Rigid Frame
**Note: Deluxe Wheels feature RDC Rim.

TIRE

Vee Rubber VRM302 Whitewall

46-0456

46-0457

Feature specially formulated compound to deliver great grip in day and wet riding, all weather tread pattern, H rated construction and heavy duty sidewall construction for superior weight carrying capacity for larger displacement motorcycles. Tubeless construction.

VRM302 Rear Tires		VRM302 Front Tires	
VT No.	Size	VT No.	Size
46-0450	150/60B x 18"	46-0457	120/70H x 21"
46-0451	180/50R x 18"	46-0458	130/50B x 23"
46-0452	200/50R x 18"	46-0459*	130/70H x 18"
46-0453	200/55R x 17"	46-0460	MT90HB x 16"
46-0454	MT90HB x 16"		
46-0455	150/80HB x 16"		
46-0456	200/60B x 16"		

*Note: Can be installed on front or rear wheels.

46-0300

46-0301

46-0302

H.D. 240 Classic Tires by Shinko

"Speed Grip" designs of the 1960's, 510 x 16 (MT-90-16).

VT No.	Item
46-0300	Wide Whitewall, 1.20"
46-0301	Dual White Stripe
46-0302	Blackwall

Shinko SR777

Front		
Blackwall	Whitewall	Size
46-0483	46-0484	130/90H x 16"
46-0485	46-0486	130/80H x 17"
46-0487	46-0488	100/90H x 19"
46-0489	46-0490	90/90H x 21"
46-0491	46-0492	120/70V x 21"
Rear		
Blackwall	Whitewall	Size
46-0475	46-0476	130/90H x 16"
46-0477		140/90H x 16"
46-0478	46-0479	150/80H x 16"
46-0480	46-0481	180/65H x 16"
46-0482		160/70H x 17"

Super Eagle 1960s Style

Feature classic Goodyear style of the 1960's. Available in black, wide and pinstripe whitewall, full 5.00 x 16" height and profile for the needed ground clearance on full dress models. Choose Coker or Shinko HD 270.

Coker	HD 270	Type
46-0304	46-0322	Blackwall
46-0305		3/8" Double Whitewall
46-0306		1-3/4" Wide Whitewall
46-0307		1" Whitewall
	46-0323	1-1/4" Whitewall
	46-0125	Replica Super Eagle Blackwall
	46-0039	Safety Mileage

46-0304

46-0305

46-0306

46-0307

46-0322

46-0323

46-0304

37-8887

Wheel Balance Weights

For spoke wheels. 10pk.

VT No.	Oz	Finish
37-8887	½	Chrome
37-8888	¾	Chrome
37-8889	1	Chrome
37-9100	1	Lead

52-0235   52-0200   52-0231

52-0360   52-0173

Chrome Spool Wheels

Billet hub with 3/4" inner diameter bearings.

The wheels have 40 spokes.

VT No.	Size	Bearing
52-0235	21" x 1.85"	3/4"
52-0061	21" x 1.85"	3/4"
52-0200	21" x 2.15"	3/4"
52-0231	23" x 3.00"	3/4"
52-0055	23" x 3.00"	3/4"
52-0771	17" Wheel with tire	No
52-0173	21" x 1.85" Flat Rim	5/8"
52-0360	21" x 2.15" Drop Center	5/8"

Parts		Parts	
12-0163	5/8" Bearing - pair	44-0211	5/8" - 9" Pike Style Axle
36-0612	Brake Cable for Above	44-0332	Axle Spacers
23-0588	Front Brake Arm	45-0290	5/8" Spool Hub
23-0589	Front Brake Stay Bar	45-0105	3/4" Spool Hub
44-0210	5/8" - 9" Acorn Style Axle	45-0106	Front spool hub for 1957-72 XL

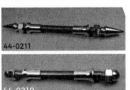

44-0211

12-0163

36-0612

44-0210

23-0589

44-0332   23-0588

Mini Air Compressor

Powered by cigarette lighter socket or connects to battery with cables supplied. Features a compact design to fit inside a saddlebag.
VT No. 16-1634

INNER TUBE

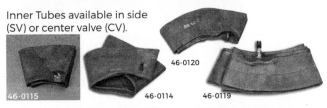

Inner Tubes available in side (SV) or center valve (CV).

46-0120

46-0115   46-0114   46-0119

*Note: VT No. 46-0116 and 46-0118 have a 11.5 mm diameter valve stem for OEM type rims. VT No. 46-0124 and 46-0101 have a 16 mm valve for custom rims.

VT No.	Size	Item	Stem	Type
46-0114	16"	5.10-16	Rubber	SV
46-0115	16"	5.10-16	Metal	SV
46-0120	16"	5.10-16	Metal	CV
46-0121	16"	200/60-16	Metal	CV
46-0133	16"	180/65-16	Metal	CV
46-0160	17"	130/80	Metal	CV
46-0147	17"	160/70 & 180/60	Metal	CV
46-0161	17"	200/55R17	Metal	CV
46-0132	17"	130/80-17	Metal	CV
46-0122	18"	180/55	Metal	CV
46-0123	18"	240/40	Metal	CV
46-0127	18"	3.00/3.50	Metal	CV
46-0116*	18"	3.75/4.00	Rubber	CV
46-0101*	18"	3.75/4.00	Rubber	CV
46-0129	18"	3.75/4.00	Metal	CV
46-0117	19"	3.25/50-19	Metal	CV
46-0131	19"	4.00/19	Metal	CV
46-0118*	19"	3.25/50-19	Rubber	CV
46-0124*	19"	3.25/50-19	Rubber	CV
46-0119	21"	MH80/90 x 21"	Metal	CV
46-0150	21"	100/90-21 (3.50)	Metal	CV
46-0158	21"	120/70-21	Metal	CV
46-0159	23"	130/60-23	Metal	CV
46-0065	23"	3.25/3.50-23	Metal	CV

WHEEL 15

Chrome Valve Stem Covers

37-9091   37-9092   42-0207   42-0016   37-9218   42-2037   42-5040

VT No.	Type	U/M	VT No.	Type	U/M
37-9091	Steel	Each	37-9218	Skull	Pair
37-9092	Steel	Each	42-2037	Piston	Pair
42-0207	Rubber	10 pack	42-5040	Bullet	Pair
42-0016	Steel	10 pack			

33-0946
33-0944

LED Valve Stem Cover Cap Sets

Include batteries.

Red	Blue
33-0946	33-0944

Maltese Valve Stem Cover

37-9381   37-9380

3/4" x 3/4" x 1/2".

Chrome	Black/White
37-9381	37-9380

V-TWIN

SOLO SEAT

CH Style Solo

47-0158   47-0164

Black	Brown
47-0158	**47-0164**

Invictor Flatlander Saddles

Feature low frame hugging design. Fits 2004-06 models.

VT No. 47-0864

Invictor Series Saddles

Fit 2004-2006 XL.

47-0990

VT No.	Type
47-0990	Bucket
47-0861	Smooth

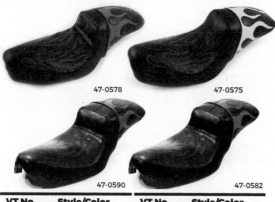

47-0578   47-0575

47-0590   47-0582

VT No.	Style/Color	VT No.	Style/Color
47-0578	Purple Flame	**47-0590**	Teal Flame
47-0575	Yellow Flame	**47-0582**	Aqua Flame

Voyager Series

Fit 2004-up XL models, and feature full comfort design for the longest ride.

VT No. 47-0270

Rear Seat Tab

Chrome. Fits 1979-96. models.   VT No. 31-4018

Black Naugahyde Solo

Features ribbed metal baseplate. Universal mounting.

Solo	Chopped Style
47-0165	**47-0021**

Invictor Gunfighter Saddles

47-0856   47-0852   47-0854

Feature sewn inlay of colored flames on rear pad area with matching flame stitch and thread in front driver area. Original style includes textured top panel in driver area and silver chrome accent to separate the driver and tail area.

2004-06	Style/Color	2004-06	Style/Color
47-0851	Black Flame	**47-0855**	Purple Flame
47-0856	Yellow Flame	**47-0852**	Teal Flame
		47-0854	Aqua Flame

Invictor Smoothie Saddles

Solo and pad on a single piece steel baseplate.

47-0866 Installed   47-0867 Installed   47-0868 Installed

Original	Chrome Spot	Black Spot	Fitment
47-0866	**47-0867**	**47-0868**	2004-2006

Seat Mount Pins

A   B

Available as quick release push pin in stainless steel in natural finish with O-Ring and extra stud. Thread into existing seat mount hole with 1/4 - 28 threads. Replacement pin available for 37-8902

VT No.	#	Type
37-8902	A	Quick Release with Pin
37-9179	B	Chrome Knob
31-0348		Kit

MOUNT KITS

Solo Hardware Mount Kits include nose brackets, springs and rear brackets. To fit police style solos purchase cross bar 31-0473. 2" spring. 31-4063 includes black frame lower.

31-4044

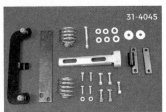

31-4045

31-4045 Kit Installed

31-4086

31-4063

31-0433 Installed

Bates Solo 47-8655 Shown Mounted with 31-4063 Mount Kit

VT No.	Model	Frame Cover
31-4044	1952-78	
31-4045	1982-2003	42-0979
31-4063	2004-06	Included
31-0433	1979-81	
31-4086	2010-up	Included
31-1740	2007-2009	

51-0539 Weld On Mounts

Solo Seat Mount Hardware. This seat tee & weld on mount tabs provide a substantial mount system from K to 1957-70 XL model solos. Order pieces separately.

VT No.	Item
31-0512	T - OEM 51902-54
37-9114	Pivot
51-0539	Mount Tab Set

Chrome Swingarm Rear Spring Support Bar for 1952-78
VT No. 31-0501

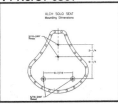

SOLO FOR XL

Contour Solo Seat

Fits XL. Bolts on.

VT No.	Year
47-0788	1982-2003
47-0723	2004- Up
47-0789	2004-14

47-0723

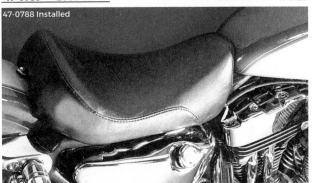

47-0788 Installed

47-0789 Installed

SEAT

16

47-0723 Installed

Model 57 Solo

Kits include replica genuine leather solo seat with complete mount kit. Replica seat is as offered on original 1957 Sportster 50 years ago. 47-0782 includes frame cover.

VT No.	Year	Cover
47-0781	1982-2003	42-0979
47-0782	2004-06	Included

 # SOLO

Leather Solo Seat Kits

47-0131

47-0134 with 50-0246 Luggage Rack

47-0133 Installed

47-0811

For XL with tuck & roll. includes K-model seat, chrome 2" springs and mount hardware. *47-0134 includes frame cover.*

VT No.	Fits	Cover		VT No.	Fits	Cover
47-0131	1952-78			47-0134	2004-09	Included
47-0132	1979-81			47-811	2004-09	Bates Style
47-0133	1982-2003	42-0979				

BATES

Rigid Frame Solo Seat and Mount Kit

47-0130 Installed

31-0608

Includes chrome 3" hairpin springs. Mount kit and seat are also sold separately.

VT No.	Item
47-0130	Seat Kit
31-0608	Mount Kit Only
47-0110	Replica Seat Only

47-0119 Installed

Rigid Seat Kit

Includes 3" springs and solo seat.

VT No.	Item
47-0119	Seat Kit
31-4043	Mount Kit Only
47-0110	Seat Only

Black Solo Seat Kit

Fits Big Twin and XL Rigid frames. Includes mount kit with hair pin springs included.

VT No. 47-0152

SADDLEBAG SUPPORT

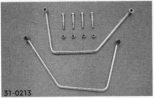

31-0213

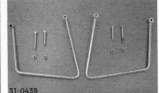

31-0439

31-9909

31-9924

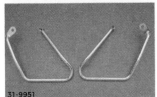

31-9951

49-0888

49-0889

XL Saddlebag Supports

Designed to fit the contour of the fender struts and protect your bags from the brake caliper and swing arm.

VT No.	Year	Note
31-0213	1952-78	
31-0439	1979-81	
31-9909	1982-93	1
31-9924	1994-03	2
31-9951	2004- Up	
49-0888	Black	1,2
49-0889	Chrome	1,2

Note 1:
Requires 31-9913 Signal Relocation Kit for 1982-89 models. Require signals to be moved to rear fender strut mounting hole.

Note 2:
Requires 31-9925 Signal Relocation Kit

31-9913

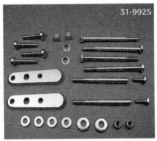

31-9925

Directional Signal Relocation Kits

Includes special hardware and extension for models listed to provide clearance for saddle bags.

VT No.	OEM	Fits
31-9913	90504-82A	1979-1989
31-9925	68471-94A	1994-2003

SADDLEBAG

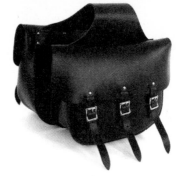

Black Leather 3-Buckle Saddlebag

Extra large leather thro-over style.
VT No. 48-3127

Large leather thro-over style is glued, sewn and riveted.
VT No. 48-3127

SEAT

16

Tool Roll

Double strap tool roll with duo strap is a heavy leather roll that measures 10" x 4-1/2" x 3" tall.
VT No. 48-3112

Heavy Leather tool bag with duo strap measures 10" x 4-1/2" x 3" tall, and is 8oz. Full grain top leather is tanned, oiled, and wax treated. Features 4-way adjustable straps for easy mounting. **VT No. 48-3113**

Soft leather tool roll features fully padded inside zipper and velcro secured flap. Includes 2 heavy leather mount straps with roller buckles. Measures 11-1/2" x 4" x 4-1/2".
VT No. 48-3116

BOBBER

©2003

197

SISSY BAR

50-1621   50-1623

50-1622   50-1624   50-1558   50-1559

50-1512   31-1315   31-1304

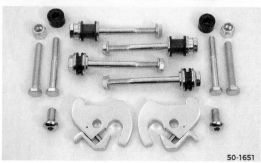

50-1651

Detachable Side Plates and Dockable Hardware

Side Plate	Hardware	Item/Fitment
50-1621	50-1622	2004-Up
50-1623	50-1624	1994-03
	50-1558	Cam Lock, Chrome
	50-1559	Cam Lock, Black
	50-1651	Mounting Kit for detachable rack
	31-1315	Bushing Set (2)
	31-1316	Bushing Set, Narrow (2)
	31-1304	Bushing Set for docking points (2)
	50-1512	Stainless Steel Bushing Set (2)
	31-1300	Bushing Set, Narrow, Chrome
	31-1301	Bushing Set, Narrow, OEM 53697-06
	31-1302	Bushing Set, Narrow, OEM 53942-04
	31-1303	Bushing Set, Wide, 53943-04
	31-1312	Bushing Set, Narrow, OEM 53967-06

Chrome Sissy Bar Luggage Rack

Solid steel rack fits all 16" tall sissy bars, unique design for easy installation or removal. Mount holes are 2-5/8" center to center and 5-1/4" wide. May require drilling for some applications.
VT No. 50-1011

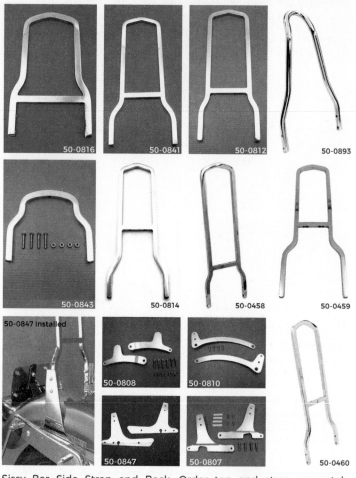

50-0816   50-0841   50-0812   50-0893

50-0843   50-0814   50-0458   50-0459

50-0847 Installed   50-0808   50-0810

50-0847   50-0807   50-0460

Sissy Bar Side Strap and Back. Order top and strap separately.

Fitment	Side Straps	16 in.	11 in.	20 in.	Sissy Bar Back Width
2004- Up	50-0847	50-0841	50-0842	50-0461	7-1/2"
					50-0843 Grab Rail, 6-1/4" ht.
	50-1198				13" x 7-1/2" Side Plates, Black
		50-1514			Round, Black
		50-1192			Round, Chrome
1994-03	50-0807	50-0812	50-0816	50-0458	6-3/4"
		50-0893			Round
1979-93	50-0808	50-0813	50-0817	50-0459	8"
		50-0320			8" Round
1957-78	50-0810	50-0814	50-0818	50-0460	7-3/8"
		50-1192			7-3/8" Round
		50-0323			Round
	37-1509				Screw Set, All models

Sissy Bar Grab Rail Combo

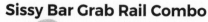

50-0503

LUGGAGE RACK DETACHABLES

Chrome Luggage Racks for XL

50-1018 Installed

50-0246 Installed

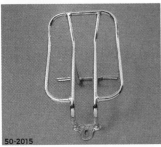

50-2015

50-2015

50-0235 Installed

50-0239 Installed

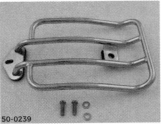

50-0239

Measure 6" x 8" for fender mounting. Loads of 10 pounds or less.

VT No.	Fits	Seat
50-1018	1979-2003	Two Passenger
50-2015	1994-2009	Solo
50-0235	1985-2003	Solo
50-0239	2004-2009	Stock Solo
50-0246	2004-up	Stock Solo

50-0589

50-0847

Bolt On Luggage Racks

Chrome finish racks mount to rigid side straps of sissy bar for 2004-up XL.

VT No.	Item
50-0589	Rack
50-0847	Side Plates

Detachable Luggage Rack

Fits 2004-up XL models. Order hardware kit separately.

50-1550

VT No.	Item
50-1550	Rack
31-1315	Mount Kit
50-1564	Complete Kit

Docking Hardware for 2004-Up XL

50-1527

50-1512

50-1558

VT No.	Item
50-1527	Stud Set
50-1558	Rotary Latch Kit, Chrome
50-1559	Rotary Latch Kit, Chrome
31-1304	2 Bushings Wide Style, rubber between chrome ends
31-1315	Bushing Set, rubber between chrome ends
50-1512	Stainless Steel Bushing Set (4)

31-1315

31-1304

SEAT

16

2004 - Up XL Sissy Bar Kits

SOLID			
Assembled	Bar Only	Plates	Height
50-0464	50-0320	50-0810	16"
50-0466	50-0893	50-0807	13"
50-0467	50-1192	50-1621 / 50-1651	13"
50-0469	50-0320	50-1621 / 50-1651	16"
50-0477	50-0322	50-0826	10"
50-0478	50-0819	50-0826	8-13/16"
50-1506			1-piece, Chrome
50-1511			1-piece, Black
DETACHABLES			
50-1542	50-1192	50-0847	13"
50-0468	50-0320	50-0847	16"
50-1630	50-0843	50-0847	6.25"
50-1626	50-0841	50-0847	16"
50-1628	50-0842	50-0847	11"

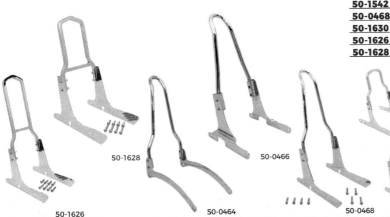

50-1628

50-0466

50-0478

50-1630

50-1626

50-0464

50-0468

50-0469

50-1511

REAR PADS

47-1964

47-1963

47-1972

47-0913

Leather Rear Pads

47-0914

VT No.	Type
47-0913	Smooth
47-0914	Tuck and Roll
47-0188	Tuck and Roll, wide

Button Sissy Bar Pads

Mount to square stock sissy bars, Mini fits 12" bar, 2 button fits 16" bar. Chrome mount clamps included, black only.

31-1987

47-0457

VT No.	Type	VT No.	Type
47-1963	Mini	47-0457	Buttoned
47-1964	2-Button	31-1987	Brackets for Above
47-1972	Smooth	47-0478	Sissy Bar Buttoned Pad
		47-0632	Black Vinyl

Pillion Rear Seat Pad

Smooth vinyl and has a welted edge. Bolt holes in the steel baseplate are used for direct fender mount. Size is 5" W x 9" L with a 2" thickness.
VT No. 47-0786

Replica Pads

7-1/2" W x 9" L.

47-0098

47-0045

VT No.	Type	VT No.	Type
47-0098	K- Replica, Leather	47-0045	K- Tuck & Roll

Stick-On Rear Passenger Pillion Pad

Vinyl with suction cups. For custom applications.

VT No.	Size	VT No.	Size
47-0348	9" x 6" x 2-3/8"	47-0349	9" x 5-3/4" x 2-3/8"

Mini Back Rest

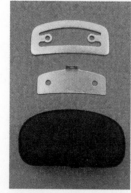

In black features a stainless steel insert with chrome frame mounting system for short sissy bars.
VT No. 47-0753

Sissy Bar Inserts

50-0820

42-0532

42-0045

42-0156

VT No.	Type	Finish
50-0820	Cross	Chrome
42-0045	Skull	Brass
42-0156	Eagle	Brass
42-0532	Eagle Spirit	Chrome, Adhesive back

 **WINDSHIELD**

Ranger Heavy Duty

Low Profile and narrow proportions. Light Tint, DOT and TUV approved. Approved for night use. Hardware sold separately. Fits all 1957-up XL. Mounting Kit VT No. 31-9930 required. For 35mm Fork Legs order VT No. 28-0335 bushings in addition to mounting kit.

Measures: 13-1/2" H, 16-1/2" W.

VT No. 51-0246

Custom Heavy Duty

51-0248

Taller and slightly wider than the Ranger. A trim and lean custom look. Light Tint, DOT approved. Approved for night use. Hardware sold separately. Fits all 1957-up XL. Mounting Kit VT No. 31-9930 required. For 35mm Fork Legs order VT No. 28-0335 bushings in addition to mounting kit.

Measures: 19-21" H, 18-3/4" W.

VT No. 51-0248

Low Boy Heavy Duty

Light tint. D.O.T. approved hardware sold separately. Fits 1957-up. For 35mm Fork Legs order VT No. 28-0335 bushings in addition to mounting kit.

31-9930

VT No.	Item
51-0330	Shield
31-9930	Mounts
38-0335	Rubber Bushing

National Cycle Deflector Screen LX

Features rake adjustment and quickset mounting hardware for 1" handlebars. Available in Lexan or Hard Coated Polycarbonate, and either clear or medium tint. Both types are D.O.T. and T.U.V. approved. Fits all 1957- Up.

Lexan	Polycarbonate	Tint
51-0245	51-0368	Clear
51-0244	51-0369	Medium Tint

SEAT 16

National Cycle Wave QR Windshield

51-0283

Manufactured from dark tint polycarbonate that features free flowing lines, adjustable rake partitioning and quick release mounting. Order mounting hardware separately. Fits 1996-up XL.

VT No.	Hardware
51-0283	31-9936

Streetshield EX

Features 4 point ball socket mount with Quickset hardware. Smoke tint. Fits all 1957-2000 XL. D.O.T. approved.

Measures: 18" H, 19-1/4" W.

VT No. 51-0325

National Cycle Spartan Quick Release Windshield

51-0288

Features full size quantum clear hand coated polycarbonate windshield, quick release hardware and a black powder coated mounting frame. Available in 16-1/4" and 18-1/2" heights, measured from head lamp cutout to top of shield. Both fit 1996-2010. *Order mounting hardware 31-9936 separately.*

VT No.	Height
51-0288	16-1/4"
51-0289	18-1/2"

Flyscreen LS

Small windshield with a very custom appearance. Triple chrome front plate. Flush counter sunk hex bolts. Fits all 1957-Up. Bronze tint.

Measures: 1-1/2" H, 9-3/4" W.

DOT and TUV approved. Approved for night use. Hardware packaged with windshield.

VT No. 51-0243

Bracket Set Fits 1957-78 XL.
VT No. 49-0879

51-0244

National Cycle Streetshield

Features U-clamp mounting for 1" handlebars. Available in Lexan or Hard Coated Polycarbonate and either clear or medium tint. Both types are D.O.T. approved. Fits 1957- Up XL,

51-0324

Lexan	Polycarbonate	Tint
51-0323	51-0366	Clear
51-0324	51-0367	Medium Tint

 # 1-1/4" BUFFALO HANDLEBAR

1982-Up XL	Rise	Grips
25-0714	12"	36"
25-0682	13"	36"
25-0715	14"	36"
25-0716	16"	36"
25-0656	18"	37"
25-0717	20"	37"

1-1/4" Flat Track Bar

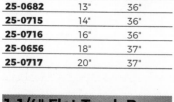

Fits 1982-Up XL. Riser 1/2-20 thread.

VT No.	Wid.	Rise	Pullback
25-0653	30"	3"	14.5"
25-0652	29"	4"	12"

Dresser Buffalo Bars

25-0690   25-0693

1982-Up XL	Width	Height	Pull Back
25-0690	38"	5"	10-1/4"
25-0693	35"	6-1/2"	10-1/2"

1-1/4" Beach Bars

Pre-drilled for internal wiring. The shape provides comfort with control. Use with stock risers and clamps. Fits 1982- Up XL.

VT No. 25-0709

1-1/4" Bikini Beach Bars

36" wide with 3.5" rise with 8" at the center. Fits 1982-Up XL.

VT No. 25-0699

7" Buffalo Drag Bar

25-2185

30-1/2" width. 1982-Up XL.

VT No.	Dia.
25-2185	1-1/4"
25-0685	1-1/2"

Dresser Style Bar

With indents. Features 1-1/4" diameter, 34.5" width, 2" rise and 11" pull back with 1/2" - 20 threads. Fits 1982-Up XL.

VT No. 25-0651

Buffalo Style Dresser Bar

Features 4" end riser, 14" pullback and 12" center width with grips at 35" wide. Designed for tall riders. Fits 1982-Up XL.

VT No. 25-0655

HANDLE

17

BLACK BARS

For 1980- Up XL.

Black Z Bar

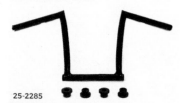

25-2285

VT No.	Rise	
25-2275	15"	*Note: Throttle by wire.
25-2285*	11"	

Black T Bar

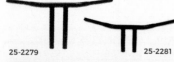

25-2279   25-2281

VT No.	Rise
25-2279	10"
25-2281	6"

V-BARS

For 1982- Up XL.

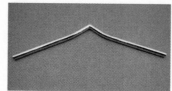

V-Bars with indents have a 1" outside diameter.
VT No. 25-0702

Flying V-Bar

25-0706

25-0707

8" rising with 1-1/4" outside diameter. For stock or raked forks.

VT No.	Type
25-0706	Stock
25-0707	Raked

17" Black Z-Bar with Indents

Slotted and drilled for internal wirings and is notched for throttle by wire application. 1982-Up XL. Also available in chrome.

Black	Chrome
25-0461	25-0460

1-1/4" HANDLEBAR

1-1/4" Chrome Ape Hangers

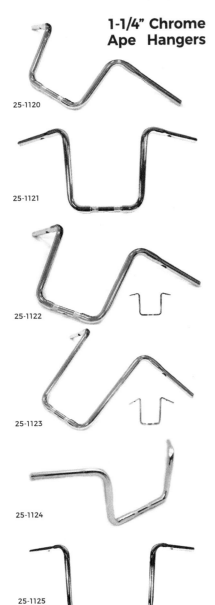

25-1120

25-1121

25-1122

25-1123

25-1124

25-1125

Custom application. Feature tapered design at hand control area, to allow use of custom or OEM controls (including hydraulic clutch). Wide bars are also notched for throttle by wire applications.

Narrow	Wide	Rise
25-1120	25-1124	11"
25-1121	25-1125	14"
25-1122	25-1126	17"
25-1123		19"

1-1/4" "T" Bars

Fit 1982-Up XL models. Chrome finish.

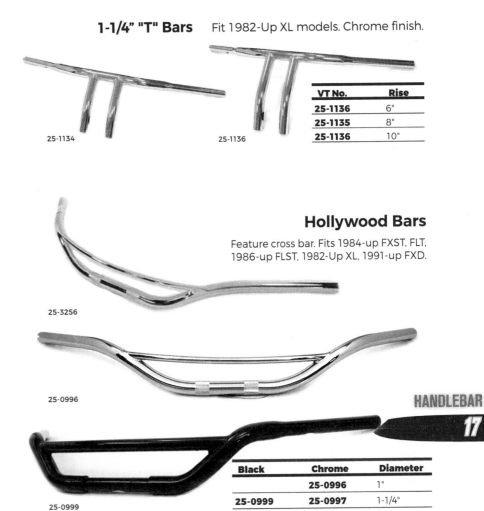

25-1134

25-1136

VT No.	Rise
25-1136	6"
25-1135	8"
25-1136	10"

Hollywood Bars

Feature cross bar. Fits 1984-up FXST, FLT, 1986-up FLST, 1982-Up XL, 1991-up FXD.

25-3256

25-0996

25-0999

Black	Chrome	Diameter
	25-0996	1"
25-0999	25-0997	1-1/4"

HANDLEBAR 17

8.5" Mini Ape Hanger

25-0198

Chrome	Black	
25-0196	25-0197	
25-0198	25-0199	For XL without indents

WYATT GATLING *Styled in Steel*

Z-HANDLEBAR

Fits 1982- Up XL unless noted for other years.

1980-up XL.

ChiZeled Chrome Handlebar

VT No.	Height
25-0632	11"
25-0633	13
25-0634	15"
25-0635	17"

1" Z Bars

25-3253

Slotted and drilled for internal wiring. Feature notches for throttle by wire applications.

VT No.	Rise
25-3257	10"
25-3252	10-1/2"
25-3253	15"
25-1179	17"

Mini "Z" Bar

Features 25" width, 4" drop with indents.

VT No. 25-0704

1-1/4" Z Bars with Knurls

VT No.	Hght	VT No.	Hght
25-1178	10"	25-1177	12"

Dropped Z Bars

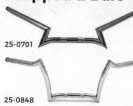

25-0701

25-0848

Feature long handles in 1" with knurl without indents.

VT No.	Type	Fits
25-0701	Single	1974-81
25-0848	Double, Chrome	1982-Up
25-0851	Double, Black	1982-Up

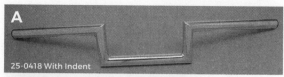

A

25-0418 With Indent

B

25-0433 With Indent

Chrome 1" Z Type Handlebars

Feature early chopper styling without knurling. Available with or without indents.

1982-Up XL With Indent	1974-81 XL Without Indent	#	Height
25-0418	25-0429	A	4"
25-0430		B	4"
25-0426	25-0419	A	6"
25-0433		B	6"
25-0427	25-0420	A	8"
25-0431		B	8"
25-0428	25-0421	A	10"

Incysa "Z"

Use with 1-1/4" diameter risers. Fits 1974-81 XL. 6.5" rise, 8" pull back.

VT No. 25-0748

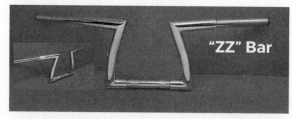

"ZZ" Bar

1.25" outside diameter with indent for wiring. 7-3/4".

VT No. 25-1095

1-1/4" Low Rise Z Bar

Features 4.5" pullback and 4.5" rise with indents.

VT No. 25-0791

25-0755

25-0753

Fatty Z Bars

1-1/4" outside diameter fit 1974-81 XL models.

VT No.	Height
25-0753	12"
25-0754	14"
25-0755	4"

Vintage Bars

25-1832

25-1836

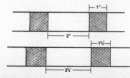

25-1833

Fit 1982- Up XL models.

VT No.	Rise
25-1832	Shorty Bar, 3"
25-1833	7.5"
25-1836	12"

Note: We suggest using our chrome control and housing sets on 1-1/4" bars such as 26-0405 or 26-0410.

Note: Handlebars include knurls with 2" spacing.

1" DRAG HANDLEBAR

15°

30°

25-0879

25-0544

25-2215

1"Drag Bars sweep back angle style with 15 or 30 degree bends and 30" overall width.

Chrome	Black	Sweep	XL Fitment
25-0539	25-0561	15°	1974-81
25-0540		30°	1974-81
25-0544	25-0456	15° Indented	1982-84
25-0897		15° Indented, w/o Knurls	1982- Up
25-2144		30° Indented	1982- Up
25-2215		30° Indented	1982- Up
25-2216		30° Indented	1982-Up

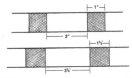

Note: Handlebars include knurls with 2" spacing.

Chrome Riser Sleeves

For use with riser drag bars.

VT No.	Size
28-0441	1"
25-0442	1.25"

1" Wide Drag Bars

25-0423

25-0424

25-0422

25-0425

Feature knurls at riser area. Available with or without indents.

1982-Up XL With Indent	1974-81 XL Without Indent	Width	Finish
	25-0422	32"	Chrome
25-0424		32"	Chrome
	25-0423	36"	Chrome
	25-0458	36"	Black
25-0425		36"	Chrome
25-0459		36"	Black

2" Rise Drag Bars

25-0563

25-0531

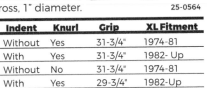

Offer pullback style yet retain the drag bar look. Measure 8" across riser, 2" rise, 7-1/2" grip, 31-3/4" across, 1" diameter.

25-0564

Chrome	Black	Indent	Knurl	Grip	XL Fitment
25-0531	25-0563	Without	Yes	31-3/4"	1974-81
25-0666	25-0564	With	Yes	31-3/4"	1982- Up
25-0847		Without	No	31-3/4"	1974-81
25-0727		With	Yes	29-3/4"	1982-Up
25-2216*		With	Yes	28-1/4"	1982- Up

*Note: has 2-1/2" rise.

HANDLEBAR

17

1" HANDLEBAR

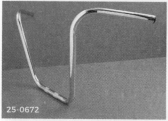

25-0672

25-0685

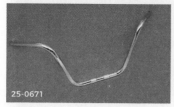

25-0671

25-0687

Chrome Ape Hangers
Made of heavy steel tubing.

Pre-1982 No Indent	1982-Up Indent	Rise	Pre-1982 No Indent	1982-Up Indent	Rise
25-0532	25-0713	8"	25-0672	25-0673	15"
25-0533	25-2146	10"	25-0684	25-0686	16"
25-0534	25-0671	12"	25-0685	25-0687	18"
25-0529	25-0576	14"	25-0855	25-0856	20"

Chrome Speeder 1" Bars

Featuring a knurled center.
VT No. 25-0990

25-0951

Narrow Ape Hangers

VT No.	Size
25-0951	13"
25-0952	15"

Stainless Handlebars

With knurl. Replaces 56083-74 on XL models 1974-81. Stock Pre-1982. 1" diameter.
VT No. 25-0416

How Bars Are Measured

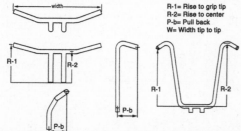

width

R-1 = Rise to grip tip
R-2 = Rise to center
P-b = Pull back
W = Width tip to tip

R-1   R-2

P-b

R-1   R-2

P-b

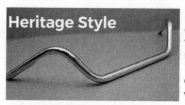

25-0884   25-0885

25-0886   25-0887

Handlebars for 1982-Up

VT No.	Style	VT No.	Style
25-0884	Mid Rise	25-0886	Cruise
25-0885	Mid Rise	25-0887	Police

Heritage Style

Indented and pre-drilled for hidden wiring, 32" wide, 6" rise, 10" pullback with 13" center width. 1" diameter. 1982-Up XL.
VT No. 25-2149

Chrome Mini-Buckhorns

A modified scaled down look and size of the original 70's buckhorn for 1974-81 XL.
VT No. 25-0542

Two Piece Bars

Original Buckhorn type, knurled to fit stock riser block on 1957-81 XL. 1" diameter on both ends enables snap throttle to be used.
VT No. 25-0663

Chrome Beach Bars

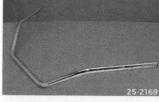

VT No.	Indent	Fits
25-2169	With	1982-Up
25-2170	Without	1974-81

25-2169

39" wide at grip with a 5" rise. 1" diameter.

Police Bars

25-0408

Wide style 33" across with 4" rise, tour bar 12" across riser mount; excellent for dog bone or Flanders style risers. The 1982-up is available with indents.

VT No.	Type
25-0399	Pre 1982
25-0408	1982- Up, with Indents

Check out our website for detailed dimensions on handlebars at www.vtwinmfg.com

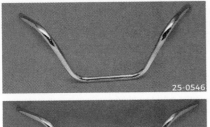

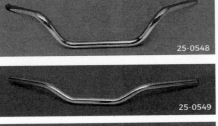

1" Handlebar

Style	1974-81 XL Chrome	1982- Up XL With Indent	Width	Rise	Pullback	Center Width
High Buckhorn	25-0530	25-0546	33"	9"	11"	8.5"
Med. Buckhorn	25-0520	25-0547	33"	7"	7.5"	10"
Low Buckhorn		25-0548	32"	3.5"	10"	8.5"
Superbar	25-0660	25-0549	29"	2"	5"	5.5"
		25-0443*	29"	2"	5"	5.5"
High Chopper	25-0650	25-0550	24.5"	6"	15"	6"
Low Chopper	25-0630	25-0551	23"	6"	13.5"	5"
Drag Bar		25-0412	28.5"		5.5"	8.5"
		25-0442*	28.5"		5.5"	8.5"
		25-0445*	29"	6"	13"	7"

Note: All 1982-up handlebars with indents are for external wiring only.

*Note: Denotes without knurl.

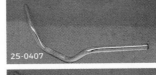

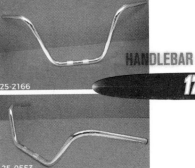

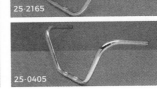

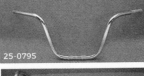

Chrome Products

1" Stock Replacement Handlebars
Chrome with indents and knurled center. Fitment as noted.

VT No.	OEM	Type	XL Fitment	VT No.	OEM	Type	XL Fitment
25-2143	56082-83	883 XL Low	1982- Up	25-2166	56079-93	FXDWG	1982- Up
25-0407	56085-83	XLX	1982- Up	25-2165	56569-86	FLSTC	1982- Up
25-0410	W/O Knurl XLX	3.5"	1982- Up	25-0553	56557-95	FLSTF-FLHR	1982- Up
25-2156**	As Above	XLX	1974-81	25-0696	56086-81	FX-FXE	1982- Up
25-0694	56473-98	XL Sport	1982- Up	25-0405**	55950-80	FXWG	1974-81
25-0543	56081-82	FXR	1982- Up	25-0667	55950-80	FXWG	1982- Up
25-2167	56081-82	FXST, XL 1200	1982- Up	25-0417**	55963-77	FXS	1974-81
25-0795	56962-07	FXST	1982- Up	25-0403	56003-75	FXE	1982- Up
				25-0404**	56003-76	FXE	1974-81

**Note: Denotes without indents

Check out our website for detailed dimensions on handlebars at www.vtwinmfg.com

RISER BARS

1.5" Fatster "T" Bar

3.5" bolt centers for 1/2 x 13 bolts.

25-1163

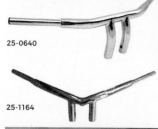

25-0640

25-1164

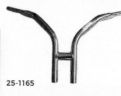

25-0641 Installed

25-1165

VT No.	Rise	VT No.	Rise
25-0640*	6"	25-1163	Gothic
25-0641	8"	25-1164	V-Bar
25-0874**	8"	25-1191	V-Bar, Black
25-0642	10"	25-1165	Flyer

*Fits 1974-81   **Custom application
All others fit 1982-Up

25-0670   25-0536

1" Pullbacks

1982-Up	1974-81	
Indents	**No Indent**	**Rise**
	25-0536	4"
25-0669	25-0537	6"
25-0670	25-0575	8"

Bolt to 3 1/2" bolt centers, mounts with 1/2-20 bolts. Grips 22" apart.

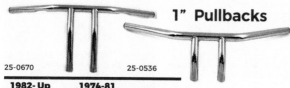

Riser Bars

25-2161

Available with indents for 1982-up models or without indents, feature 3 1/2" center to center, to accept 1/2 - 20 thread bolts

1982-Up	1974-81	
Indents	**No Indent**	**Rise**
25-2152	25-2161	5"
	25-2162	6"
25-2153		7-1/2"
	25-2163	8"
25-2154		9"

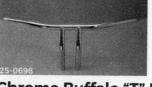

25-0698

25-0678

Chrome Buffalo "T" Handlebars

1-1/4"bars with indents and drilled for internal wiring. 3.5" bolt spacing. *Note: Without indents.

VT No.	Width	Height	Pullback	Fits
25-0698	32.75"	10.5"	8.5"	1982- Up
25-0679	32"	8.5"	10.5"	1974-81
25-0678*	32.5"	6.5"	9"	1982-Up
25-0708	29"	7"	6"	1974-81
25-0721*	32.5"	10.5"	5"	1974-81

1-1/4" Lean Back Riser Handlebar

Swept back design with indents for extended neck-fork applications. 1974-81 XL.

VT No. 25-0703

Radius Handlebar w/ Indent

9" tall "V"design, 9" rise with wire indent, and 1-1/4" diameter. Fits 1982- Up XL.

VT No. 25-0725

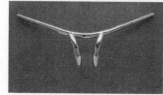

1.25" Curve Riser Bar

26" wide, 9.5" pullback, 1-1/4" diameter. 1982- Up.

VT No.	Rise	Knurl
25-0718	7"	With
25-0720	8.5"	Without

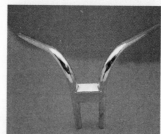

Buckhorn 1" Riser Bar

11" rise to center, 12" rise to grip, 11" pullback and 22-1/2" end to end. Mounts to 3-1/2" center to center with 1/2"-20 bolts. Available with or without indents.

VT No.	Indent	Fits
25-0625	With	1982- Up
25-0626	Without	1974-81

Swing Back Handlebar

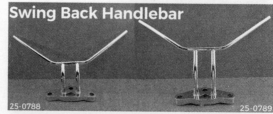

25-0788   25-0789

1" outside diameter with indents. 1982- Up XL.

VT No.	Size	VT No.	Size
25-0788	6"	25-0789	7-1/2"

1.25" Way Back Bar

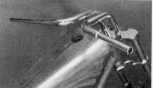

Features 10" rise and 12" pull back. No holes or indents for wiring. 1974-81 XL.

VT No. 25-0582

Check out our website for detailed dimensions on handlebars at www.vtwinmfg.com

Chrome Stock Riser Stems

Sold in pairs, order top clamp and screws separately. 1-1/2" height, fits 1974- Up XL.

VT No.	Attribute
25-2101	Drilled Through for Bolt
25-2115	Threaded

Black Solid Riser Sets for 1"

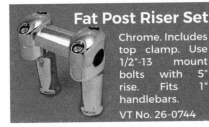

Application for 1" handlebars.

VT No.	Item
26-0646	4" Hourglass
26-0647	6" Solid Billet

Fat Post Riser Set

Chrome. Includes top clamp. Use 1/2"-13 mount bolts with 5" rise. Fits 1" handlebars.
VT No. 26-0744

Chrome Tapered Stock Type Risers

Original tapered type, through bolt design, chrome steel. Bolts not included.

VT No.	Rise	VT No.	Rise
25-2171	3"	25-2176*	3"
25-2129	4", Threaded	25-2250	3"
25-2173	5"	25-2208	6", Threaded
25-2130*	5"	25-2209	8"

*Note: Feature rubber Iso-inserts, and 5/16"" allen screws

Chrome Riser Cap Set

For 3" riser set.
VT No. 25-2212

Polished Stainless Steel 1-3/4" Riser

Set is for 1" handlebars. Has 1/2"-13 thread.
VT No. 26-0555

RISERS

6" Post Risers

25-0556

Chrome Solid Billet Riser Sets

Feature 1/2" x 13 mount threads. For 1-1/4" handlebars.

VT No.	Size	VT No.	Size
26-0597	3"	26-0600	6"
26-0599	4"	26-0601	8"
26-0598	5"		

Chrome 3-1/2" Riser Set

Fits 1-1/4" bars.   VT No. 26-0252

HANDLEBAR

17

Chrome Stock Riser Set

25-2100 Assembled

Includes finned riser cap and screws. Use 1/2" x 13 mounting bolt. Fits 1977-up XL.

VT No.	Item
25-2100	Complete Kit, 1-1/2"
25-2132	Complete Kit, 1-1/8"

Chrome Steel Glide Risers

VT No.	Item
25-2202	4"
25-2203*	4"
26-0595	8
25-2204	6"
25-2205	8"
25-0556	6" without tops

25-2202   25-2203   25-2204   25-2205

Steel risers have 1/2"-20 threads. *Note: 25-2203 has hole through for bolt, not threaded.

T-Bar Clamp

Used in mounting tee bar handlebars with built in risers to custom Paughco or Wyatt Gatling spring forks which have 1/2-20 threaded hole in top. Top clamp fits on top of existing triple tree.

VT No.	Item
25-0782	T-Bar Clamp
25-0783	Mounting Hardware Kit

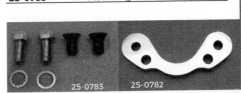

25-0783   25-0782

RISER TOP CLAMP

25-2104

25-2107 Without Skirt

26-2161

25-2138

25-2109

25-2210

25-2135

25-2120

25-2128

26-0795

25-0200

25-0201

25-0202

25-0203

24-1155

24-1163

24-1164

25-0592

25-0593

25-0590

25-0591

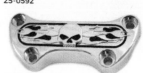
24-1161

24-1162

Handlebar Top Clamp

Chrome Skirt	Item	Chrome Skirt	Item
25-2104	Smooth	25-0203	Skull, black
25-2108	Finned	24-1163	Chrome Skull w/ flames
25-2138	Antique		
25-2155	Raised Top	24-1164	Chrome Skull w/ flames on black
25-0200	Skull, Chrome		
25-0201	Skull, skirt	26-0592	Chrome
25-0202	Skull, black	26-0593	Black

1974-Up XL. Front Panel as long or short skirt.

No Skirt	Item	No Skirt	Item
25-2128	Raised Top	25-2120	Smooth Hidden
25-2107	Smooth	26-0795	USA Hidden
25-2109	Finned	25-2210	Skull, Hidden
25-2135	Eagle Spirit	24-1155	Touring
26-2161	Live to Ride	24-1161	Chrome skull w/ flames
25-0590	Chrome		
25-0591	Black	24-1162	Black skull with flames

Chrome Billet Style Riser Cap
Set replaces 56057-00 and is a curved 2 piece design. For risers which accept the 1 piece clamp. 1974- Up.
VT No. 26-0540

Chrome Handlebar Screw
Caps snap over allen head screws to cover hole. 10 pack.
VT No. 37-7966

Riser Links
Cover top of glide type risers. 3-1/2" center. Studs and acorns included.

VT No.	FITS
49-0418	1973- Up XL
37-8810	4 Studs, 4 Acorns -Set

Chrome Handlebar Top Clamp Bolt Sets

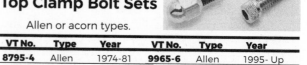
Acorn   Allen

Allen or acorn types.

VT No.	Type	Year	VT No.	Type	Year
8795-4	Allen	1974-81	9965-6	Allen	1995- Up
8796-4	Allen	1982- Up	9636-8	Acorn	1982- Up

Handlebar Reducer Sleeves
measure 7/8" ID, 1" OD to grip 7/8" bars in ID risers, set of 4.
VT No. 25-2174

RISER BUSHING & BOLT

BUSHINGS

Riser Mount Set

1/2" x 13 threads. 1973-Up XL.

VT No. 25-0953

Handlebar Riser Damper

Kit includes all rubber bushings, threaded studs, washers and cups. 1985- up XL.

VT No. 28-2118

28-2118

Handlebar Damper Kit

One pair damper, spacers, top and bottom washers. Replaces 56153-73, 46159-73. Fits 1973-84 XL-FX-FL.

28-0221   28-0228   37-8881

VT No.	Item	Finish
28-0221	Kit FX-XL-FXST-WG	Zinc
28-0228	Kit FX-XL-FXST-WG	Chrome
37-8881	Washers, four pieces	Chrome

Chrome Solid Mount Kit

Replaces stock rubber bushings and cap washers. Order bolt set separately.

28-0673   28-0675

VT No.	Item	Thread	VT No.	Item	Thread
28-0673	Kit	Billet	2132-4	Bolts	1/2" — 20
28-0675	Kit	Steel	2094-4	Bolts	1/2" — 13

Poly Urethane Riser Bushing Set

Includes 4 bushings with chrome covers.

28-0276   28-2260   28-0284

VT No.	FITS
28-0284	1962- Up XL
08-2260	1973- Up XL
28-0276	1997-2003 XL OEM:56165-03

BOLTS
COLONY

28-0951

28-0950

28-0744

Chrome Billet Cone Head Riser Mount Kit

Includes washers, cones and bolts 3-1/2:" long.

VT No.	Item
28-0950	1/2" — 20
28-0951	1/2"— 13
28-0744	1/2" — 13 Chrome 1973-up (Washers Not Included)

Chrome Riser Bolt Kit

Includes bolts with integral lower flange washer, and allen flush head for installation. Includes spacers and chrome top washers.

37-0878

VT No.	Item	VT No.	Item
37-0881	1/2" — 13	37-0878	1/2"— 20

2135-4

Chrome Riser Bolt Sets in allen or hex style includes lock washers. Order cupwashers separately.

Hex	Allen	Len.	Thread	Fit
2135-4	2094-4	2-1/2"	1/2" — 13	
	2132-4	2-1/2"	1/2"— 20	
	2133-4	2-3/4"	1/2"— 20	
2136-4	2095-4	2-3/4"	1/2" — 13	
2137-4	2129-4	3"	1/2"— 13	1984
	2134-4	3"	1/2"— 20	1984
2138-4	2130-4	3-1/2"	1/2"— 13	1974-79
2139-4	2131-4	3-3/4"	1/2"— 13	1979-Up

Handlebar Riser Bolts

Replacement for the stock type riser bolts. Can also be used with V-Twin risers. Sold as pair.

VT No.	Length	Application
37-8451	1/2" — 13 — 3-1/2"	1980-83 FL, 1983-up XLX
37-8452	1/2"— 13 — 2-3/4"	1984 FL, 84-up FXWG
37-8453	1/2"— 13 — 3-3/4"	1979-up XL-XLCH 1979-82 FX 1974-up all FX-FXE
37-8454	1/2"— 13 — 2-1/2"	1979-80 XL,
37-8455	1/2"— 13 — 3	1984 XL-XLX 1984-up FXE 80
37-8456	1/2"— 13 — 3-1/2"	1974-79 all XL

HANDLEBAR

17

1996-UP LEVER ASSEMBLY

26-2158

26-2211

26-2184

26-2186

26-2163

26-2212

26-2182

26-2204

32-1219

1996-2003 Type Clutch Lever Bracket

Includes 2 halves.

VT No.	OEM	Finish	
26-2184	38608-96	Chrome	
26-2186	As Above	Black	
26-2163	45044-96	Chrome	Clamp Only

Clutch Handle Assembly

Includes mount bracket, clamp and handle, assembled.

VT No.	Fits	VT No.	Fits
26-2158	1996-03 XL	26-2211	2014-up XL
26-2182	2004-2006 XL	26-2212	As Above Black
26-2204	2007-13 XL	32-1219	Switch; 1996-03 XL

26-2194

26-2195

26-2196

2004-13 Chrome Pieces for XL

VT No.	OEM	Item
26-2194	42807-4	Clamp/Bracket
26-2195	38671-04	Bracket
26-2196	42807-4	Lever Pin
26-2198	45799-04	Spring

HANDLEBAR 17

48-1714

48-0550

Black Leather Accessories

VT No.	Item
48-0550	Lever Covers
48-1714	Lever Covers with 16" Fringe

LEVER CONTROL HARDWARE

26-1979 · 26-2129 · 12-0944

Hand Lever Pivot Pins for brake and clutch sides.

VT No.	OEM	Item/XL Fitment	U/M
26-1979	45032-82	Pin 1982-03	5pk
26-0507	45031-65	Pin and Clip 1965-81	10pk
26-0544		Pivot Pin Set w/ Grease Fitting 1971-81	
12-0939	11036	Clip for above 1957-90	10pk
26-2129	45032-82	Pin 1982-03	Each
12-0944	11143	Snap Ring for Above 1982-95	10pk

Skeleton Lever

Chrome skeleton brake and clutch hand Lever fits 2004-13 XL.

VT No. 26-0119

26-0505

26-1979

26-2129

26-2138 · 26-2132 · 36-2559

Brake Cable Clamp

Universal style clamp.

VT No. 26-0508

Cable Clamp

Fits to hand lever for emergency or permanent use. Easy to install .460" diameter, 1 pair.

VT No. 26-0509

Chrome Lever Pins

Allen style for pivot point on 1982-03 XL.

VT No. 37-8823

Allen Screw Set for Lever Clamp

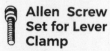

4-piece set for 1965-72 levers.

VT No. 8797-4

Lever Pins / Bushings

VT No.	OEM	Item	Year	U/M
26-0505	45036-68	Bushings	1968-87	10
26-2138	45039-68	Nylon Bushing	1968-87	25
26-2129		Pin	1982-14	Each
26-1979		Pin	1982-14	5
26-2132*	45036-88	Bushings	1988-up	Each
36-2559	45423-92	Lever Bushings	1992-up	10

*Note: Teflon pin fits 1988-up eyelet clutch cables

1996-UP HAND LEVER SET

CHROME SMOOTH

CHROME SKULL

BLACK SKULL

CHROME DRILLED

BLACK DRILLED

CHROME V-CUT

BLACK V-CUT

CHROME 5 HOLE

Contour Levers Designed for Easy Grip

Sold pairs.

Chrome	Black	Year	Type		Chrome	Black	Year	Type		Chrome	Black	Year	Type
26-2178		1996-03	Smooth		26-0785		1996-03	5 Hole		26-0797	26-0980	2007-13	Smooth
26-0788	26-0984	1996-03	Drilled		26-2193		2004-06	Smooth		26-0786	26-0820	2007-13	4 Hole
26-0789	26-0111	1996-03	Slotted		26-0783	26-0819	2004-06	Drilled		26-0466	26-0467	2014-up	Smooth
26-2189	26-2109	1996-03	Skull Ends		26-0782		2004-06	Slotted		26-0802	26-0805	2014-up	OEM Style
26-0787	26-1156	1996-03	Skull Ends		26-0784	26-0114	2007-13	Slotted		26-0803	26-0806	2014-up	2 Slot
26-0780	26-0982	1996-03	V-Cut		26-2203	26-0983	2007-13	V-Cut		26-0804	26-0807	2014-up	4 Hole
										26-2156		1985-95	Skull Girder Style

26-0984

26-0783

Skull End Detail

26-0982

26-0983

26-0783

HANDLEBAR 17

26-0786

26-0785

26-0797

26-0788

26-2193

26-2203

26-0784

26-2178

Trigger Lever Sets Replace stock levers. Fit 1996-03 XL.
VT No. 26-0415

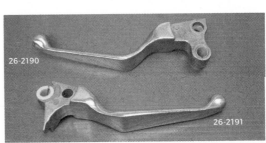

26-2190

26-2191

Replica Polished Levers 1996-03 XL

VT No.	Type	VT No.	Type
26-2190	Clutch	26-2191	Brake

Chrome Billet Flame Control Set

Fits 1996-07 FX-FXD and 1996-03 XL.
VT No. 26-0989

HANDLEBAR CONTROL

Black Front Master Cylinder

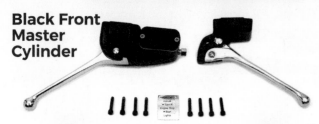

Has a 1/2" bore and includes the brake lever, stop light switch, reservoir cover, and all internal components. OEM 45010-73. Fits 1972-1981 XL,

VT No. 26-2097

Chrome Adjustable Lever

Set features hidden adjustment screw that allows the lever to be moved in closer to handlebar controls. 2004-12 XL.

26-0116

Power Wide Lever

Chrome lever set replaces stock lever on 1972-81.

VT No. 26-0580

1972-95 Lever

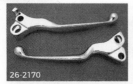

26-2170

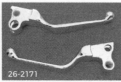

26-2171

26-2162- Polished

Chrome contour levers designed for easy grip, sold pairs.

VT No.	Year	VT No.	Year
26-2170	1972-81	26-2162	1982-95
26-2171	1982-95	26-2110	1982-95

Soft Pad Lever

26-1975

26-1974

VT No.	Year
26-1975	1982-95
26-1974	1972-81

Feature a comfortable rubber insert 3/8" thick locked into a tongue-and-groove channel.

Chrome Handlebar Control Cover Kits

26-0746

Include master cylinder cover, clutch mount and two clamps for single disc application.

VT No.	Year	Disc	VT No.	Year	Disc
22-0876	2007-13 XL	Single	26-0537	1996-03 XL	Dual
26-0536	2996-03 XL	Single			

Chopped Handlebar Master Cylinder and Control Housing

Set for 1996-10 models. Fits 1996-10 FXST, FLST, 1996-up FXD, 1996-up FLT without cruise radio controls, 1996-03 XL.

VT No.	Bore
22-0813	9/16"
22-0814	11/16"

26-0527

26-0528

26-0519

26-0531

26-2136

26-2133

26-0532

26-2135

Clutch and Brake Levers

Polished or chrome finish. Sold individually.

Chrome	Polish	OEM	Years	Type
26-0527	26-0528	45016-72	1972-81	Brake
	26-0517	Power	1972-81	Brake
	26-0519	Power	1972-81	Brake
26-0531	26-2136	45017-82	1982-95	Clutch
26-2133		45017-88	1988-95	Clutch
26-0532		45016-82	1982-95	Brake
	26-2135	45016-82	1982-95	Brake

Extended Turn Signal Caps

Fits 1996-up XL models.

32-1669

32-1668

VT No.	Finish
32-1668	Chrome
32-1669	Black

Standard Back-lit LED Handlebar Switches and Wiring Harness

Without switch housing. LED is amber and wires are 60" in length.

VT No.	Fitment
32-1135	2007-up XL
32-1272	1996-03 XL
32-1273	1996-03 XL

CONTROL KIT

22-0813

22-1076

22-0836

22-0804

22-0838

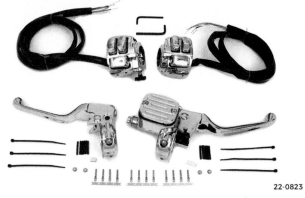

22-0823

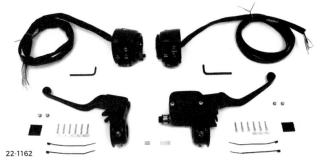

22-1162

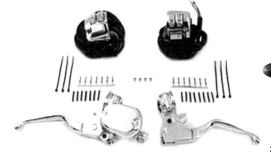

22-0885

HANDLEBAR

17

Description	Bore	Kit w/ Wiring		Brake Assembly	
		Chrome	Black	Chrome	Black
82-95 Dual Disc	3/4"			26-2145	26-2153
82-95 Single Disc	5/8"			26-2120	26-2122
82-95 Dual Disc	11/16"				26-2154
96-03 Single Disc	9/16"	22-0823	22-1162	26-2180	
96-03 Dual Disc	11/16"	22-0824	22-1167	26-2179	
96-03 Single Disc w/ Slight Hole	9/16"	22-0817	22-1168		
04-06 Single Disc	1/2"	22-0857			
04-06 Dual Disc	9/16"	22-0858			
07-13 Single Disc	1/2"	22-1524			
07-16 Dual Disc	9/16"	22-0885			
2014-Up w/o ABS	1/2"			26-2213	26-2214
2014-Up w/o ABS				26-2215	26-2216

Description	Bore	Kit w/o Wiring	
		Chrome	Black
82-83 Dual Disc	3/4"	22-1069	
84-95 Single Disc	5/8"	22-1076	22-1164
96-03 Single Disc	9/16"	22-0804	22-1165
96-03 Dual Disc	11/16"	22-0803	22-1166
96-03 Single Disc w/ Slight Hole	9/16"	22-0820	11-1161
04-06 Single Disc	1/2"	22-0825	22-0835
06-06 Dual Disc	9/16"	22-0826	22-0836
07-13 Single Disc	1/2"	22-0876	22-0837
07-13 Dual Disc	9/16"	22-0884	22-0838
2014-Up w/o ABS	1/2"	22-0839	22-0840
2014-Up w/o ABS	14mm	22-0841	22-0842

Handlebar Cable and Brake Line Kit

VT No.	Length	Fitment
36-1608	12"	2014-2017 XL
36-1609	14"	2014-2017 XL
36-1610	12"	2007-2013 XL
36-1611	14"	2007-2013 XL

CONTROL DRESS KIT

Dress Kit with Switch Housings

Fits 1996-03 XL models with single disc.

VT No. 26-0546

 22-0804

 22-0823

Chrome Handlebar Control Kit

Includes complete chrome master cylinder, clutch handle with clamp and two pairs of chrome switch housings. Available with or without chrome switches as listed. All kits include stainless steel hardware.

Switches		Fits	Bore	Disc
With	Without			
22-0823	22-0804	1996-03 XL	9/16"	Single

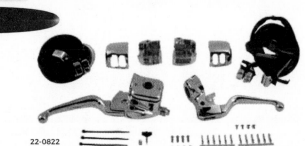 22-0822

Smooth Contour Handlebar Control Kit

For custom applications.

Snap On Switch Covers

 32-1091

26-0991

 32-0562

Replace existing black switch covers. Available in chrome or gold.

Gold	Chrome	Year
32-1091	32-0562	1996-13 XL
	26-0844*	2014-up XL
	26-0991	2014-up XL

Note: Includes switch cap for cruise control equipped models.

1996-up Chrome Control Dress Up Kit

 26-0538

Includes clutch lever bracket, handlebar control clamps, master cylinder top and body cover with levers and hardware for 1996-03 XL. Disc models as noted.

VT No.	Disc	VT No.	Disc
26-0538	Single	26-0549	Dual

Chrome Smooth-Contour Control Kit

22-0378

26-0590

Features a hidden underside mounting on the switch housings for an unobstructed smooth, rounded surface on the top housing. Switch housings use stock or chrome rounded switches (introduced on 1996 models). Complete kits include clutch and brake levers, master cylinder, hydraulic clutch, switch housings, brackets and hardware. Both master cylinders have 11/16" bore for single or dual disc.

VT No.	Style	VT No.	Style
22-0378	Contour	26-0590	Lever Set

 26-0536

 26-0537

Chrome Handlebar Control and Reservoir Cover Set

Includes clutch lever bracket, handlebar control clamps, master cylinder top and body cover, and hardware for complete installation. Fits 1996-03 XL models.

VT No.	Disc	VT No.	Disc
26-0536	Single	26-0537	Dual

HANDLEBAR 17

V-TWIN

HANDLEBAR CONTROL 1996-UP

32-0752

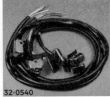

32-0540

32-1272

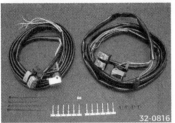

32-0816

32-1273

Handlebar Switch Kits with Wiring.

VT No.	OEM	Year/Model	Item	Finish
32-0752	Set	1996-06	7 Piece Set, (60")	Black
32-0540	Set	1996-06	7 Piece Set, (48")	Chrome
32-0816	Set	1996-06	7 Piece Set, (106")	Chrome
32-0578	Set	1996-06	7 Piece Set, (60")	Chrome
32-1272	Set	1996-up LED	60"	Chrome
32-1273	Set	1996-up LED	60"	Black
32-0848	Set	2007-up XL		Chrome
32-0849	Set	2007-up XL		Black
32-7000	71589-96		Engine-Start-Stop	Black
32-7001	71590-96		Stop Light 6" Wire	Black
37-0994	71509-00		Stop Switch Shim	
32-7002	71591-96		Right Turn Signal	Black
32-7003	71597-96		Dimmer Horn	Black
32-7004	71598-96		Left Turn Signal	Black
37-0882	2955		Switch Mounting Screw	10 pk
32-1219	71584-96B		Clutch Handle Switch	

Chrome Switch Housing Kit

Includes 48" long wiring harness, chrome switch housings with chrome switches and hardware screws. Fits 1996-2007 XL.

VT No. 32-0561

32-7817

32-7820

20" Wire Extension Kit for Handlebar Switches

VT No.	Fits
32-7817	2007-up models w/o Cruise Control 14 Wires
32-7820	2007-up models w/ Cruise Control 17 Wires

HANDLEBAR

17

Allen Chrome Handlebar Switch Housing Screw Kit fits 1996-up.

VT No. 9776-10

26-2175

26-0793

Switch Housing Kits

26-0007

26-0986

Includes left and right upper lower housing. Order switches, wiring and adjuster separately.

VT No.	Type	Year	Finish
26-2175	Stock	1996-up	
26-0976	Stock	1996-2011	
26-0793*	Stock	2007-11	*Note: Has provision for clutch lock-out switch
26-0986	Stock	2014-up	Chrome
26-0988	Stock	2014-up	Black
26-0007	Kit	1996-03	Throttle Adjuster Kit

Ready to Install Handlebar Extension Harnesses

All the items needed to successfully extend wiring to handlebar switches. Harnesses include both male and female Molex terminals crimped on each end. Feature color matching wire as per original.

Fit 2014-up XL			Fit 2014-up XL		Fit 2014-up XL	
			Fit 2007-13 XL		Fit 1996-06 XL	
32-6676	+ 4"		32-6656	+4"	32-6664	+4"
32-6677	+8"		32-6657	+8"	32-6665	+8"
32-6678	+12"		32-6658	+12"	32-6666	+12"
32-6679	+15"		32-6659	+15"	32-6667	+15"

LED Gear Indicator Kit

Features a chrome housing and a bright LED display. Kit control module, housing, and wire harness for easy plug and play installation. Fits 2007-up XL models.

VT No. 32-0296

Turn Signal Kit

32-6672	4" Length
32-6673	8" Length
32-6674	12" Length
32-6675	15" Length

Front Turn Signal Extension Harness

For installing taller handlebars when keeping turn signals mounted on handlebar switch housings. No crimping required. De-pin factory harness and connector and install new extension harness.

Fit 1996-up XL		Fit 1996-up XL	
32-6557	+ 4"	32-6559	+12"
32-6558	+8"	32-6560	+15"

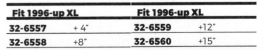

1982-95 CONTROL KIT

Chrome Switch Housings and Assembly

Includes 48" long leader wires and internal mount screws. Fits 1982-95 XL.

VT No. 32-0560

Includes complete master cylinder, clutch handle with clamp and 2 pairs of switch housings in chrome finish. Master cylinder includes a clamp with both a 10mm and 12mm bolt. All kits include stainless steel hardware.

When rebuilding 1982-95 front master cylinder check that bleed back passage is clear

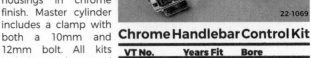

22-1069

Chrome Handlebar Control Kit

VT No.	Years Fit	Bore
22-1069	1982-83	3/4"
22-1076	1984-95	5/8"

26-2149

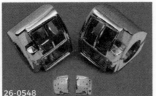

26-0548

4-pc Handlebar Switch Housing Set

Four piece chrome set replaces upper and lower of right and left sides including stainless buttonhead screws. Use existing wiring and switches for assembly.

VT No.	Item
26-2149	1982-95 XL
26-0548	1982-95 Set, All Models
37-8940	25 Screws, OEM 2508 (Buttonhead Stainless)

Allen Chrome Handlebar Switch Housing Screw Kit fits 1982-95.
VT No. 8767-10

HANDLEBAR 17

1982-95 Handlebar Switch Kit

32-9208

Includes complete right and left switch assemblies, brake light switch, mounting screws and clips. Individual switches also available.

Black	Chrome	Item
32-8084	32-9208	1982-95 Switch Kit
32-8000	32-9070	Left Turn Signal
32-8001		Engine Stop-Start
32-8002		Right Turn Signal
32-8003		Dimmer and Horn
32-7782		Stop Switch, Front
Hardware for Above		
	37-8966 Zinc	Screws, 25pk
	37-0006 Zinc	Spacer, 5pk

Handlebar Wiring Harness Kits

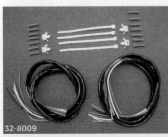

32-8009

Color coded.

VT No.	Type
32-8010	Stock
32-8009	Extended

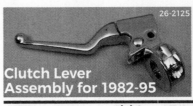

26-2125

26-2137

Clutch Lever Assembly for 1982-95

VT No.	Item	Finish	VT No.	Item	Finish
26-2125	Assembly	Chrome	26-2137	Clamp and Bracket	Chrome
26-2188	Assembly	Black	26-2165	Clamp and Bracket	Black

1982-95 Clutch Lever Components

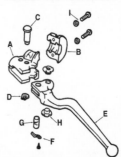

26-2129

26-1979

26-2140

26-2130

26-2138

26-2132

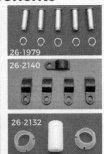

VT No.	#	OEM	Item
26-2137	A	38608-82A	Bracket and
	B	45044-82	Clamp, Chrome
26-2165		As Above	Black
26-2146	B	45044-82	Clamp, Black
26-2147	B	45044-82	Clamp, Chrome
26-2129	C	45032-82	Lever Pin with Snap Ring
26-1979		45032-82	Lever Pins Only, 5pk
12-0944	D	11143	Snap Ring
26-0531	E	45017-82	1982-88 Clutch Lever
23-2133		45017-88	1988-Up Clutch Lever
26-2164		45017-93	Clutch Lever
26-2140	F	45021-86	Anti-Rattle Spring
26-2130	G	45036-82	Cable Pin
26-2132		45036-88	Nylon Cable Pin
26-2138	H	45039-68	Pin Bushing
26-0400	I		4pc Kit, Chrome

1972-81 CONTROL

Switch Housing

VT No.	#	Years	Finish	Item
26-0513	A	1973-81	Chrome	Switch Housing
26-2093			Black	
26-0628	A	1973-81	Black	As Above
26-0642	A	1973-81	Polished	As Above
26-0631	B	1972	Chrome	Horizontal Switch Housing
26-0629	B	1972	Black	As Above
26-0514	C	Smooth	Chrome	Plain Switch
26-0630	C	Smooth	Black	As Above
26-2160	C	Smooth	Polished	As Above

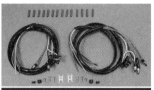

Handlebar Wiring Harness

Chrome or black switches and pre-soldered hardware. Includes wire connectors, buttons, screws, stop light switch rubber boot, and switch retaining plates. Fits 1973-81. Color coded to match stock wires. 40" long, kit will fit tall handlebars.

VT No.	Finish
32-8071	Black
32-8208	Chrome

32-0403   32-0404   32-0402   32-0406   32-0405

Handlebar Switches

Available with or without wire for 1972-81. *Note: 32-0395 is 5 pack.

W/o Wire 10pk	W/o Wire Ea.	W/Wire Ea.	Type	Style
32-0395*	32-0403	32-8933	Hi-Low	Rocker
32-0391	32-0404	–	Plain	Rocker
32-0394	32-0402	32-8931	Run-off	Rocker
32-0392	32-0406	32-8930	Brake	Button
32-0393	32-0405	32-8919	Starter	Button
32-0393	32-0405	32-8920	Horn	Button
32-0408			Long Cap 5/16"	1972- E73
32-0407			Short 3/16"	L1973-81

Switch Control Assortment for 1972-81

Qty	Switch	Qty	OEM	Switch
2	Hi-Low	10	71535-72	Long
6	Brake	10	71534-72	Short
2	Run-off	2	71482-72	Plain
6	Starter and Horn			

Saves time and money on dimmer, starter-horn button hardware. *Note quantities supplied. Included are the following: *VT No. 32-0320* for entire assortment.

Handlebar Wiring Harness Kits

Color coded. 1973-81.

VT No.	Type
32-9316*	Stock
32-8005	Stock
32-0708	Extended

*Note: fits 1970-71

32-8005

8766-10   Allen

Chrome Switch Housing Allen Screw Sets for 1973-81.

Colony	VT No.
8766-10	8766-10T

Control Box Decal Set

Turn-L ➡
Horn ➡
◀ Turn-R
Engine Stop
◀ Start
Lights

Decals for both right and left handlebar switch boxes for 1973-81.

VT No. 48-0415

Handlebar Control Kit

26-2148

26-2185

1972-81 kit includes complete master cylinder with clamp, clutch handle with clamp, switch housings and bracket. Order with or without black switch kit.

VT No.	Item	Finish
26-2148	Without Switch Wiring	Chrome
26-2185	With Switch Wiring	Chrome
26-2187	Without Switch Wiring	Polished
26-2209	With Switch Wiring	Polished
26-2093	Without Switch	Black

26-0535   26-0511

Clutch Lever Assembly

Order switch housing separately. Fits 1973-81.

VT No.	Finish	Item
26-0535	Chrome	Clutch Lever Assy.
26-2131	Polished	As Above
26-0511	Chrome	Clutch Lever Mount
26-0512	Polished	As Above
26-0627	Black	As Above

Rubber Stop Switch Caps

Protect the stop switch from moisture.

VT No.	Application	VT No.	Application
28-2114	1972-81 Front	32-0748	Switch Terminal

Chrome Switches and Buttons 1972-81

32-9060   32-9061   32-9062   32-9063

32-9064

VT No.	Item	Type
32-9060	Rocker Switch	Run-off
32-9061	Rocker Switch	Hi-Low
32-9062	Rocker Switch	Plain
32-9063	Button Cap (10)	Long
32-9064	Button Cap (10)	Short

Handlebar Switch Repair Kit

4 screws, 2 retainer clips for button switches (71533-72) .and 4 button black caps. Fits 1973-81.

VT No.	Item	VT No.	Item
32-1555	Kit	31-1988	Clips, 10pk

HANDLEBAR
17

MASTER CYLINDER COVER

Front Master Cylinder Covers

VT No.	Years	VT No.	Years	VT No.	Years	VT No.	Years
Smooth		**24-0604**	1996-05	**Milled**		**Finned**	
23-9188	1972-81	**23-0779**	1996-05	**24-0927**	1985-95	**24-0601**	1979-81 Kelsey Style MC
23-9189	1982-84	**24-1279**	1996-05	**23-0781***	1996-05	**23-9190**	1982-86 Rear
23-9187	1985-95	**23-0782**	1996-05	**23-9160**	1986-95 XLH	**23-0617**	1979-81 Kelsey Style MC
24-0649	1985-95	**23-9263**	2004-06				
23-0901	1985-95	**23-0944**	2004-16				
23-0794	1985-95	**23-9267**	2007-up				

HANDLEBAR

17

Vertical Style

Horizontal Style

Front Master Cylinder Assemblies

Complete with internals and lever, assembled.

VT No.	OEM	Item
26-0513		Vertical Switch Housing 1973-81
26-0631		Horizontal Switch Housing 1972 Only
26-0514		Smooth Cover
23-1719	45063-72	Rebuild Kit

Front Master Cylinder Assemblies

Complete with internals and lever, assembled. 1972-81.

VT No.	OEM	Item	Finish
26-0456		Assembly	Chrome
26-0457		Assembly	Polished
26-0458		Assembly	Black
26-0624	45010-73	Assembly	Chrome
26-2099	45010-73	Assembly	Polish
26-0110	45010-73	Body Only	Raw
23-9267	2007-up		

Eagle Spirit Master Cylinder Covers

Chrome or with gold inlay.

Chrome	Gold	Fitment
	24-0631	1982-85 Front
24-0629	**24-0632**	1985-95

Front Master Cylinder and Reservoir Top Gaskets

VT No.	Year	VT No.	Year
15-0188	1972-81	**15-0242**	1985-95
15-0204	1982-84	**15-0250***	1996-2005
		15-0373	2004-up

MASTER CYLINDER REBUILD

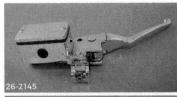
26-2145

26-2147

26-0576

23-1055

26-2153

26-2154

26-2166

26-2179

Front Master Cylinder Assemblies complete with internals and lever, assembled.

Chrome	Black	OEM	Item
1982-95			
26-2145	26-2153	45013-82A	3/4" Bore, 10mm banjo line
26-2120	26-2122	45019-85	5/8" Bore, 12mm banjo line
26-2166	26-2154	45013-85B	11/16" Bore, 12mm banjo line
26-2147	26-2146	45044-82	Clamp
26-0400			Screw Kit for Clamp
32-7782		71574-82	Front Brake Switch
23-1716		45063-82	Rebuild kit 3/4"
23-3021		45069-84	Rebuild kit 5/8"
23-3020		45006-87A	Rebuild kit 11/16"
1996-2003 XL			
26-2179		45013-96	Complete 11/16" bore, Dual
26-2180		45019-96	Complete 9/16" bore, Single
23-1714		45006-96	Rebuild Kit 9/16"
23-1715		45072-96	Rebuild Kit 11/16"
26-2163		45044-96	Clamp
2004-06 XL Only			
26-0576		42307-04	Complete, Single
26-2201		45052-04	Complete, Dual
23-1788		42803-04	Rebuild Kit, Single
23-1787		42809-04	Rebuild Kit, Dual
2007-up XL Only			
26-0582		45146-07	Complete, Dual
23-0288		42803-07	Rebuild Kit, Single
2014-up XL			
26-2213	26-2214		Without ABS
26-2215	26-2216		With ABS

Handlebar Master Cylinder Rebuild
Each kit contains parts necessary for complete rebuild.

23-1719 28-2002 23-1738

VT No.	OEM	Years	Fits
23-1738	Complete	1972-81	
23-1719	45063-72	1972-81	
23-1739	Complete	1972-81	
26-0622	Fitting	1972-81	
23-1716	45063-82	1982-85	3/4" Bore
23-3021	45072-87	1985-95	5/8" Bore
23-1714	45006-96	1996-2003	9/16" Bore
23-1715	45072-96	1996-2003	11/16" Bore
23-1787	42803-04	2004-06	Dual Disc
23-1788	42809-04	2004-06 /2007-up	Single Disc
23-1825	42809-07	2007-13	Dual Disc
23-1826	4170087	2014	Single Disc Non ABS
23-1827	4170084	2014-up	Single Disc w/ ABS
23-1825	42809-07A	2007-13	Dual Disc
23-1826	41700087	2014	Single Non-ABS
23-1827	41700084	2014-up	Single With ABS
12-0984	11063	Retaining Ring, 1972-81	
23-0590	45059-72	Spring Cup	
23-0825	45056-77	Piston Cup	
28-2002	45042-82	Fluid Level Window, 1982-2005 w/ seal	
13-0152	45071-72A	Plunger Spring	1972-81

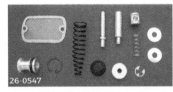
26-0547

26-0616

Master Cylinder Plunger Assembly Complete Kit 1972-81

VT No.	Type
26-0547	w/ Master Cylinder Rebuild
26-0616	Hardware Only

1982-95 Front Brake Pushrod Parts

VT No.	OEM	#	Item
26-2141	45051-82 A / 45031-82 B	A/B	Rod/Barrel Set
26-2139	45031-82	B	Pivot Barrel

HANDLEBAR 17

 BILLET MIRROR

Chrome Billet Mirrors

34-0122

Chrome Billet Mirrors with Stem

34-0152

34-0788

34-0154

34-0789

34-0151

34-0790

34-0143

34-0791

34-0153

34-0794

34-0788

34-0147

Crescent style sold in sets. Rotar style sold each and can be used for either right or left hand side.

Crescent	Rotar	Stem Only
34-0152	34-0788	
34-0154	34-0789	34-0145
34-0151	34-0790	34-0146
34-0143	34-0791	34-0147
34-0153	34-0794	34-0148

34-0124

34-0125

34-0127

34-0128

34-0129

VT No.	Style	U/M
34-0122	Oval, Right/Left	Each
34-0123	Oval, Right/Left	Each
34-0124	Oval, Right/Left	Each
34-0125	Diamond Right and Left	Set
34-0127	Diamond, Right and Left	Set
34-0128	Oval, Right and Left,	Set
34-0129	Diamond, Right and Left	Set

34-0123

Billet Mirror with Adjustable Stem

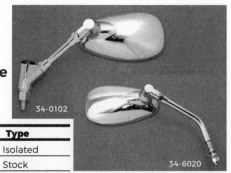

34-0102

34-6020

VT No.	Type
34-0102	Isolated
34-6020	Stock

Billet Mirror Set, Sculpted Stem

34-0354

VT No.	Finish
34-0354	Chrome
34-1964	Black

Chrome Convex Tinted Mirror Set

Includes billet stems.
VT No. 34-0371

MIRROR 18

BILLET MIRROR

Billet Mirrors Pairs

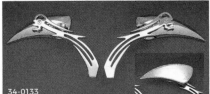
34-0133

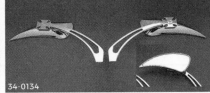
34-0134

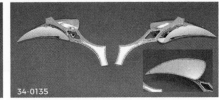
34-0135

34-0136

34-0137

34-0866

34-0865

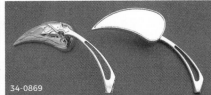
34-0869

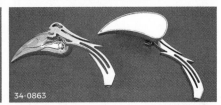
34-0863

34-0864

34-0867

34-0868

34-0861

34-0859

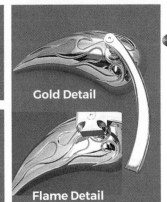
Gold Detail
Flame Detail

MIRROR
18

34-0870

34-0860

Flame	Smooth	Face	Stem	Flame	Smooth	Face	Stem
34-0863	34-0133	Tear Drop	Skull	34-0859	34-0136	Tear Drop	Normal and Short Stem
34-0864		Gold Inlay	Skull	34-0860		Gold Inlay	Two Stems
34-0867	34-0134	Tear Drop	Cross Head	34-0865	34-0137	Tear Drop	Flame
34-0868		Gold Inlay	Cross Head	34-0866		Gold Inlay	Flame
34-0861	34-0135	Tear Drop	Twisted	34-0869		Tear Drop	Spear
				34-0870		Gold Inlay	Spear

Billet Oval Mirror Set with 3-slot Stem

Sold pair. Replaces 91513-99.

VT No.	Finish
34-0328	Chrome
34-1955	Black

All Mirrors are covered under "Replacement Only" Provision. No credit will be issued for these items as they are exchange only.

BILLET MIRROR

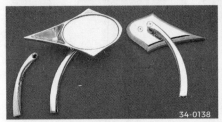

34-0138   34-0140

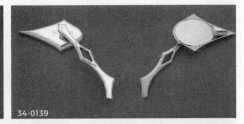

34-0139

34-0155

34-0141

34-0142

34-0157

34-0156

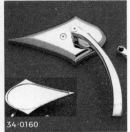

34-0160

Chrome Billet Spike Oval Face Mirror

Featuring smooth face or face with inset. Sold each.

Full Face	Face w/Inset	Stem
34-0160	34-0138	2-Stems
34-0155	34-0139	Twisted
34-0156	34-0140	Flame
34-0157	34-0141	Skull Stem
34-0158	34-0142	Cross Head

34-0158

Billet Baroque Mirror Set

With billet stems.
VT No. 34-0777

Chrome Snake Eye Mirror

Set features billet stems.
VT No. 34-0369

Villain Style Mirror

34-0768

34-0769

VT No.	Stem
34-0768	Long and Short
34-0769	Spear

Odins Mirror Set

34-0858

Features offset billet stems with curved mirrors.

34-1966

VT No.	Finish
34-0858	Chrome
34-1966	Black

Odins Arrow Style Mirror

34-0717

All Mirrors are covered under "Replacement Only" Provision. No credit will be issued for these items as they are exchange only.

MIRROR

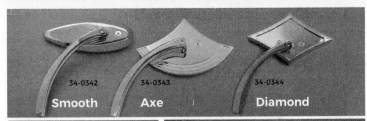

Smooth 34-0342   Axe 34-0343   Diamond 34-0344

34-0356 Oval

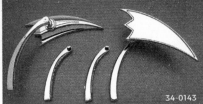

34-0143

Chrome Slim Line Mirrors

Include 2 stem sets, 5" and 3-3/4" long with complete mount hardware to fit right or left side. Sold each unless noted

VT No.	Style	VT No.	Style
34-0342	Smooth	34-0356	Oval
34-0343	Axe	34-0143	Crescent, Sold as pair
34-0344	Diamond		

Oval Mirrors
Fit right or left, sold each.

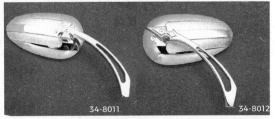

34-8011   34-8012

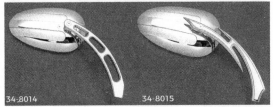

34-8014   34-8015

VT No.	Style	VT No.	Style
34-8011	Maltese	34-8014	Slot
34-8012	Spear	34-8015	Sickle

Die Cast Cobra Mirror

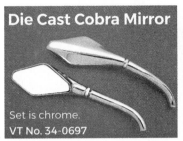

Set is chrome.
VT No. 34-0697

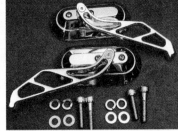

Mod Custom Mirrors
Chrome with stem included. Pairs.
VT No. 34-0349

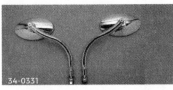

34-0331

34-1965

Radii™ Oval Mirror Set

Contour round stem with oval face. Hardware included. Sold in pairs.

Chrome	Black
34-0331	34-1965

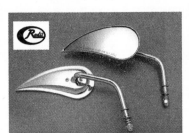

Radii Mirror Set

7" long and 3" wide at widest point.
VT No. 34-0785

34-1212

34-1215

34-1214

34-1213

34-1216

Eagle Eye Shaped Mirrors
With stem. Sold in pairs.

VT No.	Style	VT No.	Style
24-1212	Long and Short	34-1215	Spear Stem
34-1213	Crane Stem	34-1216	Sickle Stem
34-1214	Twisted Stem		

MIRROR 18

Oval Girder Mirrors

Include mount stems and have a chrome structural brace. Stems included but sold separately. Note: R/L fits right or left.

34-1059

34-2023

34-1058

34-0324

VT No.	Style	Type
34-1058	Smooth Flat Back	Right/Left
34-2023	Smooth Flat Back	Right
34-0719	Smooth Flat Back	Left
34-1059	Groove, Back	Left
34-0323	Smooth Radius Back	Right
34-0324	Smooth Radius Back	Left
34-0994	Stem only, 6"	Right

All Mirrors are covered under "Replacement Only" Provision. No credit will be issued for these items as they are exchange only.

MALTESE MIRROR

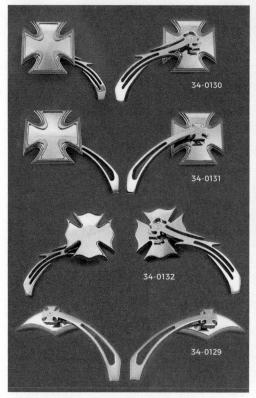

34-0130

34-0131

34-0132

34-0129

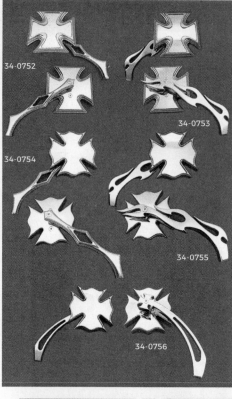

34-0752

34-0753

34-0754

34-0755

34-0756

Chrome Billet Mirrors

Sold ea, fit Right and Left

VT No.	Stem	Style
34-0130	Skull	Maltese
34-0131	Maltese	Maltese
34-0132	Skull	Fireman
34-0129	Maltese	Spear

Sold each

VT No.	Stem	Style
34-0752	Diamond	Maltese
34-0753	Flame	Maltese
34-0754	Diamond	Fireman
34-0755	Flame	Fireman
34-1957*	Flame	Fireman
34-0756	Maltese	Fireman

*Black Finish

Mini Red Baron™ Mirror

2.5" square with 2 stems.
VT No. 34-0757

Chrome Firefighter Billet Mirror

Has 2 stems, one long and one short.
VT No. 34-0390

 34-8007

 34-8008

 34-8009

Kaiser Billet Mirrors

Include stem. Fit right and left side.

VT No.	Stem	VT No.	Stem	VT No.	Stem
34-8007	Ball Milled	34-8008	Curve Stem	34-8009	Maltese

Billet Firefighter Mirror

Includes both 3" and 5" arms. Sold each.
VT No. 34-0394

 34-0120   34-0121

 34-0450

Red Baron™ Billet Mirrors

Sold each with billet stem(s) as noted.

VT No.	Stem
34-0450	Billet, (2)
34-0120	Girder, Ea.
34-0121	LED, Ea.

Maltese Set w/ Curved Stem

Chrome finish.   **VT No. 34-0382**

Maltese Mirror Set

3.5 x 3" profile. Sold as pair.
VT No. 34-0796

Black Wrinkle Maltese

Mirror features black wrinkle finish, plastic head with chrome stem and clamp.
VT No. 34-0315

GIRDER STEM

ROUND STEM

"Chopper Chrome" Die Cast Maltese Mirror

Available with round or girder stem, each.

VT No.	Stem	VT No.	Stem
34-0345	Round	34-0351	Girder

FLAME MIRROR

34-0786   34-1593

34-1245   34-1590

Fireball Mirror

VT No.	Type	VT No.	Type
34-1245	Overlay	34-1590	Chrome Over Black
34-0786	Chrome	34-1593	Black

Flame Stem

34-0433   34-0446

Mirror with stem sold each. Fits right or left side.

VT No.	Type	VT No.	Type
34-0433	Tear Drop	34-0446	Diamond

34-0398   34-0489

34-0490

Fire Ball Mirror Sets

With long flame stems or curved stems types. Include both long and short stems. Mirrors feature full chrome, chrome with gold inlay or black finish.

VT No.	Stem	Finish
34-0398	Curved, Long and Short	Chrome
34-0490	Curved, Long and Short	Gold Inlay
34-0489	Flame, Long	Chrome
34-1958	Fireball, Long	Black

34-0885

Teardrop Mirror Sets w/ Stem

34-0212

VT No.	Stem
34-0885	Flame w/ Lady Luck
34-0759	Skull
34-0212	Rogue
34-1232	Rogue, Raised Design

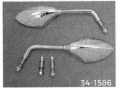

34-1586   34-1588   34-1589

Chrome Mirror Sets with Billet Stems

VT No.	Type	VT No.	Type
34-1588	Flame	34-1586	Lazer Wing
34-1589	Oval		

34-0366

Flame Tear Drop Mirror

Sets feature slotted stem with full chrome or gold inlay finish.

VT No.	Finish	VT No.	Finish
34-0365	Chrome	34-0366	Gold

34-0720   34-0721

34-0729   34-0727 34-0730

Billet Druid Mirrors for Left Side

Sold each for left side or as pair.

VT No.	Style	U/M	VT No.	Style	U/M
34-0720	Oval Flame	Each	34-0727	Oval Flame	Pair
34-0721	Druid Spear	Each	34-0730	Druid Flame	Pair
34-0729	Druid Flame	Each			

Lady Luck Sets

34-0797 Installed

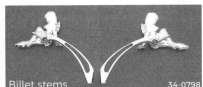

Billet stems.   34-0798

VT No.	Stem	VT No.	Stem	VT No.	Stem
34-0797	Long-Short	34-0798	Spear	34-0795	Body Set Only

34-0145   34-0146   34-0147   34-0148

34-0871   34-0159   34-0856   34-0761

Billet Mirror Stems

Fit Wyatt Gatling mirrors. Sold each.

VT No.	Style	VT No.	Style
34-0145	Spear	34-0159	Lady Luck
34-0146	Diamond	34-0856	Spinner Lady
34-0147	Curved	34-0871	3-Spade
34-0148	Maltese	34-0761	Tri Skull

All Mirrors are covered under "Replacement Only" Provision. No credit will be issued for these items as they are exchange only.

 # TEAR DROP MIRROR

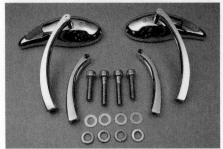

Chrome Tear Drop Mirror Set

Available with curved stems and mount hardware.

VT No. 34-0357

Teardrop Mirrors w/ Tribal Design

Solid stem.

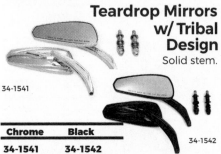

Chrome	Black
34-1541	34-1542

Offset Stem Teardrop

"Apache" style with offset stems.

VT No. 34-1566

MIRROR 18

VT No.		VT No.	
34-1217		34-1218	

Deco Mirror Pairs with Stem

VT No.	Stem	VT No.	Stem
34-1217	Long-Short	34-1219	Slot
34-1218	Sickle	34-1220	Spear

Tear Drop Mirror Set

Retro styling. Sold in set for right and left for 1982-up models. *Use on pre-1982 models requires spacer VT No. 37-0587.*

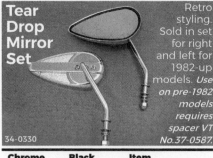

Chrome	Black	Item
34-0330	34-1962	Mirror Set
34-0587		Spacer Set

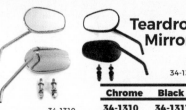

Chrome Tear Drop Mirror Set Features Radii stems, right and left.

VT No.	Brand	VT No.	Brand
34-0358	V-Twin	34-0188	Wyatt Gatling

Teardrop Mirrors

Chrome	Black
34-1310	34-1311

Billet Teardrop

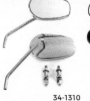

VT No.	Style
34-1594	Tribal w/ Short Slotted Stem
34-1595	Tribal w/ Sickle Stem
34-1597	Sickle w/ Spear Stem

Ace Mirrors for Left Side

Feature billet stem.

VT No.	Style
34-0722	Smooth
34-0723	Ball Milled

Billet Profile Mirror

Features hidden mount bolt.

VT No.	Stem
34-0388	Smooth
34-0395	Slotted
34-0396	Slotted

Tear Drop Mirror fits right and left sides. Each.

VT No. 34-0360

Micro Tear Drop

Features slotted stem. Sold each. Fits right or left side.

VT No. 34-0359

Billet Deco Mirror Set

34-0887

MIRROR

Deco Mirror

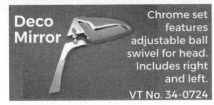

Chrome set features adjustable ball swivel for head. Includes right and left.

VT No. 34-0724

Billet Mirror

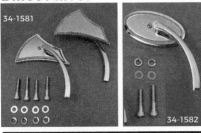

34-1581

34-1582

VT No.	Type	U/M
34-1581	Axe	Pair
34-1582	Oval	Each

Chrome Curvado Mirror Sets

VT No. 34-8214

Siege Billet Mirror

Set with twisted stem. VT No. 34-6016

34-0320

Chrome Oval Mirror

Fits right and left sides 1965-up.

VT No.	Type
34-0320	Smooth
34-0327	Stem w/ Yoke

Chrome Billet Slasher Mirror

34-1834

34-1833

VT No.	Type	U/M
34-1833	Oval	Pair, Slotted Stem
34-1834	Oval	Pair

Chrome Oval Mirror

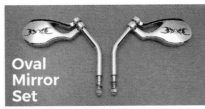

With ring and billet 3 slot stem. Use for the right or left side.

VT No. 34-0384

Oval Mirror Set

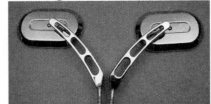

Features adjustable lens.

VT No. 34-8019

Oblong Billet Mirror Set

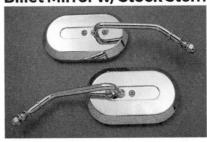

Feature slotted stem. Fit 1982-up control handles, sold in pairs.

Chrome	Black
34-0675	34-1963

Billet Mirror w/ Stock Stem

Chrome mirrors feature stock style steel stems for right and left fitment.

VT No. 34-0373

Taper Mirror Set

Billet stems.
VT No. 34-0333

Chrome Billet Replica Mirror Set

VT No. 34-0758

MIRROR

Wyatt Gatling

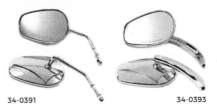

34-0391   34-0393

34-1960   34-0392

34-0402   34-0403

34-1959   34-0404

Wyatt Gatling Mirror

Available with stock or billet stems.

Chrome	Black	Stem
34-0391	34-1959	Short Stock
34-0392	34-1960	Long Stock
34-0393	34-1961	Billet
34-0402		Short Round
34-0403		Billet
34-0404		Short Round

MIRROR 18

Oval Vision Deep Dish

Mirror with radius stem. Sold each for right or left side.

VT No. 34-0348

Billet Style Cat Eye Mirror

With tinted glass and girder stem, mirror measures 2-3/4" x 5". Each fits right or left.

VT No. 34-0347

MIRROR SETS

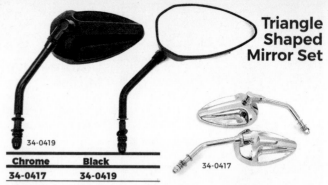

Triangle Shaped Mirror Set

Taper Convex Mirror Set

Chrome	Black	Stem Type
34-0410	34-0411	Long
34-0412	34-0413	Short

Chrome	Black
34-0417	34-0419

With round steel stems, includes right and left sides with hardware top mount to handlebar controls. Plastic back.

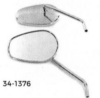

Oval Mirror Sets

Round stems for right and left sides.

Chrome	Black
34-1376	34-1377

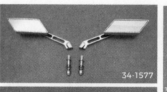

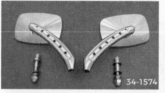
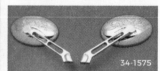

Arrow Billet Mirror Set

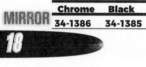

Chrome	Black
34-1386	34-1385

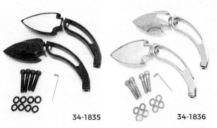

Mirror Sets		
VT No.	Item	Stem
34-1577	Parallelogram Mirror Set, Chrome	5"
34-1578	Teardrop Mirror Set, Chrome	4"
34-1579	Teardrop Mirror Set, Chrome w/ Steel Stems	6"
34-1580	Round Mirror Set, Chrome	4"
34-1574	Oval Mirror Set, Chrome	4"
34-1575	Oval Mirror Set, Chrome	5"

Rectangle Taper Set

Chrome	Black
34-0333	34-0459

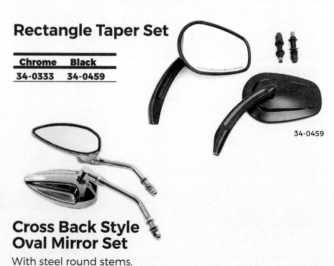

Mini Tapered Mirror

VT No.	Item
34-1598	Short Slot Stem
34-1599	Long Slot Stem

Billet Mirror Set w/ Sculpted Stems

Chrome	Black
34-1837	34-1838

Cross Back Style Oval Mirror Set

With steel round stems.

VT No. 34-1375

2" Cone Billet Mirrors

34-0368

VT No.	Type	U/M
34-0368	Cone	Pair

VT No.	Type	U/M
34-0383	Tear Drop	Each
34-0793	Tear Drop	Each

34-0793 34-0383

MIRROR

Racer Mirror Set

With adjustable face.
VT No. 34-0397

34-8001

34-8003   34-8002

Lucifer Billet Mirror Sets

Include right and left side with stems.

VT No.	Type
34-8001	Scroll
34-8002	Curve Stem
34-8003	Sickle

34-8004 34-8005 34-8006

'Zoid Mirrors
Sold each with stem.

VT No.	Stem	VT No.	Stem	VT No.	Stem
34-8004	Sickle	34-8005	Smooth	34-8006	Spike

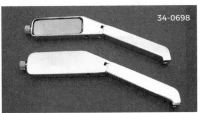

34-0389 34-0698

Adjustable Angle Mirror

Chrome billet mirror pairs feature adjustable angle face.

VT No.	Type
34-0389	Ball Milled
34-0698	Smooth

MIRROR 18

34-8113

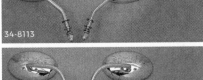
34-8114

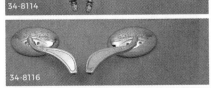
34-8116

Mirror Set with Stems

VT No.	Stem Type
34-8113	Angle
34-8114	Curve
34-8116	Wide Curve

Die Cast Mirrors

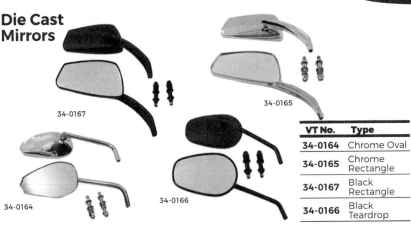

34-0167 34-0165 34-0164 34-0166

VT No.	Type
34-0164	Chrome Oval
34-0165	Chrome Rectangle
34-0167	Black Rectangle
34-0166	Black Teardrop

Chrome Billet "S" Curve

Mirror set includes stems.
VT No. 34-0381

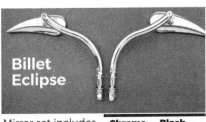
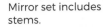

Billet Eclipse

Mirror set includes stems.

Chrome	Black
34-0380	34-1967

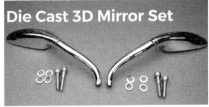

Die Cast 3D Mirror Set

Die cast chrome mirror (left and right).
VT No. 34-0350

SQUARE MIRROR

34-1069

34-0297

34-0298

Eagle Spirit Sets

Include stems and acorn nuts for handlebar lever mounting. Available in sets, right and left sides.

VT No.	Type	Stem
34-1069	Chrome Set	Girder
34-0298	Chrome Set	Stock
34-0297	Gold Inlay Set	Stock
34-0988	Chrome, Right	Stock
34-0989	Chrome, Left	Stock
34-0731	Chrome	Right Head

MIRROR
18

Rectangular Mirror Set
Includes billet stems.   VT No. 34-0386

34-6023

Chrome Rectangular Mirror

Die cast. Sold each.

Round Stem	Billet Stem
34-0294	34-6023

34-0301

Chrome Steel Mirror

Mounts on hand lever through existing hole.

VT No.	Type	VT No.	Type
34-0301	Stock	34-0310	Stock Scroll
34-0302	Clamp on		

34-1011   34-1013

Chrome Styler Mirror Set

Girder stem design. Sold pairs.

VT No.	Type	VT No.	Type
34-1011	Eagle Spirit	34-1013	Smooth

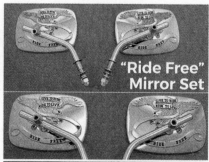

"Ride Free" Mirror Set

Chrome	Gold
34-1234	34-1235

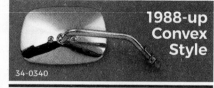

34-0340

1988-up Convex Style

Left	Right
34-0341	34-0340

 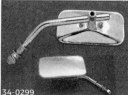

34-0289   34-0299

34-0290   34-0291

Rectangle Mirror

Chrome	Black
34-0299	34-0289
34-0290 Die Cast	34-0291 Die Cast

Chrome Mirror Stems

With acorn nut, pairs.

VT No.	Len.	Rise
34-0334	11"	8"
34-0335	8"	4"

Replica Die-Cast Chrome Mirrors

A   34-0531

B   34-0317   34-0309

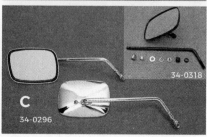

34-0318

C   34-0296

1-pc swivel-head design as original for 1965-up, all models.

VT No.	#	Item	Type	Note
34-0531	A	Each	Short	Right
34-0319	A	Each	Short	Left
34-0295	A	Set	Short	Set
34-0309	C	Stock	Short	Plain
34-0314	B	Each	Long	Right
34-0317	B	Each	Long	Left
34-0296	B	Set	Long	Left/Right
34-0318		Each	Long	Black Left/Right

34-0872   34-0873

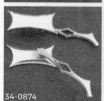 

34-0874   34-8010

Oblique Mirror Pairs

VT No.	Type	VT No.	Type
34-0872	Plain	34-0874	Diamond
34-0873	Girder	34-8010	Slot

All Mirrors are covered under "Replacement Only" Provision. No credit will be issued for these items as they are exchange only.

Pork Chop Mirror Sets

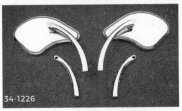

34-1226

Feature billet stems. Sold as right and left set.

34-1228

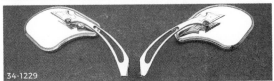

34-1229

34-1230

VT No.	Stem	VT No.	Stem
34-1226	Long Short	34-1229	Spear
34-1228	Twisted	34-1230	3-Skull

Parallelogram Style

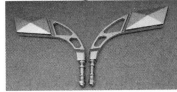

One piece design. Sold as pair.
VT No. 34-0346

Black Triangle Mirror

Mirror set is black powder coated PVC type. Set includes right and left sides with hardware.
VT No. 34-0416

SPLIT VISION

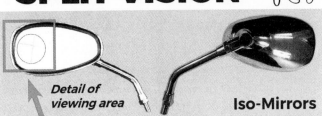

Detail of viewing area

Iso-Mirrors

Iso-Mirrors feature isolated mirror at head mount with far view. Viewing area encircled.
VT No. 34-1225

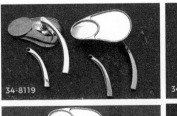

34-8119

34-8120

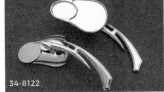

34-8122

34-8121

Split Vision Mirror Set

Features out board convex mirror for wide angle view. Split Vision Mirror has small outboard inset for seeing panoramic view of the scene behind you. The main mirror is for normal view and the small convex inset shows wider field.

VT No.	Stem	VT No.	Stem
34-8119	2 Stems	34-8121	Spear Stem
34-8120	Slot Stem	34-8122	Sickle Stem

Split Vision Mirror with Lower Convex

VT No. 34-1592

MIRROR 18

EXTENSIONS AND MOUNTS

Mirror Extension Kit

Replaces 91907-87 for relocating mirrors 2" higher on all models.

Chrome	Phosphated Black
37-9188	37-9397

31-0519

34-1968

Mirror Mount Block

Fits 1996-2007 handlebar master cylinder to allow use of custom mirrors with larger than stock stem by moving the mirror stem up and out from the master cylinder.

VT No.	Item
31-0519	Right
34-9158	Right and Left
34-1968	As Above, black

Deco Mirror Bracket

Die cast. Attaches any stock stud mirror mount to 1" handlebars.

31-0045   31-4025

Chrome	Black
31-4025	31-0045

Black Deco Clamp

Black Deco Clamp is die cast and is used to clamp to 1" handlebars to mount a mirror with stud.
VT No. 31-4180

SKULL MIRROR

3-9/16" Diameter Round Skull

Features bone stem, pair.

VT No. 34-0367

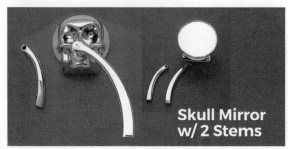

Skull Mirror w/ 2 Stems

Two length stems fit right or left side. VT No. 34-0111

Skull Teardrop

Sets include stems.

VT No. 34-0759

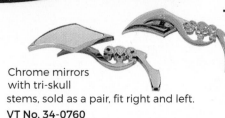

Tri-Skull Gothic Billet Mirror

Chrome mirrors with tri-skull stems, sold as a pair, fit right and left.

VT No. 34-0760

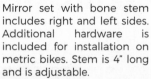

Chrome Skull, Black Eyes

Mirror set with bone stem includes right and left sides. Additional hardware is included for installation on metric bikes. Stem is 4" long and is adjustable.

VT No. 34-1274

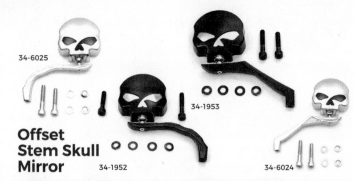

Offset Stem Skull Mirror

VT No.	Stem	VT No.	Stem
34-6025	Worm	34-6024	Wing
34-1952	As Above, Black	34-1953	Skull w/ billet stem

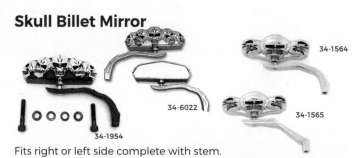

Skull Billet Mirror

Fits right or left side complete with stem.

VT No.	Skull #	Stem	VT No.	Skull #	Stem
34-6022	5	Worm	34-1564	3	Worm
34-1565	3	Wing	34-1954	5	Worm

Skeleton Hand w/ Wrist Bone Stem

VT No.	Type
34-0782	Chrome / Chrome
34-0783	Chrome / Gold
34-0784	Black / Black
34-0319	Black / Chrome

LED LIGHTED MIRROR

ALL CUSTOM TURN SIGNAL/LIGHTS REQUIRE LOAD EQUALIZER.

Sequential LED Turn Signal

34-9163
34-9157
34-9157 Installed

Billet mirror set features sequential LED turn signal on back side.

VT No.	Style
34-9157	Slotted
34-9163	Oval

34-6019
34-0293

Ellipse LED

Chrome mirror set features built in LED turn signal. Mirror measures 5" x 2-3/4", with 7" long stem.

VT No.	Lens	LED
34-0293	Clear	Amber
34-6019	Amber	Clear

Lighted Stem

Round Mirror has turn signal strip in die cast stem. Fits right or left side. Sold Each.
VT No. 34-0387

Chrome Billet Maltese Mirror Set

Built in LED turn signal matrix on back side
VT No. 34-0681

Evil Eye Set

Chrome plated die cast mirror, right and left, available with or without LED turn signals.

34-0022
34-0021

LED	Non-LED
34-0022	34-0021

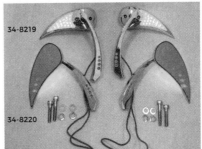

34-8219
34-8220

LED Billet Mirror Sets

Drilled stems with teardrop shape head with built in LED in back side.

1 SIDE LED	2 SIDE LED
34-8219	34-8220

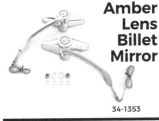

34-1378
34-1353

Amber Lens Billet Mirror

Set features amber lens with full LED turn signals.

Flashing	Rotating
34-1378	34-1353

Black LED Billet Mirror Set

34-1950
34-1951

Round	Tear Drop
34-1950	34-1951

MIRROR 18

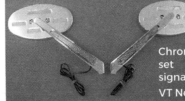

Cat Eye w/ Turn Signal

Chrome cat eye mirror set with amber turn signals built in.
VT No. 34-0372

Evil Eye LED

Chrome mirror set features amber LED turn signals built into the stems.
VT No. 34-1832

LED Skeleton Hand Mirror Set

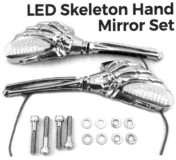

VT No. 34-0072

All Mirrors are covered under "Replacement Only" Provision. No credit will be issued for these items as they are exchange only.

ROUND & CLAMP ON MIRROR

3-3/4" Smooth Round Mirror

Chrome set is die cast with 4-3/4" long stems, pair.
VT No. 34-0364

3" Cafe Style Mirror Sets

VT No.	Finish	VT No.	Finish
34-1969	Black, Fits 1" bar	34-1971	Black, Fits 7/8" bar
34-1970	Chrome, As Above	34-1972	Chrome, As Above

34-0363   34-0037

Billet Smooth Round Mirror

Set is die cast with curved stem. Sold pair.

3.5"	2.75"
34-0363	34-0037

MIRROR 18

3" Billet Round Mirror w/ Flame Stem

Sold each.
VT No. 34-0448

3.5" Babyface

Billet with round stem. Use for right or left.
VT No. 34-0716

Chrome Groove Back

Mirror Set features die cast construction and 4-3/4" slotted stems set. Includes right and left side.
VT No. 34-0361

Chrome Round

With billet stem.
VT No. 34-1585

34-0378

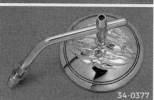

34-0377

Round Flame Mirror

4-3/8" outside diameter.

VT No.	Finish	Stem	U/M
34-0376	Chrome	Round	Pair
34-0377	Gold	Round	Ea.
34-0378	Chrome	Slot	Ea.
34-0379	Gold	Slot	Ea.

34-0427

34-0426

Round Black

VT No.	Fits
34-0426	Clamp on round stem for stock lever brackets
34-0427	Custom round - 4" round stem

Billet Air Flow Sets

34-0016

34-0017   34-0018

Chrome mirror sets have 4" diameter face. Available with straight, curved, or round billet stem. Features raised center portion with relief cuts.

VT No.	Stem Style
34-0016	Straight
34-0017	Curved
34-0018	Round Steel

4" Round Chrome Mirrors

34-0313

34-0399

34-0312

34-0306

Include stems in either clamp on or threaded end to fit stock lever brackets. For 1965- up models.

VT No.	Type
34-0313	With stud
34-0399	With stud
34-0312	With stud
34-0306	With clamp

34-0308

34-0300

34-6014

34-1514

34-0418

3" Round Chrome Mini-Mirrors

Clamp or stock stem to fit standard lever mount.

VT No.	Type	VT No.	Type
34-0308	Clamp on	34-6014	Lever Mount, Black
34-0418	Clamp Black		
34-0300	Lever Mount	34-1514	Mirror Head

34-0995   34-0997

Round Mirrors

34-0999

Clamp on long or short stem in right or left mounting. All sold each unless noted.

Chrome	Stainless	Side	Stem
34-0995	34-1573	Set	Clamp on
	34-1572	Right & Left	Stud & Nut
34-1317		Right & Left	Telescope
34-0997		Right	Short
34-0998		Left	Short
34-0999		Right	Long
34-1000	34-1569	Left	Long

4 & 4.5" HEADLAMP

33-0030

33-0077

Chrome Deco 4" Bottom Mount Headlamp

Features longer tapered shell fitted with 12 volt H-4 60/55 watt bulb. Includes mount block and stud.

Chrome	Black
33-0030	33-0077

Chrome 4" Round Diamond Cut Style Headlamp

Add a custom touch of style to your bike with this chrome 4" diamond cut halogen headlamp. Includes 12 volt 60/55 watt H-4 bulb and mount stud.

VT No. 33-0079

4" Chrome Halogen Lamp

33-0030   33-1466

Includes H-4 12 volt 60/55 watt bulb and mount stud.

Visor	No Visor
33-1466	33-0030

Deutsch Headlamp Connector

Use when installing custom lamps on 1996-up models.
VT No. 32-0487

4.5" Round Headlamp

33-4071

33-4072

33-4073   33-4074

VT No.	Type
33-4071	Chrome
33-4072	Black
33-4073	Copper
33-4074	Visor

Chrome Billet Headlamp

33-0660

Available with visor or plain no visor type. Features seamless type construction and includes and halogen bulb. Headlamp is 4-1/2" in diameter.

33-0659

33-0997

33-0997 Installed

Pointed Visor	Smooth Visor	No Visor
33-0659	33-0997	33-0660

4.5" Billet Projection Headlamp

33-0925 Installed

With bracket and 75 watt H-1 bulb for bottom mounting.
VT No. 33-0925

Custom Driving Lamp

33-0012   33-0054

4-1/2" diameter bottom mount. Features 12 volt sealed dual beam indicator and stud mount. Sold each.

VT No.	Type
33-0054	Headlamp Shell
33-0012	Complete Light, w/ bulb
33-0153	Replacement Bulb

4.5" Cyclops Headlamp

8.5" long with 55/60 W H-4 bulb.
VT No. 33-0960

LIGHTING

19

5-3/4" HEADLAMP

5-3/4" LED Headlamps

33-1015

33-1013

33-1014

These universal tear drop lights are machined from billet and feature LED lighting installed.

Black	Chrome	LED Insert
33-1013	33-1014	33-1015

33-0196 Back

33-0197 Back

33-0189 Back

33-1418 33-1419

33-0189

Stock Replacement Headlamp With H-4 unit.

Chrome	Black	Year	Fits
33-0189		1995-2003	XL
33-0196	33-1418	1974-84	XL-FX
33-0197	33-1419	1954-73	XL-FX

5-3/4" LED Daylight Headlamp Unit

Black shaded reflector and daytime running light LED ring. Fits1985-up.
VT No. 33-1043

33-2155

33-2178

33-2250

33-0085

Teardrop Headlamp

Includes mount eye bolt. Complete with bulb.12 volt.

VT No.	Type
33-2155*	Paughco *Note: Does not include mounting eye bolt
33-2178	Halogen H-4
33-2250	As Above Black
33-0200	Lamp Unit with glass lens for VT No. 33-2178
33-0085	Diamond Cut
33-0536	Lens Retainer Clip Set

33-0232

33-0231

33-0230

5-3/4" Stock Headlamp for XL

Fits FX-FXE-FXD-XL. Includes 12v sealed beam. Late type replaces 67705-74, has rectangular hole in shell for wiring. Early type has 2 connections on shell back. Order rubber insert 28-2004 separately for late type.

28-0223

VT No.	Finish	Year
33-0232	Chrome	1971-73
33-0233	Black	1954-73
33-0231	Chrome	1974-84
33-0230	Black	1974-84
28-2004	Rubber Boot	1974-83
28-0223	Rubber Ring	1954-83
33-0522	Chrome, Outer Rim Set	1963-up XL

Lamps listed are for show or decorative use only, not D.O.T. approved.

Original Bates Style!

33-0001

33-0019

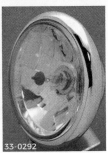
33-0292

33-0078   33-1297

33-0293

33-0958

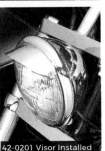
42-0201 Visor Installed

Black 5-3/4" Bates Style Headlamp Assembly

33-3042

VT No.	Type
33-3042	Black Headlamp
33-0078	Black Faceted Headlamp with copper rim
33-1297	Black Faceted Headlamp

33-2058

33-0229

33-0003

5-3/4" Bates Style Headlamp Assemblies

Include indicator bulb and mounting eye bolt and beam assembled. 60/55W H-4 installed

*Note: Hi-Beam does not have indicator lamp.

BATES
LONG BEACH CALIFORNIA
48-1325

VT No.	Type	VT No.	Type
33-0001	Wagner (12 volt)	33-0229	Shell only
33-0002	Wagner (6 volt)	33-0358	Brass Rim
33-2058	Faceted	33-0003	Complete w/ Sealed Beam
33-0019*	Bates Replica		
33-1197	Clear Dome	**Components**	
33-0292*	Blue Faceted	33-0520	Rim only, chrome
33-0293*	Clear Faceted	33-0518	Mounting Eye Bolt, chrome
33-1172	Clear Faceted		
33-0958	Reverse Cup	37-8457	Rim Screw (10 pack)

33-4075   33-4076   33-4078

5-3/4" Diamond Cut Headlamps

	H-4 Bulb Installed Lamp	
Chrome	Chrome w Visor	Black
33-4075	33-4078	33-4076

5-3/4" Teardrop

Features tear drop design with milled grooves. Includes H-4 12V 60/55 watt bulb.
VT No. 33-0606

5-3/4" H-4 Headlamp

Features domed glass and built in visor.
VT No. 33-2038

5-3/4" H-4 Headlamp

H-4 designed.

33-1321

33-1321

VT No.	Type
33-0078	Black with brass rim
33-1321	Chrome Stretched, H-4 bulb

BILLET HEADLAMP

5-3/4" Teardrop Billet Headlamp with Visor

Includes Halogen bulb and features seamless type construction.

VT No. 33-0658

33-1615

33-1614

33-1617

33-1616

4-1/2" Prototype

Includes 55/60 W H-4 bulb with tri bar lens, mount included.

VT No. 33-5050

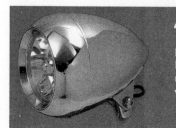

5-3/4" Synapse Style Headlamp

Features a outer ring lamp, which acts as a marker light, with a 60/55 watt H-4 bulb.

Black	Chrome	Type	Black	Chrome	Type
33-1614	33-1616	LED	33-1615	33-1617	CCFL

A cold cathode fluorescent lamp (CCFL) is a lighting system that uses two phenomena: electron discharge and fluorescence. CCFLs are mainly used as light sources for backlights, because they are smaller and have longer lifetimes than ordinary fluorescent lamps.

5-3/4" Billet Rocket Headlamp

Features H-4 60/55 bulb and bottom mount.

33-0664

33-1205

60/55 Watt	100/55 Watt
33-0664	33-1205

Axel's Billet Headlamp

Features oval shaped design with 60/55 H-4 bulb installed.
VT No. 33-0647

33-1541

33-1542

33-1543

33-1544

Oval Style Headlamp

60/55 watt H-4 bulb. Lens color as noted.

Chrome	Black	Lens	Chrome	Black	Lens
33-1541	33-1542	Clear	33-1543	33-1544	Blue

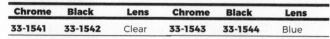

33-0786

Bi-Focal Headlamp

Includes mount and 55-55W H-3 bulb.

Clear Lens	Blue Lens
33-0784	33-0786

Lamps listed are for show or decorative use only, not D.O.T. approved.

BILLET HEADLAMP

5-3/4" Headlamps with Trim Ring and H-4 60/55 Bulb

VT No.	Style	Type
33-0628	Rocket	Billet
33-0928	Bullet	Billet
33-0591	Bullet	Steel
31-0642	Bracket (33-0585), (33-0681)	
31-0796	Bracket (Extended)	

Headlamp Mount Eye

Square top mount bolts for 5-3/4" Bates Style headlamps.
VT No. 33-0518

Dual Headlamp

9" x 5" x 4" deep, unit includes twin bulb at 60/55 watt, each.
VT No. 33-1134

Triangle Headlamp

Includes lower mount and 12v 35/35w H-6 bulb. Sold each.

1" Beam	2" Beam
33-4077	33-1122

33-0591 Installed

33-0591

33-0628   33-0928

31-0642

31-0796

Wyatt's Glow Style Headlamp Assembly

VT No.	Type	Bulb
33-0981	5-3/4" Round	H-4 60/55
33-0982	7" Rectangular	H-3 55W

33-0981 includes 5 watt parking bulb.

33-0982   33-0981

Chrome Caddy Type Rectangular 12V Beam Headlamp

LIGHTING
19

33-1323

Has bottom or side mounting, measures 4-1/2" x 7-1/2" outside. Includes sealed beam bulb and high beam indicator light on bulb type lamps.

33-1211

VT No.	Item	VT No.	Item	VT No.	Item
33-1323	Bottom Mount	33-1211	Side Mount	33-1212	Replacement Bulb

5-3/4" LAMP UNIT

33-0881   33-0203   33-0755

33-1043

33-1015   33-1029   33-1040

LED Units

Diamond Cut Reflector Lamp Units

Include 12 volt H-4 60-55 watt bulb.

VT No.	Type	VT No.	Type	VT No.	Type
33-0881	Tri-Cut	33-0203	Reverse Cup	33-0755	Faceted

VT No.	Item
33-0834	Bates H-4 Insert
33-1015	Complete Kit for Bullet Style Headlamps
33-1040	Complete for 5-3/4" Custom Housings
33-1043	Headlamp Unit for 5-3/4" Housings
33-1029	OE Type 2004-up XL

33-0200   33-0894

H-4 Lamp Unit

Features glass lens 55/60w bulb included.

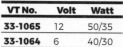

Beck Replacement Round Sealed Beams

VT No.	Volt	Watt
33-1065	12	50/35
33-1064	6	40/30

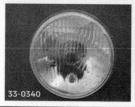

33-0100   33-0340   33-0472

VT No.	Lens	VT No.	Lens
33-0200	Flat	33-0100	Round by Candle Power
	Round	33-0894	Tri Bar with H-4 Bulb
		33-0472	Rubber Boot Only

33-0112   33-0144

Rainbow H-4 Insert

Allows lamp to radiate soft colorful light

VT No.	Qty
33-0112	Pair
33-0144	Each

33-1234   33-1191

H-4 Xenon Blue Bulb

VT No.	Type
33-1234	60/55
33-1235	100/55
33-1238	100/90
33-1242	130/90
33-1495	Cyron for 5-3/4" Housing

For superior night visibility. In the construction of the Xenon Blue Bulb, the Xenon gas is used to cool the filament and allow the halogen process to produce a higher light output. The special blue coating increases the whiteness of the light with only a trace of blue at the headlamp periphery. Unit fits all H-4 applications.

H-4 Replacement Bulbs

33-1217

VT No.	Watt	Volt
33-0181	55-60	12
33-1217	55-100	12
33-1218	55-60	6V
33-1782	LED	Clear

5-3/4" Chrome Bullet Style Headlamp Trim

Held in place by existing headlamp bulb and rim.
VT No. 33-0173

HEADLAMP VISOR

 33-2024
 33-2025

33-2022

 39-0122
 33-2026

42-0306   42-0307

Chrome Headlamp Visor Cover

VT No.	Cutout
42-0306	With
42-0307	Without

Fits over existing head light visor on 1971-up XL models. Available with or without cutaway for oil and generator lights.

Indicator Lamps

Fit visors and dash for high beam, neutral and generator.

12-0553

VT No.	OEM	Color	Type	Fits
39-0122	67891-75B	Blue	HiBeam	A-1977-85
33-1956	67851-75	Green	Neutral	C-1975-83
33-1957	68536-75	Red	Oil Pressure	C-1975-83
33-2022	68489-86	Red	Oil Pressure	C-1986-up
33-2023	68574-86	Green	Neutral	C-1986-up
33-2024	68023-92	Blue	HiBeam	C-1986-up
33-2026	68002-92A	Red		1986-up
33-2025	68695-91	Green	Turn Sig	C-1991-up
12-0553	7614	Speed	Nut 1/2	D-1975-83

Chrome Headlamp Visor Plug

 37-0538

Fits die cast headlamp mounting visor center hole.

VT No.	OEM	Fits	QTY
28-1500	67830-59	1959-88	5pk
37-0538	67865-89	1989-Up	Set

Chrome Sunvisor

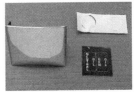

Shields LED lights on the headlamp mounting bracket from the sun.
VT No. 42-0321

 31-0958
 31-0959

Billet Headlamp Mounts

Adapt to stock forks. *Note: Tall bracket can be reversed for some applications.*

VT No.	OEM	Fits	Type
31-0958	68595-06	1996-Up XL	Short
31-0959	69611-06	1996-Up XL	Tall

Headlamp Bracket Extender

Fits 1971-up FX-XL-FXD.
VT No. 31-0143

Chrome Headlamp Mount Kit

Includes nut, tapered spacer, lockwasher and chrome cap plug

1954-88	1989-Up
37-8855	37-9006

Headlamp Mount Blocks

 31-0576
 31-0793

1987-Up XL	1988-Up XL
31-0576	31-0793

Side Mount Headlamp Bracket Set

Clamps on to 39 and 41 mm fork tubes.

Black	Chrome
31-1351	31-1353

Chrome Headlamp Visor Mount Bolts

Acorn	Allen
8717-4	9783-4

Bottom Mount Headlamp Bracket

Chrome. Fits 1957-86, 35 & 33mm forks.
VT No. 31-4192

Extended Billet Headlamp Mount

Allows lower lamp position. For use with custom lamps with narrow spacing.
VT No. 31-0944

1pc Side Mount Headlamp Bracket

Chrome. Fits Bates style lights.
VT No. 31-0603

Lamps listed are for show or decorative use only, not D.O.T. approved.

TAIL LAMP FENDER MOUNTED

33-0990   33-0991

Radii Style Tail Lamp Assemblies

LED installed.

VT No.	Year	Type	Includes
33-0990	1978-98	Complete	4" wires
33-0991	1999-up	Lens/LED Only	36" Wire, no OE plug

Webbed Reflector LED Tail Lamp Assembly

Clear Lens.

33-1523   33-1524

Top Window	Bottom Window
33-1523	33-1524

Red Slice Style LED Tail Lamp

VT No. 33-1550

LED running and brake light and red lens. Features low profile design to mount to the edge of a chopped rear fender. Replaces 73420-11.

LED Slimline Tail Lamps

Fit 1989-2010 XL.

33-0940   33-0939

Smoke	Red	Clear
33-0940	33-0939	33-1084

33-1531

Chrome Body LED Lamps

VT No.	Color
33-1531	Red
33-1549	Smoke

Chrome Adjustable Bobbed Tail Lamp Bracket

Adjusts 7.5" to 9" wide to accept cat eye or similar tail lamps.

VT No. 31-0097

33-0832   33-0833   33-0831

LED Conversion

Fits 1999-up XL.

VT No.	Color
33-0832	Red
33-0833	Smoke
33-0831	Clear

33-0892

LED Tail Lamp Kit

Fits 1973-99 by removing stock tail lamp. Covers existing lamp cut out.

VT No. 33-0892

33-0301   31-0271

Chrome License Plate Bracket Lamp Kit

Includes stock style 3-hole bracket assembly, backing plate, frame and four krommets. Order tail lamp and blue dot lens separately. Fits 1973-up.

Plate Kit	Tail Lamp	Blue Dot Lens
31-0271	33-0301	33-0507

LED Tail Lamp for 2007-Up XL

33-1491   33-1492

Black	Red
33-1492	33-1491

Big Eye Tail Lamp

VT No.	Lens	Type	
33-0643	Clear	LED	Constructed of ABS.
33-0644	Red	Bulb	

TAIL LAMP FENDER MOUNTED

Chrome Radii™ Tail Lamp Assembly

Full LED matrix with amber turn signal bulb built in. Measures 6" long by 2-1/2" high at center.
VT No. 33-0605

Thin Cat eye Tail Lamp

Only 3/4" thick with LED.
VT No. 33-0807

33-0306

33-0028

33-1966

33-0286

33-1967

Die Cast Chrome Cat Eye Tail Lamp

VT No.	Item	Type
33-0306	Light	Complete
33-0028	Light	Complete, LED
33-1966	Red	Lens Plain
33-0286	Grill	Arrow
33-1967	Red	Lens with Blue Dot
33-1996	Clear	Top Lens
15-0665	Gasket, 5 pack	

15-0665

Chrome Die Cast Box Tail Lamp

12 Volt

Lamp	Lens
33-0310	33-2119

Cyclops Tail Lamps

33-0886

With studs for mounting.

VT No.	Type	Mounting Studs
33-0886	LED	5-1/2" C-C
33-0887	Bulb	4-3/8" C-C

33-0887

Chrome Billet Oval Tail Lamp

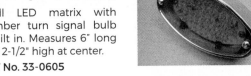

LED array with clear window. 12 volt.

VT No.	Item
33-0443	Tail Lamp
33-0655	LED Array Only

Cat eye Tail Lamp with Ridged Body

33-0680

33-0919

Features smooth red lens with LED board installed. Chrome body has stepped design for updated look.

VT No.	Item
33-0680	Red Lens
33-0919	Clear Lens

Replica Lucas Lamps

33-1972

33-0302

Large	Small
33-1972	33-0302

33-1325

33-1326

33-1099

33-1096

33-1094

33-1093

LIGHTING
19

Tail Lamps

VT No.	Item
33-1325	Chrome Round Tail lamp
33-1326	Black Round Tail lamp
33-1093	LED type with bracket red plastic lens & chrome housing
33-1094	LED type with bracket red plastic lens & black housing
33-1096	Chrome Universal Tail lamp
33-1099	Black Universal Tail lamp

Oval Chrome Tail Lamps

33-1910

33-1911

With visor and LED internals.

VT No.	LED	Lens
33-1910	Red	Clear
33-1911	Red	W/turn signal

Lamps listed are for show or decorative use only, not D.O.T. approved.

FENDER TAIL LAMP 1973-UP

Mount to 3 bolt position on stock fenders. Rubber pad included.

Chrome Billet Fender Mount LED Tail Lamps

VT No.	Item	VT No.	Item	VT No.	Item
33-0353	Diamond	33-0765	Maltese	33-0460	Katz Eyez
33-0567	Slice	33-0216	Iron Cross	33-1919	Clear
33-0385	Skull	33-0289	Zoid	33-1904	Slice

Chrome Fender Mount Oval Tail Lamp

Assembly mounts to stock 3 hole style pattern.
VT No. 33-1905

Tail Lamp with red bulb with a red lens. Lamp has swivel 2 hole mounting bracket.
VT No. 33-0061

Fresno Teardrop Tail Lamp Assembly

Features chrome die case construction and stainless strap license plate bracket.

VT No.	Type	Lens Color	VT No.	Type	Lens Color
33-3036	Bulb	Red	33-3037	LED	Red
33-0198	LED	Clear	31-0663	Bracket	

Deco Style Lay Down Tail Lamp

Fits stock location.

VT No.	Fits XL
33-0335	1973-98
33-0336*	1973-2008
31-0594	1999-up Bracket

*Note: Requires wiring harness modification

Radii LED Fender Mount Tail Lamp

Billet bracket with Billet oval LED lamp with LED amber turn signals.
VT No. 33-0609

Radii LED Tail Lamp

Includes clear LED for license plate illumination. Fits 1993-98 XL
VT No 33-0624

Chrome Fender Mount Tail Lamp features clear lens red LED bulb.
VT No. 33-0885

Chrome Billet Fender Mount Tail Lamp

BACK VIEW

LED slice tail lamp. Unit bolts in 3 hole license plate bracket location.
VT No. 33-0917

FENDER TAIL LAMP 1973-UP

33-2140

33-1977

33-0600

33-0617

33-1972

33-0302

33-0621

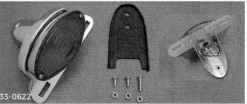
33-0622

Sport Tail Lamp Assembly
Features aluminum body and lamp. For show use only.

VT No.	Item	VT No.	Item
33-2140	Complete, Aluminum, large	33-2126	Lens Only for 33-2140 & 33-1977
33-1977	Complete, Chrome, large	33-0302	Lamp Cpt for 33-0600/33-0617
33-0600	Complete, Aluminum, small	15-0543	Lens Gasket for 33-1972
33-0617	Complete, Chrome, small	33-0621	Complete Chrome, 12 V with cat eye
15-0577	Gasket for 33-2140 and 33-1977	33-0622	Complete Chrome LED with cat eye
33-1972	Lamp Only for 33-2140/33-1977		

Chrome Fender Mount Tail Lamp w/ Plate Mount

Assembly includes license plate mount and fender bracket in chrome steel.

VT No. 33-0308

Snake Eye Tail Lamp
Lens measures 16 cm x 4 cm, with alloy license plate bracket.

VT No.	Item	Type
33-0435	Kit	Bulb
33-0651	Kit	LED
33-0439	Lamp Only	LED
33-0902	Lamp Only	LED

Mini-LED Cat Eye Tail Lamp

33-0911

33-0912

15 LED in a 4-1/2" W x 1" H lamp with alloy 6-3/4" W plate mount.

Clear	Red
33-0911	33-0912

33-0301 33-0029

1973-1998 XL Tail Lamp

Includes chrome base, lens, wire and bulb. Utilizes 12-0575 speed nuts for mounting as stock.

LED	Bulb
33-0029	33-0301

LIGHTING
19

33-1531 33-1549

Chrome Tail Lamp with Red LED
1999-Up.

Red	Smoke
33-1531	33-1549

42-0216 42-9966 42-0000

Visors

Chrome Tail Lamp Visors for 1973-up units in plain and louvered. Fits with inverted light.

VT No.	Type
42-0216	Smooth
42-9966	Louvered
42-0000	Smooth

Lamps listed are for show or decorative use only, not D.O.T. approved.

1955-72 TAIL LAMP   STOCK LENS

33-0300

33-0299

33-0838

33-0519

1955-72 XL Stock Type Tail Lamp

Includes lens housing and internals, complete.

VT No.	Item	VT No.	Item
33-0300	Chrome Complete Lamp	33-1963	Red Lens Glass
33-0299	Primer Complete Lamp	33-0504	Red Plastic Lens
33-0838	Chrome with Blue Dot	33-0519	Blue Dot Red Plastic Lens
15-0209	Fender Gasket (Rubber)	33-1964	Chrome Rim
15-0322	Fender Gasket (Foam)	33-0530	Clear Top Lens only, 1969-72
15-0760	Fender Gasket (Sponge)		
15-0301	Lens Gasket, 5 pack	15-0302	Top Lens Gasket

Round "STOP" Tail Lamp

33-1949   33-0087   33-3055

31-0874   33-1916

VT No.	Item	VT No.	Item
33-1950	Kit, bulb	33-3055	LED w/Bracket
33-3039	Kit, LED		
33-1949	Lamp	33-0087	LED w/ Bracket
33-1346	Lamp, LED		
33-1916	Lens Kit	31-0874	Bracket

Lens and Rim Kit

Chrome rim, lens gasket, 2 screws, and red lens. Fits 1955-72.
VT No. 33-0550

Chrome Tail Lamp and License Plate Bracket Kit

1955-72 FL-XL models.   **VT No. 33-1955**

Chrome Tail Lamp Visor

Fits 1955-72.
VT No. 42-0206

Plastic dots w/ rim.
VT No. 33-0283

Blue Dots

License Plate Brackets

For fender mounting.

31-0157

31-0158

33-0503

33-0238

33-0040

33-0507

33-0668

33-0669

33-0241

33-0048

33-0049

Lens in red, clear or red with a blue dot installed.

Stock	Dot	Clear	XL Fitment
33-0503*	33-0507	33-0241	*1973-84/1973-1998
33-0238	33-0668	33-0048	1999-E03
33-0040	*33-0669	33-0049	2004-07/*2003-2004

Caution: Blue dot lens may not be approved for use in your state.

Chrome Lens Grill

Available as lens w/blue dot and grill assembled or as grill only for 1973-up.

VT No.	Type	Style
33-2021	With Dot	V
33-2020	Grill only	V
33-0109	Grill	Slot

Lens Screws 10pk

VT No.	Year	Use
12-2520	1973-98	Tail Lamp
12-0590	1999-up	Tail Lamp
12-2526	1939-72	Tail Lamp
12-2521	1973-85	Signals

12-2520

15-0206

12-0575

15-0207

Tail Lamp Hardware and Gasket

Fits 1973-1998 XL

VT No.	Item
15-0206	Lens Gasket
12-0575	Mount Nuts
15-0207	Beaded Rubber Base Gasket

Blue Dot Tail Lamp

VT No. 33-1435

Chrome	Black	Fitment	Type
31-0157	31-0476	1955-72	2-Bolt
31-0158	31-0086	1973- Up	3-Bolt

MALTESE TAIL LAMP

33-0749

33-0750

33-0751

33-0587

Maltese Inset Oval Tail Lamp

VT No.	Oval Color	Inset Color
33-0749	Red	Clear Cross
33-0750	Clear	Red Cross
33-0751	Red	Red Cross
33-0587	Red	Clear Skull /Bulb
33-0031	Red	Clear Skull/ LED

33-0964

33-0965

Maltese Tail Lamps with LED

Clear	Red
33-0964	33-0965

Diamond LED

Tail Lamp has bolt pattern to fit cat eye applications.

Flat	Angled
33-0354	33-0858

LED Maltese with Bracket

Maltese LED Lamp Kit is 2-3/8" square with red lens mounted black bracket separately.

VT No.	Item	VT No.	Item	VT No.	Item
33-0824	Kit	33-0820	Maltese Lamp	31-0866	Black Bracket

33-0414

Maltese Side Mount Kit

Includes chrome steel plate, bracket and lamp with bulb.

VT No.	Item
33-0414	With Bracket
33-0347	Without Bracket
31-0175	Bracket Only

Maltese Vertical Side Mount

Includes light, chrome backing plate and side mount bracket to fit 5/8" axles.
VT No. 33-0363

33-0343

33-0312

Maltese lamps fit flush mounted to steel backing plates.

VT No.	Item
33-0312	Light
33-0343	LED
33-0595	Lens Only

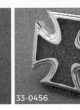
33-0454   33-0456

4" Maltese Billet Tail Lamp

VT No. 33-0454 Wire Functions

Black Wire - Ground
White Wire - Running Light
Orange Wire - Brake Light
Red Wire - Blinker Brake Light
Green Wire - Blue LED Light

Clear	Red
33-0454	33-0456

Center portion acts as brake lamp. 33-0456 features red lens and all red LED. 33-0454 features clear lens and red/blue LED.

Iron Cross Oval Tail Lamp

Features LED design with red lens and two clear LEDs for plate illumination. Mounts where any cat eye tail lamp with mount.
VT No. 33-0477

Spike Tail Lamp

With license plate lamp.
VT No. 33-0619

Cat Face Tail Lamp

Mounts on flat plate.
VT No. 33-0915

LIGHTING
19

33-0900

33-0901

Model "A" Style Chrome Round Tail Lamps

Red	Dot
33-0900	33-0901

Model "A" Style Glass Lens Tail Lamps

33-1312

33-1313

33-1314

VT No.	Finish
33-1312	Chrome
33-1313	Black
33-1314	Stainless

Lamps listed are for show or decorative use only, not D.O.T. approved.

LED SIDE MOUNT TAIL LAMP

Diamond 33-0685 — Slice 33-0686 — Maltese 33-0687 — Cat eye 33-0690 — Iron Cross 33-0693 — Lady Luck 33-0809 — Baron 33-0803

Chrome Billet Curved Tail Lamp

Installed Position

Assembly mounts to outboard starter housing on York, BDL and Primo 3", 3-3/8" and 3-1/2" belt drives. Complete assembly includes curved plate/tail lamp holder and mounting bracket. Curved Plate / Tail Lamp Assembly also sold separate.

VT No.	Type	VT No.	Type	VT No.	Type	VT No.	Type	VT No.	Type
33-0685	Diamond	33-0687	Maltese	33-0693	Iron Cross	33-0463	Katz	33-0809	Lady
33-0686	Slice	33-0690	Cat eye	33-0462	Odin	33-0795	Spike	33-0803	Baron

33-0224 — 33-0842 — 31-0721 — 31-0732

Plate and Lamp Set

VT No.	Type	VT No.	Type	VT No.	Type
33-0234	Diamond	33-0488	Katz	31-0721	Bracket for Belt Drive Mount
33-0223	Slice	33-0800	Spike	31-0732	Bracket for Axle Mount
33-0224	Maltese	33-0802	Lady		
33-0225	Cat eye	33-0801	Baron		Available separately w/o bracket.
33-0226	Iron Cross	33-0842	Pirate		
33-0487	Odin				

LED Billet Side Mount Lamp

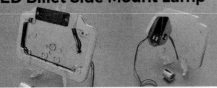

1/2" mount hole, with 1/2 x 1" spacer for shock or frame mounting.
VT No. 33-1249

33-0771 — 33-0770 — 33-0768 — 33-0772 — 33-0769

V=Vertical / H=Horizontal — 33-0865

LED Chrome Billet Vertical Side Mount Tail Lamps

Feature LED lamps with plate illumination and unique mounting design which incorporate adjuster block. Tail lamp and plate available without bracket.

1979-96 XL	Style	Type	Plate/Lamp	1979-96 XL	Style	Type	Plate/Lamp
33-0773	Diamond	V	33-0222	33-0769	Maltese	H	33-0262
	Cat Eye	V	33-0461	33-0770	Mini	H	33-0264
	Maltese	V	33-0357	33-0771	Slice	H	33-0265
33-0768	Iron Cross	H	33-0263	33-0772	Diamond	H	33-0266

Chrome Billet Side Mount Assembly LED Maltese Lamp

33-0455 — 33-0366 — 33-0367

VT No.	Type	Mounting Type
33-0367	Vertical	1/2" or 3/8" Stud
33-0365	Vertical	5/8"Axle Nut
33-0366	Horizontal	Axle Nut
33-0455	Lamp Only	

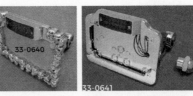

33-0640 — 33-0641

Side Mount Billet Chrome Mini Tail Lamp Assemblies

VT No	Type	Mounting Type
33-0722	Skull	1/2" or 3/8" Stud
33-0723	Plain	1/2" or 3/8" Stud
33-0640	Skull	5/8" Axle Nut
33-0641	Plain	5/8" Axle Nut
33-0654	LED	Array only for Above

33-0345

Side Mount Cat eye Tail Lamp Kit

Die cast cat eye lamp with chrome recessed plate. To fit 5/8" axles.

Horizontal	Vertical
33-0345	33-0364

SIDE MOUNT TAIL LAMP

Chrome Billet Side Mount Tail Lamp Assemblies

33-0772
33-0769
33-0768
33-0771
33-0770

Feature LED lamps with plate illumination and unique mounting design which incorporate adjuster block. Tail Lamp and plate available without bracket.

79-96 XL	Style	Type	Plate/Lamp
33-0773	Diamond	Vertical	33-0222
	Cat Eye	Vertical	33-0461
	Maltese	Vertical	33-0357
33-0768	Iron Cross	Horizontal	33-0263
33-0769	Maltese	Horizontal	33-0262
33-0770	Mini	Horizontal	33-0264
33-0771	Slice	Horizontal	33-0265
33-0772	Diamond	Horizontal	33-0266

Inspection Tag Holders

REMOTE INSPECTION TAG HOLDER FIRST OFFERED BY V-TWIN MFG. IN 1969

31-0201   31-0264   31-0282   31-0983   31-0933

Available in stainless or chrome. Measuring 3-1/2"square with 1/2" or 3/8" mounting hole which can mount to footpeg or shock studs.31-0282 is square type which clamps on to 1" to 1-1/8" tube with worm clamp included.

VT No.	Item	Type	VT No.	Item	Type
31-0201	Stainless	.5"	31-0983	Chrome	3/8"
31-0264	Chrome	.5"	31-0282	Chrome	Clamp
			31-0933	Black	.5"

33-0611

33-0613

Tail Lamp & Mounting Plate Set

Includes lamp and backing plate which may be sissy bar or side mounted (by purchase of bracket).

VT No	Type	Size
33-0611	Lucas	4" x 7"
33-0612	Lucas	5" x 7"
33-0613	Cat eye	4" x 7"

Side Mount Cat Eye Lamp

Fits 2004-Up XL.

Vertical	Horizontal
33-1811	33-0852

Swivel Side Mount Bracket Kit

42-1529

Mounts in horizontal or vertical position with a set screw mounts to side mount brackets.

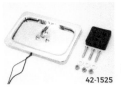

42-1525   33-1031

VT No.	Item
33-1929	Bracket Kit
42-1525	Plate Holder
33-1031	Chrome Kit

Billet Clamp On Side License Plate Mount

Accepts 3-bolt plate units for left side mounting. Order flat or curved lamp assembly separate.

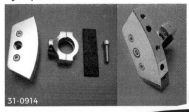

31-1204

31-0914

Curved	Flat
31-0914	31-1204

LIGHTING
19

Billet Side Mount Bracket

31-0729   31-0732

VT No.	Item
31-0729	Flat
31-0732	Curved
44-0660	3/4" -1" Bushing

Chrome Billet Side Mount Brackets

Fit stock swing arm.

VT No.	Year	Model
31-0727	1979-96	XL
44-0682	5/16 x 24	Nut Set
44-0683	5/16 x 18	Nut Set

Chrome Side Mount Tail Lamp Kit

Originally developed in 1970 by Clown Cycle, NYC.

Fits right or left side.
VT No. 33-0307

LED Round Tail Lamp

Mini Cat eye Tail Lamp Kit

Includes chrome tail lamp and alloy mount bracket. Not approved for street use.

VT No.	Size	Item	VT No.	Size	Item
33-0315	Small	Kit	33-0381	Small	Lamp Only
33-0316	Large	Kit	33-0382	Large	Lamp Only

Chrome	Black	Lens
33-1526	33-1527	Red (2-bolt)
33-1528	33-1529	Smoke

Chrome	Item
33-1036	Round Tail Lamp
33-1037	Torpedo Bullet Style
33-1038	Round Lamp, 12v Bulb
33-1039	Wipac British Style

LIGHTING
19

Chopper Tail Lamp

Chopper 12 Volt Tail Lamp with red lens are not DOT approved and are for decoration or show use only.

Chrome	Black	Item
33-1022		Warbird LED
	33-1023	Finger LED
	33-1024	Warbird with hinged
33-1025		Maltese LED
	33-1026	"FCUK" LED
33-1028	33-1027	Round

Lamps listed are for show or decorative use only, not D.O.T. approved.

The LED (Light-Emitting Diode)

is an electronic light source invented in the early 20th century and introduced as practical electronic component in 1962. All early devices emitted low-intensity lights, but modern LEDs are available across the ultraviolet and infrared wavelengths with very high brightness.

THE LED

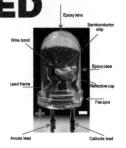

Typical indicator LEDs are designed to operate with no more than 30-60 milliwatts of electrical power.

Solid state devices such as LED are subject to very limited wear and tear if operated at low currency and at low temperature. Many of the LEDs produced in the 1970s and 1980s are still in service today. Typical life times quoted are 25,000 to 1,000,000 hours, but heat and current settings can extend or shorten this time significantly.

SUPER FLUX LED BULB

Super Flux LEDs have four pins, so that up to 3 chips within one casing can be controlled independently. Moreover, the pins provide a better thermal behavior, which results in a longer life expectancy and stronger power.

33-1378   33-1922

33-1386

Super Flux LED Filament Bulb

VT No.	Description	VT No.	Description
33-1378	Dual filament, amber	33-1291	Single filament, clear
33-1266	Dual filament, red	33-1922	Single filament, red
33-1267	Dual filament, white	33-1923	Single filament, amber
33-1377	Single filament, amber		
33-1379	Single filament, red		
33-1380	Single filament, white		
33-1382	Dual filament, amber/white		
33-1384	Dual filament, red/white		
33-1381	Single filament, amber/white		
33-1383	Single filament, red/white		

Super Flux LED Bulb Wedge Style

VT No.	Description
33-1386	Dual filament, amber
33-1268	Dual filament, red
33-1269	Dual filament, white
33-1385	Single filament, amber
33-1387	Single filament, red
33-1388	Single filament, white
33-1390	Dual filament, amber/white
33-1392	Dual filament, red/white
33-1389	Single filament, amber/white
33-1391	Single filament, red/white

SMD

SMD Stands for Surface Mounted Device. An electrical component that is usually mounted on the surface of a circuit board. Advanced technology has made these components smaller and smaller. Manufacturers are now making SMD LEDs (Light Emitting Diodes). These incredible small SMD LEDs are extremely bright and allow for more light in a compact bulb. Replace an old conventional bulb with these super bright, extended life, low energy bulbs.

SMD BULB

LIGHTING
19

SMD Filament Bulb

VT No.	Description
33-1351	Dual filament, amber
33-1353	Dual filament, red
33-1355	Dual filament, white
33-1350	Single filament, amber
33-1352	Single filament, red
33-1354	Single filament, white

SMD LED Wedge Style Bulb

VT No.	Description
33-1357	Dual filament, amber
33-1359	Dual filament, red
33-1361	Dual filament, white
33-1356	Single filament, amber
33-1358	Single filament, red
33-1360	Single filament, white

TAIL LAMP BULB

33-0158 33-0168 33-0165 33-0188

Rotating

LED Bulb is unaffected by vibration, making for longer life. Available in 1157 (brake and tail lamp) or 1156 (signal lamp) types.

VT No.	Volt	Color	Type
33-0158	12	Red	Brake
33-1292	6V	Red	Brake
33-0165	1157 Rotator	Red	Brake
33-0168	12V	Amber	Brake
33-0188	12V	Amber	Brake 5pk

Rotating type features LED's that rotate and reverse direction every two seconds and when brake light is activated the LED's pulse 2 two times per second.

33-1266 33-1268 33-1269 33-0219

33-0207 33-0208 33-1267

Lazer LED Bulb

Features colored LEDs with clear band for license plate. *Note: Includes clear band for license plate.

Flux	VT No.	Type	Fit	Year	Color
33-1266	33-0207*	1157	Tail-Brake	1965-02	Red
33-1267		1157	Tail Lamp	1965-02	Clear
	33-0208	1156	Signal	1965-up	Amber
33-1268	33-0219*	3157	Tail-Brake	2004-up	Red
33-1269		3157	Tail Lamp	2004-up	Clear

33-0194 33-0195

Tail Lamp Bulb for 2004-up

Push in wedge style to replace 3157.

Stock 10pk	LED Each
33-0194	33-0195

33-0214 33-0213

LED Turn Signal Bulb

VT No.	OEM	Color
33-0214	1156	Red
33-0213	1156	Amber

33-0212 33-0169 33-0193 33-0211

Flat	Lollipop	OEM	Color	Type
33-0211	33-0169	1156	Amber	Turn Signal
33-0212	33-0193	1157	Red	Tail Lamp

12V Halogen

Tail Lamp Bulb. Extra bright with stop and tail lamp.
VT No. 33-2105

12 Volt Bulbs Filament Type

VT No.	OEM	Description
33-0116	68727-64	4-1/2" Spotlamp Seal Beam Red Clear, Single Filament
33-0297		4-1/2" Spotlamp Seal Beam, Single Filament amber, bulb with clear smooth lens
33-0161		4-1/2" Spotlamp Seal Beam, Single Filament Two prong screw type with fluted lens with a 30 watt bulb
33-1980		4-1/2" Spotlamp Bulb, Early Single Function
33-0153		4-1/2" Seal Beam for Round Headlamp 35w
33-0134	53439-79	Speedo Tach Hi Beam Indicator
33-0137	68024-94	1994-up Speedo and Indicator Lamp
33-0131	68165-64	Brake and Tail Lamp
33-0056	68165-64	2 filament
33-0138		Front Fender Light
33-0136		Turn Signal Indicator
33-1971		Bullet Light
33-1982		Bullet, dual filament w/offset mounting pins
33-1913		As Above with inline mounting pins
33-2047		Mini Bulb for Mini-gauge
33-0170	68572-64A	Directional for Turn Signal, Single
33-1958	71099-74	Directional for Turn Signal, Dual
33-0133	71090-64	All Speedo, Hi Beam Mini Indicator, 75-up XL,
33-0135	71092-68A	Hi-beam Mini Bulb,
33-0138	71099-74	Tachometer Hi beam indicator. Bates Style Headlamp

LED Valve Stem Cover Cap Set

Includes battery.

Blue	Red
33-0944	33-0946

TAIL LAMP WIRE

Tail Lamp Connector

32-0491 32-0944

Includes wire harness to be spliced to replacement.

Deutsch	6 Pin Amp
32-0491	32-0944

PVC Covered Tail Lamp Wires

1970-72 XL	1974 XL
32-9309	32-9313

Snake Eye Lamps

1.75 x 2.25 long, with 1/4" stud mount. Sold pairs.

Amber	Red
33-2131	33-2132

Chrome Marker Lamps

Clear lens. Includes 12 volt 20 watt halogen bulb. 2-1/4"diameter and 3-3/4" long, pairs.

VT No. 33-0580

Mini-Square Marker Lamp

Set is 12 volt set with chrome body.

VT No. 33-0672

Evil Eye Marker Lamp

Set with amber LED, and clear lens. Set of 2.

VT No. 33-1130

MARKER LAMP

ALL SOLD AS SET OR PAIR UNLESS NOTED.

Mini Marker Lamp

Feature rounded profile and smooth half moon lenses. They mount to any flat surface single filament lamps. Comes with both amber and red lenses, mounting hardware and rubber base gasket. 1" diameter lens, 3-1/4" overall length. Sold pair.

VT No. 33-0819

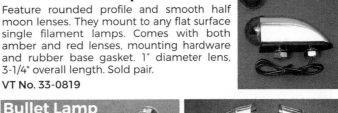

Bullet Lamp

33-0437

33-0436

Features built in 360° turnable visor, with clear lens and an extra yellow lens, pair, 1-7/8" diameter.

Grooved	Smooth	Bulb Set
33-0436	33-0437	33-0143

Baby Bullet

1-1/8" diameter x 2-1/4"" from tip to top with a 5/16" - 18 x 1" long mounting stud and features a glass lens with a chrome body. Sold in pairs.

Red	Amber	Blue
33-0440	33-0441	33-0442

Mini Speeder Bullet

Lamp Set includes a red lens.

VT No.	Filament
33-0629	Single
33-0665	Dual
33-0728	Amber Lens

Clear Bullet Lamp

Set features red LED bulbs. Pair. Includes turn signal load equalizer.

VT No. 33-0674

Black Mini Bullet Lite Set

VT No. 33-3045

Chrome Bullet Lamp

Set includes LED units. Body measures 2-1/4" OD x 3-3/4" long.

VT No. 33-0763

2" Chrome Skull

Decoration only, lighted eyes.

Bulb	LED
33-2146	33-0626

Mini Cat eye Winker Set

VT No. 33-6493

Black Missile Light Set

Sold pair.

VT No. 33-1334

LED Bullet Lamp Set

1.5" OD x 2.75" long with clear lens and amber LED. Sold pair.

33-1003   33-1009

Chrome	Black
33-1003	33-1009

LED Arrow Lamps

Include clear lens with 28 colored LED units.

Red	Amber
33-0846	33-0847

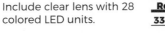

33-6056   33-6057   33-6058

Mini-Marker Lamp Sets

Amber bulbs.

VT No.	Style	Lens	LED
33-6056	Cat Eye	Amber	Amber
33-6057	Maltese	Clear	Red
33-6058	Maltese	Red	Red

Missile Head LED Marker Light

Set features a chrome 4" long body and is available with either amber or red lens. Includes 5/16" mounting stud and two wire leads for either running light, brake, light or turn signal use.

33-1310   33-1311

Red	Amber
33-1311	33-1310

LIGHTING

19

MARKER LAMP

ALL CUSTOM TURN SIGNAL/LIGHTS REQUIRE LOAD EQUALIZER.

Standard

33-0418

33-2059

Diamond

33-0423

Mini

33-0420

Chrome Die Cast Tour Lamps

Available in mini, standard or diamond shape. Wire exits through mount for sanitary mounting. Amber or red, 12 volt.

VT No.	Type	Lens	U/M
33-0418	Standard	Amber	Pair
33-0419	Standard	Red	Pair
33-0420	Mini	Amber	Each
33-0421	Mini	Red	Each
33-0423	Diamond	Amber	Pair
33-0422	Diamond	Red	Pair
33-2059	Standard	Blue Lens	Pair
33-2061	Diamond	Blue Lens	Pair
33-2085	Standard	Amber Lens	Pair
33-2060	Mini	Blue Lens	Pair
33-1131	Mini	Red Lenses	Pair
33-0138		Bulb for Above	Pack

33-0419   33-0421   33-0422

33-0060   33-0058   33-0059

Hi-Glide

Universal LED round Hi-Glide lamps, sold each.

VT No.	Size	Color	Lens
33-0058	1.50 D x 2.75L	Amber	Amber
33-0059	1.50 D x 2.55 L	Amber	Clear
33-0060	1.60 D x 3.00 L	Amber, Dual	Clear

Firefighter Marker Lamp

Set features 3" x 3" red lens with full LED matrix.
VT No. 33-0874

Chrome Maltese Marker Lamp

LED design. Measure 2.5" x 2.5".

Lamp Set	Bolt Set
33-0671	33-0679

Hot Spot Indicator Lamp

Sold set. 12V mini bulbs w/ amber lens.
VT No. 33-0947

Torpedo Lamp

Sold set. 4 x 2-5/16" body with 12 volt halogen bulb.

VT No.	Item	Type
33-0618	Lamp Set	35W
33-0987	Lamp Set	50W
33-0988	Bulb Set	50W

LED Micro Lamp Set

Features 12V LED units, red bulbs with clear lens.
VT No. 33-0683

Center Mount

33-0274

LED marker lamps sold as pairs.

VT No.	Color	VT No.	Color
33-0271	Amber	33-0275	Purple
33-0272	Green	33-0276	Red
33-0273	Blue	33-0277	Clear
33-0274	Orange		

Chrome Pony Lamp Set

2-1/4" L x 3/4" H, single filament with red and amber lens sets.
VT No. 33-0761

Maltese Bullet Lamp

LED bulbs w/ red lens. Pair.

	Amber	Red
	33-0675	33-0688

Chrome Mini Decoration Lamp

33-0879

ABS assembly with LED. Operates by air current without wiring system.

VT No.	Color
33-0879	Amber
33-0880	Green
33-0876	Blue
33-0877	Red
33-0878	White

Missile Marker Lamp

33-1004

Set. LED construction with stud mounting.

Amber	Red
33-1005	33-1004

MARKER LAMP
ALL CUSTOM TURN SIGNAL/LIGHTS REQUIRE LOAD EQUALIZER.

33-2209   33-2212

Hyper Lamp Sets
Four choices of lens color; amber, red, smoke, or clear. Total of 8 pieces of lens.

Large	Mini
33-2209	33-2212

LED Diamond Marker Lamp Sets
Colored lenses with LED bulb.

Red	Amber	Blue
33-0446	33-0447	33-0448

33-0473 Installed

33-0473

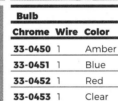
33-0486

Bulb

Chrome	Wire	Color
33-0450	1	Amber
33-0451	1	Blue
33-0452	1	Red
33-0453	1	Clear

LED

Chrome	Wire	Black	Wire	Color
33-0473	1	33-3044	2	Amber
33-0474	1			Blue
33-0475	1	33-3047	2	Red
33-0476	1	33-3048		Clear
33-0486	2		3	Amber
33-1912	3			Clear
33-0959	6pc Lens Set 3 color			

33-0556

33-1056

Flush Lens Bulb Deco Lamp Set
*Note: with two sets of lenses, one red set and one amber set, 12V.

Red/Amber	Red /5 watt	Red
33-0556*	33-1920	33-1056

Styler Marker Lamps

A

B
33-2092

33-0827

C
33-2210

33-2093

Die cast and chrome. Styler Lamp I are 2-3/4" long 1" wide and 1-1/8" deep. Red lamps have 3/8" mount holes for strut mounting. Amber have 5/16" holes for front fork mounting. Styler Lamp II flush mounts to fender struts or flat surfaces. Sold pairs.

VT No.	Type	Filament	#	VT No.	Type	Filament	#
33-2089	Red I	2	A	33-2093	Amber II	1	C
33-2090	Amber I	1	A	33-2210	Amber II	1	C
33-2091	Amber I	2	A	33-0827	Red	LED	
33-2092	Red II	1	B	33-2094	Bulb 10 pack	1	

 33-2011
 33-2012

Flush Mount Marker Lamps
Die cast and chrome, measuring 3-1/2" L x 1" W x 2-1/4" D. Sold in pairs. Mounts to any flat surface with ease. Gasket included.

Red	Amber
33-2011	33-2012

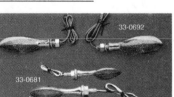
33-0692 / 33-0681 / Length

Eagle Eye
Set features amber lens and billet extension stem.

2.75"	3.75"
33-0681	33-0692

33-0065

33-0074

Skull Billet LED
LED marker lamp set is a 3 or 4 wire type for use as a brake light or marker lamp. These can be installed in any flat panel such as saddlebags, tourpaks or fender surface. Features threaded back with aluminum panel mounting nut. Requires a two 1/8" hole for mounting. Sold in pairs.

VT No.	Style	Finish
33-0065	3-Wire	Chrome
33-0074	4-Wire	Red

LIGHTING 19

MARKER LIGHT

Mini LED Marker Lamp Set

Lens Color	Chrome VT No.	Lens Color	Chrome VT No.
Amber	33-1327	Clear	33-1330
Blue	33-1328	Set w/all 4 color lenses	33-1331
Red	33-1329		

Bates Turn Signal Lamp Pairs

Lens Color	Black	Chrome
Amber	33-1125	33-1124
Smoke	33-1127	33-1126
Red	33-1138	33-1137

LED Turn Signal Lens Conversion

Lens Color	Black	Chrome
Amber	33-1340	33-1338
Red	33-1339	33-1337

Bates LED Tail Lamp

Black	Chrome
33-1046	33-1045

33-1045   33-1046

FENDER LAMP

LIGHTING 19

LED Gear Indicator Kit
Features chrome housing and a bright LED display. Kit control module, housing, and wire harness for easy plug and play installation. Fits 2007-up XL models.
VT No. 32-0296

LED Fender Edge Lamp Kit

Smoke	Red
33-1598	33-1599

Black Bullet Smooth Marker Lamp Set
Features built in 360° adjustable visor with yellow lens and an extra pair of clear lenses.
VT No. 33-0084

Eagle Front Fender Ornament
2 bolt stud mounting with gasket in chrome or with gold inlay.

Chrome	Gold Inlay	Gold	Black
48-0034	48-0039	48-0195	48-0141

Black Die Cast Lamp

33-1532   33-1534

Eagle Fender Ornament
Cast pewter with one stud mounting. Finished in a bronze patina. Mounts to any flat or curved surface.
VT No. 48-1790

VT No.	Type
33-1532	Torpedo Bullet Style Marker Lamp Set, Yellow
33-1534	Rocket Tail Lamp, Red

Lamps listed are for show or decorative use only, not D.O.T. approved.

33-0479

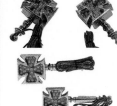

33-0479

33-0480

33-0480

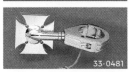

33-0480

33-0481

33-0481

33-0481

33-0482

33-0482

SIGNAL LAMPS

ALL CUSTOM TURN SIGNAL/LIGHTS REQUIRE LOAD EQUALIZER.

33-0484

33-0485

Fireman Turn Signal Sets

Fit OE style mounts. Sold pairs.

Note: Fork mount types have clear lens, amber LED. Rear stud mount have clear lens with red LED.

VT No.	Type	LED Color
33-0483	Turn Signal Mount	Short Stud
33-0484	Turn Signal Mount	Long Stud
33-0485	Turn Signal Mount	41mm Clamp Kit
33-0268	Turn Signal Mount	39mm Clamp Kit
33-0269	Turn Signal Only	

Maltese LED Lamps *Pairs w/clear lens.*

VT No.	Type	LED Color
33-0479	Turn Signal w/ 86mm Short Stud	Red
33-0480	Turn Signal w/ 96mm Long Stud	Red
33-0481	Turn Signal w/ 41mm Clamp Kit	Amber
33-0267	Turn Signal w/ 39mm Clamp Kit	Amber
33-0482	Turn Signal Only	Amber

33-0778

33-0780

33-0781

LED Turn Signals with Mount Base

Amber Maltese	Amber Firefighter	Red Firefighter
33-0778	33-0780	33-0781

Chrome Turn Signal Relocation Mounts

Move turn signal mount location to lower triple tree for a cleaner appearance. Fits 1986-2010 XL.

VT No. 31-0051

Chrome 49mm Clamp On Signal Kit

With amber lens. Mounts to forks.

VT No. 33-0904

TURN SIGNAL LENS

33-0500

33-1220

33-0492

XL/FX Signal Lens Sets

VT No.	Type	Color	Years
33-0500	Stock	Red	1973-85
33-0492	With dot	Amber	1973-85
33-1236	With dot	Red	1973-85
33-1220	Stock	Amber	1986-up
33-1221	Stock	Red	1986-up

33-1054

33-0614

33-0615

Smoked Lens Kits

Include translucent smoked lens and amber turn signal bulbs which will show amber through lens. Set of 4 lens and 4 amber bulbs.

VT No.	Years	VT No.	Years
33-1054	1973-85	33-0615	2000- Up
33-0614	1986-01	33-1209	Amber Bulb Set

TURN SIGNAL

33-0581

33-0047

Chrome Fork Mount Turn Marker Lamp Set

Die cast two piece housing with 12 volt bulb, to attach to 35, 39 and 41 mm fork tubes.

VT No.	Type	Bulb Type	
33-0581	Front Panel	Single	Bulb
33-0047	Side Panel	Dual	Bulb

FRONT		
VT No.	Filament	Use
33-0412	Single	1973-84-XL
33-1213	Dual	1973-84-XL
33-1215	Dual	1986-up XL
33-1216	Dual	1986-93 XL1100
33-0431	Single	1994-06 XL
33-0046	Dual	2001-up XL
33-1318	Dual	1994-06, 2 wire
33-1319	Single	1994-06, 1 wire
Rear		
33-0432	Single	1994-06 XL

Chrome Turn Signal Assemblies

Amber replacement turn signal unit.

Note: 33-0412, 33-1216 have threaded body, 33-1214 and 33-1215 are unthreaded at mount hole.

Check factory parts books for the application. Single or dual contacts.

33-1075 33-1076 33-1070

33-1072 33-1077

33-1074 33-1073

LED Turn Signal Set

VT No.	Style
33-1075	Bullet, Amber, each
33-1076	Bullet, Red, each
33-1077	Maltese Amber
33-1070	Bullet, Amber with light mount
33-1071	Bullet Amber with mount base
33-1072	Bullet with 41mm clamp
33-1074	Bullet Red with stud
33-1073	Bullet, Red with long stud

TURN SIGNAL EQUALIZER

Turn Signal Load Equalizer III

33-2213

33-2214

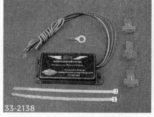 

33-2138 32-2014

Designed to specifically work on all Twins with OEM Alarm System or self canceling turn signal module. Solid state design works with Halogen or LED signals and eliminates erratic blinking of signals. All Equalizers are Plug and Play except 33-2138 and 33-2014 which are hardwire.

VT No.	Brand	Fits
32-2014	Volt Tech	XL 1991-2003
33-2213	Badlands	1999-03 XL
33-2214	Badlands	2004-13 XL
32-2147*	Badlands	2014- XL

*NOTE: The ONLY time a load equalizer is needed is when you install aftermarket turn signals on a 2011-UP FXST, 2012-UP Dyna or ANY 2014-UP model and you have rapid flashing turn signal indicator lights. The bike will also throw a trouble code. Unlike earlier equalizer modules, CAN/Bus bikes require (1) module for front and (1) module for the rear turn signals.

2004- Up Turn Signal Engine Guard

Chrome	Black
50-0021	50-0022

FRONT SIGNAL MOUNT

Amber Clamp On Signal Kit

39mm Forks	41mm Forks
33-0913	33-0914

Grooved Billet Fork Clamps

39mm Forks	41mm Forks
33-0334	33-0333

Chrome Turn Signal Clamp Kits

Mount stock or custom turn signals to fork tubes. Sold pairs.

VT No.	Size	
31-0304	35mm	
31-0300	39mm	8.5mm
31-0345	39mm	10mm
31-0320	41mm	
31-0346	41mm	10mm

Clamp Set will clamp to 1/2" bar for custom mounting.
VT No. 31-0956

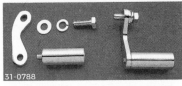

31-0789 Installed

Front Turn Signal Mount Kit

Bolts to billet headlamp lower mount.

5.5" Length	8.5" Length
31-0789	31-0788

Chrome Turn Signal Relocation Mounts

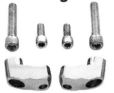

Move the turn signal mount location to the lower triple tree for cleaner appearance on 1986-2010 XL models.
VT No. 31-0051

Directional Signal Relocation Kits

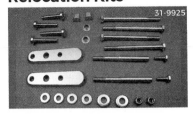

Includes special hardware and extension for 1994-03 XL to provide clearance for saddlebags.
VT No. 31-9925

Turn Signal Mounting Hardware

Fit models from 1973 to present.

VT No.	Item
31-0181	Bracket fits between turn sign lamp and handlebar clamp
31-0255	Clamp screw, 2 short, 2 long, four pieces
31-0163	Stud kit with spacer
31-0479	1993-up Bracket with screw, pair
31-0162	Clamp Set, 1973-81
31-9980	Clamp Set, 1982-up
37-9095	1990-Up XL Rear Extended

Chrome Turn Signal Mount Set

Allows bullet style turn signals to be located under control boxes on bars for 1988-03 XL. Replaces 68266-03.
VT No. 31-0687

LIGHTING 19

Chrome Turn Signal Relocation

Kit moves turn signals to post mounted to top of triple tree. Chrome mount posts wiring and hardware included. Replaces 68517-94A.
VT No. 31-9935

Lamps listed are for show or decorative use only, not D.O.T. approved.

INDICATOR LAMP

3/8" Indicator Lamps

VT No.	OEM	Color	Type	Fits XL
33-2022	68489-86	Red	Oil Pressure	1986-94
33-2023	68574-86	Green	Neutral	1986-94
33-2024	68023-92	Blue	HiBeam	1986-94
33-2025	68695-91	Green	Turn Sig	1986-94
33-2026	68002-92A	Red		1991-up

Speedometer and Tachometer Lamp Sockets

LIGHTING
19

VT No.	OEM	Fits	Model
33-1959	67327-78	1979-85	FX-XL
33-1960	92045-76	1976-77	FX-XL
33-2171	67034-83	1983-86	FX-XL
33-1933	67202-86	1986-90	FX-XL
33-1934	67107-83	1983-90	FX-XL
39-0135	71151-67B	1967-73	FX-XL
33-2008	Mini Gauge	48mm	
33-2039	Mini Gauge	60mm	

Miniature Bulbs- 10pks

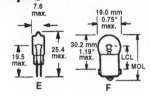
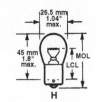

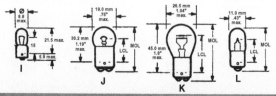

VT No.	#	OEM	Application
33-0142	H		6V 2 Pin NLN, Dual
33-0137	E	68024-94	94-up Speedo and Indicator Lamp
33-0130	K	68165-47	6V Brake and Tail lamp
33-0131	K	68165-64	12V Brake and Tail lamp
33-2105	K		As Above, Halogen 12V
33-2046	F	68165-15	6V Early Dash and FF light
33-0139	B	68462-49	6V 33-0408 FF light
33-0138	B		12V 33-0408 FF light
33-1970	H	68572-50	6V Bullet Light
33-1971	H		12V Bullet Light
33-1982	J		12V Bullet, dual filament with offset mounting pins
33-1913	J		As Above with inline mounting pins
33-2047	E		12V Mini-gauge
33-0170	H	68572-64A	12V Directional, Single
33-1958	K		12V Directional, Dual
33-0132	I	71090-47	6V Speedo and Hi Beam
33-0133	L	71090-64	12V Speedo 75-up XL
33-0135	D	71092-68A	12V Hi-beam , all dash panels
33-0138	D	71099-74	12V Tachometer, Bates Style Headlamp
33-0139	B	68462-49	6V High-Beam Indicator, Bates Style Headlamp (#55)
33-0244		68561-50	6V 1948-64 Dash Base

33-0399   33-2198   33-2173

33-0397   33-8925

Flashers for Indicator Lamps

VT No.	OEM	Item	Volt	U/M
33-0399	68543-64A	Round	12	Ea.
33-0848	68543-64A	Round	12	10pk
33-0916	68543-64C	12V, Round Solid State		Ea.
33-2198	As Above	Rectangle, Replica	12	Ea.
33-2173	As Above	Rectangle, Plastic	12	Ea.
Flasher for hazard or four flashing lights.				
33-0397	68541-64	Round	12	Ea.
33-2039	Mini Gauge	60mm		

Flasher Connector and Mount VT No. 32-8925

12 Volt 2 Pin Flasher Units
With built in bulb failure indicator.

10 Watt	21-23 Watt
33-2350	33-2351

33-0033   33-2097   33-0016

33-0221

Adhesive Backed OE Reflectors

DOT approved. Sold in pairs.

VT No.	Type	Fits XL
33-0033	Front, Amber	1972- up
33-0039	Rear Red	1972- up
33-2097	Rear Amber	1979-up
33-0016	Rear Red	1990-91
33-0221	Rear Red	1992-up

32-1542   32-1543

Mini Push Button Switch Kits
Include 25" colored wires.

Black	Chrome	Button
32-1541	32-1543	Dual
32-1542	32-1544	Single

SIGNAL FLASHER

33-0713

Illuminator Module

Allows turn signals to be used as running and brake lights, without losing their turn signal abilities. Features built in load equalizer and works with stock or custom turn signals. Security system compatible.

33-0816

VT No.	Module Type	Fits
33-0713	Hardwire	1973-98 XL and all custom wiring applications without self canceling turn signals
33-0815	Plug & Play	1986-90 XL
33-0816	Plug & Play	1999-03 XL
33-0817	Plug & Play	2004-13 XL
33-1195	Plug & Play	2014-up XL

Turn Signal Flasher

For use with LED turn signals. 2 pin type attaches by tie wrap.
VT No. 33-0938

3-Prong Wiring Flasher Connector

With mounting bracket riveted on. Flasher connector includes bracket and plug.
VT No. 32-0570

Badlands ATS-03 Self Canceling Modules

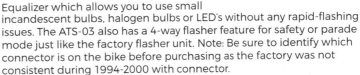

33-2071

Designed to provide a less expensive alternative to the factory flasher module. The ATS-03 module not only has a built in 11-second flasher but it also is a Load Equalizer which allows you to use small incandescent bulbs, halogen bulbs or LED's without any rapid-flashing issues. The ATS-03 also has a 4-way flasher feature for safety or parade mode just like the factory flasher unit. Note: Be sure to identify which connector is on the bike before purchasing as the factory was not consistent during 1994-2000 with connector.

VT No.	Type	Fits XL
33-2071	Hand-Wire, Self Canceling	Universal on 1973-90 models without self canceling module on custom builds.
Plug & Play Self Canceling Modules		
33-2276	Amp Style, 6 Pin Plug	1992-93 XL
33-2277	8 Position Male, Deutsch Connector w/ Delphi TSM	1997-2000 XL
33-2278	8 Position Male, Deutsch Connector w/ Delphi TSM	1997-2000 XL
33-2279	12 Pin Deutsch Plug, Plug w/ Delphi TSM	1997-2000 XL

LIGHTING
19

HORNS FOR XL

42-0755

42-9936

42-0304

42-0052

42-9939

42-0303

42-1174

42-0305

42-0015

42-1106

33-2110

Stock Replacement Horns
Order covers separately.

Horn	Cover	OEM	Fitment
33-2109	42-0303	69000-76	1965-85 All XL - Low Note
33-2110	42-0304	69016-76	1965-78 All XL - High Note
33-2116	42-0755	69060-90D	1991- Up XL 1200
33-2206			1991- Up XL 1200

Chrome Horn Covers

VT No.	OEM	Fitment
42-0015	69012-86	1988-92 XL
42-0755	69012-93A	1993- Up XL
42-0305	69141-70	1970-76 - High Note
42-1174		1993- Up LED Skull Design
42-9936	69138-65	1965-76 XL
42-9939		1965-76 XL
42-0304	69017-76	1965-78 XL - High Note
42-0052	69012-86	1986-92 XL 1100, 1988-Up 1200 w/ tab
42-0303	69140-76	1976-85 XL - Low Note
42-1106		1976-85 XL - Low Note, Skull Design

HORN 20

33-2109

33-2206

33-2116

Chrome Trumpet Horn Kit

Includes bugle, power pack and mount hardware. Fits 1957-85.

33-0699

42-9924

VT No.	Item	VT No.	Item
33-2013	6V	33-1985	6V Horn Pack
33-0699	12V	33-0736	12V Horn Pack
		42-9924	Horn Cover

 Horn Bumper Bracket
Replaces 69041-73 on 1973-85 XL.
VT No. 31-0133

 Trumpet Horn Mount Bracket
Fits 1954-66 XL. Power Pack. Replaces 69031-57.
VT No. 31-5012

 2004-up XL Horn Mount Bracket
Replaces 69135-04.
VT No. 31-0299

 Horn Mounting Plate
Replaces 69117-65. Use on all 1965-85.
VT No. 31-0129

Chrome Grill Face

Will fit late model XL horn.

Complete Horn	Grill Only
33-2099	33-2100

Left Side Horn Kit
Bracket and horn fit 1952-85 XL.

6v	12v
33-0696	33-0697

 GM Restoration Parts.

Replica Horn Kits

Kit is bracket, horn cover, and iso mount rubber stud.

VT No.	Year	Model
33-2189	1971-85	XL
33-2191	All	Horn only

Horn and Bracket
Fits 1996- up XL.

VT No.	Item	Finish
33-0324	Horn	Black
33-0369	Horn	Chrome
31-0299	Bracket	Chrome

 31-0369
 31-0299

Horn Kit

34-1039 33-1468

Bracket, horn cover, and related hardware for installation.

VT No.	Year	OEM
34-1039	1986-91	69014-88A
33-1468	1993-up	69112-95E

Horn Mount Nut
For mounting stock horns.

VT No.	Year	OEM
12-0550	1965-85	69149-65
12-0624	1986-up	7495

Horn Cover Mounting Hardware
Includes (3) 1719W screws, (8) 7015 lockwashers, (2) 7608 nuts, (1) 8125 nut and (1) spacer. Use to mount 1965-up XL horns.

Kit	Nut Only
37-8804	12-0554

HORN COVERS

Round Horn Cover

42-0588

42-1036

42-1526

42-1527

42-1182

42-1194

VT No.	Style	Fits
42-0588	Smooth	1993-up XL
42-1036	Skull	1991-up XL
42-1526	Skull	1991-up XL
42-1527	Flame	1993-up XL
42-1182	Black Gloss	1993-up XL
42-1194	Black Wrinkle	As Above

42-0588 Installed

Waterfall Style Horn Cover

42-1520

Fits 1993-up XL. OEM# 61300523.

Chrome	Gloss Black
42-1520	42-1519

1993- Up Round and CVO Horn Cover

42-1134

42-1135

42-5041

42-1053

42-1084

42-1179

42-5047

VT No.	Style
42-1134	Round Spoke Chrome
42-5041	Skull
42-1135	Round Slotted Chrome
42-1053	Chrome CVO
42-1179	Black CVO
42-1084	Louvered Chrome
42-5047	Black Skull
42-1545	Raised Skull, Chrome and Black

Universal Horns

Chrome	Black
33-1469	33-1470

HORN

20

SPRING FORK

Spring Fork Kits include 1" stem for use on XL models 1982-2003. *Order 24-0192, 7/8" stem to adapt kit to 1952-1977 XL models.*

Kit includes:
- Fork
- Caliper Kit,
- SS Rotor,
- Fender,
- 21" Wheel,
- Axle,
- Riser Studs
- Avon AM20 Tire

VT No.	Length
24-1300	28"
24-1301	30"
24-1302	32"
24-1303	34"
24-1304	36"
24-1305	38"

OE Square Springs

Wound with square wire, AEE chopper style.

VT No. 13-0960

24-1305

STIRRUP SET

Heel Stirrups

27-1813

27-0792

27-1812

27-1529

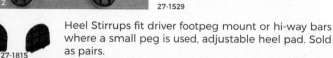

27-1815

Heel Stirrups fit driver footpeg mount or hi-way bars where a small peg is used, adjustable heel pad. Sold as pairs.

VT No.	Type
27-1813	Stirrups with large pegs
27-1812	Stirrups with small pegs
27-1529	Stirrups with small pegs
27-0792	Stirrups without pegs
27-1815	Replacement Soft Pad Inserts

Chrome Footpeg Set with Heel Rest

Features rubber insert and retractable heel rest to fit female peg mounts.
VT No. 27-0765

27-0241

27-0432

27-0521

27-0433

Combat Vintage Pegs

These hollow style steel pegs fit male peg applications.

VT No.	Finish
27-0432	Black Oxide
27-0433	Chrome
21-0521	Parkerized Shifter
27-0241	Combat Peg Set, Parkerized

SHIFTER PEG

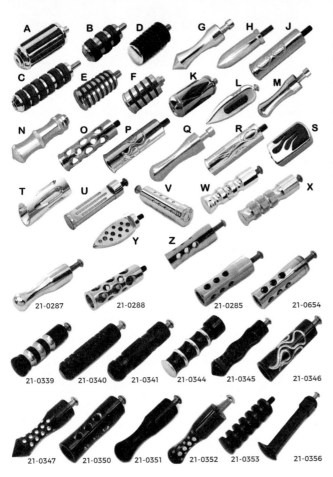

21-0287 21-0288 21-0285 21-0654

21-0339 21-0340 21-0341 21-0344 21-0345 21-0346

21-0347 21-0350 21-0351 21-0352 21-0353 21-0356

#	Chrome	Black	Brass	Style
A	27-1633			Railer
B	21-2025			Cats Paw
C	21-1665			Cats Paw, extended, 4.5"
D	21-0407			Chrome Cap
E	21-0402			O-Ring
F	21-0640			O-Ring (Rotates)
G	21-0408			Pirate
H	21-0689			Bullet Shift Peg
J	21-0790			Skull
K	21-0260			Diamond
L	21-0542			Dagger
M	21-0540			Batique Grooved
N	21-0641			Druid
O	21-0674	21-0355	21-0288	Swiss Cheese
P	21-0789	21-0346		Flame
Q	21-0541	21-0351	21-0287	Contour
R	21-0683			Hollow Flame
S	27-0559			Rectangular Flame
T	21-0620			Slasher
U	21-0277			Ball Milled
V	21-0278			Colt 45
W	21-0279	21-0339		Contour Groove
X	21-0280			Convex Knurled
Y	21-0281			Teardrop
Z	21-0292	21-0350	21-0285	Concave
	21-0357	21-0340		5 Groove
	21-0569	21-0341		4 Groove
	21-0358	21-0347		Spike Agostinni
		21-0344		Tribal
		21-0345		Form Druid
		21-0352		Agostinni
		21-0353		Deep Groove
		21-0356		Railroad
		21-0926		Cobra Shifter Peg
			21-0654	Shot
			21-0450	Pirate Spike
	21-0725	Stainless Steel		Swiss Cheese

Stock Rubber Shifter Footpegs

White or black, long or short stud. The 7/8"long stud is used when the lever is unthreaded and stud accepts a nut. Short 5/8" thread screw into lever. Includes a 10 pack of 5 long and 5 short.

VT No.	Color	Type
21-0901	Black	Short
21-0317	Black	10 pack, includes 5 long, 5 short
21-0902	White	Short
21-0903	Black	Long
21-0908	Black	Long
21-0904	White	Long

21-0902

21-0903

21-0904

21-0908

21-0749 21-0910 21-0872 21-0952

Shifter Pegs with 1/4 x 28" End Stud

VT No.	Type	VT No.	Type	VT No.	Type
21-0749	Shooter	21-0952	Comfort	21-0872	Skull
21-0910	Speeder	21-0620	Slasher		

PEGS & GRIPS
21

27-0797 Installed

Has right and left heel rest arms. Serrated clevis allows heel rests to be fixed at the driver's selection. Kit mounts on XL models w/ forward controls which accept male pegs. Includes flame rider male peg set to complement the flame heel rest set.

VT No. 27-0797

Flame Heel Rest and Footpeg Kit

27-0146

27-0142 Kit Installed

27-0142

VT No.	Item
27-0146	Peg and Bracket Kit, Fits male applications
27-0142	Bracket and Arm Kit
27-1582	Footpegs
21-2025	Shift Peg

Heel Rest Kit allows extra set of pegs to be used for rider position where male peg is used on forward control. Order appropriate matching foot and shift pegs to complete installation.

FOR MORE SELECTION - WWW.VTWINMFG.COM

CAT PAW PEG

27-1581

27-1768

27-0042

Cat Paw Footpegs

Unique soft rubber pad is an inserted cleat isolastically mounted on chrome allen socket bolt and yoke stem. Vibration is reduced. Sold in pairs, matching shifter sold each.

VT No.	Type
27-1581	Large driver female end
27-0042	Mount Yoke for above, female
27-1586	Large Driver, male
27-0041	Male Yokes for Above Footpegs
27-1582	Passenger, Rear, male
27-1768	As Above ET Brand
27-0041	Stock size Mount Yokes for Above, male
27-1457	Passenger Black, small
27-1646	Kicker Pedal, 1957-1959 XL
27-1583	5/8" Female type for custom Hi-way Footpegs
27-1623	As above, Clamp-on set for 1" engine bars
27-1699	3/8" x 24 Stud Mount Footpeg Set
27-1700	1/2" x 20 Stud Mount Footpeg Set
21-2025	Shifter Footpeg Complete, 1952- Up XL
21-1665	Shifter Footpeg 1" longer, 1952- Up XL
28-2009	27-1582 1583, Rubber only 8 piece
28-2018	21-2025, Rubber only 3 piece
27-1800	Small ISO Footpeg, male
27-0873	Mount Kit for 27-1582 & 27-1586

27-1586

27-1457

27-0041

27-1582

27-1583

27-1646

27-1623

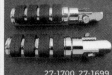
27-1700, 27-1699

21-2025

21-1665

28-2009

28-2018

27-1800

27-0873

Lion's Paw Footpeg

Wide style for male peg application.

Black	Chrome
27-1059	27-2100

27-1059   27-2100

Offset Driver Peg Set

Male style pegs that "drop" the footpeg height.
VT No. 27-0006

Chrome Footpeg Kit

Includes offset mount bracket and 1-1/8" clamp set. Fits Custom application for 1-1/8" bar
VT No. 27-0986

Soft Footpeg Set

Includes male peg set with a matching shifter peg.
VT No. 27-0583

27-1646

27-1647

Large Cat Paw Footpegs

Available with 3/8"flush mounts for forward controls and kicker pedal.

Kick Start Pedal	Flush Mount
27-1646	27-1647

Male Mount Foot Peg	
27-0096	Black with clear cuts
27-0097	Stealth Tone Black
27-0098	Shot Peened, Chrome
Brake and Shifter Peg	
21-0261	Chrome
21-0262	Black with clear cuts
21-0263	Stealth Tone Black
21-0264	Shot Peened, Chrome

Replica Chrome Rear Footpeg Mount

Adds style and comfort to your ride. Fits custom application. Utilizes a 1/2" mounting hole.
VT No. 27-0028

27-0096
21-0261
21-0262
21-0263

21-0264

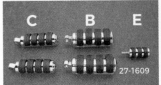

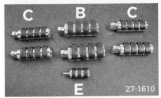

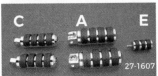

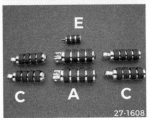

FOOTPEG SET

Silver Knurled 4-Groove Footpeg Set

Silver anodized finish.

VT No.	Style
21-2100	Shifter Peg
27-2103	Large Male Mount Footpeg Set
27-2104	Large Female Footpeg Set
27-2105	Small Male Mount Footpeg Set
27-2106	Small Female Mount Footpeg Set

Cat Paw Footpeg Kit

Includes chrome and soft rubber insert pegs. Display packaged as complete kits. Included are a driver, passenger, and shifter peg, also available with our optional hi-way bar peg sets. Type of pegs are denoted by the following VT Nos.:(A) 27-1581, (B) 27-1586, (C) 27-1582, (D) 27- 1583 and (E) 21-2025. See the web for full description of peg and model year fit.

VT No.	XL Year	Includes
27-1607	1970-90	A, E, C
27-1608*	1970-90	A, E, (2) C
27-1611*	1970-90	A, E, C, D
27-1609	1991-up	B, E, C
27-1610*	1991-up	B, E, (2) C

*Note: Includes extra peg set for hi-way bar (27-1582) kit. 27-1611 includes (27-1583) 5/8" type for hi-way bar.

Offset Driver Peg

Male style pegs that "drop" the footpeg height.

VT No.	Type
27-0857	Stock
27-0006	Soft Peg
27-0403	Railer

Black Footpeg Extension Set

For 2014-up XL.   VT No. 27-0975

Shaker Driver Footpegs

PEGS & GRIPS

21

Vibration absorbing pegs with chrome end caps. Both male driver pegs are larger diameter. With extra cushion built into the rubber shank.

VT No. 27-1616

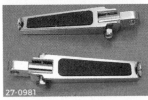

Stock Footpeg Rubbers for 1957-84 XL

Sold in pairs.

VT No.	OEM	Color	Models
28-0201	50940-52	Black	Driver large diameter
28-1954	10 pack	Black	Driver large diameter
28-0202		White	Driver large diameter

Chrome Cap Footpegs

Rubber covered with chrome end caps.

VT No.	Item
27-1215	1952-84 Driver, Large Female
21-0407	Shifter Peg, 1/2" Stud

Skull Pegs

Male end mount pegs for female mount blocks.

Driver	Shifter
27-0083	21-0872

Rubber Insert Pegs

VT No.	Type
27-0979	Clamp
27-0981	Male
27-0982	Male with clevis mount rotated 30°
27-1524	Clevis Only

FX Driver Footpeg

Replaces 50939-52. Fits 1952-84 K and XL.

27-1225	27-1226

O-RING FOOTPEG

21-0402

27-1221

27-1220

27-1222

27-1223

27-1585

27-1580

27-1626

17-0299

Chrome O-Ring Footpeg Sets

Die-cast pegs with o-rings installed.

VT No.	Type/Model	OEM
27-1221	Rear Passenger Pegs male end, small dia.	50901-84T
27-1626	Extended As Above, 1-1/2"	
27-1220	Large Driver peg, female	52651-85T
17-0299	Flat Kicker Pedal 1957-79 XL	50908-88T
27-1222	Clamp on Set 1"	
27-1223	3/8"Stud Mount Pegs	
27-1580	Pegs only - 5/8"square blocks	
27-1585	Large driver peg, male	50913-89T
21-0402	O-Ring Shift Peg each, 1/2" stud 1952-Up XL	34631-84T
14-0901	O-Rings for Large Pegs, 100 pieces	49028-85T
14-0902	O-Rings for Flat Kick Pedal,100 pieces 1957-79 XL	49029-85T

27-0897   27-0896

Diamond O-Ring Footpegs w/ Clamp Set

V-Twin Logo	Plain
27-0896	27-0897

PEGS & GRIPS

21

1" Extended Footpeg

27-1601

27-1509

27-1626

27-1627

27-1717

27-1665

27-1643

Extended footpegs are 1" longer than stock male yoke end pegs. Available in pairs. Fit all models with female mounting block.

VT No.	Style
27-1601	Rubber with Chrome Caps
27-1509	Rubber without Chrome Caps
27-1626	O-Ring style
27-1627	Cats Paw Style with Yokes
27-1643	Extended Yoke only for above
21-1665	Extended Cats Paw Shifter 1952-Up XL
27-1717	Cats Paw Style Peg, Male End 1" Extended

27-1661

27-1660

27-1662

27-1716

Magna Footpeg Set

Feature heavy duty flat rubber ring with chrome center shaft and tapered end cap, sold pairs.

VT No.	Style	VT No.	Style
27-1661	Driver, male	27-1662	5/8" square mount, female
27-1660	Driver, female	27-1716	Passenger Male 1" Extended

THROTTLE

Chrome Throttle Clamps and Tube Set

Feature smooth design, upper and lower pieces with screws and nylon throttle tube, for single cable application. For use with 1982-95 type cables.

VT No. 35-0253

35-9871 · 36-0151 · 36-0564

Radii Billet Throttle Housing

VT No.	Type	Cable
35-0255	Single	1981-95 XL throttle
36-0151	Single	1974-80 XL throttle
36-0564	Dual	1981-95 XL throttle or idle

Donkey Handlebar Grip Set

Installed

Dual cable has chrome end caps.
VT No. 28-0934

28-0116 28-0786 35-0832 35-0261

28-0002 28-0003 28-0004

Original Jack Hammer Handlebar Grips

1960's style, thick rubber.

VT No.	Type	Size
35-0071	Grip Throttle	
28-0786	Grip Set with tube	
28-0116	Grip Set	
35-0347	Grip Kit	
28-0002	Brown	
28-0003	Red	

VT No.	Type	Size
28-0004	White	
28-0182	Grip Set	7/8"
35-0261	Grip & Throttle	7/8"
35-0832	1/4" Turn	7/8"
35-0779	1/4" Turn	1"

BILLET GRIP

28-0297 · 28-1506 · 28-0799

Chrome Handlebar Grip Set
Billet alloy w/chrome.

VT No.	Style	VT No.	Style
28-0297	Band	28-1506	Banded, Skull
28-0001	Band Wrist	28-0799	Wrist Rest

Banded Grip Set with Wrist Rest

VT No. 28-0001

Billet Rocket Handlebar Grip

Features jumbo O-rings for good grip. 1982-up.
VT No. 28-0588

Iso-Billet Handlebar Grip Design

Fits 1982- up XL dual throttle.
VT No. 28-0607

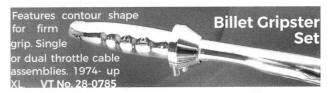

Features contour shape for firm grip. Single or dual throttle cable assemblies. 1974- up XL. VT No. 28-0785

Billet Gripster Set

Odins Contour Handlebar Grip

Set is constructed of billet alloy with chrome. 1982-up XL.
VT No. 28-0784

PEGS & GRIPS 21

Nylon Throttle Tubes

35-9073 · 35-9870 · 28-1981

VT No.	Type	XL Year
35-9073	Single	1974-80
28-1981	Dual	1982-95
35-9870	Dual	1996-up (Black)

HANDLEBAR GRIP

28-0579

28-0580

28-0581

28-0057

Chrome Billet Grip Sets

Accept single or dual cable assemblies.

28-1987

28-0678

28-0567

28-0586

28-0279

28-0569

28-0741

28-0326

28-0596

28-0595

28-0759

28-0597

VT No.	Style	VT No.	Style	VT No.	Style
28-0579	Spiral	28-0567	Phat	28-0759	Skull
28-0580	Diamond	28-0586	Faceted	28-0595	Ventilated
28-0581	Smoothie	28-0279	Druid	28-0596	Vintage with Grooves
28-0057	Maltese	28-0569	Batique	28-0597	Slugger with Grooves
28-1987	Swiss Cheese	28-0326	Flame		
28-0678	Slugger	28-0741	Flame		

Foam Grips

Full foam grips with chrome end caps.

VT No. 28-0573

Chrome Rail Grip Set

Use with 28-1981 nylon tube.

VT No. 28-0742

28-0563

28-0446

Chrome Diamond Insert Handlebar Grips

Die cast construction for 1974-up models.

Die Cast	PVC
28-0563	28-0446

Profile Barrel Handlebar Grips

Chrome accents with barrel shape rubber insert for comfort.

28-0570

28-0571

Rail	Twist
28-0570	28-0571

Handlebar Grip Adhesive

Fastens grips to bars.

VT No. 41-0190

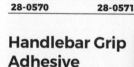

28-0454

28-0451

Dual Hot Rod Flame Handlebar Grip Set

Features molded cushion rubber inner sleeve with chrome flame outer sleeve, for looks and comfort.

1982-Up	1996-Up
28-0454	28-0451

Chrome O-Ring Insert Handlebar Grip Set

Includes nylon throttle tube for dual or single cable operation.

VT No. 28-0585

HANDLEBAR GRIP

Handlebar Grip Sets

28-0247

28-0245

28-0246

28-0248

28-0925

1982-15		1982-15	
28-0245	Plain, Chrome	28-0247	Black With cut
28-0246	Shot Peened, Chrome	28-0248	Stealth Tone Black
		28-0925	Cobra Black

28-0456   28-0452   28-0206

Custom Handlebar Grip Sets

28-0150

VT No.	Item	Years
28-0452	Iso Bar	1996-up
28-0150	Deco	1996-up
28-0206	Chrome End	
28-0456	Chrome End	2004-up XL

Skull Chrome End Handlebar Grip

Order throttle inner sleeve separately. 1974- up.

Grips	Sleeve
28-0144	28-1981

O-Ring Handlebar Grips

Machined chrome grips with O-Rings. 1" and 11/8" size for 1974-up controls. Show use only.
VT No. 28-2011

Shooter Handlebar Grip

Set feature brushed metal finish with holes.
VT No. 28-0590

28-0125   28-0124

28-0445   28-2015

Chrome End Handlebar Grip Sets

Soft touch grip area with foam or leather covering to reduce vibration. Available in chrome plated end cap with smooth cap or embossed emblem. Fit 1974-up models.

VT No.	Type
28-0125	Embossed Cap
28-0124	Smooth Cap
28-2015	Smooth Cap, Leather
28-0445	Pebble

Heated Handlebar Grip Set

Fits 1996-up XL models. Includes end caps.
VT No. 28-0589

PEGS & GRIPS

21

28-2211

28-2212

L E D

28-2211

28-2212

5 LED bulbs. Powered by 3 small batteries, the end caps light up when pressed. There are 3 patterns.

1. On steady
2. Flashing on/off
3. Single bulb circular flashing pattern
4. Off

Billet Handlebar Grip Sets

Groove	Knurl
28-2211	28-2212

Flame Billet Handlebar Grip

For single or dual throttle application

Barrel	Flanged
28-0741	28-0845

Billet Handlebar Grip

Multi-Band	6 Flat Band
28-0642	28-0643

Chrome V-Tech Handlebar Grips

Available in flat o-ring or rubber rail design in die cast grip.

Iso Rails	Chrome O-Ring
28-2229	28-2251

Chrome Delta Handlebar Grip Set

Features 3-point eccentric form with rubber cushion inserts.
VT No. 28-0153

1953-1961 Grip Hole Plugs

Zinc plated with groove, pair. Replaces 56239-53.
VT No. 28-0625

Fat Billet Grips

Match outside diameter of large bars for symmetry. Both have inner diameter for fit ends and accept single or dual throttle cable.

1-1/4"	1-1/2"
28-0583	28-0582

Single or dual cable use.

Chrome Billet Throttle Handlebar Grip Set

VT No.	Style	VT No.	Style
28-0051	Twist	28-0050	Groove
28-0576	Flame	28-0052	Groove Grips

Vintage Style Grips

Retro molded rubber design with chrome accent band throttle grip. Includes nylon sleeve for dual cable operation.

1973-95	1996- Up
28-0149	28-0148

Chrome End Plug

Sold pairs. 10 pk.
VT No. 28-0618

1962-72 Handlebar Grip Sets

Sets are 1-1/8" ID on both sides to fit internal throttle control. 28-0113, 28-0114 include chrome end plugs.

VT No.	Color	Note
28-0113	Black	With plugs
28-0114	White	With plugs
28-2021	Black	Without hole

Black Rubber Hillclimber Grip

1940s design with Beck logo.
Fits 1976-98 1" and 1-1/8".
VT No. 28-0479

STOCK GRIP

Replica Waffle Handlebar Grips

28-0159   28-1985   28-0121   28-0111

28-0601   28-0602   28-2000

28-0131

28-2016   28-2126   28-0628

28-0110

Replacement for 56212-53 on 1949-61 models. 1-1/8" x 1-1/8" size or 1974-up late type 1"- 1-1/8" size. Available in pairs.

VT No.	Color	Year	Size
28-0159	Black w/o plug hole	1949-72	1-1/8"
28-0110	Black w/ plug hole	1949-72	1-1/8"
28-0111	White	1949-72	1-1/8"
28-1985	Black	1974-up	1" and 1-1/8"
28-0121	White	1974-up	1" and 1-1/8

Replica Stock Handlebar Grip

Set includes chrome plugs 1-1/8 and 1" size for 1974-up replacing 56206-74 for XL models.

Black	White	Fits
28-0601	28-0602	1974-up
28-2000*		1974-up
28-2016**		1981-up
28-0131***		1974-80, left side, each
28-2126**		1981-96, left side, each
28-0628		2004-up XL

*Note: Grip set less plugs.

**Note: Does not accept chrome plugs

***Note: Order chrome plugs separately.

Metal Flake Handlebar Grip Sets

28-0798   28-0797

28-0107   28-0972   28-0160   28-0975

28-0792   28-0794   28-0795   28-0793

VT No.	Color	VT No.	Color
28-0792	Charcoal	28-0794	Silver
28-0793	Red	28-0795	Blue
28-0798	Yellow	28-0797	Aqua

28-0108   28-0594

Vintage Style Handlebar Grip Set

For use on 1974-up with 1" & 1-1/8" size for twist grip assemblies. Translucent colors as noted.

VT No.	Color	VT No.	Color
28-0594	Black, dual cable	28-0160	Red
		28-0972	Brown
28-0107	Black	28-0973	Yellow
28-0108	White	28-0974	Blue

PEGS & GRIPS

21

Beck Plastic Grips

28-0960

28-0958

28-0961

28-0931   28-0957   28-0959

1962-72 Rib Style Grips

28-0119   28-0184   28-0185

28-0186

28-0187

28-0118

VT No.	Color	VT No.	Color	VT No.	Color
28-0118	Black	28-0119	White	28-0185	Blue
28-0186	Yellow	28-0184	Red	28-0187	Green

VT No.	Color	VT No.	Color
28-0931	Black	28-0961	White
28-0959	Yellow	28-0957	Red
28-0958	Blue	28-0960	Green

FOR MORE SELECTION - WWW.VTWINMFG.COM

VENTED GAS CAPS

Note: XLs use one vented cap.

Cam Style Spinner Gas Caps

Chrome	Black	Style	Years
	38-0459	Vented	1941-82
38-0409		Vented	1983-95
38-0429		Set	1983-95

1983-up Ratcheting Style Caps

Made of steel, featuring low pressure relief vent recessed in cap to clear the filler neck vent tube on 1985 and later tanks. *Note: For 96-99 models.

VT No.	Finish	Type
38-0317	Chrome	Metal
38-0307	Chrome	Plastic
38-6684	Stainless	Metal
38-0325*	Chrome	Metal

Gas Cap Gasket replaces 61109-85, on 1983-up ratcheting caps.
VT No. 14-0561

Chrome Billet Gas Cap

Features cross design. Fits 1996-up XL, sold each.
VT No. 38-0391

Flame Gas Caps

Fit vented applications, 1996- Up
VT No. 38-0541

Billet Flame Cap

Fits 1983-99
VT No. 38-0405

Air Craft Gas Caps

38-0350   38-0426

38-0347   14-0188

Fit tanks which accept air craft style caps.

VT No.	Description
Caps w/o Mount Rings.	
38-0350	Vented Cap Only
Caps w/Mount Ring, Gasket & Screws	
38-0347	Vented Cap w/ ring, gasket & screw, w/o keys
38-0426	Vented Cap Only w/ lock
38-0352	Vented Cap Only w/ lock
14-0188	Gasket and Seal Set

Locking Gas Caps

38-7028

VT No.	Type	Fits XL
38-7028	Bung Type Vented Cap w/ 2 keys	1996- up
38-0981	Stainless Steel, Cam Lock Design	1959-1981
38-1642	Eaton Style Bayonet Cap Opening, w/ 2 keys	1960-1981

38-0793   38-0789   38-0439

Chrome	Black	Years
38-0789	38-0793	Vented (Right), 1996-up
38-0437		Vented, 1984-96
38-0439		Vented, 1997-up

Billet Red Baron Cap

Fits 1983-up
VT No. 38-0423

Chrome   **Gold Inlay**

Eagle Spirit Gas Caps

VT No.	Style	Year	Type
38-7001	Chrome	1983-95	Right, Vent
38-7003	Gold Inlay	1983-95	Right, Vent
38-7038	Gold Inlay	1996-99	Right, Vent
38-0412	Gold Inlay	2000-up	Left Dummy

Bayonet Style Eagle Spirit

Fit 1971-82 tanks.. Chrome finish.

Vented	Set
38-6687	38-6688

Skull Caps by Wyatt Gatling

Black   Chrome

*Note: Sets include vented cap and dummy cap for left side to replace fuel gauge.

Chrome	Black	Style	Years
38-0953	38-0954	Vented	1984-95
38-0955	38-0956	Vented	1996-12
38-0961	38-0962	*Vent/Dummy	1996-up

38-0927

38-1132

Skull Caps

	Chrome Body	Black Body
	38-0927	38-1132

Cap body is black or chrome with a chrome or black mesh insert skull with black or chrome eyes. Vented, sold each. 1962-1982 XL.

GAS CAPS 1952-UP

38-0310   38-0313   38-0539

Chrome Stock-Style Gas Caps

Vented cap fits right side of dual or single cap tanks.

VT No.	XL Fitment	Type
38-0310	1971-82	Right, Vented
38-0534	1971-82	Painted, Black
38-0313	1973-82	Right, Vented
38-0539	1973-82	Vented, each
38-7050	1998-up	Vented, for 2.1 or 4.5 gal tanks

Scalloped Deluxe Chrome Cap

With vent. Replaces bayonet type early caps. Fits 1971-82 XL.
VT No. 38-0304

1952-70 Large Chrome Cap

VT No. 38-0329

38-0440

Replica Chrome Caps

Replica Eaton Style Gas Caps with correct knurls, depth and markings. Cam lock style.

VT No.	Item	Fitment
38-0440	Vented Cap Set	1959-69 XL
38-0535	Vented, sold each	1965-81 XL

KROMMET   38-0336 Installed

Chrome Krommet Style Gas Cap Cover

Fit over existing caps. Sold Each.

Fits 1973- up XL	Fits 1983- up XL
38-0336	38-0551

38-7029   38-7041 Installed   38-7032   38-7032 Installed

Gas Tank Filler Rings

Polished stainless steel rings prevent paint from blistering and flaking around filler neck and conceal existing paint damage in this area.

VT No.	Type	XL Fit
38-7029	Bayonet	1971-82
38-7041	Bung	1983-96
38-7032	Bung (Smooth Top Tanks)	1996-Up

LOW PROFILE CAPS

38-0344   38-0395   38-0343

Low Profile Vented Cap Set for Bob Tanks

VT No.	Finish	XL Fit
38-0344	Stainless Steel	1983-91
38-0343	Stainless Steel	1996- Up
38-0395	Chrome	1983-91

Lone Star Low Profile Cap

Set available in pairs (vented or non-vented). Features star type emblem on low profile pointed style gas cap. Fits 1983-91 XL.
VT No. 38-0277

Chrome Vented Retro Gas Cap

With air craft style ring.
VT No. 38-0745

Gas Tank Gaskets

GB No.	James	OEM	Fits
	15-1065	61109-85	1983-up Gas Cap
15-0182	15-1066	61111-77	1958-85 Gas Cap
15-0265	15-1068	62172-75	1975-up Fuel Valve
15-0328	15-0201	62628-66	1957-66 Oil Filler Cap

BILLET CAPS

Weld In Air Craft Cap Kit

Includes machined insert and chrome vented aircraft cap. Insert must be welded in.
VT No. 38-0746

Mini Screw-In Vented Gas Cap

Includes weld in bung. VT No. 38-0749

Chrome Pop Up Cap

Fits XL models with 2.4 gallon tank.

1996- Up	1998- Up
38-5551	38-5557

38-0494   38-0493

Air Flow Gas Cap

Features raised center section with contrast relief lines in either a black or chrome. Fits 1996- up XL.

Black	Chrome
38-0490	38-0489

EMBLEMS

22

POP-UP GAS CAP

Chrome Pop-Up Cap features built in dress ring with O-ring for seal at cap area. Fits 1996-up XL.

VT No. 38-0757

38-0403
38-0402

Smooth Vented Pop Up Cap by Wyatt Gatling

1996-05	1982-95
38-0403	38-0402

Black Vented Pop Up Gas Cap

Cap features a smooth finish. Fits 1996-up XL.

VT No. 38-0565

EMBLEM MOUNTS

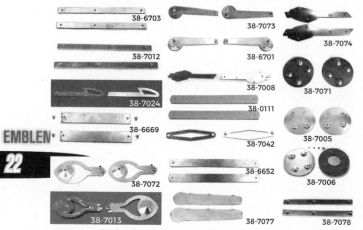

38-6703
38-7012
38-7024
38-6669
38-7072
38-7013
38-7073
38-6701
38-7008
38-0111
38-7042
38-6652
38-7077
38-7074
38-7071
38-7005
38-7006
38-7078

EMBLEM

22

Weld On Emblem Mounts can be spot welded or blazed to Bobbed Tank sets. Order emblems and screws separately.

Note: Denotes Adhesive Mounts. NOS = New Old Stock

VT No.	OEM	Years	VT No.	OEM	Years
38-6703	61794-51	1951-54	38-7072		1959-60
38-7012*	61784-92T	1951-54	38-7013*	61742-93T	1959-60
38-7024*	61840-94T	1955-56	38-7073		1961-62
38-7071	61780-91T	1957-58	38-6701*	61740-90T	1961-62
38-7005*	61781-91T	1957-58 Curved	38-7008*	61782-91T	1963-65
38-7006*	61780-91T	1957-58 Flat	38-6652	61254-79	1979-84 Thick
38-6669		1959-60 NOS	38-7078		1951-53
			38-7074		1963-65

EMBLEM

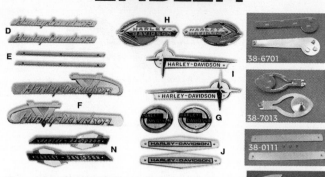

D
E
F
H
I
G
J
N
38-6701
38-7013
38-0111
38-7024

Gas Tank Emblems & Mounts

Stock type, in pairs. Mount strips available separately w/ adhesive back or weld-on. Order screws separately.

Emblem	Mount	Note	Years	#	Color
38-6670	38-6669	1	1959-60	H	Red
	38-7013	2	1958-85 Gas Cap		
	38-7072	1	1975-up Fuel Valve		
38-6162	38-6701	2	1961-62	I	Black/White
	38-7073	1			
38-1961	38-6701		1961-62		Patina
	38-7008	2	1963-65	N	Silver
	38-6703	1	1951-54	D	Chrome
	38-7012	2	1951-54		
38-7044	38-6704	1	Strips	E	Stainless
38-7045	38-6704	1	Strips		Chrome
38-7022	38-7024	2	1955-56	F	Chrome
38-6698	38-7005	2, 3	1958	G	Black/Gold/Silver
	38-7006	2, 4	1957-58		For Above
38-6682	38-0111	1	1966-71	J	Black
	38-7042	2			

Mount Type Note
1. Weld On Type
2. Adhesive Backed Type Mount
3. For Curved Surface Application
4. For Flat Surface Application

Tank Emblem Sets

Include steel mount strips that can be installed with adhesive strips supplied or welded on. We suggest welding.

VT No.	Year	Color
38-0801	1961-62	Black/White
38-0802	1951-54	Chrome
38-0806	1955-56	Chrome

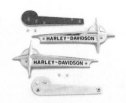

38-0801

38-0802

38-0806

eXceptional PRODUCTS

WR-KR-XL Wheels

	Front						
Wheel	Rim Size	Hub	Hub Finish	Spokes	Rim	Rim Finish	Axle O.D.
52-0013	18"	45-0102	Nickel	45-0587	52-0785	Black	3/8"
52-0014	18"	45-0102	Nickel	45-0587	52-0025	Alloy	3/8"
52-0065	18"	45-0106	Alloy	45-0936	52-0785	Black	9/16"
52-0075	18"	45-0106	Alloy	45-0936	52-0025	Alloy	9/16"
52-0020	18"	45-0109	Nickel	45-0936	52-0025	Alloy	3/8"
52-0085	18"	45-0109	Nickel	45-0936	52-0785	Black	3/8"
52-0083	19"	45-0106	Alloy	45-0932	52-1016	Black	9/16"
52-0079	19"	45-0106	Alloy	45-0932	52-0026	Alloy	9/16"
52-0080	19"	45-0106	Alloy	45-0932	52-1016	Black	9/16"
52-0024	19"	45-0102	Nickel	45-0932	52-0026	Alloy	3/8"
52-0023	19"	45-0102	Nickel	45-0932	52-1016	Black	3/8"
52-0019	19"	45-0109	Nickel	45-0846	52-0026	Alloy	3/8"
52-0087	19"	45-0109	Nickel	45-0846	52-1016	Black	3/8"
52-0018	21"	45-0102	Nickel	45-0948	52-1208	Black	3/8"
	Rear						
52-0067	18"	45-0107	Alloy	45-0936	52-0785	Black	9/16"
52-0070	18"	45-0107	Alloy	45-0936	52-0025	Alloy	9/16"
52-0071	19"	45-0107	Alloy	45-0149	52-0026	Alloy	9/16"
Carrier Sprocket		45-0115	Alloy				
Sprocket 46T		19-0454					
Disc 11.5"		23-0182					

Spool wheels with alloy or nickel plated hubs, stainless spokes, and rim finish as noted.

52-0785

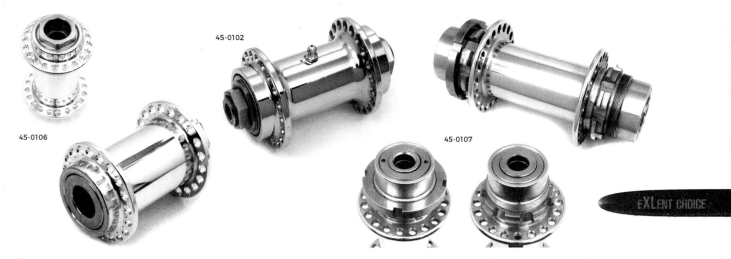

45-0106

45-0102

45-0107

eXLent CHOICE

eXceptional PRODUCTS

Cam/Sprocket Cover Sets, 2004-Up XL

10-1431

Set	Finish	Cover Only
10-0348	Black	10-1431
10-0489	Chrome	10-1432

27-0832 Installed

Outlaw Sprocket Cover Kit and Belt Guard

27-0833

For 2004-Up XL. Replaces stock pulley cover, fills in the center of pulley for clean, detailed, high-performance look.

43-0388   43-0389

Chrome	Black	Item
43-0388	43-0389	Pulley Cover Kit
27-0832	27-0833	Pulley Cover Guard

eXLent choice
Alternator 17 Amp Charging System Kit

Kit includes alternator rotor clutch shell assembly with bearing and ring gear installed. Alternator rotor clutch shell assembly features vibration proof magnet construction. Magnets are held in place by stainless steel non-magnetic insert, stator, and chrome regulator. Charging kit fits 1984-1990 XL models with alternator in clutch drum.
VT No: 32-0473

Cam Cover Trim

42-0138   42-0138 Installed

42-0137   42-0137 Installed

Cam Cover Trim installs over original cover for 2004-up XL

VT No.	Finish	VT No.	Finish
42-0138	Alloy	42-0137	Black

Outer Primary Cover Kit

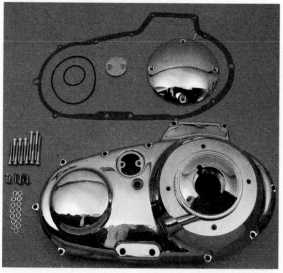

Chrome outer primary cover kit includes cover, allen screw set, inspection cover and gasket. Fits: XL 1991-2003
VT No. 43-0235

eXceptionaL PRODUCTS

Transmission Sprocket Conversion Kit

Used to convert belt drive models to chain drive. Kit includes 23 tooth front sprocket and 51 tooth rear sprocket with special nut to accept sprocket and a chain breaker tool. The metal spacer features a 2.1" inner diameter. Fits 2000-2006 XL models. Suggested to use with 20-0215 Pulley Indexing Flange Nut. Includes 20-0324 Transmission Drive Sprocket Nut.

*NOTE: Chain must be cut to correct length.

VT No.	Item
19-0761	Conversion Kit
19-0402	23T Transmission Sprocket Kit
19-0250	51T Rear Sprocket Chrome
20-0324	Transmission Drive Sprocket Nut
19-0725	Nickel Plated Chain - 120 Link

19-0761

Aluminum Kick Starter Conversion Kit

Kit includes aluminum sprocket cover with V-Twin logo, transmission mainshaft, kick starter arm, rubber pedal, and kick shaft. Retains the electric start system. Does not require removal of electric start feature. Kit uses the stock pulley with no requirement to convert to a chain/sprocket. Works with stock or aftermarket exhaust systems. Requires transmission mainshaft to be changed, which is included in the kit. Will not work with stock mid controls. Must used with forward controls, or relocation of master cylinder. Fits XL 1991-2003 5-speed models.

**Note: Assembly should be carried out by an experienced mechanic or home hobby mechanic with patience.

22-0213

Installed

eXceptional PRODUCTS

XR Style Gas Tank

Original shape for the "750" look.

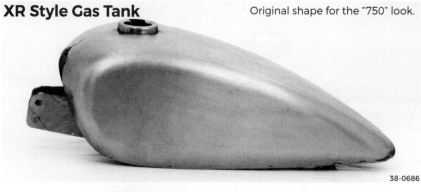

38-0686

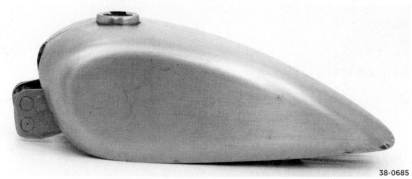

38-0685

38-0687 Rear View

38-0687

EXLENT CHOICE

VT No.	Year	VT No.	Year
38-0686	1957-78	38-0688	2007-up
38-0685	1982-03	38-0636	XR 750 1957-78 w/o brackets, universal
38-0687	2004-06		

V-Race Patch

SPEEDSTER V-TWIN 750 WR · KR · XR

An authentic V-Twin racing patch that represents the WR, KR and XL speed products.

VT No. 48-1641

Oil Pump Assembly

Replica oil pump is fully assembled. Replaces 26204-86. Fits 1986-1990 XL models.

12-1563

eXceptional PRODUCTS

Shotgun Duals

For Evolution and Sportster swing arm frames.

VT No.	Frame
29-0201	Swing Arm

9-0201 Installed

Sumax Braided Cloth Spark Plug Wires

7mm black silicone with synthetic jacketing resists heat, oil and abrasion. A combination Kevlar Helically Spiral Wound Core at 350 ohm per foot resistance delivers greater spark energy, improving power, idle, and fuel efficiency. Matching black silicone boots protect from high exhaust temperatures. Double spring locking terminals for secure vibration proof connections. Cloth jacket is rated at 450°F. Will work on all models with point or electronic ignitions. Custom fit and universal sets available.

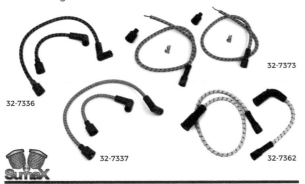

32-7373

32-7336

32-7337

32-7362

Universal Fit		XL			Type
90° Boot	Straight Boot	1965-85	1986-06	2007-Up	
32-7364	32-7365	32-7336	32-7341	32-7359	Black/Blue Tracer
32-7366	32-7367	32-7337	32-7342	32-7360	Red/Black Tracer
32-7368	32-7369	32-7338	32-7343	32-7361	Yellow/Black Tracer
32-7370	32-7371	32-7339		32-7362	Grey/Brown Tracer
32-7372	32-7373	32-7340		32-7363	Orange/Black Tracer

"Poor Boy" Sissy Bars by Wyatt Gatling

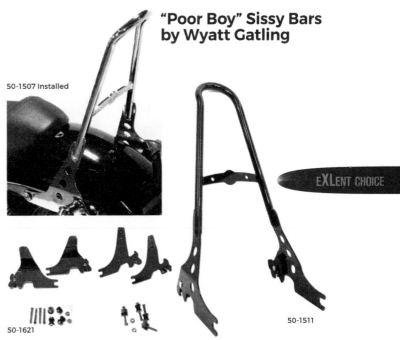

50-1507 Installed

eXLent CHOICE

50-1621

50-1511

Original solid steel design for XL models 2004- up. Use with detachable lat sold separately.

VT No.	Item	Finish	VT No.	Item	Finish
50-1511	Sissy Bar	Black	50-1621	Kit	Detachable
50-1507	Sissy Bar	Chrome			

eXceptional PRODUCTS

Wyatt Gatling Side Slash Slip-On Muffler

Side slash slip-on muffler set features a dura-chrome finish with a side slash cut and 2" removable baffles. Set of 2 Superlow XL 883L mufflers will give you a horsepower increase straight out of the box. Features dura-chrome processing and baffles wrapped in a high-tech mat designed to disperse heat and retain sound. Engineered through thousands of hours of development and real world application, and independently dyno tested to guarantee you the best performance and sound in the market. Order end clamp set and cross tube gaskets separately. *NOTE: Side slash slip-on muffler set features cross tube nipples to connect to OE bracket and installs to stock header pipe. Baffles have an inner diameter of 1-13/16". Baffles can be removed by simpling removing a single bolt on the backside of the muffler. Some applications will require drilling a 1/4" hole into the header pipe. OEM No: 80424-04 Fits 2004-2013 XL models.

VT No. 30-0359

Replica tapered muffler set has a 2-3/8" body diameter, a 1-3/4" inlet inner diameter, and a length of 19". Sold in a quantity of 2. Fits XLCH 1965-1970. OEM 65231-65A is embossed.

VT No. 30-0795

Chrome Tapered Replica Muffler Set

CAUTION: These exhaust products are not legal for sale or use in California on pollution controlled vehicles. These products are intended for non-highway only.

30-0795

Magnum Exhaust Drag Pipe Set

30-1286

eXLent CHOICE

Constructed of steel featuring heat shields. For 2004-2013 XL.

30-1285

VT No.	Finish
30-1286	Black
30-1285	Chrome

Wyatt Gatling 2-into-1 Exhaust Header

1986-03	2004-Up	Finish
29-0932	29-0934	Chrome
29-0933	29-0935	Black

One piece design featuring turn out mufflers. Fits 1986-2003 XL with stock foot controls.

BATES eXceptionaL PRODUCTS

Bates Style Tuck and Roll Genuine Leather Solo
13" wide x 16" long with mount holes 6-5/8" c/c.

Seat	Kit
47-0162	47-0601

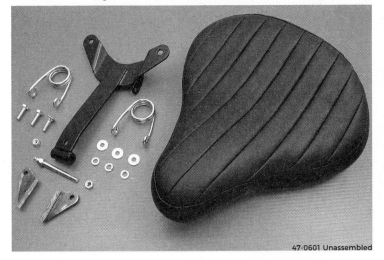

47-0601 Unassembled

47-0601

Replica K-R Saddle

Features thin profile with leather construction on stock formed steel baseplate. Edge is original cobble style with ground and sanded edge. Seat measures 14" rear width, 4-1/2" front width, 16" length.

47-0159

47-0923

Brown	Cowboy Brown
47-0159	47-0923

Chrome Seat Rail Kit

Fits small solo seats. Mount tabs may be required for some applications. Rail and mount tabs are available separately.

VT No.	Item	Rail Only
47-0263	Kit	31-0978
47-0158	Seat	
47-0165	Seat	

eXLent choice

Features this profile with leather construction on stock formed steel baseplate. Edge is original cobbler style, ground and sanded. Seat measures 13"w x 16" l, with 6-5/8" c/c on rear bolt holes.

VT No.	Color
47-0157	Black
47-0159	Brown
47-0605	Brown, Kit
47-0606	Black, Kit

Velo Racer

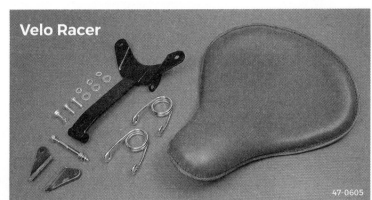

47-0605

eXceptional PRODUCTS

Leather Solo Seat Kits

47-0782

47-0782 Unassembled

Kits include replica genuine leather solo seat with complete mount kit. Replica seat is as offered on original 1957 model, 50 years ago. Includes front cover

57 Solo	Bates Solo	Fitment
47-0781	47-0810	1982-2003
47-0782	47-0811	2004-2009
47-0803	47-0812	2010- Up

Note: 2007-2009 models require regulator under the seat to be relocated, or remounted in current position to seat mount plate.

Solo Seats

Fit 2004-2006 and 2010- up XL models.

VT No.	Finish	Style
47-0321	Black Leather	Bobber
47-0322	Black Leather	Solo Spring Saddle
47-0323	Black Synthetic	Solo Spring Saddle

47-0323

Seat Mount Brackets

For 2000-up XL models.

31-1542

31-1543

VT No.	Type	Fitment
31-1542	Solid	2010- Up
31-1543	Spring	2004-06, 2010- Up

eXLent CHOICE

Leather Police Solo

47-0114 Installed

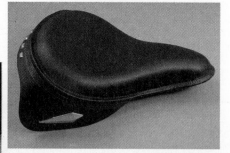

Corbin Gentry leather police solo seat is smaller scale for use on XL models. Measures 14" rear width, 4-1/2" front width, and 16" long.
VT No. 47-0114

INDEX

INDEX